WAR
GAMES

*Conn Smythe and
Hockey's Fighting Men*

DOUGLAS HUNTER

VIKING

VIKING
Published by the Penguin Group
Penguin Books Canada Ltd, 10 Alcorn Avenue, Toronto, Ontario,
Canada M4V 3B2
Penguin Books Ltd, 27 Wrights Lane, London W8 5TZ, England
Viking Penguin, a division of Penguin Books USA Inc., 375 Hudson Street,
New York, New York 10014, U.S.A.
Penguin Books Australia Ltd, Ringwood, Victoria, Australia
Penguin Books (NZ) Ltd, 182–190 Wairau Road, Auckland 10, New Zealand

Penguin Books Ltd, Registered Offices: Harmondsworth, Middlesex, England

First published 1996
1 3 5 7 9 10 8 6 4 2

Printed and bound in Canada on acid free paper ⊜

Canadian Cataloguing in Publication Data

Hunter, Doug, 1959-
War games: Conn Smythe and hockey's fighting men

Includes index.
ISBN 0-670-86901-5

1. Hockey - Canada - History. 2. National Hockey League - History.
3. Smythe, Conn, 1895–1980. I. Title.

GV848.4.C2H85 1996   796.962'64'0971   C95-933396-7

Map illustration by Douglas Hunter

For Herbert and Thomas,
who went the first time

The history of the Second World War
has not yet been written.
—*John Keegan*
The Battle For History (1995)

CONTENTS

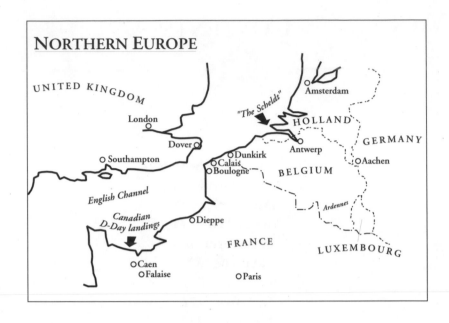

NORTHERN EUROPE

UNITED KINGDOM

London

Dover

Southampton

English Channel

Canadian D-Day landings

Dieppe

Caen
Falaise

Paris

FRANCE

"The Scheldt"

Amsterdam

HOLLAND

Antwerp

BELGIUM

GERMANY

Aachen

Ardennes

LUXEMBOURG

Dunkirk
Calais
Boulogne

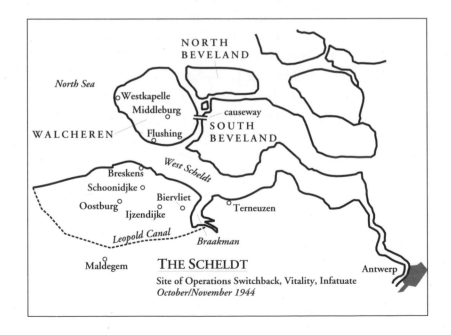

North Sea

NORTH BEVELAND

Westkapelle
Middleburg

WALCHEREN

Flushing

causeway

SOUTH BEVELAND

West Scheldt

Breskens

Schoonidjke

Oostburg

Ijzendijke

Biervliet

Terneuzen

Leopold Canal

Braakman

Maldegem

THE SCHELDT

Site of Operations Switchback, Vitality, Infatuate
October/November 1944

Antwerp

PROLOGUE

A NEW SEASON

October 15, 1944

SNOW.

He draws back the curtains, raises the blinds and confronts a glittering landscape on this Sunday morning. The sight draws an "Oh!" of delight from him, and his dogs join him at the window and share in his childlike enthusiasm over this marvel. Snow not falling, but fallen, overnight rolling a carpet of virginal white atop the fading summer's fertile green. There are still leaves in the trees, and their bright colours provide a dazzling counterpoint to the downy hush of the first full promise of winter. Prime Minister William Lyon Mackenzie King dresses and takes the dogs out of Kingsmere cottage to frolic in this signal day.

It *is* a sign, the snow: not merely a change in weather, but an affirmation of change in his political life. King subscribes to mystical interpretations, readily reading into the minutiae of the natural world winkings from the spiritual plane—a consciousness in the universe of his own life and its urgencies. The significance of incidents and windows of opportunity for action are revealed to Mackenzie King when the celestial machinery's sympathetic motions are transmitted by the semaphore signals of clock hands. A glance at a clock might reveal the hour and minute hands aligned, the minute hand at twelve and the hour at six, or the hour of noon and midnight framed perfectly with the hour hand at eleven and the minute hand at one. Symmetry; portent.

The snow—he sees a fresh beginning in its newness. In the past is a war made glorious by the success of D-Day and the advances the Allied armies have made since then. It has been almost a week since Canadian infantry made an amphibious assault against the Germans holding out in Holland's Scheldt pocket. The Low Countries are about to fall; Germany itself can only follow. And in the future is a Canada blossoming in peacetime, with two gifts he has determined to make to the Canadian people—a flag of their own, and the first Governor General to have been born among them, on their own soil.

After lunch, he works through papers and dispatches, admiring the progress of the war in Europe. He learns that Field Marshal Erwin Rommel, commander of the German ground forces in France at the time of D-Day, died yesterday, presumably from wounds suffered when his car was strafed by Allied aircraft two months earlier. On October 20, his death will be attributed by British military intelligence to Canadian and British Typhoon fighter-bomber pilots of the RAF Tactical Air Force, operating near Dozule, east of Caen, on July 17. Although Rommel was wounded in a strafing on that day, he has, in fact, committed suicide. Three days after Rommel's wounding, Hitler narrowly escaped death in a bombing attempt on his life. Though Rommel was in hospital at the time, his involvement in the plot was suspected by Hitler, and the hero of the Afrika Korps was given two alternatives—face death by firing squad as a traitor, and so place the lives of his family in grave danger, or take his own life and enjoy a hero's funeral, his death attributed to his wounds. And so, on Saturday, Rommel took a stroll in the woods in the company of fellow officers and accepted the vial of poison offered him.

Rommel is dead, and the world from the vantage point of Kingsmere is renewed. It has been a difficult war for King, politically and personally. When hostilities broke out, King, a lifelong bachelor, further pledged himself to an ascetic existence until peace was regained. There would be no drinking, no entertaining, no pleasures that would cloud his mind and inhibit his reception of messages from the spiritual plane in those most crucial days. Those days are now, surely, coming to an end. The possibilities the immediate future hold out, the magical transformation of the landscape, the general gladness of the day, fill him with euphoria. He has been impatient to put the war behind himself, the Liberal Party and the nation. Two months away from his seventieth birthday, King has spent almost eighteen years in the prime minister's office; having returned to power in 1935, he was leading the country when war was declared, and he leads it still. More than four years have passed since the last election, a campaign that rewarded him with a majority government. He must renew his mandate with the electorate by next summer, and he is eager to secure for himself an unfettered run at governing in the postwar years.

A month earlier, King met with Churchill and Roosevelt at Quebec City for their second wartime conference in that redoubt. Two days before leaving for Quebec City, King had bid adieu in Ottawa to Princess Juliana of the Netherlands, who was preparing to return home after spending the war in exile in Canada. *I began to feel that the war was ending,* he wrote in his diary that September day. *It was one of those memorable scenes that helped in a way to recall its early beginning but some new orientation was clearly coming into being.* King was already making plans for the postwar economy, plotting changes in his cabinet.

With the war in Europe having swung in the Allies' favour, elections were on the minds of all three leaders converging on Quebec City for the conference known as Octagon. It was essentially a meeting between Churchill and Roosevelt, but King as host had the opportunity to play equal partner in the Allied cause. King arrived by train on September 10, the fifth anniversary of Canada's formal entry in the war. The following morning, before waking, he was gripped by a vision, which seemed to him to augur an improvement in Liberal electoral chances. Quebec premier Maurice Duplessis, leader of the isolationist Union Nationale, had reacted to the approach of war by dissolving the legislature and calling an election in October 1939, gambling on a French-Canadian distaste for imperial wars delivering him a secure majority. But Quebec ministers in King's cabinet, led by Justice Minister Ernest Lapointe, insinuated themselves into the election, telling voters that if Duplessis were re-elected, they would resign their portfolios, thereby leaving Quebec without a strong voice at the federal level as war was being waged. Québécois fearful of a repeat of Conservative Prime Minister Sir Robert Borden's imposition of conscription during the Great War were they to lose their champions in the King cabinet dutifully lined up behind the Liberal party. Duplessis was swept from office by the provincial Liberals, who stood foursquare on all policy fronts with King. After four years of war, however, Quebec has swung back in Duplessis' favour, delivering him the premiership on August 8. And on August 18, fifty thousand Montrealers welcomed back their old mayor, Camillien Houde, who had spent four years in military prison after encouraging Quebecers not to register for the draft, and promptly re-elected him. King's vision nonetheless gives him hope. *The vision was like a beacon [of] light spreading its light over the country from*

Quebec. But what was noticeable in it was that this light symbol-
ized Liberal thought. It was a golden light and seemed as I have
said to be shed over the entire country.

On the eleventh, King was abruptly summoned to meet with the
freshly arrived Roosevelt in his car, a breach of protocol that ruffled King: it was as if Roosevelt considered himself still to be on
American soil. King was surprised by the president's frailty.
Roosevelt asked him directly about election plans—Roosevelt must
face the American electorate on November 7. King told him there
would be no Canadian election this year, and was uncertain of what
the outcome of one would be. He then joined Churchill alone in
Churchill's car for the formal motorcade. It is an understatement to
say that, in the course of this war, King and Churchill have been
through much together. King respects, even venerates, Churchill's
opinions—about the course of the war, even about Canadian politics. King's solidarity extends to holding a membership in
Churchill's Conservative Party. Riding with Churchill in the car, *I*
asked him if he expected the war to be over this year. He said the
military authorities believed it will, "I don't." ...He spoke about the
political situation in Canada. He said: your party looks a little in a
better position. Spoke of the results in Quebec. Of what they
demonstrated of the difficulty we had. Talked of the President's
chances. He could not see that the President would not win. Said
that it would be ingratitude itself. At the luncheon table, he spoke of
never having based his own actions on merely public opinion. That
he had yet to find that the people themselves would not respond to
service. He thought it would be gross ingratitude if they did not.

On the evening of the twelfth, King met with Field Marshal Sir
John Dill, the British representative on the Combined Chiefs of
Staff, the British-American strategic directorate in Washington. A
reputation for being overcautious had led to his being replaced by
Alan Brooke as Chief of the Imperial General Staff in December
1941—he had, for one thing, recommended to the War Cabinet that
Britain withdraw from Hong Kong rather than try to defend it. In
conversation with King, he was anything but cautious about the
war's progress. *I asked when he thought the war would be over. He*
said without hesitation that he felt quite sure that it would be at an
end in November. I mentioned having, in November of last year,
said the war might end about that time a year hence. He said you
could not have made a better estimate. Dill's confidence, noted
King, was based on having been told that the Germans didn't have

the reserves to hold out beyond that month. The general mood at Octagon was that victory in Europe was imminent; it was agreed during the conference that resources originally earmarked for that theatre would be switched over to the Pacific.

With Octagon still under way, with a war still to be won, King's mind began to turn increasingly to re-election. *The more I think of it, the more I feel that whether it will be winter or not, once the Germans have surrendered, we should go at once to the country. The last thing I relish is an election in mid-winter. The problems, however, will be so many, particularly related to demobilization, that we should not delay. Also I feel certain that Churchill plans to do that and it would not do to delay long after him. Moreover the country will expect it and except for the winter, take no exception to it.*

King has led the country through the war, but he has not been a wartime leader in the Churchillian mould. Churchill graduated from the Royal Military College, experienced combat in South Africa, devised military strategy during the Great War and was serving as Lord Admiral when Neville Chamberlain's prime ministership was handed to him in May 1940. King had no personal experience of war or military command when hostilities erupted in 1939, and he has produced no stirring pledges of fighting on the beaches, of blood, toil, tears and sweat.

King is a seemingly unlikely combination of anti-imperialist and ardent supporter of the British Commonwealth. He has a modern view of the Commonwealth as a family of equals, not as a mother country and its semi-independent colonies. After all, his grandfather, William Lyon Mackenzie, led an armed rebellion against a colonial clique in control of Upper Canada in 1837, which resulted in reforms granting new powers of self-government. As the Second World War began, and traditionally imperialist groups called upon King to place the country and all of its resources at the disposal of the British government, he was not in the least likely to respond with enthusiasm. He hoped initially that Canadians would not have to do any actual fighting. With combat for Canadians having inevitably arisen, he has shown himself to be traumatized by the deaths of the volunteers ultimately under his command. He is not, like Churchill, predisposed toward waging war for the glory of it.

King also senses a battle approaching that he has no desire to fight, a battle over conscription, and his political instincts run along the lines of denial, evasion and deferment when confronted with an issue that could cost him support of a critical segment of the electorate.

With D-Day's success and the war's momentum in the Allies' favour, he wants nothing more than to put the war in the past, beneath that opaque carpet of snow. Once buried, it will take conscription with it. The country has done more than her fair share, he is ready to argue. He has no ambition to see a Canadian soldier become the first Allied warrior to rush into Hitler's bunker. His priorities have shifted to a peace that the country has yet to reach. On Friday evening, with Canadian troops fighting to open the Belgian port of Antwerp, King announced several key changes in his cabinet with a view to peacetime rule. He gave his minister of transport and of munition and supply, C.D. Howe, the additional duty of reconstruction, a new post. King has created a new department of veterans affairs of which Ian Mackenzie will be minister. His parliamentary assistant, Brooke Claxton, a forty-four-year-old veteran of the Great War, will become minister of the newly formed department of health and welfare, charged with creating the bureaucracy necessary to dispense the funds in the new family allowances program that will come into effect next July.

King of course does not want the country still to be at war next July. He knows, as the European theatre's fortunes have turned for the better, that a Pacific war awaits. He wants as little to do with it as possible—not only to speed along the conclusion of Canada's involvement in the war, but also to avoid having the Liberals tarred by the Pacific theatre's imperial overtones. Superficially, this war has unfolded along much the same lines as the Great War for Canadians. At first, the call to arms was a rallying cry to the aid of England, the mother country. As demands for more enlistees increased in both wars, the cause of democracy and world peace was more emphasized, even though in both wars there was nothing democratic about the harsh regime of a crucial ally, Russia. It has been the way of Canadians to embrace what others might see as turf wars between empires as causes on which hinge the fate of mankind's most noble values. This rationale helped justify the appalling losses of the Great War, as Germany was demonized beyond recognition. It could be said that Canadian soldiers demonstrated a talent for fighting with exceptional courage in the name of causes that might not actually exist. The Second World War has had enough ingredients to make it a potential repeat of the futility and horror of its predecessor. Italy is an inept and unlikely opponent. Propelled by delusions of resuscitating the ancient Roman empire, Mussolini has blundered into an alliance with Hitler, committing his people to fight against enemies—British, Americans and Canadians—that class ties and emigration give them little enthusiasm to oppose. Hitler's treachery has driven Stalin into the Allied camp, thereby making a tyrant as murderous as Hitler into a realpolitik partner of the idealistic Canadians. It will be difficult for veterans, politicians, civilians and historians alike to concede that the battles of western Europe might, in the long view, prove to be a sideshow to the fundamental struggle in the east between Stalin and Hitler, between a pair of merciless totalitarian regimes intent on ruling the continent between Berlin and Moscow. Worse, that the war in western Europe served as a diversion that allowed Stalin's army to swallow Poland, Czechoslovakia, Rumania, Hungary and half of Germany. That said, no sober second thought will deny that Canadians have thrown themselves against a despicable enemy. The Nazis are monsters, and their essential evil has made the sacrifices of the Canadians in combat in this latest European inferno an achievement that cannot fade. It has turned out to be a battle worth fighting. The war, King has been convinced, is right and just: *No wor[l]d drama of the kind could have been conceived in proportions so great and dramatic that it discloses "the hand of God in history.["] God rules in this world; not Satan and his soldiers.*

The Pacific theatre, however, is another matter. The Japanese have demonstrated aggression and cruelty, not least against Canadian troops killed or captured in the fall of Hong Kong, but this component of the global conflict has too many overtones of warring empires for King to want to have much to do with it. The fall of Hong Kong leaves a bad taste in the mouth of Canadian anti-imperialists, certain that British commanders threw away Canadian volunteers in a hopeless defensive assignment to retain a far-flung corner of the Empire. Japan may have embarked on a rapacious conquest of Asia and the Pacific, but her war is essentially with western powers who are not prepared to surrender their own established interests. Britain was an ally of Japan from 1902 until 1922, when strategic ties were broken at the insistence of Australia and the United States. When the British and the Americans, who had thrown in their lot with Chiang Kai-shek's China, attempted to hold back Japan with an oil embargo, the result was the strike on Pearl Harbor, designed to deny the U.S. Navy the ability to enforce the embargo.

Southeast Asia is a quilt of western colonial holdings. When Japanese troops drove the British from Singapore, the local population treated them as liberators, although their subsequent experience with Japanese rule quelled their enthusiasm. Burma, spun off from India by the British in 1935, harboured its own nationalist movement, which openly collaborated with the Japanese invaders. Nationalists led by Mohandas Gandhi launched a "Quit India" campaign to rid the jewel in the Imperial crown of the British defence forces, and in his prewar rhetoric Churchill was wont to make Gandhi sound as dangerous as the Kaiser or Hitler. In a meeting on September 13 with his war cabinet—an assembly of key cabinet members and senior military staff—King recorded, *I held very strongly to the view that no government in Canada once the European war was over would send its men to India, Burma and Singapore to fight with any forces and hope to get through a general election successfully. That to permit this would be to raise at a general election, a nation-wide cry of Imperial wars versus Canada as a nation.* A meeting of the full cabinet resolved that Canada indeed would prefer to fight in the North Pacific, not in the South, while being agreeable to actions extending as far south as Formosa and the Philippines. Ultimately, it is agreed that Canadian troops should participate in the land invasion of Japan.

To conclude Canada's war participation with grace and electoral promise, King needs above all to avoid the political disaster of introducing combat service for conscripts. Canada has resolved to fight this war only with volunteers, although in 1940 the National Resources Mobilization Act resulted in the conscription of men solely for the purposes of home defence. In the process, two Canadian armies were created—one of volunteers fighting in Europe, another of conscripts training, retraining and tending to home-defence duties in Canada alongside volunteer home-defense militia. King has managed to soldier through five years of military and political manoeuvres without having to commit the NRMA men to combat duty overseas. They have remained on the home front as an army of defence and, to the NRMA's detractors, of political compromise. They have attracted the sobriquet of Zombies—the living dead of wartime, not civilians, but not full-fledged fighting men either, loathed and resented at every turn.

For more than two years, King has been dodging the results of a national plebiscite on compulsory overseas service for conscripts. Held on April 27, 1942, the plebiscite uncovered a serious division in the country along a painfully familiar fault line. In Ontario, 82.3 per cent of respondents agreed that conscripts should be committed to overseas service, and not continue to be limited to home defence duties. In Quebec, 72.9 per cent opposed the idea. The plebiscite freed King of his promise in 1940 not to send conscripts into battle, though it did nothing to shake him of his reluctance, as he realized how overwhelmingly opposed Quebec was to such a move.

The Liberal response to the plebiscite, Bill 80, passed in the summer of 1942, deleted the clause in the NRMA limiting service to home defence, and left the door open for the commitment of conscripts to overseas service at a future date, if circumstances warranted, through an order-in-council. But what, in King's mind, would constitute those circumstances? And how would he go about calling them up? To pro-conscription forces, particularly those in his own government, he has been conveniently evasive. Fundamentally, King has maintained that he would call up conscripts only if it was a question of winning or losing the war. But even at that, there has been serious dispute within the King government over *how* they would be called up, if King were ever persuaded to do so. At the conclusion of debate on Bill 80, King declared that before he would send conscripts overseas, he would first seek the approval of the public in another plebiscite. This was too much for his own defence minister, Colonel J.L. Ralston, a Great War veteran, who felt committing conscripts when they were deemed necessary should require nothing more than a wave of the legislative hand to activate the powers the government had just granted itself in Bill 80. Ralston tabled his resignation with King, and the two men were left at an impasse, King declining to accept the resignation, Ralston declining to withdraw it—King appreciating Ralston's skills and commitment to a significant cabinet post in a time of great crisis, Ralston too loyal and too dedicated not to strive to retain his position.

Their standoff was allowed to recede into the background in the ensuing years—so long as volunteer recruitment remained high, and so long as Canada's volunteer army was in camps in England and not in combat, there would not be a manpower crisis in the Canadian active army. Canada's decision in 1943 to commit two divisions and a brigade to the Sicilian and Italian campaigns naturally resulted in battle casualties, and along with needing reinforcements the Canadian army requested another full brigade for Italy in August 1944. King agreed, on the assurance that even this additional commitment of men to the battlefield would not overtax the pipeline of volunteers.

The Normandy invasion unfolded in June 1944 with a Canadian army exclusively manned by volunteers—a proud accomplishment for the country, as the British and Americans used conscripts in their invading forces, and no fighting men made more progress on the first day of the invasion than those of Canada. So long as the conquest of Germany continues with manageable losses, King will be able to avoid sullying his political record by sending in the conscripts as reinforcements. It is an issue on which his political future would seem to hinge—in the election of 1940, Quebec delivered sixty-one of sixty-five possible seats to the Liberals, more than one-third of King's caucus.

He also fears, legitimately, for the country's future. King was first elected to Parliament in 1908, lost office in the rout of Liberals that ended Sir Wilfrid Laurier's reign in 1911, and watched the Great War of 1914–18 nearly destroy his party and the country at the same time. The country had responded to Britain's declaration of war on Germany with imperialist fervour; even Laurier supported the cause as just, provided enlistment was voluntary. Canadians performed magnificently in battle, and the Borden government called for ever higher levels of enlistment, until a target of half a million men was set for a nation of only eight million people. It would mean placing in uniform half of all eligible males, a proportion that would have seemed incomprehensible had not the hyperpatriotic New Zealanders managed to achieve it, with 129,000 men participating.

But as casualties mounted in the bloody stalemate of trench warfare, it was clear the nations of the British empire could not sustain massive armies and their huge losses without compulsory service. Britain and New Zealand introduced conscription in early 1916. Would the other dominions prove patriotic enough to follow suit? South Africa wouldn't even try—there were too many Boers who, having been subjugated by Imperial forces at the turn of the century, could hardly be expected to answer a call-up willingly. The Australian government was similarly hamstrung by a large immigrant Irish population, who were in no mood to come to England's aid when she had backed away from granting Home Rule to Ireland after the Easter Uprising in the spring of 1916. Australia tried through plebiscite to impose conscription for foreign service on its population and failed—twice, in October 1916 and December 1917—even though it, like New Zealand, had already introduced compulsory service before the war for home defence in fear of the threat the Yellow Peril posed in their hemisphere by Japan.[1]

That left Canada. While Canada had its share of Irish Catholic immigrants reluctant to march under the King's orders, the most significant bloc of anti-conscription sentiment was in Quebec, which recognized that the government had no constitutional right to demand combat service from young men for any cause other than home defence. Canada, went the objections of Quebec, was responding to Britain's declaration of war as a de facto colony; her citizens had no representation in the British parliament. Back in 1899, when war between France and Britain seemed imminent, Canadian politicians had warned their British counterparts that compulsory service would not be possible if it meant ordering Quebecers to storm the French possessions of St. Pierre and Miquelon in the Gulf of St. Lawrence.

Two schools of nationalism came clearly into focus: the *autonomiste* movement of Quebec, which viewed Canada and Quebec as an independent political entity without imperialist ties and obligations, and the subservient nationalism of Anglo-Canadians who saw Canada's greatness on the international stage achieved and measured within the context of her relationship with the mother country, Great Britain. Once Canada was deep in the mire of the Great War, Borden's critics argued he was trying to purchase greatness within the Empire with the blood of the country's young men. The more of them in the battle line, the greater the contribution of Canada to the imperial cause, and so the greater Canada's status.

Following the introduction of conscription in Britain and New Zealand, the Empire slogged through a series of costly, ineffective offensives, at the Somme, Arras and finally Passchendaele beginning in July 1917. Borden introduced conscription without resorting to a plebiscite in November 1917 while Canadians were falling by the thousands in a renewed offensive at Passchendaele. Pro-conscriptionist Liberals abandoned their own party to form a Unionist government with Borden. The election of December 17, 1917, was sealed up by the Unionists through voter manipulation—measures were taken to ensure that the ballots of soldiers overseas would be marked practically by default for Unionist candidates, to disenfranchise voters at home determined to be enemy aliens, and to grant votes only to women who were relatives of men overseas. Quebec, which had been engaged in an informal boycott of volunteer enlistment since 1916, erupted in riots in the spring of 1918 when the draft became too much to bear.

It was a shameful, dangerous period in Canadian history, and the country emerged from the killing fields of the Great War and her home-front battles with two distinct, irreconcilable experiences: on the one hand, that of a nation that had suspended the basic rights of its citizens and sacrificed so many bright young lives in a misguided effort to earn itself a place among leading nations in an irrelevant foreign war; and on the other hand, that of a nation that had been able to define itself as such through the valour and sacrifices exhibited at places like Vimy Ridge while helping contain an expansionist Germany whose victory would have been calamitous for Britain and her dominions.

With the death of Laurier, King, who had failed to win a seat in the 1917 election, took over the leadership of the shattered federal Liberals in 1919 at the first leadership convention ever held by a Canadian political party. The Great War has fed an undercurrent of antagonism into his political life. King was not afraid to tar Conservative leader Arthur Meighen with the brush of conscription when campaigning against him in Quebec, and the Conservatives, for their part, endured with a power base in Orange Ontario, devoted to the idea of a Canada defined within the British empire, her greatness a consequence of this association, her obligations to the mother country paramount. Many issues occupied the forefront of the public stage in the 1920s and 1930s—issues related to labour and social programs—but the essential paradox of the country's experience in the Great War remained. Twenty-five years after Canadians first answered Borden's call to come to England's aid, the call went out anew. An old and bloody war was reborn, and with it those powerful undercurrents resurfaced. In responding to the outbreak of hostilities in Europe in 1939, Canada was destined to relive all the emotional upheaval and antagonisms of 1914–18.

After five years of war, it seems that the country will be able to emerge from the experience stronger than she entered it, with old wounds, if not fully healed, then at least not so aggravated that they will never heal. Yet with the hour of victory seemingly at hand, the country is sinking into dispiriting contrariness. Ontario premier George Drew, a Progressive Conservative who came to power with a minority government in 1943, and a Great War veteran besides, has been a longstanding critic of federal defence policy. He caused the King government considerable embarrassment when he received a tip that the Canadian regiments sacrificed at Hong Kong were sent on that garrison assignment without their trucks, which had been shipped to the Philippines. He has been relentlessly critical of King's government and Quebec's alleged failure to pull its weight in the war effort. Having returned from a summer's tour of Canadian troops in Europe, he and his fellow Conservatives have been calling vociferously for the commitment of conscripts to combat. They have been supported unconditionally by conservative newspapers such as the Toronto *Globe and Mail*, whose editorial page on Friday declared Drew to be "the most outstanding, most honest public man now holding office in Canada."

The most persuasive arguments, however, have been made by a fellow Conservative, Major Conn Smythe, wounded at Caen, now recovering from his injuries at Chorley Park Military Hospital in Toronto. In a September 19 article in the *Globe and Mail*, Smythe charged that King's government was sending untrained volunteers to the front line as reinforcements rather than commit overtrained conscripts to combat duty. The practice was costing the lives of volunteers. On Saturday, John Bracken, national leader of the Progressive Conservatives, made a typical contribution to the recent rhetoric on the issue, calling the practice Smythe described "criminal folly." Denials from the government have not satisfied the *Globe and Mail* and the rest of the conservative press, Conservative politicians, Smythe himself, or the soldiers and voters who side with him. Indeed, there are men within King's own party and cabinet who would like to send the conscripts into battle. Smythe's charges carry extra weight beyond his front-line experience. He is also a charismatic public figure, the driving force behind the Toronto Maple Leaf hockey club and an enthusiastic racehorse breeder. The *Globe and Mail*'s president and publisher, George McCullagh, happens to be a director of Smythe's Maple Leaf Gardens Ltd., and McCullagh's *Globe* has made Smythe's charges an ongoing priority. Supportive letters are printed, some having been received by Smythe personally.

The conscripts issue has given Drew fresh cause to further inflame relations between Ontario and Quebec. Already he has expressed his disapproval of the federal family allowance legislation, vocally displeased with the prospect of Ontario tax dollars underwriting the production of Quebec babies. Four days ago, Ontario Liberal leader Harry Nixon announced on the CBC that his party's legislative truce with the Conservatives was over, disparaging what he called Drew's effort to "pit race against race and province against province."

On this Sunday freshly dusted white, his dispatches read and digested, King is nonetheless optimistic. The Nazis will soon be driven from the Low Countries. By this evening, three sectors of Canadian infantry will be within two miles of cutting off the German pocket of resistance south of the river Scheldt, the artery that can feed materiel to the advancing Allies through Antwerp. *In the light of the European picture thus disclosed, and this by intelligence officers in reporting to the Cabinet in Britain in September, I do not see how for a moment there could be entertained thought of conscription in Canada at this period of the war.*

That evening at Kingsmere, King ponders two glass swans in a silver centre dish, their hollow bodies filled with water upon which float pansy blossoms. He recalls a recent sight, a piece of paper floating in water, its folds revealing to him the image of a swan. There is some significance in this, the swans, still to be ascertained. He goes for another walk in the hushed landscape. The swans, the downy snow; the flower petals, the bright leaves still caught up in the trees—these metaphoric mirrors do not rise to his conscience. When he returns from his walk, he glances at the clock. It is 10:23. The clock hands are in perfect alignment. Portent. King retires, a perfect future his principal hope and concern.

The next day, Monday, at 5:30 p.m., he ventures to Government House to call on the Governor General, Alexander Augustus Frederick William Alfred George Cambridge, better known as the Earl of Athlone. The two men get along and are the same age, both now sixty-nine, but come from different worlds of experience. King presents him with a special bound volume, Ludwig's Portrait Sketch, created by an artist friend. *He thanked me for it cordially, mumbling something I did not wholly understand but intended as a word of appreciation. It is this kind of thing that disgusts me—a supposed attitude of royalty in showing no enthusiasm, it being out of form for royalty to express any particular enthusiasm.* King feels out the G.G. on the best way to present a copy to the King and Queen, proposing that he do it through one of the secretaries. *The reply was to the effect that that would be the way. I was going to say I suppose an inscription would hardly be proper, but I omitted that. It is this sacred personage business that sickens one. One would have felt in the intimate relationship we enjoyed, there might have been some expression [that] would have shown a bit of personal interest. It is all part of the affectation of English superiority which in the end may cost those who follow this method more heavily than they imagine. It was all quite amusing to me. Not unkindly*

*meant but just part of the order of things that has persisted through
centuries, of idol worship.*

Their conversation turns to the war. The earl is also a major-general, and served with distinction in South Africa and the Great War,
meriting a mention in dispatches and the DSO. Originally marked
out as Governor General in 1914, the war in Europe intervened,
and he did not begin his five-year term until the spring of 1940,
when Germany was again on the prowl.

Four years later, with his term as King George's representative in
Ottawa coming to an end, he can confidently discuss with King the
issue of demobilization. Except in extreme circumstances, the
Canadian volunteers overseas have not been granted home leave.
Some have not seen their families for five years. No other Allied
army has imposed such a lengthy isolation on its soldiers. The G.G.
speaks of having some of the Canadian forces demobilized. The
war in Europe, after all, is in its final phase; the German back has
been broken. But there is this matter of Conservative rabble rous-
ing, principally by Drew and Smythe. The Conservatives have been
hammering away at the defence department, and while Ralston has
been loyal to King in his responses, the defence minister has no
personal enthusiasm for shielding the NRMA men.

King reflects on the Smythe–Drew–Ralston set-to, and the G.G.
assuages his concerns about the allegations made by Smythe and
Drew: typical of the things said about the war. King notes that
Ralston will be returning from his overseas tour of the troops on
Wednesday, and is braced for the worst. Ralston's telegram on
Friday suggested that he will be seeking front-line duties for the
conscripts. This, King maintains, *would be madness at this stage of
the war.* The G.G. agrees. It is getting late, he says, for anything of
the kind.

Time is of the essence. The past speaks to him—through spirits,
through experience, through shrewdly observed lessons of past triumphs and follies. He is keenly aware of his revolutionary grandfather. King is no firebrand, though he has a capacity for reform
when the political winds warrant. But where his ancestor incited
revolution, King is desperate to avoid one. He places his faith in the
cleansing, unifying light of his vision. In his mind, the war is all
but over because it must be. He suspects a war in the Pacific would
keep Canadians in combat for another eighteen months after the
fall of Germany, an intolerable scenario. He must have peace. He
must have an election. And Canadians must have their own flag and

their own Governor General. While the earl's term is up in the spring, King doesn't want him to leave his posting until the war is won, and tells him so. But once he does leave, King wants a Canadian as his replacement. He sets before the G.G. the name of his candidate; the earl is surprised that this man would be interested in the post, but nonetheless approves.

King leaves Government House with the future within his grasp, if only he can outmanoeuvre a present heavily freighted with the past. Ralston will be back from his tour in two days, bearing a message King cannot stomach. The prime minister is in for the fight of his life—a fight in which he sees at stake not only his own political future, but the very survival of the nation. Canada will emerge from the coming winter either as a nation triumphant, a leading player on the world stage, or as a nation in ruins, tearing itself apart as loyalty to an outdated notion of Empire compels the military infrastructure to keep on fighting past the point of the country's moral obligation. The latter is King's own vision: not the one he experiences in his dreams, but the one he projects to his colleagues and his cabinet. They will either acknowledge its likelihood as solemnly as he does, or turn away from it and in so doing make it his living nightmare.

King's manner is to seek the meaning within messages, to ponder significance where others see no messages at all. You must look, and listen, and learn. But King is only seeing and hearing reassurances, affirmations instead of warnings. He is careering toward a fate he cannot foresee, though he calculates every possible movement with an eye to consequence. The foreshadowing is in Rommel's camouflaged death. King's walk in the snow; Rommel's walk in the woods with his comrades. The vial of poison Rommel is forced to drink by erstwhile allies. He really had no choice. King will not have one either. His handpicked champion will leave him no alternative but to accept a bitter solution. It is a time of betrayal defying loyalty, shame sullying honour, action obscuring motive. Winter has lowered a blinding disguise over William Lyon Mackenzie King's world.

RITES OF SPRING

You have to admit that one NHL player is worth
2 wartime NHL'ers.
—April 9, 1944, letter from Conn Smythe
to Leaf scout Squib Walker[1]

April 10, 1939

IT has been a long campaign for the Edmonton Athletic Club
Roamers. It actually began back in 1934, when a struggling young
attorney named Clarence Campbell, who will go on to become
president of the National Hockey League, persuaded two other
Junior clubs in Edmonton to suspend operations so that the city's
young talent could be pooled in one lineup, the EAC Roamers.
That team, with brothers Neil and Mac Colville up front, made it to
the Memorial Cup finals, the national Junior hockey championships, against the St. Michael's College Majors of Toronto, a
club sponsored by Conn Smythe's Toronto Maple Leafs. The
Roamers lost the best-of-three final 5–0 and 6–4 (in overtime), and
have spent the last five seasons trying to earn another shot at the
championship. When the 1938/39 Roamers defeated the Brandon
Elks to win the western Junior title and advance to the Memorial
Cup finals in Maple Leaf Gardens, the possibility of a national title
for an Edmonton Junior club at last arose.

At 1:07 of the first period of the opening game, Edmonton moves
ahead on a goal by Bob Carse. The Roamers are soon up 2–0. Then
Billy the Kid Taylor puts on a show.

Taylor is a razzle-dazzler, a dipsy-doodler, a 143-pound crowd
pleaser, and no one in the Gardens crowd is more pleased than
Conn Smythe, managing director, part owner and motivating force
of the Maple Leafs. Smythe's Leafs hold the professional rights to
the Winnipeg-born phenomenon who is about to turn twenty.
Taylor unstitches every seam in the Roamers' defensive cloak. He
scores once in the first period and twice in the second, halfway
through which the Roamers collapse. Taylor comes out for the third
period and scores three more times; when sixty minutes are up,
Oshawa has won 9–4 on the strength of six Taylor goals.

The next game is another showcase for Taylor's stickhandling, deking, passing and shooting. He scores four times and assists on five other goals as the Generals win 12–4. The Roamers check Taylor more assiduously in the third game and win 4–1, but they cannot turn around the series, losing 4–2 in game four. Although prevented from scoring in the last two games, Taylor has scored ten times and registered six assists in producing the best personal performance of the series.

Bob Carse, who opened the scoring for Edmonton in the first game, produces the best offensive effort of any Roamer, finishing fourth on points in the series. After scoring twice and assisting on one other goal in the 9–4 loss of game one, the five-foot nine-inch, 170-pound left-winger was stymied by Generals' checking, and ends the series with three goals and three assists. Two months younger than "Kid" Taylor, the nineteen-year-old Carse, who has played in the EAC system for seven years, is a young man in a hurry to get on with life. He is already married with a two-year-old daughter, and his wife Betty is expecting a second child in the fall. As sure as Taylor is to star with the Maple Leafs, Carse has a future mapped out as a Chicago Blackhawk.

Last autumn, it looked as though Carse was destined to be a New York Ranger. General manager Lester Patrick has been paying attention to the Edmonton hockey scene since Neil and Mac Colville came out of the 1933/34 EAC Roamers lineup to star for him. Patrick has been helping underwrite the EAC bottom line and in August 1938 he came to Edmonton to see what sort of boys the athletic club had to offer. Carse was one of two invited to a school the Rangers ran for amateur prospects in Winnipeg in October. The Rangers already owned Bob's brother Bill, five years older, who was on the 1933/34 Roamers team with the Colvilles and has played for the Rangers' American Hockey League affiliate, the Philadelphia Ramblers, since 1937.

But the Carse brothers' professional futures have been remapped by the collapse of the Chicago Blackhawks. After winning the Stanley Cup in 1937/38 (admittedly after winning only fourteen of forty-eight games that season), the defending champions failed to make the playoffs in the spring of 1939. The team embarks on a youth drive and issues a four-page flyer for its fans, outlining its rebuilding strategy.

"The unpredictable and disappointing showing of the veteran team during the 1938/39 season clearly demonstrated that new blood, mainly youths with speed, stamina and hockey brains, was badly needed to give Chicago a representative team. To this end the Black Hawks'* management decided on two important, and what they believe will be beneficial steps—

"First—To purchase the outstanding rookies of the Minor Leagues.

"Second—Planning not only for 1939–40 but for the coming years as well, the Hawks decided on a thorough scouting of the amateur players throughout the entire Dominion of Canada."[2]

Late in the 1938/39 season, Paul Thompson came to Edmonton to have a look at Bob Carse. The Blackhawks organization has considerable Alberta roots. Although Thompson, a Calgarian, was a charter member of the New York Rangers lineup assembled by Conn Smythe in his shortlived stint as Rangers general manager in 1926, the left-winger was an All-Star with the Blackhawks in the 1930s. And while Paul was starring with the Blackhawks, his older brother "Tiny" was in Boston, where in the 1930s he became the first goaltender to win four Vezinas. Paul played his last thirty-seven NHL games with Chicago in 1938/39, then at season's end took over as coach of the floundering defending champions. Tiny, who has been traded to Detroit to make way for a new Bruins goal-tending star, Frank Brimsek, will play one more NHL season before joining the Blackhawks as a scout. And running the Blackhawks day-to-day is assistant general manager Bill Tobin, who played goal for the Edmonton Eskimos of the old Western Canada Hockey League. When it folded in 1926, Tobin headed to Chicago with little more than a suitcase to his name to see if there was a living to be made with the new Blackhawks franchise. He will take over as general manager in 1942.

The Rangers have decided to pass on Bob Carse, or Bob Carse has decided to pass on the Rangers; whichever is the case, in the spring of 1939 the Roamers star is available. Paul Thompson puts Bob Carse on Chicago's negotiating list and then secures his professional rights. In May the Blackhawks also buy from the Rangers the contract of Bill Carse, who finished second in the AHL scoring race. These are days when brother acts are a novelty item. The Rangers already have Neil and Mac Colville and Lester Patrick's sons Lynn and Murray ("Muzz").

In the fall of 1939, Bob and Bill Carse are at the Blackhawks

---

*At the time the club was spelling its name as two words. "Blackhawks" was eventually settled on.

training camp. Twenty-three-year-old Doug Bentley, one of five hockey-playing brothers from Delisle, Saskatchewan, who played Senior hockey in Drumheller in 1938/39, makes the team, and will be joined by brother Max in 1940/41. Also on hand is a young Calgary goaltender named Frank McCool, who doesn't make the cut.

At the end of training camp, Bob Carse is offered a contract by Bill Tobin. He will be paid $2,000, with a $200 signing bonus. Bob balks—he wants a $500 bonus. Tobin then hands him two envelopes, and tells him: pick one. One has $200 in it; the other has a train ticket back to Edmonton. He takes the $200. He is not complaining. Coming out of the Depression, two thousand dollars is an enormous sum of money. "Heck, those were the days when you couldn't carry five dollars worth of groceries," he will recall. "I was paying $46 a month for my apartment and I thought that that was high." He also has to consider the welfare of a wife and daughter, with a second daughter about to arrive, at a time when the world is making a convulsive break with the Dirty Thirties. While the United States is still a neutral nation, Canada has just gone to war with Germany. Bob Carse heads south of the border to earn a living.

The Blackhawks plan is to assign Bob to their American Hockey League affiliate, the Providence Reds, for a year or two of seasoning. The Reds are a very good tier-two pro outfit, owned by Lou Pieri and coached since 1937/38 by Fred "Bun" Cook, a star left-winger with the New York Rangers for ten seasons. Bob makes a positive impression very quickly. While Billy Taylor is struggling in his debut as a Maple Leaf, collecting only ten points in twenty-nine games, Bob ends up splitting his season between Providence and Chicago, joining his brother Bill with the Blackhawks for twenty-two games. The Blackhawks overall aren't much in the scoring department—Bill collects twenty-three points, Bob eight—but after winning only twelve games and finishing last in 1938/39, the Blackhawks of 1939/40 win twenty-three games, only two less than Toronto, and finish fourth in the seven-team league, thereby making the playoffs.

Bob plays for both Chicago and Providence in the playoffs that spring. The Leafs sweep Chicago in two games in their semifinal matchup, and Bob is held without a point. Providence, on the other hand, goes all the way and defeats the Pittsburgh Hornets three straight in the American league championship finals. In six playoff games, Bob Carse contributes three goals and two assists.

The 1939/40 season has played out against a background of the

deceptively idle months of the phony war; Germany has been girding itself for its next phase of conquest, leaving the rest of the world
to wonder what all the militaristic fuss is about. But in the midst of
the playoffs in the spring of 1940, the war, like some somnolent
monster, suddenly awakens. On April 9, Germany invades Denmark
and Norway. On May 10, the Nazi blitzkrieg begins its western
offensive by sweeping into Luxembourg, Holland and Belgium.
That day, Neville Chamberlain, he of the hollow "peace in our time"
accord with Hitler of 1938, calls upon the Liberal and Labour parties to form a coalition government to make possible a united
response to the emergency. When the Labour members refuse to sit
in a government under his command, Chamberlain is forced to hand
over the prime ministership to his Lord Admiral, Winston Churchill,
who assumes the defence minister's post as well. On May 13,
Churchill makes his "blood, toil, tears and sweat" speech to the
British public. Holland capitulates to Germany two days later, and
the day after that, May 16, the German Wehrmacht breaches the
supposedly impermeable Maginot Line of France. With the Low
Countries, Norway and France collapsing, the British Expeditionary
Force, First French Army and surviving remnants of the Belgian
army are trapped at Dunkirk.

   In the span of a year, Bob Carse has gone from being a star of
Canadian Junior hockey to being an emerging star of the professional game in the United States. He has a promising career ahead of
him, and a growing family around him. But now there is real war,
which also bears the very real possibility of defeat for Britain.
Official American isolationism is dissolving behind closed doors. It
is only a matter of time, it seems, before everyone and everything is
mobilized to beat back the Nazis. The game in which Bob Carse
earns his living is about to become part of that war—not simply
affected by it, but caught up in its objectives and controversies. The
game will come on side, but in some minds it will also let the home
side down. For many athletes, the war will be an exercise in absurdi-
ty and camouflaged heroics. For others, it will play out tragically.
The deaths of a handful of young men will allow hockey to emerge
from a global firestorm stronger than it entered it. Because so few
will give so much, the game will emerge scarcely singed. It will, in
fact, be better than it ever was. Faced with the privations of war, the
game will prove to be cunning, resourceful, where necessary decep-
tive, and for the most part profitable. With one very large exception,
the men in suits who manage and amass fortunes from the game are

not compelled to make personal sacrifices to bring an end to international tyrannies. By the time Bob Carse has made his mark as a
Providence Red and Chicago Blackhawk in the 1939/40 playoffs,
Conn Smythe, managing director of the Toronto Maple Leafs, is well
on his way to realizing an irresistible ambition: killing Germans.

THE WARRIOR

June 5, 1940

ADOLF Hitler's invasion of France is under way, having begun at
four o'clock this morning, Paris time, and about 100 German aircraft
are flying sorties over England as Conn Smythe, Toronto hockey
impresario, makes his first flight in twenty-three years. A flight student aboard one of the Toronto Flying Club's DeHavilland Moth
biplanes, he is thousands of miles from the 120 German divisions
driving toward the Seine or the Heinkel bombers pounding British
airfields, several thousand feet above a landscape that has not seen
conflict of any dimension since the prime minister's grandfather led
an armed mob out of a Toronto tavern in 1837 in an attempt to flush
the ruling class from the seat of power in Upper Canada. Below and
around him stretch the city, the farms, the rim of the blue bowl of the
lake, the rail lines snaking east and west, and north, into transitional
terrain, farmland giving way to wilderness, wilderness yielding tim-
ber, minerals various, arboreal vistas of crown land. The King's land,
claimed in the monarchy's name, governed with his blessing and
under his authority. The threshold of this wilderness is obvious from
a height of six thousand feet; its receding vastness is the magnitude
of the kingly realm—literally majestic—an awesome expanse.

When he was only seventeen, in 1912, Smythe had headed alone
into the north to try his hand at homesteading, building a cabin on
150 acres in Clute township, about ten miles west of where the
Temiskaming and Northern Ontario Railway met up with the new
National Transcontinental line, then under construction. Land grants
were available to veterans of the South African War, payment from
the crown in bites of trackless territory for services rendered. That
war, a war that had nothing to do with Canada's domestic security,
had elicited a remarkable stampede to enlist among the country's
young men, a budding of imperial patriotism that would flower

dramatically in a few short years when the nations of Europe fell upon each other. How Smythe came to acquire his land is unknown, but here is a small clue: the crown lands agent for the region, S.J. Dempsay, happened to hail from the same Protestant niche of Northern Ireland, County Antrim on the outskirts of Belfast, as Smythe's father, Albert. Smythe is—becomes—a great believer in connections, in patronage. He believes in obligations, which are debts as well as duties, and often the happy consequence of acquaintances gathered and nurtured. His loyalty can be fiercely resolute, though prone to abrupt reversals when he suspects not simply an easing in reciprocity but outright treachery. You do not cross Conn Smythe. You do not let him down.

This is one consequence of a life shaped by its own loyalties to absolute principles. Smythe does not always succeed—the homestead venture sputters out in one summer—but he rarely demonstrates regret. He can be, despite his public forthrightness, self-deprecating with friends; he understands himself well enough to know when he is being a handful, but it does not temper his intrinsic drive, which by any measure is extraordinary.

Nearly a quarter-century before this flight, Smythe soared above a very different landscape in his devotion to the Empire. The King's rule can be measured out in acres and apportioned to different corners of the globe, but the topography of Empire for men like Smythe is not about borders but about race: a people's destiny. He had put behind him his dalliance with wilderness, and his subsequent studies at the University of Toronto, to rush to the aid of England in its battles on French and Belgian soil against Bismarck's hated Germans—a situation precipitated by a Serbian terrorist's assassinating the crown prince of Austria. Having been shot down in 1917, Smythe took away from the Great War no fondness for aircraft yet an unshaken faith in the Empire and its subjects' obligations. The faith is so great that it has put him back in the cockpit of the hated device and sent him aloft to survey the domain and seek out, as it were, the surest, not necessarily the safest, route back to the battlefield.

❧

Helena Petrovna Blavatsky saw it all. She saw the past in the present, and in the future too. She saw the future in the present, and in the past too. She saw repetition: periodicity. The sun rising, and setting, and rising again. Man born, man dying, man born again. The soul, that is, in its journey toward perfection. A person's soul has visited many, many times, among many races of men, some of them never physically realized, and it will be back, among that person's descendants, among new races more perfect than their predecessors. And then—a glorious winking out of all life as the universe is suffused with a spiritual completeness. Evolution will have reached its zenith, and there will be nothing except unbridled bliss.

Madame Blavatsky was intimate with the spiritual plane. At her séances, it rapped on tables for her. Sometimes it tipped them. Henry Steele Olcott was less intimate, though a seeker of spiritual truth nonetheless. The Civil War Union Army veteran and leading New York lawyer was introduced to the Ukrainian-born emigré in 1874 at the hub of spiritualist phenomena in New York State, whereupon their minds met; no one knows if their bodies did as well. By the autumn of 1875, they had formulated a cohesive spiritualist doctrine where none had truly existed before. They called it theosophy, and it embraced all religions because it claimed to be based on an ancient wisdom that was the root belief of all subsequent theologies. Its foremost accomplishment was to ground the spiritualist movement's unelaborated convictions of an intertwined life and afterlife in the borrowed tenets of Hindu's Brahmanism. Deities and other prominent figures of the major religions such as Christ, Buddha and the mahatmas were embraced as great teachers, universal beings. All souls were deemed part of a brotherhood linked to one great entity, the Over-Soul, and their passage through successive reincarnations, reaching toward an ultimate perfection, was a reflection of the truth of nature's periodicity, the measurable rhythm of change that is repetition.

Madame Blavatsky explained it as best she could in her best-selling *Isis Unveiled*, published in 1876. Though not always cohesive, it nonetheless spelled out an extraordinary belief system that liberal reformers, artists and spiritual seekers of the upper classes found irresistible. Blavatsky produced a more explicit theology in *The Secret Doctrine* (1888) and *The Voice of Silence* (1889)—by then theosophy was an international sensation.

Like all spiritualists, the theosophists believed in the immortality of the soul, which was engaged in a cycle of progress both in the physical world and in the higher spheres of existence beyond this mortal realm. Theosophists rejected the Catholic concept of redemption, holding that it was up to the individual soul to make its own way toward betterment under the watchful eye of karma, the law of justice. Theosophy also rejected the idea of predestination of the soul, the idea that some of us are condemned to burn in hell the moment we are born, adhered to by dour Protestants like the Puritans and Jansenists. And unlike traditional Christian belief, the theosophical soul did not simply ascend to heaven after its mortal phase on earth; it entered into a kind of ecstatic purgatory for some 1,500 years before returning to the material realm in another human form.

Darwin's evolutionary theory had a tangible influence on Blavatsky's wisdom. The planets moved through successive phases of existence—at any given time the earth existed on no less than seven planes, one physical, the rest unknowable to us. Humanity was moving simultaneously through a cycle of seven, progressively superior races. The first two had existed on a purely spiritual plane. The third race, the Lumerians, were the first to replace spiritual with sexual reproduction, not necessarily a good thing. About eighteen million years ago, in the middle of the Lumerian reign, humanity acquired a physical existence and learned about good and evil. Then came the Atlanteans, the last of whom perished a few thousand years ago after their continent disappeared beneath the sea. The fifth—and modern—race, the Aryans, emerged from northern Asia, diffusing into seven subraces, the fifth of which was the Anglo-Saxons. As Madame Blavatsky composed theosophical thought, a sixth race was beginning to supplant the Aryans: the first signs of this were appearing in America, where she happened to live. Once the sixth and seventh races appeared, humanity would reach the end of its corporeal cycle and move to a purely spiritual plane as the life impulse of the Over-Soul withdrew from earth.

There was more—much more—and theosophy found a wide following internationally. Ostensibly egalitarian in its creed, it nonetheless left plenty of room to manoeuvre for the consciences of the privileged. Madame Blavatsky warned her adherents of the "curse of karma," or the idea that transgressions in a past life produced suffering in the present one. Ergo, if people were suffering in this life, it was because of something they had done in a previous one, at least 1,500 years ago, which had nothing to do with those who were doing perfectly fine, thank you. If your life was in a hole, it was up to you to climb out of it, to seek the karmic betterment that would improve your lot in your next life. While theosophy emphasized that personal privilege was only justified if gained by merit, and stressed the importance of charity in a soul's progress, it also accommodated a notion of heredity of family karma, which allowed an adherent to accept the elevated standing of royalty, the nobility and dynastic wealth. (Madame Blavatksy's father, an officer in the Russian army, was descended from petty German nobility.)

Blavatsky had not yet published two of her most influential works, *The Secret Doctrine* and *The Voice of Silence*, when the essential message of *Isis Unveiled* captivated a twenty-three-year-old poet, essayist and Dickens enthusiast in Northern Ireland named Albert Edward Stafford Smythe. He made his acquaintance with the theosophist canon in Belfast and then Edinburgh in 1884, just when the reputation of its architect faced total ruin. The newly formed Society for Psychical Research had an opportunity to inter-view Madame Blavatsky and other leading theosophists while they were in England and investigate their claims of paranormal occur-rences. In December of that year they issued a preliminary report stating "it is certain that fraud has been practised by persons con-nected with the Society." Madame Blavatsky's purported liaisons with the spirit world were, they concluded, entirely worldly, and in hindsight it seems a little more than likely, for example, that letters she claimed were addressed to her from across the great divide were of her own hand, not to mention on her own stationery. Theosophy survived this scandal, which did not seem to shake the faith of a fresh recruit like Albert Smythe. Immigrating to Canada in 1889, he began proselytizing with such vigour that by 1891 he had enough adherents to form a theosophical lodge.

It was a seminal year in the movement as a whole. Madame Blavatsky died on May 8, 1891, a date thereafter marked by theosophists as White Lotus Day. After a scuffle over the transition of power, the leadership moved to Annie Besant, a charismatic reformer and brilliant orator who championed the independence of India. In the United States, W.Q. Judge led a breakaway movement, the first of many over theosophy's history. Under Besant's leader-ship the movement grew as never before, deftly putting behind it the scandal of Madame Blavatsky's psychic sleights-of-hand while upholding her teachings and revering her memory. In Toronto, Albert Smythe became a charter member of the Theosophical Society of Canada and the editor of its monthly newsletter, a responsibility he fulfilled until the final years of his life.

In 1911 Besant caused another rift in the theosophical movement by presenting her young Indian apprentice Jiddu Krishnamurti as a World Teacher and making him the focal point of the Order of the Star of India. Rudolf Steiner, whose authority rivalled that of Besant, chose to break away with a large number of followers to found the Anthroposophical Society. By this time the Smythe family was experiencing a leadership crisis of its own. Albert's first wife, Amelia Constantine, had borne him a son—Constantine Falkland Cary—on February 1, 1895. The boy never liked the ring of his mother's maiden name, and when he was finally christened at age nine, he insisted that his name be shortened to Conn, as in King Conn, the Irish ruler who fought one hundred battles.

Amelia, who liked to drink and was a bit of a hell-raiser, died in 1906. After her death, Conn became estranged from his father, a circumstance exacerbated by Albert's new relationship with Jane Henderson. Conn bolted for the woods west of Cochrane in the spring of 1912, in defiance of his father's wishes that he study law at the University of Toronto.

Conn was a fine athlete, and bright and ambitious. Though the Smythes at times lived not far beyond the reach of poverty, Albert made sure Conn had every opportunity to appease karma by enrolling him in Upper Canada College, the High Anglican private school favoured by Toronto's Protestant upper crust. (Albert had begun working for the *Toronto World* in 1903, and by 1908 was the newspaper's editor. Twice a week he wrote a front-page column of a spiritually uplifting nature.)

Conn Smythe grew up in one of the most fervently Imperialist periods in the history of Britain and her colonies, when boys were inundated with a barrage of propaganda on the greatness of the Empire and their duties to defend it. As historian Lawrence James will relate, "A generation of university teachers, schoolmasters, clergymen, poets, journalists and boys' fiction writers concentrated their minds and energies on popularising the cult of the new imperialism. At its heart lay the concept of 'Anglo-Saxon manhood,' an abstraction compounded in equal parts of patriotism, physical toughness, skill at team games, a sense of fair play (sometimes called 'sportsmanship'), self-discipline, selflessness, bravery and daring." J.E.C. Weldon, headmaster of Harrow from 1891 to 1895 and later the bishop of Calcutta, observed: "If there is in the British race, as I think there is, a special aptitude for 'taking up the white man's burden'...it may be ascribed, above all other causes, to the spirit of organized games." The Battle of Waterloo, after all, had been won on the playing fields of Eton.

Smythe will recall attending a Woodcraft Indians camp* and

---

*The Woodcraft Indians movement was founded in 1902 by nature writer Ernest Thompson Seton, who went on to help establish the Boy Scouts.

becoming involved in a competition for points with six other boys. On the last day of the contest, the boys had to track an "Indian" across the camp and into the woods. At the end of this trail, the successful contestant would find a wooden dummy that he had to shoot with his bow and arrow.

"Just as we started out," he will relate, "my shoelace came untied. By the time I'd stopped and done it up, the rest of the kids had disappeared into the woods. I thought I heard them off to one side, so I took a shortcut through the woods and what do you think? There's the dummy figure right in front of me.

"It's only ten feet away and I take aim with my bow and arrow and missed. So I got the arrow and plunged it into the dummy's heart and then I yelled that I had found it. I won the competition."

G.A. Henty, one of the most successful "boys' tales" authors of the era, summed up concisely the qualities the son of the Empire should embody in his youth novel *Through the Sikh War*:

> Think it over yourself, Percy. Can you thrash most fellows your own age? Can you run as far and as fast as most of them? Can you take a caning without whimpering over it? Do you feel, in fact, that you are able to go through fully as much as any of your companions? Are you good at planning a piece of mischief, and ready to take the lead in carrying it out?... It is pluck and endurance and the downright love of adventure and danger, that have made us the masters of the great part of India, and ere long makes us the rulers of the whole of it.[1]

Young Conn was moulded by precisely this curriculum of duty and daring at Upper Canada College; when not in class, he sometimes found himself street-fighting with the city's many Irish Catholic youth. After his outburst of pluck and endurance sputtered out in the bush northwest of Cochrane in the summer of 1912, he enrolled at the University of Toronto that autumn in pursuit of a degree, not in law, but in civil engineering, even though his father had lost his admission papers. In 1913 Albert and Jane married, and there followed a stepsister, Moira, for Conn.

Conn became one of the more accomplished young hockey players in Toronto, scoring prolifically as a centre. He was nineteen when his University of Toronto Varsity squad won the Ontario Junior hockey title in the spring of 1915. The clinching game was

on a Friday. On the Monday, Conn and the rest of the fully vested
Imperialists in the Varsity lineup took the next logical step in their
sporting careers: they enlisted en masse in the Canadian army.
(Smythe will recall that the team had tried to enlist at the start of the
season, but were told to come back when they had beards.) After
securing a provisional rank of lieutenant with 2nd (Ottawa) Battery,
8th Brigade, on July 17, he headed to the Royal School of Artillery
in Kingston, Ontario, in August for five weeks of training. On
September 11, he was made a full lieutenant, and managed to get
himself transferred to the 40th (Sportsmen's) Battery of Hamilton,
organized by publishing figure Harry Southam. In 40th Battery, the
British public school idea of athletics serving as a proving ground
for those who would be called upon to defend the Empire was
enshrined. The boys were off to make mischief with the Hun.

Conn Smythe's private notebook in the year leading up to his
venture into soldiering is a unique amalgam of topics: racetrack
bets, hockey scores and lists of theosophical reading. Conn wasted
little time with sentences: he itemized.

On February 22, 1914, he took stock of a dozen pamphlets,
among them Evolution and Occultism, Life After Death, Esoteric
Basis of Christ, Transparent Jewel, Astral Light, Sankara Charya,
Love's Chaplet, Voice of Isis, Esoteric Buddhism and Introduction
to Yoga. On March 28 came more reading: Studies of Lesser
Mysteries, Great Law, Bhagwad Gita, The Other Side of Death,
Growth of Soul. Still more reading appeared: Some Questions
Concerning Theosophy, Feet of Masters; and manuals on reincar-
nation, karma and the astral plane.

Near the end of his life, in 1977, Smythe will offer in an interview that his father taught him the principles of theosophy. "I'm a
theosophist today," he will say. "Very straightforward religion. Just
believe in the basic things. The Golden Rule. As ye sow, so shall ye
reap. Things like those two. *Cast* your bread on the *waters*! That's
the best one of 'em all. Great truth in it. But I'll tell ya what it all
comes down to in theosophy, the reason I've stayed a theosophist
all my life. It's because theosophy teaches you that ya can't get
away with anything in this life anyway!"[2]

He seems to have been most affected by theosophy's essential
dictum that a man controls his own destiny, that his betterment is
within his own hands. He will not reflect upon theosophy's sterner,
ascetic measures as laid down by Madame Blavatsky. In *The Secret
Doctrine,* for example, she stated that the curse of karma would be

suffered for "desecrating the divine gift, and wasting the life-essence for no purpose except bestial personal gratification."

Madame Blavatsky taught that a theosophist disciple has two Selves, a Self of Matter and a Self of Spirit. The two Selves, she lectured, can never meet, and ultimately one must eradicate the other. With the spiritual realm's superiority over the mortal one, there could be no doubt which Self must prevail. "Ere thy soul's mind can understand," she wrote, "the bud of personality must be crushed out, the worm of sense destroyed past resurrection." In a chilling passage, she proclaimed, "The Mind is the great Slayer of the Real. Let the Disciple slay the Slayer." The disciple, she wrote, must "kill out desire.... Kill love of life.... Merge the two into the One and sacrifice the personal to SELF impersonal." She went on to write, as one academic study of her work will sum up, "of passing the threshold into the realm in which love of pleasure is destroyed forever, and the roots of one's will to live are torn out."[3]

These were powerfully self-destructive ideas for a young man to carry into what proved to be the greatest killing ground yet experienced in the history of warfare. Some twenty million Selves of Spirit were liberated from their Selves of Matter in four years of combat, among them 56,700 Canadians. Had Conn Smythe absorbed these pronouncements at the core of theosophy, they might have been enough to provoke an acceptance of death, even an active death-wish. The Empire was already telling him to accept it. An ABC primer on patriotic duty, given to Canadian soldiers in 1916, prescribed: "E is for Empire for which we would die." It was possible that Smythe was prepared to accept it not only because it was his duty as a soldier to lay down his life in the name of his king, but because his own soul's transcendence demanded it.

We can imagine him as a young man at a suggestive age in desperate circumstances. We can imagine him in a world tailor-made to Madame Blavatsky's most dire vision of the mortal realm, a wasteland demanding resistance to all feeling: no pleasure, no pain, the roots of one's will to live torn out, leaving one deadened, seeking a release into spiritual bliss, free of any notion of sin.

In early 1917 he made a singlehanded charge on the enemy, armed only with a service revolver. The rashness of the act defies explanation; even Smythe will have a hard time accounting for it. In his version, the incident began when he decided to countermand the orders of his superiors and instructed his gunners to lower their aim, as he thought that his shells were overshooting their targets.

To his horror, he saw white puffs of smoke erupting in the midst of friendly infantry. "I felt the only thing I could do was to run down there and join the men and take the beating they were taking."

He discovered that the puffs of smoke were from German stick bombs. He kept going, running right into a trench. What did he find? Not a wooden dummy at the end of a trail in a Woodcraft Indians camp, but a German with fixed bayonet. He had no bow and arrow on this occasion, just a service revolver.

"I put the pistol in his stomach and fired, and he cursed me all the way down to the ground—at least I think he cursed me, I didn't understand that much German," he would tell a newspaper reporter late in his life. He kept up his shooting on this strange spree until the click-click of the revolver told him he had spent all his ammunition.

On March 5, he was awarded the Military Cross for his rash, even suicidal gallantry. The bizarre incident marked the end of his Great War career as a gunner. Following the death of his commanding officer, Major Gordon Sutherland, he decided to transfer to the Royal Flying Corps, the most dangerous assignment in all of the armed forces. No longer tossing shells into the bruised sky, he now hurled his own self into its hurly-burly, scouting the enemy terrain for the benefit of the gunners he left behind. During the disastrous offensive at Passchendaele in November, he was called upon to direct artillery from the air. He was green, and the cloud cover was low, and he was flying too close to the ground. A *bang* and his rudder control was shot away. For the past year, he had been carrying on a debate with a Catholic comrade about the destination of one's soul at the moment of death. "As I frantically tried to get her out of a flat spin," he will recollect in 1945, "I remembered that I should have been scared to death, because here was the World coming up to me, upside down and inside out, but the only thought I had at that time was this: 'In about ten seconds I'm going to prove that Bill O'Brien was wrong and I was right.'"*

No one was proved right, or wrong. Smythe survived the crash, and subsequent internment as a prisoner of war at Schweidnitz (Swidnica) in Upper Silesia, and two failed escape attempts, and the

---

*The above account was delivered by Smythe in a speech on April 30, 1945, at St. Michael's College in honour of its Junior hockey team. In another account he gave of this incident late in his life, Smythe identified his Catholic debater as his observer, riding with him in the plane at the time. "What now, Conn?" he had the observer asking as the plane spun out of control. Smythe replied, "In a couple of minutes we're gonna find out who was right and who was wrong."

solitary confinement that resulted. He also survived Madame
Blavatsky. How much of her teachings he ever truly ascribes to we
do not know. Albert Smythe endures not as a spouter of scorched-
earth death-wish screeds, but as a gentle, good-humoured man who
was fond of life and the arts and people, who loved his children and
was proud of a son whom he happened to resemble not at all. Albert
Smythe grew a great Shavian beard and looked every inch the Irish
poet. In a photograph taken while imprisoned at Schweidnitz, Conn
appears twice his actual age, his prematurely thinning hair close-
cropped, his trademark pencil moustache already apparent. He never
smokes or drinks, and he maintains his virginity until marriage in
1920. Conn Smythe seems determined to wring every karmic possibility out of this most recent visit to the material realm. Theosophy
must speak to him most persuasively on the plane of potentiality.
You are what you make of yourself. This life is yours to shape. You
are the master of your own destiny. And perhaps, Conn Smythe
understands, as Madame Blavatsky directed, there is a pattern to be
discerned, not only over eons, but within a lifetime as well.

Periodicity.

We move back nine months from his training flight to September
1939. Conn Smythe receives the news of war in Europe as more
than a personal call to arms, a consequence of living a life in which
the security of king and country and empire are paramount. It's true
that, as the son of an Irish Protestant father and an English mother,
he always closely held the sentiments of the Orange Order. When
Great Britain last went to war in Europe, and Canada dutifully followed, Smythe enlisted the moment he was deemed acceptable.
Now he is determined to go back, in both space and time, as it
were, to virtually the same bloodied ground, fighting virtually the
same enemy, compelled to act as the dutiful young subject he once
was. He no longer has an idealistic naivete to shield him or excuse
him. He knows war is not some grand and glorious game, but
Smythe has elevated the play of children to the sport of men in the
years since he embraced and survived the Great War, and his willingness to equate sport and war has turned round on him and encir-
cled him. He feels not so much summoned as judged by the news
that England and Germany are, once again, at each other's throats.

He accepts the war as a litmus test of his character and credibility.
It is not simply a matter of his going to fight because he should—it
is a matter of what other people will think if he doesn't. This has

nothing to do with being young and able-bodied, which he is not: at the outbreak of war Smythe is nearly forty-five, a small (five feet seven inches), stocky man, a husband and father of three, hardly someone at the risk of withering looks from patriots (the women, the citizens of standing, the veterans of the last terrible campaign) who could hold him, at a glance, in contempt for not being Over There. Smythe feels compelled to play a front-line role in the call to arms because his experience of the last war allowed him to articulate and legitimize his ideas of duty and obligation and sacrifice in his professional life. Warfare became a ready and compelling analogy, never more evident than when he was in and around his beloved Maple Leaf Gardens, home of his beloved Toronto Maple Leafs.

The language of combat has always been within easy reach of sportsmen, and since levering himself into control of the team in 1927, Smythe's actions and rhetoric have resounded with parade-ground sentiments. And why not: thanks to the English public school example of the model young defender of Empire, athletes roam the same linguistic landscape as warriors, called upon to make sacrifices, smite enemies, stand by comrades, display courage, triumph with honour. Indeed, military historian John Keegan will describe the qualities of regimental culture as "total obedience, single-minded courage, self-sacrifice, honour."* Smythe has made these sentiments explicit in his management of the team.

The regiment, a cornerstone in the formalization of national armies in the eighteenth century, is generally a force of about one thousand men, formed from a group of smaller companies. It was common for a regiment to become affiliated with a particular community—a garrison town or city—drawing upon its greater population in recruitment. Sworn to the service of a monarch, the regiment naturally became a source and an emblem of civic pride. It also came to be seen as a force of moral improvement for the uneducated young men of the underclass drawn to its ranks. With the Maple Leafs, Smythe fused the tradition of the regiment with the emerging phenomenon of the professional sports franchise. In essence, he participated in the commercialization of the ethic of the regimental

---

*Keegan is also not far off the professional athlete of Smythe's time when he describes the Roman professional soldier thus: "His values were…pride in a distinctive (and distinctly masculine) way of life, concern to enjoy the good opinion of comrades, satisfaction in the largely symbolic tokens of professional success, hope of promotion, expectation of a comfortable and honourable retirement."

culture along with the imperative of gamesmanship contained within the duties of Empire.[4]

Already in the late nineteenth century, athletics began to emerge
from its ordained role as a training regimen for schoolboys who
would be expected to defend the King's realm. The modern
Olympic movement, founded in 1896, helped make sports an end
in themselves in sparring between nations, and not simply an
abstract training ground for conventional combat. Athletics that
represented more than the skill of the athletes themselves, athletics
that proclaimed superiority to whatever lump of geography and
associated culture the victor purported to represent, was irresistible;
a commercial version was inevitable. The for-profit version was not
merely a pale imitation of the Olympic ideal—it brought the winning formula to the lucrative frontier of the city states.

In team sports, the ensuing professionalism meant that a team
might still be called a "club," a nod to the roots of elite teams in the
private athletic club system, but the expense of maintaining a top-
calibre professional club—and the reaction of many private clubs
against professionalism—meant that commercial teams were
attached to and identified with an entire city. Professional sports
teams marketed with tremendous success in the decade following
the Great War a sporting reincarnation of the wars between the city
states of ancient Greece. When New York took on Boston, Thebes
and Athens clashed anew.

Outright professional hockey had only begun to gel about ten
years before the Great War, and during the war it struggled to survive. The National Hockey League emerged from the discord of the
four-team National Hockey Association in the autumn of 1917, just
as Conn Smythe was beginning his stint as a prisoner of war, and
only three teams—in Montreal, Ottawa and Toronto—made it to the
end of the inaugural season. When Smythe gained control of the
Toronto franchise in 1927,* the NHL was expanding as professional

---

*Smythe took $10,000 he received in severance from the New York Rangers in
1926 and with successful bets on a University of Toronto football game against
McGill and an NHL game between the Ottawa Senators and the St. Patrick's,
was able to lever a purchase of the St. Pats on February 14, 1927, with the participation of partners J.P. Bickell, Hugh Aird and Peter Campbell. Smythe became
managing director of the venture, called the Toronto Maple Leaf Hockey Club,
in 1928, and served as the team's coach until 1930/31. On February 24, 1931,
Maple Leaf Gardens Ltd. was incorporated to buy the assets of Toronto Maple
Leaf Hockey Club and to build and operate the new arena. In the process,
Smythe added the duty of secretary-treasurer to his managing directorship.

sport as a whole was blossoming in the Roaring Twenties. Smythe breathed life into a tentative franchise, the St. Patricks, by discarding the name of an Irish saint in favour of a national symbol drawn from the Great War.

The experience of that war was explicit in the motivations of Smythe and his partners in the Toronto franchise, every one of them a veteran. According to Smythe, they saw the team commemorating their own experiences, capturing in sport the spirit of camaraderie and will to win of the Canadian army that fought at Vimy Ridge and in so many other nation-building contests, instilling in returned men like Smythe a patriotism they had never known before. "Now the Maple Leaf to us," he will recall in 1945, "was the badge of courage, the badge that meant home. It was the badge that reminded us of all our exploits and the different difficulties we got into and the different accomplishments that we made. It was a badge that meant more to us than any other badge that we could think of, so we chose it, hoping that the possession of this badge would mean something to the team that wore it, and when they skated out on the ice with this badge on their chest, they would wear it with honour and pride and courage, the way it had been worn by the soldiers of the first Great War in the Canadian Army."[5] As a final motivator, Smythe and his partners hired Robert Barker, who had won the Victoria Cross as a Canadian flying ace, to serve as the club's first president. They could think of no greater example of courage for the players to follow than a man at the head of the company with a VC on his chest.*

With the Leafs, and with so many other teams of the age, triumph in the sporting arena required in players some facsimile of the loyalties that drive the warrior forward. These loyalties are substantively to the teams themselves; their grand traditions upheld the way modern members of a particular regiment respect and even claim as their own the feats of long-gone heroes who carried their standard at Waterloo. It is the way of the regiment not only to honour its traditions, but to pursue an unfolding glory, gathering new conquests to celebrate alongside the old. While a regiment's soldiers might not

---

*Smythe also may have been inspired by the example of the New York Rangers, whose lineup he had been hired to assemble in 1926. Rangers are elite fighting units specializing in operating behind enemy lines whose roots reach back to the War of Independence in New York State. Team lore, however, has it that the name was a pun inspired by Madison Square Garden impresario "Tex" Rickard. Thus, the team was known as "Tex's Rangers."

experience such an opportunity in their own lifetime, Smythe's regiment of hockey stars embarked on a new campaign of glory with the clockwork start of every NHL season.

The timing for such a change in the culture of the professional game was perfect from Smythe's perspective. Professional hockey had struggled through its first mercenary years; it was established, however tentatively in some markets, and so could be inspiring to and emulated by the new generation of players. When Smythe was playing for the Ontario Junior championship in 1915, professional hockey, in the form of the National Hockey Association, the NHL's forerunner, had only been in Toronto for three years. By the time he had survived the Great War, completed his engineering degree and established himself in the construction business, the professional game had something approaching a heritage, albeit one he was eager to shuck. If Smythe had any hope of making professional hockey something greater than a diversion for the city's underclass, if he had any hope of turning what at times was little more than a bloodsport into a cause célèbre of rich and poor alike, there would have to be sweeping changes that reached beyond the uniform.

Toronto fans had been entertained unevenly by the Blueshirts, the Arenas and finally the St. Patricks when Smythe entered the picture. After turning the St. Pats into the Maple Leafs, Smythe was still forced to entertain the spectators in the dingy confines of Mutual Street Arena. Smythe's ultimate coup was to give his Maple Leafs their own garrison, a place in which to assemble, to train, to display their war prizes, to fight their battles. He marshalled the construction of Maple Leaf Gardens in defiance of the Depression; it officially opened, at the corner of Church and Carlton streets, on November 12, 1931—the day after the thirteenth anniversary of the armistice that ended the Great War. Appropriate to the date, the bands of the 48th Highlanders and Royal Grenadiers played that night.

Toronto became a garrison city in the sense that the Maple Leafs had right of first refusal in recruitment within its allotted territory. And the team became something, as a player, worth shaping your life around and within; as a spectator, worth accepting as an embodiment of civic values, a barometer of your own esteem, a standard-bearer for your own community. The heritage of the Leafs was not the heritage of the Blueshirts or the Arenas or the St. Pats. It was the heritage of Canada at war; within Maple Leaf Gardens, the warriors of the Great War were reincarnated as the Maple Leafs. Ironically, the warriors on ice took precedence in the public imagination over warriors in fact, as funding for the Canadian permanent force dried up and a career as an officer and a gentleman became not nearly as appealing to a youngster as a career as a Maple Leaf.

Smythe has been instrumental in the maturation of professional hockey. He has helped it evolve from a sometimes seedy pursuit not far removed from boxing or wrestling to an almost noble sporting phenomenon. He has achieved this in no small part by giving the game stability—by moving it away from the days of outright mercenaries, who switched teams according to the highest salary bid, and into a new configuration in which the team took precedence over the player. Amateur sport had come to see itself as a refuge of dignity and fair play as professional sports came to the fore. With the Maple Leafs, Smythe managed to steal the thunder of amateurism's self-proclaimed superiority. He made an exercise in virtue out of a game that paid its players to play and charged its spectators to watch.

During the 1930s, when Canada suffered through the Depression along with the rest of the world, sport became a valued distraction to an enervated public. There were still enough people with money to fill the Gardens' 12,000-plus seats, and those who could not afford to attend could tune in to Foster Hewitt's game broadcasts, which began in 1931 and reached a national audience from 1933, or read about the team's exploits in the newspapers. The rise of professional sport was aided and abetted, and capitalized upon, by newspaper publishers, who found in the Leafs and other sporting enterprises a subject that rewarded regular coverage with boosted readership, which was vital to publishers at a time when advertising lines were drying up and street-corner sales of individual issues kept the presses running. It was not difficult, with so much attention being paid to sport in the Dirty Thirties, for Conn Smythe to become a leading public figure through the attentions of a good news–starved medium. He provided the good news by icing a charismatic, winning team, and by offering himself as a dynamic patriot who thumbed his nose at the Depression and built the Gardens for the benefit of the citizenry. It has been of great good fortune to Conn Smythe that the city's leading conservative newspaper, the *Telegram*, is also a leader in sports coverage.

By 1939, Conn Smythe has been running the Maple Leafs for twelve years; the team is sufficiently established to serve as its own inspiration, more so than the men of the Great War who provided the symbol on the jersey and the essential military model of the franchise. But when the Great War is reborn through Hitler's Germany, Smythe's regimental past and regimental present cause him to embrace this new/old war as a deeply personal challenge. It is all about what he is made of, if he has really been saying what he means all these years when he has lectured his Leafs about things like commitment and courage and sacrifice. He has, he will reflect, made himself out to be a warrior, and has tried to make his players into warriors, too. Now what of it? What sort of warrior is he? A warrior of cheap and easy dressing-room analogies, or a warrior in flesh and spirit? What else can he do, when he finds himself within earshot of this clarion call, but run after it, right past the fear and exasperation of his own wife?[6]

All private motivations aside, as a staunch Conservative and royalist, Smythe reacts as might be expected to Britain's declaration of war on Germany on September 3, 1939, and to Canada's hesitant decision, one week later, to follow suit. He is a member of the Canadian Corps Association, a forthright lobby group that grew out of a 1934 reunion of "returned" soldiers from the Great War. The Corps is, in its own words, "a medium through which ex-servicemen from the Great War might exert their influence for the public good."

At a reunion in 1938, these men were moved to express on paper their sense of continuing purposefulness, which included a sense that the values for which they had fought and for which comrades had died needed a champion in the public arena. They feared that the Empire had slid in the nation's priorities in the years following the war; that the importance of belonging to and defending this Empire, of being able to say that Canada was a British institution, was in dangerous decline. In truth, Canada as a nation had been drawing away from a subservient role to the mother country even before the first shot in the Great War was heard. Britain was finding her global power challenged by ambitious nations with far more powerful economies such as Germany and Russia, and relations with the French were so poor that the ancient rivals had nearly gone to war at the turn of the century over competing colonial claims; only two years before the Great War, Britain and France were still enemies. It was during this period of anxiety over her status as the dominant world empire that imperialism as a social movement took hold, encouraged by those who held that the citizens of Britain and her colonies had a life-and-death stake in the security of the Empire.

There was a strong belief that Canadians owed Britain for their basic security (a belief actively promoted by the British themselves).

Even when Canada became embroiled in the Great War, staking out an identity distinct from that of Britain became paramount. Canadian prime minister Sir Robert Borden, who nearly brought down Confederation by imposing conscription in 1917, nonetheless that same year insisted on a change in the format of the Imperial War Conference to reflect the autonomous status of the Empire's dominions. Borden also insisted on having the dominions sign the peace treaties of 1918 as sovereign states. In 1919 the Empire became more formally known as a commonwealth, implying an association of independent states with equal powers. And after joining the new League of Nations after the Great War as independent states, the dominions were no longer prepared to follow Britain blindly into conflicts in the name of empire. The Chanak crisis of 1922 was the turning point in relations between the mother country and her former colonies. Turkey and Greece were in dispute, and the British were preparing to intervene to maintain their strategic influence in Asia Minor. But when the British government assumed the dominions would automatically join in any fight, it assumed wrong. Canada's new prime minister, Mackenzie King, made it clear that Canada saw no reason to become involved; nor did Australia. Further erosion of Britain's control of dominion affairs followed, as Canada began to sign its own treaties and establish its own diplomatic missions through powers invested by the Statute of Westminster in 1931. By 1938, with Germany beginning to flex her military muscle, King was determined not to be drawn into a war of empires. Britain's request that Canada co-operate in a commonwealth air training plan that year was rebuffed.

The Canadian Corps Association produced a strident manifesto in 1938, a blueprint for the federal government to follow in repairing this nation's status as a member of the Empire in good standing. Of great importance, Canada was to take steps to ensure that the racial balance of its citizens remained properly tilted in favour of its British roots. The Corps called for "proper immigrations laws" to "ensure that our future citizens will be predominantly British[,] the remainder to be those whose racial origin permits rapid and complete assimilation into our social and economic life...." Furthermore, "the abuses of the system of entry to this country under special permit [are] to be abolished," a measure aimed specifically at refugees such as German Jews. The Corps also blamed "aliens" for taking jobs that should be filled by ex-service-men and Canadian citizens in general.

With Europe teetering on the brink of war, on August 25, 1939, the Corps sends to Prime Minister Mackenzie King a battle plan. "We are unanimous in our belief that, in the event of Great Britain becoming involved in an armed conflict, the entire resources of the Dominion of Canada should be placed unreservedly at the disposal of the British Government.... Should Great Britain become involved in war, we insist that a National Government, representa-tive of all groups in the country, be immediately formed in Canada, and that the Cabinet of that National Government include represen-tatives of the organized returned soldiers of this Dominion. One of the first acts of this Government must be conscription of all resources in Canada, of its wealth, its man-power and its industries, and that these resources be mobilized for the expressed purpose of making Canada's maximum contribution on the Empire's behalf."

When Britain declares war on September 3, the Corps immedi-ately calls upon King to produce the appropriate forthright response. "Canada and the Empire," the Corps argues in a September 4 missive, "now enter the most desperate struggle in the whole history of the British peoples. This is no time for half mea-sures. Everything that is Canadian must be at war." The Corps calls for a law of National Service, to marshall national resources in manpower, industry and finance. This naturally includes conscrip-tion, which the British government has implemented over the objections of the Labour Party. "National Service means that the present ineffective and inequitable system of voluntary enlistment of man-power will be discontinued, both for home and foreign ser-vice. There is no distinction between home and foreign service. We must go where duty calls."

The views of the Corps are the views of Smythe himself. He is one of its most vocal public figures, and so he helps set the pace of the country's convoluted, divisive response to Nazi aggression. The country embarks on a collision course with itself, in part because men like Smythe help fuel the suspicions of Quebecers that this war is not about freedom from tyranny, but about returning Canada to the status of an obliging British colony—a status the country had already outgrown before the Great War. If the reaction of many people in Quebec is *Not another bloody campaign in the name of Empire*, then the response of men like Smythe is *Absolutely anoth-er bloody campaign in the name of Empire*.

Smythe chafes at the indecision and tepid response of King's government, which, despite the strident urging of the Canadian Corps Association for a national mobilization, initially hopes to avoid having Canadians do any actual fighting, concentrating instead on the production of war materiel and the training of British Commonwealth pilots, as the British had requested a year earlier. Within two weeks of declaring war, however, it is clear to Ottawa that Canada will have to commit at least some troops to the conflict. Smythe begins investigating the best way for he himself to enlist with the Canadian military, to surmount a quarter-century of his own momentum and reacquaint himself with the young officer he once was.

Smythe watches the unfolding calamity in Europe and waits to make his move. In mid-September, the Soviet Union joins Germany in the invasion of Poland, and the massacre of Jews begins; on October 14, the German submarine U-47 steals into the British naval base of Scapa Flow in the Orkneys and sinks the anchored battleship *Royal Oak*, erasing 833 lives. On November 28, the Soviets scrap their nonaggression pact with Finland and, two days later, invade their neighbour.

Smythe cannot sit on the sidelines any longer. On December 9, he writes to Frank Ahearn, Liberal member of Parliament for Ottawa. He is the son of Thomas Ahearn, the wealthy self-made engineer who came to own almost everything electrical in Ottawa, including the streetcar system and the streetlights. The elder Ahearn, who died in 1938, built up a CV that included a directorship with the Bank of Canada, the chairmanship of the National Capital Commission, and a seat on Mackenzie King's Privy Council. Frank Ahearn was an officer in the 1st Canadian Division supply column in the Great War, and served as orderly officer to Lieutenant-General Sir Sam Hughes, the controversial minister of militia in the Borden government during the war. After the war the younger Ahearn promoted Junior and Senior hockey locally, and in 1924 he used the family fortune to get into the professional game, buying the Ottawa Senators franchise from Tommy Gorman. The storied Senators had won the Stanley Cup in 1922/23 and won another one just for Ahearn in 1926/27, but then the Depression hit, and the team bled a stream of money tapped from the Ahearn fortune. Frank Ahearn moved into politics with his election to Parliament in 1930, and he embarked on a sell-off of player contracts to try to keep the Senators afloat. The team had to suspend operations for the 1931/32 season, and one of the Ahearn fire sale's beneficiaries was Conn Smythe, who bought or borrowed several key players for his Maple Leafs. Among them was King Clancy, whom Smythe acquired for $35,000, plus the rights to two other players, a deal whose total value Smythe pegged at an astronomical $50,000. It was money well spent; with Clancy in the lineup, the Leafs won the Stanley Cup in 1931/32. The Senators returned to play in 1932/33, but were then moved to St. Louis, where they played out their last gasp as the Eagles in 1934/35.

Ahearn is a fine example of the depth of contacts Smythe has cultivated in his life, and he is confident that Ahearn has the ear of Defence Minister Norman Rogers. Canada has committed one division of soldiers to the defence of England, and Smythe asks Ahearn if there are any immediate plans for raising more troops. There is another important initiative in the works, but it is not about Canadians entering combat—on December 17, just as the first 7,500 Canadian volunteers arrive in England, King will celebrate his sixty-fifth birthday by announcing that Canada's major contribution to the war effort will be the British Commonwealth Air Training Plan. But another division, as it happens, will head for England in January.

If more troops are needed, Smythe is ready to supply them. He proposes to Ahearn that he be allowed to assemble a "sportsmen's battery"—an artillery outfit formed by volunteers with athletic résumés.[7] This is precisely what Smythe himself joined in 1915, and as Smythe well understands, the military still works as it did in the previous conflict, with advancement and opportunity furthered through connections and a few well-placed words. It is Smythe's way too: seeking the proper channels to power, moving over, through and around the bureaucrats and their red tape to get what he wants. Smythe's world is one in which men of daring and motivation rise as necessary to opportunities and occasions, establishing agendas rather than responding to them, becoming the events themselves rather than mere players. Those who govern and who administer the laws and whims of government are held fiercely accountable by him. He will badger, heckle, berate and insult, if necessary, publicly and privately, anyone from the most anonymous functionary to the prime minister himself to get what and where he wants, in his own name and that of his country and monarch.

Smythe explains to Ahearn that he was able to secure his commission in the Hamilton Sportsmen's Battery in the Great War through a Colonel Arnoldi in Ottawa. With his connections to the Maple Leafs,

Smythe proposes, it would not be hard to assemble another such battery, though he does not explain whether he sees actual Maple Leafs enlisting. But whether or not there are Maple Leafs in its ranks, he fully expects to have command of it. And he makes his bid for karmic betterment in his quest to reincarnate a battery of sportsmen: "Although I was only a Lieutenant in the last army," he explains, "I had three years' experience and I believe my experience in the army entitles me to a promotion, and my records in civil life since that time would not make it very hard for me to command a battery."

Ahearn goes to bat for him. And as Smythe explores the military options open to him in a country not convinced it should be fighting, he doesn't miss much. After Germany and the Soviet Union crush Poland, the war enters its lulling, phony phase: the winter passes with little happening, and the United States remains officially neutral. Smythe is willing to tell anyone who will listen that Canada belongs in the fight, that conscription should be imposed by Ottawa to mount the force necessary to stem the German tide. The conscriptionist opinions of Smythe and his fellow Canadian Corpsmen are not extreme. Sentiments in Ontario appear strongly in favour of a more forthright war effort. In January 1940, Liberal premier Mitchell Hepburn produces a formal condemnation of King's policy in the provincial legislature. But those in favour of a more aggressive policy suffer a setback in the federal election on March 26, when King's Liberals increase their total seats from 171 to 178 on the strength of 52 per cent of the popular vote. That same month, the British Columbia Youth Congress passes a resolution stating a unanimous opposition to conscription, one of its reasons being that "Canadian unity would suffer by reason of a split between English and French speaking Canadians." Whatever Smythe feels the country should be doing to combat the Nazis, the majority of the country, it seems, is fully in favour of the cautious approach of King and his Liberals.

MEN AT ARMS

BORN in 1892 in Limestone Ridge, a hamlet near Hamilton, Ontario, James Dickinson Irvin moved to Winnipeg at age nine, thereby making western Canada the site of his emerging hockey prowess. He was not a robust young man—only five feet eight inches tall with (as a medical examination in 1917 revealed) an expanded chest measurement of thirty-four and a half inches. But he was a stylish centre who could score goals, and in 1916, at age twenty-four, he went west to play for the Portland Rosebuds of the Pacific Coast league and recorded thirty-five goals and ten assists in twenty-four games, including three four-goal games and another game in which he produced a hat-trick.

Back east, in Toronto, Ottawa and Montreal, the National Hockey League, which rose from the ashes of the National Hockey Association, played its first season in 1917/18 with exquisitely bad timing, opening for business just as the draft was being introduced in Canada. The Quebec Bulldogs were unable to ice a team, and the remaining four-team loop dropped to three in mid-season when the Montreal Wanderers' rink burned down. Out west, the Patrick family's Pacific Coast league was forced to drop from four teams to three in 1917/18 as its Spokane franchise folded.

Among the able-bodied young men inducted by Prime Minister Borden's Military Service Act, passed on August 29, 1917, was Dick Irvin. He was declared category AII after his medical exam on November 6, 1917. Call-ups began in January 1918; on April 15, 1918, Irvin was taken on strength by the Fort Garry Horse, a cavalry unit that, like most every cavalry unit by then, had forgone the horse for the tank. He gave his trade at the time as "salesman and butcher," and arranged to have $60 a month in pay sent directly to his mother. Private Irvin was one of the relatively few draftees who ever got near the front. Of some 400,000 Canadians like Irvin called upon to register for the draft, about 125,000 had their services requested, and of those, only 24,132 actually got to France. Irvin was in England on May 24, and in France on August 16; on October 5, he transferred to a signals unit as a motorcycle rider. The war ended on November 11; Irvin arrived back from overseas in Halifax on May 28, 1919.

When he returned home, his old team in Portland was no more. The Rosebuds were replaced in 1918 by a Victoria team, which the Patricks had originally dropped in favour of Spokane in 1916. Thereafter the PCHA was a three-team loop (Vancouver, Victoria and Seattle). For the next three seasons, Irvin played for the Regina Victorias Senior club. He returned to the professional game in 1921 with the founding of the four-team Western Canada Hockey League as a member of the Regina Capitals. After four seasons, he was back in Portland for the 1925/26 season, when the amalgamated Pacific Coast and Western Canada leagues operated as the Western Hockey League and the Regina team was dropped in favour of Portland.

It proved to be the swan song of top-flight professional hockey in the west as the WHL collapsed after the 1925/26 season. As new NHL teams were being added in Detroit, Chicago and New York, western league player contracts were bought up en masse by the NHL, which until the WHL folded had to have its champion play a western league team in the Stanley Cup finals.

Irvin was still a capable player, having produced a league-leading thirty-six points in thirty games in his last hurrah as a western leaguer, and he was signed by the new Chicago Blackhawks, who bought all the Portland contracts. Irvin had one good season, then struggled through two more with injuries before retiring from the ice to take up station behind the bench. In his rookie season as a coach, he steered the Blackhawks into the 1930/31 Stanley Cup finals—as a player, he'd never gotten near the trophy.

Irvin showed himself to be a shrewd strategist. In 1929/30 the NHL had introduced the modern offside rule, which gave the game an entirely different tempo and flavour, doubling scoring in one season. Chicago didn't put a single player on the top-ten scorers list in 1930/31, while its cup opponents, the Canadiens, had three, including the league-leading Howie Morenz. Irvin nonetheless capitalized on the offensive possibilities of the new game in the cup finals by dressing more players than Montreal and employing shorter line shifts to maintain a wearying pace that almost, but not quite, overcame the Canadiens' firepower. Montreal had to come from behind and use all five games of the finals to subdue Irvin's Blackhawks. The Blackhawks' owner, Major Frederic McLaughlin, rewarded Irvin by sacking him. He was at home in Regina in November 1931 when Conn Smythe called.

Like Conn Smythe, Dick Irvin neither smoked nor drank. Smythe was sufficiently impressed with his skills and demeanour—his reputation was that of a taskmaster[1]—that he hired Irvin at the start of the 1931/32 season, just as the Leafs were moving into the new Gardens. The Leafs won the 1931/32 Stanley Cup under Irvin, and then made the cup final six more times over the next eight seasons, three in a row between 1938 and 1940, but were not able to win another one. They lost to the Rangers, the Maroons, the Red Wings, the Blackhawks, the Bruins and then to the Rangers again.

Waiting in the wings was Hap Day, another non-smoker and non-drinker who had been a friend of Smythe's since Day was a pharmacy student at the University of Toronto. Smythe was coaching the powerful U of T Varsity squad in 1924 when he lost Day to the St. Patricks; Day was a star left-winger when Smythe acquired control of the Toronto NHL team in 1927, and he immediately made him captain. He wore the "C" for his entire Leaf career, which ended after the 1936/37 season. About to turn thirty-six, Day stretched his career by switching to defence in his final seasons. He had one more tour of duty, with the hapless New York Americans, in 1937/38, before retiring. A minority partner in Smythe's sand and gravel business, C. Smythe Ltd., Day was ready to move behind the bench. The problem was, Smythe had a very capable coach in Irvin.

Over in Montreal, the Canadiens hired the latest in a string of coaches for the 1939/40 season, Babe Siebert, but the thirty-five-year-old Siebert, who finished his fourteen-season NHL career with Montreal in 1938/39, drowned on August 25 while trying to retrieve an inner tube for his daughter from the Lake Huron waves off St. Joseph, Ontario. Montreal scrambled to find a replacement, and opted for Pit Lepine, who had played centre for the Canadiens from 1925/26 to 1937/38. Lepine had spent the 1938/39 season in his first coaching job, guiding the New Haven Eagles of the American league. Lepine did not demonstrate a facility for turning lead into gold in New Haven. The Eagles, who won thirteen of forty-eight games in 1937/38, won only fourteen of fifty-four games under Lepine. The Canadiens might as well have hired a mannequin for all the good Lepine was able to do; the Canadiens' 1939/40 campaign was one of the worst in NHL history. Of forty-eight games, they won only five at home and five on the road, finishing nine points behind the next-worst team, the New York Americans. Their twenty-five points were the lowest produced since the league moved to a forty-eight-game schedule in 1931/32. The team only scored 90 goals and allowed 168. Boston, who finished first, scored 170 and allowed 98. Their one bright spot was a twenty-seven-year-old graduate of the Sudbury amateur hockey scene, Hector "Toe" Blake, who played his first NHL game as a Montreal Maroon in 1932/33 and became a Canadien in 1935/36. Blake was the league scoring champion in 1938/39, the only Canadien to make the top-ten scorers list in 1939/40. With thirty-six points in that dismal season, the left-winger was involved in more than one-third of all the team's goals.

The Montreal Maroons folded in 1938, and in the summer of 1940 it appears that, with another performance like the Canadiens' latest tour, Montreal may end up having no viable major-league hockey franchise. There were ten NHL teams when Conn Smythe acquired control of the Toronto franchise in 1927. Now there are seven. He well understands that the profitability of the Leafs depends on the overall health of the league. Weak teams make for poor draws on the road, and he doesn't need a lousy Canadiens squad disappointing his ticket buyers four times a year, when four games translate into at least fifty thousand tickets and when the Leaf fans already put up with the charity-case New York Americans four nights every season. True, people in Toronto are so crazy about hockey that the Gardens might sell out if the Leafs host the national team of Iceland five nights a week, but a shrinking professional loop like the NHL cannot afford the disease of ineptitude to spread. How much longer before the Canadiens go the route of the Amerks and have to be run by the league? Before the league loses both clubs and is down to five teams? Five teams, when the American league, which just got going in 1936, has nine teams, and two of them, Pittsburgh and Philadelphia, are in major markets the NHL has already tried and abandoned? When attendance in the better American league franchises is already above what Montreal is drawing at home? When the Canadiens are such dogs on home ice that their own farm team, the Montreal Senior Royals, regularly attracts more fans?

After the playoffs in the spring of 1940, Conn Smythe fears not only for the future of the British empire, but for the future of the National Hockey League as well. The Montreal Canadiens cannot be allowed to deteriorate any further. He suggests both to Montreal and to Irvin that they would make a good match. After taking the Leafs to their third straight final that spring, and with the Leafs having lost their third straight final, Irvin has probably coached the team as far as he can. The Canadiens can only improve under Irvin's guidance. And so Hap Day comes behind the Leaf bench; Irvin gets a pay raise and takes on one of the league's more problematic franchises, which happens to be in Canada's most problematic city in 1940.

During the 1930s, while Toronto was time and again falling short of another cup victory, the Canadiens were in disarray, on and off the ice. In the time Irvin was in Toronto, the Canadiens only reached the semifinals twice, lost in the quarterfinals seven times and missed the playoffs altogether twice.

To improve offence, Irvin brings aboard Elmer Lach, a twenty-two-year-old centre from Saskatchewan whose French doesn't go much beyond bonjour. He also combs through young amateur prospects. There is in particular a kid right in Montreal who is just turning nineteen, a right-winger who, after a short stint with the Verdun Junior Maple Leafs, has come to play with the Senior Royals. The second-eldest of seven children in a working-class Montreal family who began playing organized hockey at age eleven, his name is Maurice Richard.

Hap Day is a disciplinarian, someone who epitomizes the players-as-soldiers regimen Smythe has been laying down. When there are miles to run at Maple Leaf training camp Day gets out in front and leads the team the way a good officer will lead a charge, never expecting his men to do more than he himself is willing to.

Day leads by example, and so shall Smythe, now more than ever. May 23, Empire Day, 1940, is a day of bands and bunting and schoolchildren throughout King George's realm being reminded of the value and sanctity of his rule. Rarely has there been a celebration with more dire overtones, as the realm's army, trapped at Dunkirk, faces annihilation, its soil and citizens subjugation. Beginning on May 26, a remarkable flotilla of military, commercial and private vessels removes some 338,000 men, about two-thirds of them British, although much of their equipment is left behind.

Churchill has stepped with grim resolve into the calamity, and his people staunchly with him. It is a time when to be British means to stand almost alone against a terrible tyranny, and those in Canada who feel solidarity through King George's rule, or simply through a shared contempt for a cruel regime, can scarcely contain their disgust with their own government's favouring of measured political pragmatism over bold initiative.

On June 10, Italy declares war on the Allies and invades southern France. On June 12, the miracle of Dunkirk cannot be repeated as General Rommel accepts the surrender of 46,000 French and British troops who could not be evacuated from the beach at St. Valéry-en-Caux. On June 13, Canadian troops who have just been deployed around Le Mans as part of a British reinforcement contingent that landed at Brest have to be evacuated. On June 14, Hitler's awesome rout of northern Europe is crowned by his troops marching into Paris. The Wehrmacht shifts its attention to the Balkans while laying plans for the invasion of England.

The air war known as the Battle of Britain is launched in August as the Luftwaffe strives to soften up England for a seaborne invasion. As Messerschmitts and Spitfires tangle over Dover, Conn Smythe soars over greater Toronto. Such is his determination to get back in uniform that he has joined the Toronto Flying Club, taking to the skies several times a week to renew his pilot's licence. His first lesson on June 5 marked the day Hitler began his conquest of France. As Smythe makes his first solo flight eleven lessons later on June 22, a jubilant Hitler is imposing an armistice on France in the same railway car at Compiègne in which Germany had signed the surrender at the end of the Great War.

Smythe's aerial excursions sometimes take him over Scarborough, and from the cockpit of his Moth, Smythe can look down on an unlikely topography, a strange marriage of swords and ploughshares. The sprawling township to the east of Toronto is populated by some 25,000 scattered souls, its market gardens and crossroad towns interspersed with the hastily erected plants of the war materiel industry. The seeds of the great postwar boom are in these munitions factories. The war will leave the country with an impressive industrial infrastructure of factories and skilled labour; the bombs on the assembly lines will be replaced by toasters and televisions, and the fields of vegetables will give way to tracts of suburban housing, some of them occupied by his own Maple Leafs. The country has set itself on a path to becoming a producer of the goods for this war, even more than a producer of soldiers, airmen and sailors. Two-thirds of its materiel production will be consumed by armies other than its own. It angers Smythe that those in power should be satisfied that a principal contribution to the war of this country should be weapons, not warriors.

He is by now openly hostile to King's war policy, railing as much against him as he does against Hitler. On June 18, he sends King a personal telegram:

TWO WEEKS AGO YOU SAID ON THE AIR THAT YOU AND YOUR GOVERNMENT WOULD WELCOME CON-STRUCTIVE CRITICISM STOP HERE IS MINE STOP YOU AND YOUR GOVERNMENT TO CEASE ASKING THE PEOPLE TO HAVE FAITH IN THEIR LEADERS BUT RATHER FOR YOU AND YOUR GOVERNMENT TO HAVE FAITH IN THE PEOPLE STOP PUT IN EFFECT IMMEDIATELY CONSCRIPTION OF MEN MONEY AND INDUSTRY STOP TO HARNESS THE POWER THUS OBTAINED RECALL MCNAUGHTON AT ONCE ANSWERABLE ONLY TO THE GOVERNMENT WITH FULL POWER TO BUILD CANADA'S WAR MACHINE NOT ONLY TO PROTECT CANADA BUT TO TAKE THE EXTRA PART NOW NEEDED FOR ENGLAND.

The Recall McNaughton campaign is a personal hobby-horse, the centrepiece of Smythe's conviction that the Canadian war effort is being badly managed. General Andrew McNaughton, over in England in charge of the volunteer First Canadian Army, is some-thing of a renaissance man of business, technology and warfare.[2] Born in 1887 in Moosomin, in a corner of the Northwest Territories that was later added to Saskatchewan, McNaughton was the son of a trading post operator. His academic brilliance culminated in a master's degree in electrical engineering at Montreal's McGill University in 1912. He had just gone into private engineering prac-tice when Britain declared war on Germany in 1914. Military train-ing for McNaughton had begun in the cadet corps, and he had joined the militia in 1909. He rose rapidly through the ranks of the 3rd Battery, moving from lieutenant to captain to major between 1910 and 1913. When war broke out, he took the 4th (7th) Battery overseas as its commanding major in the first contingent of volun-teers in the Canadian Expeditionary Force. Befitting his academic training, he made a science not only of the ballistic behaviour of his guns, but of the tactical role they should play in support of infantry. The Great War was, after all, a war of infantry, waves of troops charging across no-man's-land to seize the enemy's entrenched positions only a few hundred yards away. McNaughton could fire guns with unprecedented accuracy and in close co-ordination with the troops expected to scramble over the top to claim the enemy positions his shells softened up for them. If Canada came of age at Vimy Ridge, McNaughton was elemental in clearing the path for the nation's rite of passage. Eighty-three per cent of German guns were said to have been silenced by his counter-battery fire before the Canadians had even left their trenches.

Promotions came rapidly. After being wounded at the second battle of Ypres in April 1915, he returned to action as the commanding major of the 21st Battery; in March 1916, he achieved the rank of lieutenant-colonel with his own artillery brigade, the 11th. The next step up was a position as Counter-Battery Staff Officer of the Canadian Corps Artillery in 1917. After being wounded at Soissons in February 1918, he was promoted yet again, to the rank of brigadier-general, in November 1918, just as hostilities ended. When the war was over, McNaughton was in charge of all heavy artillery in the Canadian Corps.

During the war he gained the admiration and loyalty of subordinates like Smythe, both for his accuracy in lobbing shells and his general disdain for the brass-hats crowd. When the war was over, he chose to stay in the permanent Canadian forces, and in 1929 was appointed chief of the Canadian General Staff. He was only forty-two when he acquired command of CGS; at every stage of his career, his rapid ascent was fuelled by ability, not patronage, and he must have become accustomed in his life to sure and steady promotion. He certainly had ambition, and it led to his first serious clash with his political superiors.

His adversary was a fellow Great War veteran, Colonel J.L. Ralston. Six years older than McNaughton, the Nova Scotia–born lawyer had an exemplary military record, though he did not reach quite the same heights as McNaughton. He went overseas as a major in October 1916 with the Nova Scotia Highlanders infantry battalion, reaching France in February 1917. He commanded the Highlanders, known as the 85th, until demobilization in June 1919, receiving a DSO in June 1917 and a bar to the DSO in August 1918; he was also mentioned twice in dispatches. When he went overseas, Ralston was a member of the Nova Scotia legislature for Cumberland, having been elected in 1911 and re-elected in 1916. But his political career thereafter was spotty. He was defeated provincially in 1920 and in 1925, and had already failed at the federal level in 1908. Mackenzie King appointed him chairman of the Royal Commission on Pensions in 1922, and Ralston suffered his third straight rejection at the hands of the electorate in 1926, when he stood for election in the federal riding of Halifax. King made Ralston his minister of defence anyway, in October 1926, and he secured a seat in the Nova Scotia riding of Shelbourne–Yarmouth in November.

As defence minister Ralston approved of McNaughton's appointment as head of CGS, but he rebuffed McNaughton's attempts to appoint himself the head of all military activity, air force and navy included. McNaughton had at last encountered the ceiling of his military career, at least in peacetime, and he debated resigning. Then came the general election of 1930, the first of the Depression years. Ralston managed to get himself re-elected, but King's Liberals were run out of office by R.B. Bennett's Conservatives, who won a majority government. McNaughton chose to stay in his post, and thereafter at least, he was viewed by some as a Conservative man.

But he faltered again. With the best of intentions, he used his military clout to arrange a works-relief project for unemployed men who built structures and airfields under the aegis of the Department of National Defence, in return for room and board and twenty cents a day. The project helped lay the foundations for Trans Canada Airways, the forerunner of Air Canada, which McNaughton also helped plan, but it made McNaughton a political target on two fronts. Some of the men who were housed, fed and employed by the department had political beliefs running to the radical, which gave McNaughton's projects the reputation of being a hive of seditious activity. The projects also attracted managers straight out of the Conservative pork barrel. By the time Bennett had to face the electorate again in 1935, the prime minister had concluded he could not do so with Andy McNaughton in charge of the army. Before the election, Bennett all but fired him in suggesting he would be much happier as the first chairman of the National Research Council. McNaughton agreed to the career change on the condition that he be seconded to the NRC by the army so that, in the event of an emergency, he would be able to return to military duties.

At the same time, James Layton Ralston also made a career change. He decided not to stand for re-election in 1935, returning to practise law in Montreal as a partner in his firm Mitchell, Ralston, Kearney and Duquet. In so doing, he missed out on King's return to power.

The military plainly was McNaughton's first calling, even though the NRC was a good fit for his talents. Military applications for science had always been a personal priority. In the 1920s, for example, while rising to the head of CGS, McNaughton invented and patented with Lieutenant-Colonel W.A. Steele the cathode ray airplane compass.

Bennett lost the 1935 election in spectacular fashion, shedding nearly 100 seats as King's Liberals formed a majority government. McNaughton stayed put at the NRC, and the Liberals chose to shelve McNaughton's plan for the defence of Canada, which centred upon a laboratory arsenal at Valcartier, Quebec, where every weapon and armament essential to a modern mechanized army would be developed, tested and produced. The country was still in the Depression, and the Liberals had no interest in spending what few public dollars there were on anything to do with the military. Friends of the militia such as George Drew were scandalized by the anaemic state of the Canadian military, and readily and publicly criticized King's defence policies. One article by Drew in 1938 criticizing King's policies attracted a personal letter of support from McNaughton.

As war returned to Europe, and once more began to draw Canada in, both McNaughton and Ralston made themselves available to King for service; both expected an active military assignment. Ralston did not get his; instead King invited the lawyer and old soldier, who was just turning fifty-eight, to come back into cabinet to serve his country as finance minister. Ralston accepted, and on January 2, 1940, was elected by acclamation in the Prince Edward Island riding of Prince—the riding King himself represented from 1919 to 1921 in his first years as Liberal leader.

Less than two weeks after war was declared on Germany, Defence Minister Norman Rogers recommended to King that McNaughton, now fifty-two, command the first of two divisions the country planned to send to England. While long allied with Bennett, McNaughton was not viewed as a political animal, and neither King nor his cabinet had any qualms about appointing someone whose ambitions had irked Ralston in the 1920s and who had then served controversially under Bennett. Admiration for

McNaughton cut across party lines. This remarkable breadth of support is illustrated in 1940 when a Liberal appointee becomes the subject of public lobbying by card-carrying Conservatives for a still-higher posting.

With little else happening to attract attention during the conflict's phony-war phase, the government bent its publicity machine to the task of creating in McNaughton a Canadian hero on the international stage. McNaughton graced the cover of *Life* magazine on December 18, 1939, (the day after the first Canadian troops arrived in England) as "Commander of the Canadians," and the January 1, 1940, issue of *Time* proclaimed "Soldiers, in Canada and elsewhere, rate him the ablest officer in the British Empire."

Upon this publicity Conservative editorialists built their own McNaughton campaign. As the Nazi blitzkrieg rolls across northern Europe, forcing the Dunkirk evacuation and producing alarm on the home front, the Conservative-backed McNaughton campaign turns out "Bring Him Home" posters and bumper stickers and articles, calling upon King to recall McNaughton and place him in charge of organizing the entire Canadian military effort as the government's minister of war, a posting that would have to be created specially for him. Conn Smythe is active in this effort, even contributing an article of his own, which appears in the Toronto *Telegram* on June 5 as he is making his first acquaintance with the DeHavilland Moth and the Nazis are beginning their drive for Paris.

Is McNaughton merely a draftee of Conservative sympathizers, or a coyly active participant in this program to secure him another promotion? The post Conservatives like Smythe have in mind for him does echo McNaughton's own thwarted ambitions in the late 1920s to have military control of land, sea and air. And certainly he moves in the same circles as George Drew and Conn Smythe. In addition to their Conservative allegiances (admittedly less fundamental to the character of McNaughton), they share the important touchstone of all having been battery men in the Great War.

George Drew has been a devotee of military matters since 1910, when he joined the 16th Battery in Guelph at age sixteen. When the 16th went active as part of the Canadian Expeditionary Force in 1914, Drew went with it, arriving overseas in 1915. He was wounded in May 1916, and returned to Canada the following July. After commanding the 64th Battery from October 1917 to the following April, he was forced to return to hospital, and received a discharge from the active army in June 1919.

Like Smythe, Drew had attended Upper Canada College and the University of Toronto; like Ralston he became a lawyer. He maintained an active interest in military matters, commanding the 16th Battery in Guelph from 1920 to 1929, at which point he took command of the 11th Field Brigade. The 11th was a model outfit, and Drew maintained its reputation as it won the Shaughnessy Cup as the most efficient brigade in Canada in 1927, 1928, 1930, 1931 and 1932. He has never been short of opinions: his books include *The Truth About War, Canada's Part in the Great War, Salesmen of Death, Tell Britain* and *The Truth About War Debts*. Politically, he made his debut in 1925 when he was elected mayor of Guelph; the leadership of the Conservative Party of Ontario came to him in 1938, and in 1939 he won a seat in the Ontario legislature in Simcoe East. As committed, active Conservatives, George Drew and Conn Smythe are well known to one another—Drew has even served as the honorary president of the Toronto Flying Club, where Smythe has come to take his flying lessons.

Three days after sending his telegram to King, Smythe invests seventy minutes in practice takeoffs and landings, his last session with a co-pilot before flying solo;[3] he also submits to *Canadian Veteran Magazine* an open letter to King. He has the courtesy to warn King what is coming, passing along a copy to King's secretary, H.R.L. Henry, on June 22, with the explanation: "Perhaps this may appear to you a crude method of drawing attention to what I personally think should be done. Nevertheless, it has been my experience that a customer who stands quietly at a crowded counter is the last one to be waited on."

Smythe has taken advantage of the unfortunate death in an airplane crash of Defence Minister Norman Rogers on June 10 to make his most concerted pitch for McNaughton's promotion. In his open letter to King, Smythe champions McNaughton in language that makes the most explicit connection between sport and war:

> What a wonderful team you must have in your cabinet. Here you have lost one of your best men and you do not need any replacement.
>
> Some of us sort of figure you at the bottom of the league (for win the war effort), considering the standings of Australia, New Zealand, South Africa and other members of the British Empire League. We sort of thought that with nine premiers of the provinces available, with heads of the great

industries and businesses ready to play for you, and a super-star like McNaughton free, you would at this time strengthen your team. You know that for a number of reasons a lot of us want you to be on the winning side very badly—some for patriotic reasons, some for selfish reasons, some from just pure fear, and a lot of us because we just don't like to lose.

Some of us think you are out of touch with the opinions of the public on this point—misled perhaps by the number of votes polled in an election where the choice was a vote for a conservative or liberal politician.

Persons who don't win, and persons who don't listen to public opinion have a great deal of difficulty holding their jobs. Don't you think, under the circumstances, the best thing to do would be to get some more good men for your side right away? And McNaughton should be the first.

Smythe's relentless championing of McNaughton is one of his life's great misguided, assuredly misinformed pursuits. It seems doubtful Smythe truly knows the man. McNaughton, for one thing, is opposed to conscription—if Smythe knew this, he certainly would not be lobbying for him to lead the country's war effort. Even as Smythe carries on his attacks on King's government, he attempts to insinuate himself into its military operations and policy-making. And Smythe is tolerated rather than shunned. The Canadian military is desperately short of officers, most of those in the militia being unfit for active duty, and the standing army having atrophied during the interwar years. His telegram to King elicits a formal acknowledgment of receipt from King's secretary. When Smythe responds by sending along the advance copy of the *Canadian Veterans* piece, he also observes that "a tremendous number of returned soldiers like myself" believe that the war effort is poorly organized. He cannot understand why McNaughton has not been brought back from England to build the powerful army necessary to defeat Germany. But he concedes that he is "tremendously pleased" to see a law, at last, for conscription.

On June 18, the same day Smythe sends his telegram to King, the Liberals table the National Resources Mobilization Act. Passed on June 21, it gives Ottawa power to direct the economic resources and manpower of the country in pursuing the government's war policy. Its manpower provision provides for a limited form of conscription, applying "solely and exclusively to the defence of

Canada on our own soil and in our territorial waters." No one drafted under this act will be expected to serve overseas. All single men
between the ages twenty-one and forty-four are required to register
for the draft by August 27.[4] The marriage cut-off date of July 15
induces a mini-boom in wedding vows.

Quebecers are not completely opposed to the war. The archbishop
of Quebec, Cardinal Villeneuve, proclaims it a just war, and volunteers fill the ranks of such regiments as the storied 22nd—the Van
Doos—as well as Fusiliers Mont-Royal, Le Régiment de
Maisonneuve, Le Régiment de la Chaudière and the bilingual Royal
Rifles. And out on the North Atlantic, where merchant sailors and
naval personnel pay dearly in the effort to keep convoys with precious war materiel moving to besieged Britain, one-third of the
Canadian navy's roll call is French-Canadian. Indeed, the enthusiasm of young French-speaking Quebecers to volunteer for combat
duty is remarkable in the face of the overwhelming indifference of
French soldiers to fight to free their own country from Nazi occupation. Nearly a quarter-million French troops have been evacuated
from their country, but less than eight thousand of them join Charles
de Gaulle's Free French Army. Those who do are technically traitors, for France has signed an armistice with Germany and the
southern half of the country is under the control of the puppet Vichy
administration. The majority of French citizens have passively
accepted the new order. Only about 100,000 become involved in the
resistance movement. For recruiters in Quebec who are wont to use
the fall of France as a call to arms for the world's francophone community, the tepid response of the French themselves to the cause of
their own freedom does little to instil a mentality of commitment
and sacrifice in a population divorced from its mother country two
centuries earlier. Nor does it help that some Quebec nationalists like
Montreal mayor Camillien Houde have Vichy sympathies (and
admire Mussolini as well). The situation is further exacerbated
when Britain launches Operation Catapult, designed to prevent as
many French warships as possible from falling into German hands.
A squadron of French ships has taken refuge from the Germans at
Mers el Kebir in Algeria, but when confronted by the British Fleet
on July 3, its officers refuse to consider any number of proposals
ranging from joining up with the British to surrendering their vessels to sailing for the Caribbean and sitting out the war. Finally, on
Churchill's orders the British simply open fire, killing more than
1,250 Frenchmen who were their allies less than two weeks earlier.

Quebec enthusiasm for the war stops abruptly at compulsory participation. And whether the war is prosecuted on a voluntary or compulsory basis, many of Quebec's francophone citizens have no interest in participating in what they continue to see as another English war, ending up in a Canadian army steeped in English traditions.[5] The Canadian war machine goes to heroic efforts to generate and promote French-Canadian officers in order to make voluntary service more attractive to Quebecers, but it is too little too late for a military system that in the interwar years was permitted both to atrophy and to become a backwater of underpaid officers with largely Imperialist sentiments. War has not only hoisted Canada into a leading role in a global crisis—it has also dragged the country's armed forces out of a time warp, unable to shed completely their institutional anachronisms. The Great War, the war of empire, is a binding experience for the majority of officers leading Canada into battle more than two decades later. As late as May 22, 1942, a memorandum from the officer in charge of records at the Ministry of National Defence indicates that the Canadian army continues to be dominated by men with experience in the Great War: all of its lieutenants-general and majors-general, 85 per cent of its brigadiers, 69 per cent of its colonels, 44 per cent of its lieutenants-colonel and 12 per cent of its junior staff appointments—even 8 per cent of those serving in the ranks, overseas and at home.[6] As selfless and devoted as so many of these men are in responding to the call to arms, their perspective on the cause at hand is as foreign to the young men of Quebec as their language.

King's wartime policies are shaped overwhelmingly by his understanding that he cannot control Parliament without the Quebec vote. He will manoeuvre, some say blunder, through the war not as an inspiring leader like Churchill or Roosevelt, but as a ham-fisted pragmatist tied in knots by the contrariness of his electorate, evading any firm action that might offend a substantial part of his constituency. Since 1896, Quebec has tended to vote en masse for the Liberals. King became prime minister in 1921 in the first Canadian election to result in a minority government. Quebec delivered every available seat to his Liberals that year. His only serious repudiation by Quebec voters came in 1930, when the Conservatives and their new leader, R.B. Bennett, managed to wrest twenty-four of the province's seats to form a majority government in the first election of the Depression years. But King rebounded in 1935 with the aid of a jaded Quebec electorate, which cut Bennett's Quebec caucus to five, granted five seats to independent Liberals and bequeathed the remaining fifty-five seats to King. He was even able to secure almost 70 per cent of the Ontario ridings, ending a Conservative domination of the province that stretched back into the previous century. In the spring election of 1940, he repeated this sociopolitical miracle, returning to power with over half the popular vote and a comfortable majority of seats in both Ontario and Quebec.

King has a clear mandate, but to do what? The fact that he has strong support from both Quebec and Ontario voters does not mean that the modern equivalents of Upper and Lower Canada are in any way unified when it comes to conducting a war. The National Resources Mobilization Act is a compromise that satisfies no one. It does not provide for the compulsory overseas service the majority of Ontarians support. And the proviso that conscription will only require service on the home front—at first requiring just thirty days of basic training on evenings and weekends—is still viewed in Quebec as the thin edge of a wedge that will inevitably result in conscripts being committed to combat. For saying so, and for encouraging Quebecers to boycott the registration, Camillien Houde is arrested at Montreal's city hall on August 5, 1940, and becomes a prisoner of his own country's army for four years.

Smythe's diatribes against King's war policy make their way to the desk of C.D. Howe, who as minister of munitions and supply is charged with overseeing the application of the NRMA. Howe is one of the King cabinet's great intellects: American-born, an MIT graduate who came into the government with the 1935 election and was given the cumbersome portfolio package of minister of railways and canals and minister of marine, which in 1940 were folded into a single transport portfolio, a portfolio he still holds. On June 28, Howe writes a rather bland letter to Smythe, inviting him to make suggestions relevant to Howe's duties. Smythe responds on July 3, his main suggestion being to put McNaughton in charge—a man, says Smythe, "known throughout Canada from coast to coast to be the best posted and most-up-to-date Canadian on modern warfare." Howe attempts to mollify Smythe. "Let me assure you," he writes back on July 5, "that I share your high opinion of General McNaughton. You need have no doubt that the Government is making every possible use of his experience and ability."

The prime minister pays no heed to Smythe's bring-back-

McNaughton chant in the wake of Rogers' death. To replace Rogers as minister of defence, King moves J.L. Ralston over from Finance. In his stead as finance minister King installs Ralston's fellow Nova Scotian James Lorimer Ilsley, first elected in 1926 and unfailingly thereafter, and minister of national revenue since 1935. Rogers' death has returned Ralston to the cabinet posting in which he had sparred with McNaughton some fifteen years earlier.

On McNaughton's own recommendation Ralston now recalls Harry Crerar, Brigadier General Staff at Canada's military headquarters in London, to make him Chief General Staff at National Defence Headquarters in Ottawa. Crerar, like Smythe and McNaughton, was a Great War gunner, and he was deeply offended by Quebec's stance during the conscription crisis of 1917. Crerar no longer believes in conscription, recognizing that a war that destroys the sociopolitical fabric of the country waging it in the name of freedom is no war worth waging.[7] And as Smythe fearlessly, even rashly, carries on his public attacks on the government in the cause of at least one man, McNaughton, who does not even share his opinions, the course of the war as prosecuted by Canada continues at right angles to the one Smythe prescribes. Desperate to join and lead, Smythe is still in civilian clothing and out of step with many of the country's key political and military leaders.

On July 11, 1940, Smythe goes right to the top in his quest to join the military, filing his application for active service enlistment with none other than Defence Minister Ralston. "The reason I am writing you personally is that I have contacted a great number of persons with unsatisfactory results to date.... If I have done something wrong in applying directly to yourself, please excuse this error, it simply being caused by the total lack of results of other efforts to date."

Smythe has one bald fact in his favour as he chases down his own commission: the Canadian military is sorely lacking in officer material. King and his military commanders have little choice but to fill officers' positions, at least initially, with aging volunteers like Smythe who saw action in the Great War.

The political–military infrastructure continues to treat Smythe with promptness and courtesy, but without a hint of willingness to cut corners for him. Colonel Clyde Scott, military secretary at the ministry, gets back to him on July 13: "I am today bringing your name and qualifications to the attention of the appropriate Officers at this Headquarters. Might I also suggest, however, that you call at

Military District Headquarters, 159 Bay Street, in order that you may be advised concerning vacancies in your own Military District."

The only person in Ottawa, it seems, willing to pull strings for Smythe is MP Frank Ahearn. On July 17, he wires Smythe:

MINISTER OF DEFENCE SECRETARY INFORMS ME THAT IF YOU WISH TO TAKE REFRESHER COURSE YOU SHOULD CONTACT BRIGADIER ALEXANDER ONE THREE [sic] NINE BAY STREET TORONTO

And so he at last gains a toehold. Through officers' refresher courses he secures the rank of captain—an improvement over his lieutenant's bars from the last war—and is given command of A Troop, A Company of the Canadian Officers' Training Corps at his alma mater, the University of Toronto, while continuing his flight training.

The German invasion of England is considered imminent. On September 8, the second day of the bombing campaign on London immortalized as the Blitz, four hundred German aircraft are met over Britain by more than two hundred fighter pilots from Britain, Poland, Czechoslovakia and Canada. On September 9, Conn Smythe receives his pilot's licence.

In Uniform

September 1940

A new hockey season is about to begin, and a new Maple Leaf club is about to make its debut. Over the summer, Conn Smythe has been transforming them into a fighting machine, on land and on the ice.

Who knows what planted the seed in his mind? The notion that the Leafs can be part and parcel of the war effort simply may have been irresistible and inevitable, with no one moment or incident provoking it. But the idea that the Leafs can act as a moral force in these dark days surfaces on June 10 in an admiring letter Smythe receives from his local MP, Conservative Rodney Adamson, who is also an army captain attached to Toronto military district.

"As the member for your Riding (York West), I would like to congratulate you on the excellence of your address at the Drumhead Service at Riverdale Park, last Saturday," Adamson writes. "If more people like yourself with energy and courage, would take part in the public affairs of our Nation, we would not find ourselves in the mess we are now. I send you a circular letter which is typical of the large number of so called Youth Associations throughout Canada." Enclosed is a news release from the Greater Vancouver Youth Council announcing the British Columbia Youth Congress's opposition to conscription, as resolved in March. Observes Adamson: "Would you could turn the Maple Leafs on them."

Smythe is not going to dispatch his Leafs to crack the heads of young conscientious objectors, but before the summer is out he has launched a campaign to make his Leafs a symbol of every able-bodied young man's patriotic duty to defend his country, the Empire and the free world.

Over that turbulent summer, Smythe takes it upon himself to write to each and every one of his Leafs, pressing upon them their duty, regardless of age or marital status, to sign up immediately with a non-permanent militia unit so that they can receive home-defence training as soon as possible. Whether or not their military services are required immediately, a long time from now, or never, isn't the issue, he explains. He wants them all ready to serve if and when they are called upon.

Smythe isn't asking them to drop their sticks and pick up machine guns and start fighting Nazis. But as Smythe leads by example, so his players are expected to do so. Even as Smythe himself is drawn fully into the war, he trains a pragmatic eye on the fate of his players. Training right away, en masse, will send out a soul-stirring message that the Maple Leafs are fully committed to king and country and empire, but it will also remove a potentially disruptive and annoying obligation, at a time when the full scale of the war and the actual obligations it will demand are not yet realized. As Smythe explains to his players that summer (while also urging that they secure passports allowing them to enter the neutral U.S.), complying now with military training requirements means they will "be free to play hockey until called upon." And, as he points out, they might never be called upon.[1]

This is as much Smythe the businessman at work as Smythe the patriot. Above all else, he wants to avoid having his players conscripted in the middle of the NHL season. If they voluntarily join a non-permanent active militia, they are free to do their training before the season starts. But if they are drafted under the NRMA, they must perform their basic training between October 1, 1940, and October 1, 1941. Half of that period falls within the upcoming NHL season. If his team does not get its home-defence duties out of the way forthwith, the lineup could be gutted in mid-season by draft notices.

And so that September, before training camp for the new NHL season opens, fully twenty-five members of the Maple Leaf organization, including the new coach Hap Day and broadcaster Foster Hewitt, are taking basic training. The militia regiment of choice for most of the Leafs is the Toronto Scottish. The Leafs spend two weeks at military camp, then invest another sixteen nights during the season in completing their thirty-day basic militia training. During their training in Port Credit, west of Toronto, team members hustle through trenches in their Maple Leaf jerseys.

The Maple Leafs are not the only professional hockey players joining militias and completing their thirty days of basic training to avoid being called up under the NRMA after October 1. Bob and

Bill Carse are two of eleven professional hockey players among the three thousand civilians taking basic training that September at the Sarcee camp, nine miles southwest of Calgary. The Carse brothers are joined by fellow Edmontonians Art Weibe, an old pro who played his first Blackhawks game in 1932, and New York Americans goaltender Earl Robertson. Also on hand are Robertson's fellow "Amerks" Lorne Carr, Pat Egan and Tommy "Cowboy" Anderson, who is from Drumheller. Sweeney Schriner of the Leafs and Eddie Wares of the Red Wings round out the NHLers. From the Cleveland Barons of the American Hockey League is Joe Jerwa, and from the St. Louis Flyers of the United States League is Fred Hergert. The four Edmontonians—the Carses, Weibe and Robertson—have joined the 19th Alberta Dragoons; Carr is in the 95th Field Battery of the Royal Canadian Artillery; Schriner, Hergert and Wares are in the 8th Field Ambulance; and Anderson is in the 6th Field Army Workshop.

Yet it is the Maple Leafs who as a team become identified as a fighting force, on and off the ice. In the space of a few short months Smythe has transformed himself and his team into warriors in every sense, uniformed and committed to the tasks before them. He must be thrilled by this, being able to build a bridge for the Leafs between literal and figurative combat, though which is which is far from firmly cast. The hockey heroics are real; it is the soldier- ing that is the facsimile. The only people these Leafs are shooting at in anger are goaltenders. Hap Day is no longer just a coach, but a lance-corporal. They pose together in their uniforms of war as read- ily as they do in their blue-and-white on the rink. Smythe prepares a flyer to be distributed to all Maple Leaf Gardens shareholders and the Leafs' 5,000 season-ticket holders, outlining the team's stalwart support of the war effort.[2]

The timing of his publicity campaign is exemplary. As the Leafs and the rest of the NHL teams are holding their training camps, the war front darkens and broadens, both at home and overseas. Camillien Houde has just been tossed into prison at Petawawa for inciting defiance of the Canadian draft law in Montreal and throughout Quebec. The still-neutral but wary United States enacts the first peacetime draft law in the nation's history, which results in the registration of seventeen million men. On September 13, 250,000 Italian troops surge across the Libyan border and drive sixty miles into Egypt as its badly outnumbered British defenders fall back; the Italians have already captured British Somaliland in

East Africa in August. The Blitz peaks on September 15, when
nearly one thousand German aircraft take aim at London, Bristol,
Cardiff, Southampton, Manchester and Liverpool. On September
17, Hitler decides to postpone the invasion of Britain but to continue the air war. By the end of the month, nearly seven thousand
British civilians have been killed by the Luftwaffe. On September
27, Japan signs a ten-year military and economic pact with Italy
and Germany, thereby creating the Axis alliance. On October 28, in
the first week of the new hockey season, Italy attacks Greece.

Though his Leafs are now war heroes of a sort, Smythe despairs
that his own participation in the war will fail to rise above the symbolic. MP Ahearn was able to arrange a meeting between Smythe
and the deputy minister of the air force, James S. Duncan, and his
staff, in the hope of directing Smythe into some kind of command
position somewhere within the military, but as Smythe relates to
Ahearn on October 2, it all came to nothing. After the meeting, he
reports, "there was considerable action, and I had hoped that I
might get in the army. However, having been disappointed in the
Hamilton battery and almost getting an active service battery at
Petawawa I am beginning to think that my chances are getting further away." He is fast approaching forty-six, and while he has been
attending a drill and a lecture on separate nights every week to further his officers' refresher training, the volunteer program is suddenly cancelled with the approach of winter. Smythe confesses to
Ahearn that he feels left "very much up in the air."

He sends Ahearn one of the pamphlets that extol the Maple
Leafs' war effort. "I may be wrong," he writes, "but I believe we
are not using to its full extent the influence that sport has on the
public to help along the morale of the public with regard to the war
itself and war work." He adds, his own morale in need of boosting:
"I hate to bother you again, but feel that you were able almost to
get me in the last time and that a second attempt by yourself might
land me in Canada's fighting forces."

The Leafs win more games than any other team in the league this
season, finishing five points behind the Bruins in the standings.
Three of the six players on the first All-Star team are Leafs, one of
whom, goaltender Turk Broda, is also the first Leaf ever to win the
Vezina Trophy. Never before has a hockey team appeared so purposeful, so well-rounded, both on the ice and on the street, as citizens and heroes. And as a draw at the gate, they are irresistible.

Patriotism, if nothing else, is good business.

The war that winter takes root in Africa: in December the British army chases their Italian counterparts out of Egypt; by February they have driven the Italians halfway across Libya. Continental Europe is almost completely dominated by the Axis powers. In March the United States takes an important step out of isolationism as Congress passes the Lend-Lease Act, which empowers the president to allow shipments of vital war materials to nations whose defence is considered necessary to U.S. security. Britain is its most obvious benefactor.

At the beginning of the new year, Smythe resolves to throw himself wholeheartedly into the war effort in whatever way possible, and applies to the Maple Leaf Gardens board of directors for a leave of absence. On January 9, he files with the board a memo detailing who should do what in his absence. Frank Selke, acting general manager, will do hockey deals in concert with coach Hap Day and director Ed Bickle, with final approval in the hands of the Gardens executive committee.

He sets down marching orders for his Gardens troops to follow. Though there is a war on, he will countenance no reduction in the quality of the product. ("Customer—hold up attraction to a standard so no reduction in price.") The Leafs are to play aggressive, entertaining hockey. ("Pro Games—all times stress offensive tactics and players.") He will not tolerate any discounts or giveaways for presumably any cause, be they enlisted men, war widows or orphans. ("No passes—very important.") Keep the team in the public eye. ("Press relations—tell them the story. Public relations—the truth and nothing but.") And, perhaps fatefully, let the Gardens board do its job. ("Directors—It's their business—treat them that way.")

On January 21, 1941, two days after the British have opened a new war front by moving against the Italians in East Africa, the Ontario council of Smythe's Canadian Corps Association passes a resolution stating it is "alarmed by (1) the apparent lack of any plan for the Canadian Expeditionary Forces; (2) By the confusion and lack of method in the training in Canada of new formations and reinforcements of the Canadian (Active) Army; and (3) By the absolute waste represented by the operation of the 30-day compulsory training scheme...

"The present emergency can recognize only two fields of service for the Canadian Army, the guarding of our coasts and vital services, and the overseas campaign." The resolution calls for garrisoning of defence posts to be limited to voluntary soldiers ineligible through age or physical disability for overseas service, supplemented by "trainees" conscripted for service in Canada. "Apart from these necessary garrisons, all of Canada's resources of men and money available for her Army must be devoted to the establishment, training and equipment of the expeditionary forces.

"Just as Oliver Cromwell created in the New Model Army to be the wonder of Europe, so has General MacNaughton [sic] created the new Canadian Corps [of overseas volunteers], whose training and military qualities are acclaimed as the very finest. Surely the system of training of McNaughton's Canadian Corps can be made the system of training of the Canadian Army in Canada."

The Canadian Corps Association continues its strange and misinformed fascination with McNaughton. McNaughton is proving to be no great commander, and his weakest point is the training of his troops; the Canadian forces in England under his command are poorly prepared for combat. Nevertheless, this Corps Association resolution will provide Smythe with a philosophical springboard for a fresh round of politicking and haranguing.

Now twenty-one, Bob Carse has a so-so season with the Blackhawks after his militia training at Sarcee, producing only eighteen points in 1940/41; brother Bill manages twenty. Chicago doesn't produce a single top-ten scorer, wins only sixteen games and slumps to fifth. Six of the league's seven teams advance to the playoffs this season, which allows every team but the New York Americans to have a crack at generating post-season gate receipts. In its opening matchup Chicago eliminates sixth-place Montreal, but is then knocked out by Detroit. Bob Carse is held without a point in all five of his playoff games; he now has no goals or assists in seven career NHL playoff games. Bill also has no points in five playoff games in 1940/41.

Conn Smythe might be off its board of directors, but he is not out of the Gardens. The Leafs are matched with first-place Boston in the semifinals in March. With Lend-Lease having just passed, Smythe is quick to see an opportunity to convince the average American citizen—and newsman—of the importance of the Canadian war effort. (As of March 27, the British and Americans have agreed to a Joint Basic War Plan, which outlines how the two powers will co-operate militarily should the U.S. enter the war.) About two dozen Boston reporters are in and out of Toronto as the series is played. Smythe's dislike of King and his war policy are not so venal that he can resist writing to the prime minister with a suggestion for his PR department. The Bruins and their attendant scribes will be back in Toronto on April 1. Why not round up these reporters for a tour of Camps Borden and Malton, with a visit to the Inglis war plant as well, where the Bren light machine gun is being produced? On the very day of the game, King's public relations director contacts Smythe's office, offering to take the reporters, given such short notice, at least on a tour of the Inglis plant.

In the meantime, Smythe carries on with his usual King bashing, hoping to engineer a public tongue-lashing of the government's blueprint for war. In February a new training plan was introduced, devised by Crerar to replace the thirty-day conscript program he had recognized as insufficient. Under Crerar's new scheme, both reserve non-combat draftees—the NRMA men—and active volunteers now train together for four months.

This does not mollify Smythe. He moves to give strength to the objections already raised by the Canadian Corps Association over the war effort by seeking out an alliance with the Royal Canadian Legion. On March 18, Smythe writes to M.S. Boehm, president of the Toronto Business Men's Branch of the Legion, and James S. Thomson, president of the Legion's Toronto Downtown Club, spelling out his battle plan. "In common with a great number of Canadian citizens, I am very worried about the Dominion Government's training plans." The idea of training for four months conscripts who won't actually have to fight in Europe galls him, as does making active volunteers learn the ropes in only four months. "When it does not produce one soldier eligible for overseas service, I am sure, as a business man, you must be appalled at the waste of money."

Smythe proposes that veterans of the Great War and businessmen get together to make "some firm suggestion as to how our money should be spent, and how our soldiers should be produced with that money." He wants the Legion branches to endorse a suggestion that the Legion and the Canadian Corps Association, in concert with the federal government, "cooperate wholeheartedly and one hundred per cent for a businesslike and soldierlike method of handling the present demand for Canadian soldiers."

While Smythe never uses the word in his letter, the heart of the matter is plain to everyone, because it's what the Canadian Corps Association has been clamouring for since the outbreak of hostilities: Smythe wants conscription to mean induction into an army that can be trained properly and then sent into battle, not an army that trains thousands of men ostensibly for home defence, but in reality as an act of political compromise—showing English Canada the government is willing to do something about the Axis threat, while appeasing French Canada's demand that no one drafted will actually have to fight overseas.

Thomson writes back to Smythe on March 19, noting that a luncheon will be held on March 21 at which his proposal can be considered. Thomson pledges to ask for a motion in favour, and shows himself capable of reading between the lines. "Personally, if I may be blunt, I am in favour of conscription."

Smythe, who is out of town with the Leafs in their playoff series with the Bruins, writes back to Thomson on March 25: "I suppose, bluntly, I am in favour of conscription too." He looks forward to hearing the results of the meeting.

On March 31, he receives the approved resolution from M.S. Boehm. In the meantime, it has been announced that British civilian casualties have reached 28,859 dead, 40,166 seriously injured. The Business Man's Branch has, on Smythe's initiative, come up with a position entirely at odds with his own. It has resolved that "without complete information as to the requirements for additional men for the armed forces and as to the possibility of equipping such men, this Executive cannot at present endorse conscription, nor condemn the existing 4 months training plan, but endorses the principle of consultation with representatives of the Canadian Corps Association, and other veterans' organization[s] with a view to approaching the General Staff and Government to ascertain the facts and thereafter to give full support and co-operation to any steps deemed desirable to further Canada's war effort."

Boehm, showing no inkling of the volcanic response such a non-statement will arouse in a man of action like Smythe, proposes that a meeting be held with Smythe in attendance to discuss the possibility of securing a hearing in Ottawa for "a small deputation representing returned men."

The volcano seethes. "I have taken several days to think over your Resolution," Smythe responds on April 7. "I am sorry that I cannot agree with you. You and I, as business men, know how hard it is to make money today, and how necessary it is to save money, with the country at war. You and I, as soldiers, know that youths of twenty-one can not be made soldiers in four months ordinary training. I hope, should the time come when our overseas troops need reinforcements, that I will not be blamed because there was no one trained in Canada who has agreed to go over and support them.

"I wonder if your good friends can remember that their wonderful military record twenty-five years ago was not obtained by sending out a number of deputations.

"I regret, therefore, that I will be unable, feeling the way I do, to concur with your group's idea that they can not condemn something that I know is wrong. Until more of your men can throw themselves back twenty-five years and get the spirit that they had then, so that the soldiers that we have now will be getting the support that is due them, we will just forget my suggestion of getting together and seeing if we can do something for them.

"With all due respect for yourself, because I believe you have really sincerely tried to get something practical under way, I must wait until your group runs out of resolutions."

Smythe sends copies of the letter to other members of the Legion branches' executives. Its acidity incites a response from James Thomson, who professes to be taken aback by the resolution. "The Resolution which [Boehm] read to me over the telephone is not in any way sponsored by the Downtown Branch of the Legion," he assures Smythe. "In fact, our views differ greatly, and we are all for some sort of action." They speak, but in Smythe's mind, to no practical end. "Following my conversation with you on the 'phone the other day," he writes on April 17, "I would like to reiterate what I said, and that is that until the Legion feels within itself that something more must be done than what the Legion is doing at the present time towards Canada's war effort, there isn't much use for fellows like you and me to try and push it.

"However, I am ready at any time to sit in on any discussion or do anything that you or Bob Thomson might think would start the ball rolling."

Captain Rodney Adamson, the Conservative MP for Smythe's home riding who had expressed his admiration for Smythe in June 1940, inadvertently wanders through Smythe's gunsights. On March 15, Adamson receives from Smythe a daunting telegram: "Toronto Star for Friday March fourteenth reports you satisfied with Government's training scheme. Is it possible they have misquoted you. If not tell me your reasons why you favour four months training with no guarantee of production of one soldier for the Canadian Army."

Adamson had indeed stood in the House of Commons on March 13 and, from the opposition benches, passed along his congratulations on the new training program. "The proposed method of training and the organization and establishment of the Canadian army for this year, 1941, have found almost universal support in the army. As far as I am concerned, the support is complete," he stated. On personal inspection, he had been pleased with the quality of intensified training provided at the No. 1 and No. 2 infantry rifle training centres at Camp Borden, and in the House he pronounces their work "excellent." "[T]he concentrated training received in these centres [is] much quicker and more intensified than any type of battalion training we have yet undertaken."

Adamson does his best to smooth Smythe's hackles in a March 18 letter. "I feel that it is an improvement and that training raw men in a training camp is better than to endeavour to do this by battalion training. I believe that it strengthens our hand if, when we see something which is commendable being done by the Government, we mention it. You may be assured that if, as seems very probable at the moment, recruiting for the active army fails to meet the requirements, I shall be the first to mention it. I can assure you that now our General Staff and the General Staff of other Dominions are in accord with regard to Empire Defence and arms production. I believe that it was my duty to mention this if for nothing else than to restore confidence in the country....

"May I wish you the very best of luck with the Maple Leafs and that you bring the Stanley Cup back to Toronto."

In the same session of the House in which he praised the training program, Adamson had also raised the possibility of wartime pork barrelling. A tender had been issued by the government in late 1940 for 100 million pounds of brass sheet and rod a year. Anaconda American Brass Co. in Adamson's riding made a bid $1.5 million lower than the one by Canada Wire and Cable Co. in Montreal, which was awarded the contract. As someone expressing himself to be so vitally concerned with government waste and businesslike cost-effectiveness in the war effort, and as someone so disgusted with Quebec's broad indifference to the cause of defending the Empire, Smythe should be expected to sit up and take notice of Adamson's charge. Instead he ignores it, furious with Adamson for saying that King's crowd of compromisers is doing anything worthwhile.

"I deeply regret that you should take the stand that a four months training plan is an improvement," Smythe writes to Adamson on March 25. "There is no question that a man will learn more in four months than he will in one month, but for the country to spend fifty or sixty million dollars of our money on sending trainees to camp for four months that does not produce one fully qualified soldier, nor does it make one man for the Canadian Active Service Force, is an act of folly that I can't see how any Canadian can endorse.... It is hard for me to conceive that you can justify in your mind the spending of all this money in a training scheme when the trainees have no obligation whatever to our country.

"I must say I am deeply disappointed in your stand, and I think you'll find hundreds of others of your returned soldier constituents of the same mind."

Smythe will always be a political animal, but never a politician. He has not yet learned in this war when to bite his tongue, when to avoid giving offence to those who are in his corner, or could be. His own convictions are paramount. They drive him forward and fuel his accomplishments, and if people are going to stand by him over the long run, it is because they, and not he, are willing to turn the other cheek.

In the case of the Royal Canadian Legion, the executive finds itself playing catch-up to maintain pace with the convictions of veterans like Smythe. By the fall of 1941, the Legion president is moved to call upon the government to demand compulsory combat service from conscripts.

The King government does modify its recruitment plans that April. NRMA men will now have to serve in uniform for the duration of the war, so that volunteers can be freed from home-defence responsibilities for overseas combat. But the spring, by any measure, is a miserable one for Smythe. Boston eliminates his Leafs in the semifinals. While continuing to fulfil his officers' training duties at the University of Toronto, he has tried making further contributions to the war effort by overseeing materiel production through the Ordnance Corps. Back in January, he accepted an assignment to monitor contract work for certain ammunition and a six-pounder gun. The legwork, as vital as it might be, leaves him unfulfilled. Promoting the sale of war bonds does little more for his esprit de corps and personal ambitions, and no good news is forthcoming from the theatre of battle. The Allied effort suffers yet another set-back when General Rommel's Afrika Korps replaces the routed Italians in Libya and launches a blistering counteroffensive at the British. Not a single Canadian soldier has experienced combat (not counting the Canadians who landed at Brest in early June 1940 and stayed just long enough to have to abandon most of their equipment and be evacuated), and the news of Rommel peeling back the gains of the British North African forces infuriates Canadian patriots who feel their boys should be in the desert, not sitting idly in camps in England. By the end of April, virtually all of Libya is in German hands.

Smythe has struck up a friendly banter, in person and by letter, with Air Commodore Gus Edwards at the Department of National Defence, whom he probably first met when he secured an audience with the deputy minister of the air force and his staff the previous autumn. Edwards is sympathetic to Smythe's determination to make a personal contribution to the war effort, and coaches him as best he can. "I am sorry that your tour with the Ordnance Corps did not go over so well," he writes Smythe on April 3, "and I firmly believe that if you had given it a more extensive trial, you would have been able to make a very useful contribution.... Many of the manufacturing concerns, upon whom we depend for the tools to carry on, apparently require new blood. This might prove an ideal field of endeavour and I am dropping this thought for your reflection."

Smythe promptly drops the thought as well. "I am now engaged in the Publicity Campaign [for war bonds]," he writes back on April 8, "having fairly well weathered the War Services Drive here in Ontario, but I find it a little more difficult to try and key myself up to publicize bonds, when I know that at least fifty million a year are being wasted on a cheap four months training course that produces no soldiers for the empire...."

On May 20, German paratroopers invade British-held Crete; from May 28 to June 1, some 17,000 British and Commonwealth men are evacuated, leaving behind about 5,000 men, with another 4,000 soldiers and sailors killed. Virtually all of non-Soviet continental Europe is now under Axis control.

🍁

MP Adamson does what he can to repair the rift between himself and Smythe, suggesting that they meet at Military District Headquarters at 159 Bay Street.

"I tried to telephone your Secretary at 159 Bay Street," Smythe writes him on April 17, "to try and make arrangements to see you, but could not make contact. Since I last wrote you I hear that the three Ministers of Navy, Air and Army appealed for over a hundred thousand recruits. Although I am ready to listen, I think it's going to take a lot of talk to convince me that you are anywhere close to the right when you suggested the government's training scheme was of some use."

They continue to converse. Finance Minister J.L. Ilsley's sweeping tax program includes a Moving Picture Amusement Tax, which at the last moment is extended to include admissions to hockey games. On May 27, Adamson attempts a rapprochement with the businessman Smythe. Adamson advises him to get a lawyer who knows a thing or two about the subject and to prepare a brief that would outline the damage the tax would do to small-town amateur hockey, "the permanent damage it will do to hockey as Canada's National sport.... Stress the value of the youth of the nation getting out and playing games rather than sitting in stuffy movie houses watching frustrated sex dramas.... The value of the Toronto Maple Leafs as an advertising medium for Canada, and other points which you can no doubt think of."

Concerned about Smythe's predilection for taking his personal crusades to the press, Adamson immediately telegraphs him, pleading that the letter be kept personal. Smythe does, in fact, take his tax crusade into the newspapers, prompting Air Commodore Edwards to write him: "I notice that you led the charge of the light brigade on our Finance Minister. I suppose you knew ahead of time that it was a forlorn hope, but I don't blame you for making a try."

Smythe writes back promptly to Adamson, promising confidentiality. "I have not been able to contact you regarding conscription," he adds. "I do hope you have changed your mind."

It is time for poor abused Adamson to come out of the closet on the conscription issue. "If you ever thought I was against conscription you had every reason to complain," he writes Smythe. "I have never been against conscription at any time since the war began and now believe that it is absolutely essential. What I said was that the scheme of training men in training centres is an improvement over giving them their initial training with service units.... As a member of the staff of [Military District] No. 2., I have been asked by the [District Commanding Officer] not to advocate conscription on the public platform as it is against the present policies of the Government. You could appreciate how embarrassing it would be for him if I disobeyed his request."

The war expands. In April the British move into Iraq to stop a German-inspired coup and so preserve a critical source of oil. Already the Vichy French have handed over the Syrian oil fields to the Germans, which Rommel was able to use in driving the British from Libya. On May 24, the British cruiser *Hood* is lost with all but three of her 1,419 officers and men after engaging the German battleship *Bismarck* and heavy cruiser *Prinz Eugen*. Three days later, a combined British air–sea operation hounds the *Bismarck* to the bottom of the Atlantic. In June the British and the Free French invade Syria from Iraq and impose an armistice, which gives the British control of Syria and Beirut. And on June 22, Hitler turns on his former ally, the Soviet Union, with the launch of Operation Barbarossa. The Second World War now has an eastern front.

On June 4, Kaiser Wilhelm II, Conn Smythe's ultimate nemesis in the Great War, dies in exile in Holland. On that day, Air Commodore Edwards writes to Smythe to congratulate him on at last getting himself into the army. Smythe the warrior is reborn.

The fact that Edwards had to read about it in the newspaper is proof enough that he had nothing to do with it. "You had better watch your step from now on as you are close to the category of 'brass hats' and will be the recipient of criticisms from individuals—well meaning and otherwise." Edwards' advice carries a note of what must be intended irony. Now that Smythe is in the thick of it, he is going to have to expect some of the very criticism he has been so enthusiastically churning out.

Smythe's conviction that advancement can or should come through who one knows proves to be correct. A Colonel Greer walks into Maple Leaf Gardens, tells Smythe he did a good job in the Great War, that maybe he hadn't done enough for Smythe in that adventure, and to make up for it he is going to give him a hand in this one. What was it that Colonel Greer should have done for him? Smythe, whose truncated anecdote this is, never elaborates. A hint of an advancement perhaps denied him on the death of his commanding officer in the Great War lies in this encounter. Perhaps it was this lack of promotion that impelled Smythe to switch to the Royal Flying Corps. With Greer now in his corner, the red tape melts away, and Smythe gets a battery of his own and a major's rank to go with it.

The military bureaucracy may have decided that it is better in the long run to have Smythe in the army and subject to its discipline and chain of command, than to have him on the outside, firing salvos at the prime minister, the government ranks, and the ministries of defence and munitions and supply. But Smythe will never be easy to corral or to muzzle. As he blithely observes in a June 5 letter to Air Commodore Edwards: "I noticed in some army orders last night that anybody talking to anyone else in another branch of the Service was to do so through the Superior Officer. However, we are just having a friendly discussion that has been going on for a year and I don't think what we say between us matters much." As the army will learn, they have accepted into their midst a man of indefatigable courage who is both a first-rate gunnery officer and a loose cannon.

He inherits an existing Toronto militia unit, the 30th Battery of the 7th Toronto Regiment, and dedicates the summer to converting it to active status, promoting it as a haven for athletes. Most of the existing militia men who want to join him either aren't fit for active duty or aren't interested in going overseas. Some of his new men he recruits from other active units, some he pulls in off the street. A few come from within the 7th.

Smythe isn't going to take just anybody. Before he has even gained the 30th, Smythe has lined up a core of officers: Sherwood Wright, who has been through officer training under Smythe at university; Jim Boekh, one of the greatest amateur golfers in the country; and Bill Leak, who had played hockey for Smythe at the University of Toronto in the 1920s. Wright is astonished that Smythe wants him, as the major is a sworn enemy of Wright's father, the secretary-treasurer of the Ontario Jockey Club.

In the beginning, when it is still practical to do so, Smythe personally interviews every man who wants to follow him into combat. His most spectacular acquisition is the starting lineup of the Mimico Mountaineers, who have just won the national lacrosse championship, the Mann Cup. Led by their star players Jackie Williams, Archie Dixon and Jessie James, they become Smythe's gunners. He acquires two of the best golfers in the country, Boekh and Clare Chinery. Several star baseball players from ball diamonds in Ontario, Nossy Atanasoff, Gordie Gill and John Kyrcia, sign on. So do two prominent Toronto sportswriters: Ted Reeve of the *Telegram* and Ralph Allen of the *Globe and Mail*. (Allen will be released by the army after two years with the battery to become a war correspondent, and will one day be managing editor of *Maclean's* magazine.) He takes on Don "Shanty" McKenzie, a hulking lineman with the Toronto Argonauts, after his mother sends along a note to Smythe asking him to take good care of her laddie. And he attracts one brand-name hockey player, Murray Ezeard of the Toronto Senior Marlies.

Buck Houle is a typical recruit attracted by the aura of the major. He happened to have played Junior hockey in the Maple Leaf system, and he was rebuffed by the Queen's Own Rifles when he tried to enlist because he had just started wearing glasses. Then he reads about Smythe forming a battery and goes to see him. You're just the fellow I'm looking for, Smythe tells him, and he's in.

Nick Hatten is a young sergeant with the 15th Battery when he and the rest of the men of the 7th line up in the University armoury to be addressed by Smythe, who has just been given command of the 30th. Smythe needs volunteers, and Hatten, for one, is ready to join him. His dad was a soldier in both the Boer War and the Great War. At twenty-one, he'd tried to join the 48th Highlanders but they were full up, and so it transpires that he decides to become a batteryman rather than a rifleman.

Hatten is granted an interview with Smythe the day after volunteering to join him. He is in awe of Smythe—he has never met a celebrity before, and Smythe is definitely a celebrity to anyone who follows the Toronto Maple Leafs. Major Smythe sizes up Sergeant Hatten and asks him, well, what sport do you play? Hatten doesn't really have any special sporting strength. It's a bit of this and a bit of that. This is a sporting battery, Smythe explains. We're supposed to have sportsmen. Then he relents. We have to have some soldiers, he decides, and accepts Hatten into his fold.

On September 12, as snow falls for the first time on the Russian front, 30th Battery officially goes "active," with Major Conn Smythe as commanding officer and its headquarters at Toronto's Exhibition Grounds. It is subsequently attached to the 6th Light Anti-Aircraft Regiment, joining the 1st Battery of Ottawa and the 112th from the Prairies. In all, 30th Battery has 300 people of various rank when it moves to Camp Petawawa in February 1942 after basic training in Brantford. But none of them are Maple Leafs.

Smythe and the Leafs are rapidly moving in different directions. He senses an inclination, even an eagerness, to be rid of him. Though he had taken a leave of absence from Maple Leaf Gardens in January 1941, he is incensed when he is barred from entering the

Leaf dressing room to give a pep talk during the 1942 Stanley Cup finals. He will begin to suspect, and ultimately be convinced, that director Ed Bickle and Smythe's deputized general manager, Frank Selke, are actively scheming to convince the Gardens board to replace him permanently. If he is disheartened that no Maple Leafs follow him into 30th Battery, he may be enough of a pragmatist not to want them to. His experience of war is that of France from 1915 to November 1917, when there was, for him, glory to be found, but also catastrophic losses. If the Maple Leafs were to abandon sticks and skates in favour of Smythe's battery, and if that battery were to be demolished in some French field, then the Maple Leafs as a hockey club would virtually cease to exist. There is no question that Smythe is prepared to die for his king, his country and his empire, but he might not be prepared to take his beloved Leafs with him.

On June 5, 1941, with the task of forming his battery before him, Smythe confides his ongoing concerns about the Canadian war effort to Air Commodore Edwards. "I have been, as you know, from the first worried about our plans. Everybody connected with the army has told me that we didn't need men—we needed machinery. Having been a contractor and a sand and gravel operator for twenty years—not a lawyer or stockbroker, I have never believed this statement. Watching us lose all our equipment at Dunkirk, again in Greece and another lot in Crete, I wonder if these men know how many man hours it takes to keep a machine running. In other words, this is the Iron Age, and when you have one division equipped fully, if you are in battle you should have, I would say, a minimum of three divisions of men ready to fight with that equipment. Yet we are waiting until we equip each division; then the divisions fight until they are exhausted; then we lose our equipment; then we start all over again. If they had, as they did in '14 and '15, called in all the contractors and handlers of men and machinery together, this problem could have been worked out.... In these days of mass production everybody figures out the number of man-hours needed to keep machines going twenty-four hours a day, seven days a week, fifty-two weeks a year, etc. In my opinion, every squadron should have five squadrons at least available to fly those machines. Every battery should have three to four batteries of men to man the guns and their equipment, and so on down the line. And yet they tell us they don't need men—that this is a Machine Age. I wonder if there are any men who have handled machines, fed the big mixers on the roads, taken away all [that] the steam shovels can dig, and put up buildings that had to be built in three months that normally took a year and a half—are there any of these men in charge of the branches of the army available to give advice to the now-appointed soldiers.

"It has been the history from all time that successful army work is simply a successful piece of contracting. What is the situation with respect to this, and if nothing has been done about it, why don't they get some of these experts, of which there are dozens in Canada and thousands in the United States, who would guarantee that when we fought a battle that any equipment that was taken from us would be in the same class as the *Hood* and the *Jervis Bay*,* which fought to a finish."

Smythe's extraordinary theory of massive overmanning goes hand in glove with his conviction that full conscription is needed. How else are all these bodies to be assembled? It also happens to be at odds with the technology-focused perspective of his hero, McNaughton. Churchill, for that matter, has described the war as machines against machines. The otherwise indulgent Edwards cannot let Smythe's theory go unchallenged.

"I do not think that you can rightly compare war machinery to that used by civilian contractors," he writes him on June 16. "You can hardly speak of cement mixers, steam shovels, etc., which can be operated unceasingly until the parts become worn and a breakdown occurs, in the same breath with guns, tanks, aeroplanes and other war materials which are under fire and often destroyed before they are worn or damaged by natural causes to even the slightest degree.... The cost of maintaining an Army, a Navy or an Air Force under the present system is drain enough on the resources of everyone without going to the expense of having men in the numbers you mention who would undoubtedly be sitting about with nothing to do and, as a result, becoming impatient and cause no end of

---

*The sinking of the *Hood* has already been mentioned. The *Jervis Bay*, an Australian passenger liner that had been converted into an armed merchant cruiser, was escorting a convoy from Halifax to Britain when attacked on November 5, 1940, by the German pocket battleship *Admiral Von Scheer*. Her captain, an Irishman named Edward Stephen Fogarty Fegen, who had served in the Royal Navy during the Great War, engaged the enemy at hopeless odds while ordering the convoy to scatter. Fegen fought on despite losing his arm, and was one of 189 members of the *Jervis Bay*'s crew to die when she went down. Fegen's stand meant the Germans were able to sink only five of the convoy's ships. He was awarded the Victoria Cross posthumously.

grief. To what avail is throwing into a battle, thousands of men without weapons—as you well know, wars cannot be won with bare hands unless the enemy is equally ill-equipped.

"Furthermore, before personnel can be placed in the front line, they must receive adequate training, and this cannot be carried out unless the necessary equipment is available. If events dictate that we accelerate our plan, any difficulties which we might experience would, I think, not be from lack of trainees, but rather from lack of the equipment with which to train them.

"In any event, as yet in Canada, there is no shortage of manpower and, as far as we are concerned, no pressure whatever has been brought to bear, since men are coming of their own free will in sufficient numbers to meet our requirements and to fill to capacity, all the schools which are in operation."

Smythe does not take Edwards' professional opinion well. "I guess I am getting too old, because when the day comes that I can't make you understand, I won't be of much value trying to train men to fight for this country," he writes on June 24. "To put it bluntly, in the artillery with eight guns there are forty-six gunners. The life of a gun is, I suppose, a good many thousand rounds. With the tactics the Germans use, such as infantry attacks, mounted and rapid moving tanks and parachutists, it is necessary to fight twenty-four hours a day until the supply of Germans coming in is exhausted. It is my belief that a hundred gunners could fight three times as long as forty-six, taking up the casualties and being able to pour fresh troops on to the machines.

"However, I suppose it will take a good licking before they call in the men that understand that flesh and blood can't run as long as iron and steel. That was the point I was trying to make. I didn't expect anyone to fight with bare fists, nor did I expect the British army to lose 1,000 guns at one time, as has already been the case."*

And that is the end of the surviving correspondence between Conn Smythe and Air Commodore Edwards.

---

*In the evacuation of Dunkirk, the British Expeditionary Force abandoned about 1,000 heavy guns, as well as some 400 anti-tank guns. It also cast off (among other things) 475 tanks, 38,000 other vehicles, 12,000 motorcycles, 8,000 Bren machine guns, 90,000 rifles and 7,000 tons of ammunition. Large amounts of equipment were also lost with the surrender at St. Valéry-en-Caux on June 12, 1940, and in evacuating Crete in late May, 1941.

RECRUITS

BILL Carse hangs on to his starting job in Chicago and has his best tour of duty in 1941/42, with twenty-seven points in forty-three games. Younger brother Bob is sent to Chicago's new minor pro affiliate, Kansas City of the American Hockey Association, for some seasoning, and in his thirty-three games back in Chicago he begins to show NHL potential, producing twenty-three points. Over in Toronto, Billy Taylor, Bob Carse's nemesis in the 1939 Memorial Cup, has also come into his own, with thirty-eight points in forty-eight games. The Blackhawks improve their record to twenty-two wins in forty-eight games and finish fourth, but are eliminated by Boston in three games in the quarterfinals; Billy Taylor and the Leafs win Toronto's first Stanley Cup since 1932. The Carse brothers at least are able to make an offensive contribution to the Chicago playoff performance, with Bill getting a goal and an assist and Bob two assists.

It proves to be Bill's last NHL season. Though he is a Blackhawks starter and has just had his best season in the National league, a leg injury that requires twenty-two stitches helps convince him to volunteer for active duty in the Canadian army on July 27, 1942, and he heads to Calgary for basic training.* A few weeks later, Canadian troops go ashore at Dieppe.

Ted Kennedy is sixteen when the Dieppe raid telegraphs a short, sharp shock to the home front on August 19, 1942. The country has

---

*Bill Carse served with the 31st (Alberta) Reconnaissance Regiment, the Royal Canadian Artillery, and the Canadian Forestry Corps in Canada and Britain. He was discharged on November 19, 1945, and returned to professional hockey with the Vancouver Canucks of the Pacific Coast league in 1948. He then had a brief stint as the Canucks' coach.

never received news like this before, not of a battle lost so quickly and with such overwhelming casualties. It was a mechanical slaughter, German mortars and machine guns wreaking havoc on a clockwork assault plan that in the moment of execution disintegrated into an obscene ritual of sacrifice, landing craft obediently dispensing wave upon wave of young volunteers into murderous crossfire.

The initial, and persistent, response to the tragedy in official ranks is to paint it as a glorious triumph. As the *Times* of London reports to its readership on September 9, Churchill rose in the British House of Commons to deliver these uplifting words: "The military credit for this most gallant affair goes to the Canadian troops—(cheers)—who formed five sixths of the assaulting forces, and to the Royal Navy, which carried all of them there and which carried most of them back. (Cheers.)"

It is soon apparent that, Churchill's assurances notwithstanding, the Royal Navy did not carry most of them back, as most of them simply did not come back. As young Ted travels that September from his southern Ontario village of Humberstone to a room at the Queen's Hotel in Montreal, his journey stitches together three locales left reeling by the disaster: Hamilton, almost none of whose Royal Hamilton Light Infantry escaped the Norman shingle beach, one hundred of them killed outright; Toronto, which provided most of the men of the Royal Regiment of Canada, the vast majority of whom (nearly 95 per cent) ended up as casualties; and, finally, Montreal, whose Les Fusiliers, a French-Canadian unit, had more than one hundred of its ranks killed as they were deposited in the German gunsights in the assault's final, wasteful moments. Other Canadians—members of the Essex Scottish, the South Saskatchewans, the Cameron Highlanders, the Calgary Highlanders—brought the day's casualties to 65 per cent of the 4,963 young men who had gone ashore.

Dieppe is one more depressing mishap in the country's war experience. Elements of the Canadian army were in France just long enough in June 1940 to have to abandon their equipment and hie away back across the Channel. The fall of Hong Kong in December 1941 cost the country the Winnipeg Grenadiers and the Royal Rifles, their members either killed outright or interned by the Japanese to waste away in harrowing prison camps. And then comes Dieppe, a folly that has destroyed the 2nd Canadian Infantry Division. Between Hong Kong and Dieppe, the Canadian army has been stripped of about 4,700 precious volunteers, who were either killed, wounded or captured.

Virtually all of Europe is held by Axis powers; there is no good news to be had from the battle theatre. And Ted Kennedy is taking up residence in a place traumatized by the war like no other Canadian city. For the past two years, Montreal's mayor-elect Camillien Houde has been shut away as a military prisoner at Petawawa. And the national plebiscite held the previous April revealed the disturbing polarization between French and English Canada on the conscription issue. The plebiscite has incited deep divisions in the country as much as revealed them. The two solitudes of the country have never been more perilously apparent. A nation at war with Germany, Italy and Japan is in serious danger of degenerating into war with itself.

Kennedy is too young for military service, and his brother Jim, three years older, is kept out of the armed forces by a leg deformity. But their half-brother, Charles Joseph "Joe" King, seven years Ted's senior, is in the thick of the Canadian war effort. He is a dynamic, impressive young man. As a star Junior hockey player next door to Humberstone in Port Colborne, he received an Ontario Hockey Association scholarship to attend the University of Western Ontario, where he excelled in the backfield of the school's football team as well as on the ice for its hockey team, and not the least in the classroom. Joe is fluently bilingual, able to speak and write French, and leaves Western with an honours B.A. in business. He is one of those gifted people who make an art of any sport they turn their minds to, but as much as he enjoys athletics, he has no interest in making a career out of it. He is set on conquering the business world, qualifying as an accountant after graduation, and while at university he enrolled, as any good future leader of men would, in officers' training. On March 6, 1942, he went active as a reinforcement officer in the twenty-fifth quota of the Highland Light Infantry of Canada, based in Guelph, with the rank of second lieutenant. In an army lacking fresh leaders, Joe King is an obvious fast-track talent. In the fall of 1942, now a full lieutenant, King is in Vernon, B.C., at the Battle Drill Training Centre, and before the year is out he is an acting captain.

Brother Ted has also already heard a call to action of sorts, but it is from the Montreal Canadiens. Conscription has left professional hockey clubs in Canada and the United States to fill their rosters with men beyond the reach of the draft: young single men, and older, married players.* Player shortages have become a threat to the viability of the National Hockey League. At the NHL's head office in Montreal, as Kennedy comes to town, league president Frank Calder is debating whether or not the league can even operate for another season. Calder concludes it can, but some franchises, particularly the Rangers, are so short of players that the league must amend its regulations to permit teams to loan them to one another.

As desperate as teams are for players, Ted Kennedy is too young and too green to play in the National league. Montreal, however, has secured negotiating rights for him, which gives them the exclusive right to approach the teenager with a contract. It was always believed (though with no way of knowing for sure) that the Canadiens had also once secured Joe King's negotiating rights. The scout who supposedly fingered Joe as a professional prospect was Dinty Moore, who bird-dogged for Montreal in the Port Colborne area while also serving as president of the Ontario Hockey Association. Moore is definitely the one to have put Ted on the Montreal negotiating list. While Ted has not agreed to sign anything, he has agreed to come to Montreal—to play for the Montreal Junior Royals, the Canadiens' farm club, and to attend school at Lower Canada College.

Ultimately, Ted has come to Montreal to get an education, not to launch a hockey career. The Junior Royals are a means to an end for a boy who looks up to his older half-brother and is bent on following in his footsteps to the University of Western Ontario. Joe is an impressive role model in a family otherwise lacking male mentors. Ted's mother, Margaret, was one of many Clarkes to leave Portadown in Northern Ireland for the New World. She married Tom King and, while she was carrying their child, Tom died of influenza; Joe was born on October 16, 1918. Margaret then married Gordon Kennedy, and together they had a daughter, Jessie, and a son, Jim, and three years after Jim was born they were expecting

---

*While the NHL continued to operate in 1942/43, team lineups were so chaotic that St. Lawrence Starch Co. of Port Credit, Ontario, which produced and distributed Bee Hive hockey cards as a sales promotion, issued the following undated memorandum, probably as an addendum to its agreement with league teams: "Because of the uncertainty about the personnel of National Hockey League teams this season and the liability of many of the younger players being called up for military service we have decided not to issue new picture lists or proceed with the production of new pictures until January 15, 1943. By that time it should be reasonably well established what players the teams will have to carry on with. Due to higher wartime cost we shall only be able to allow 1 picture for each BEE HIVE label regardless of size.

another. Two weeks before Ted (christened Theodore) was born on December 12, 1925, Gordon Kennedy was accidentally shot dead while hunting rabbits near Niagara Falls. And so Joe and Ted, two sporting sons of Margaret, have never known their natural fathers. Margaret has had to serve as both a mother and a father to the four children. She has raised them to value their educations, and Joe for one has been able to subdue his enthusiasm and talent for athletics beneath the priority of honing his wits for the white-collar world.

In the corner of Ted Kennedy's dreams that entertains the idea of hockey glory, the bleu, blanc et rouge of the Montreal Canadiens does not figure any more than the red, white and blue of the New York Rangers. It is a state of mind that owes more to indifference than hostility. Like many boys growing up in Ontario, Ted thinks the National league begins and ends with the Toronto Maple Leafs, whose exploits he follows religiously through the radio broadcasts of Foster Hewitt. Being a right-winger himself, his childhood idol was their scoring ace Charlie Conacher, the triggerman of the prolific Kid Line centred by Gentleman Joe Primeau with Busher Jackson on their left.

Kennedy was born into the era known as the golden age of professional sports, the wonderful 1920s when baseball was at the forefront of the popular American imagination and hockey began to conquer major American markets. He was not yet six years old when Maple Leaf Gardens opened for business in November 1931. The Leafs won the Stanley Cup in the spring, and the 1930s unfolded for the team as an era of gallant stars and devoted fans. The league was stumbling through the Depression, moving, then shedding, franchises left and right, but the Leafs soldiered on, capturing the hearts of not only the devoted Gardens crowds but the legions of men, women and children who tuned in to Hewitt's Leaf broadcasts. By the time Kennedy is old enough to face the prospect of a professional hockey career, the Maple Leafs of Toronto have become the Maple Leafs of a nation—or, at least, a nation as one segment of its population defines it. The Maple Leafs have virtually no standing in Quebec, French-speaking Quebecers being almost unheard of in its lineup. As for Quebec, its own hockey loyalties for years were divided between two Montreal clubs, the Maroons for the anglophones, the Canadiens for the francophones. While the collapse of the Maroons in 1938 left the Canadiens as the only professional game in town, the following of the Senior Royals clubs is as strong as, if not stronger than, that of the Canadiens.

Ted Kennedy arrives in Montreal on a morning train, and that evening is met at the Queen's Hotel by a representative of the Montreal Royals organization. As the heart of the Montreal Canadiens' development system, the Royals operate Junior and Senior teams in Quebec's nominally amateur leagues. The representative explains that Ted will stay at the hotel for a few days while a room is arranged for him in a private home in the upper-class anglophone enclave of Westmount, close to Lower Canada College. Ted enrols at LCC and begins attending classes, travelling between the school and his hotel room by streetcar.

But no room in a private home is forthcoming. For two weeks, he makes his streetcar pilgrimages, a young man of Irish Protestant stock who speaks no French from a small southern Ontario community. Though the Royals organization treats him very well, disenchantment begins to set in. He is not playing any hockey, as practices have not yet begun for the Junior Royals. It happens that the Boston Bruins are staying at the same hotel while holding their training camp in Verdun. As they prepare to leave the hotel one afternoon for their first practice, Ted Kennedy encounters Bruins general manager Art Ross, and he tells Mr. Ross of his woes. Never one to let a young talent go unattended or unfulfilled, Ross invites Ted along to the Bruins practice, which consists of little more than skating around.

The Bruins were the Stanley Cup champions of 1940/41, but the war has decimated their lineup. Their star scoring line, the "Kraut" Line of Bobby Bauer, Milt Schmidt and Woody Dumart, all natives of Ontario's Kitchener-Waterloo community (a community with so many German immigrants that before the First World War its name was Berlin), have entered the Royal Canadian Air Force and had their combo renamed the Kitchener Line as they play for its Flyers all-star team. Numerous other starting players have also gone into the military. This will be Boston's last solid season before the war's drain on its lineup drives it into the league cellar.

That evening, Ted joins the Canadiens for dinner at their training table in the hotel, whereupon he is invited along to his second NHL practice in one day. The Canadiens are a team in ascent. They will, after failing to advance beyond the quarterfinals in the past five seasons, at last gain the semifinals. Although they will win only nineteen of fifty games, it will be more than they have won in a season since 1936/37.

It's a very different training session from the one held by the Bruins. Ted watches from rinkside as a scrimmage is held—a brawling fracas complete with stick swinging. Coach Dick Irvin comes to him and says, Son, it's a little rough out there. You'd better not come out. Ted is not disappointed.

They love him, the maje. The men of 30th Battery will consistently pay Conn Smythe the highest compliment an officer can receive: firm but fair. He shows his military background in a stickling for regimental order, and a predilection for driving his men hard. He shows a great facility for leading men; his many years of coaching and managing athletes serves him well; he knows how to build a winning team. Sherwood Wright finds him very knowledgeable about people: the maje knows how far a man can be pushed without breaking. He also sees a man driven instinctively by reciprocity— you scratch my back, I'll scratch yours.

Scratching sometimes turns to stabbing. Smythe disappoints Buck Houle once, and once only, when the battery is at Petawawa. The men assemble for a routine morning inspection, and Smythe uncharacteristically fails to appear on time. After a few minutes of waiting, the battery's second-in-command decides to start the inspection himself. Just then the major comes around the corner of the barracks, and every man flinches. Houle watches from the ranks as the major barks: Captain, are you trying to steal my battery? The man is ejected from the battery with all possible speed, landing in an armoured regiment. Houle's admiration for the maje wilts momentarily with the captain's dismissal: Smythe didn't have to do that. The captain was only doing his job.

He does not countenance idleness. In the summer of 1942, the battery is moved to Tofino on the rugged and remote west coast of Vancouver Island after a scare from a Japanese submarine, which lobbed some shells ashore. Charged with fending off an enemy who never materializes, the battery could easily slip into idleness, but Smythe has a target set up on a rock offshore and keeps his men sharp by shooting at it. When an airport is built for the remote site, he puts his men to work hauling sacks of cement.

While in Tofino, Smythe has the opportunity to be promoted to colonel and remain on the coast with his battery in home-defence duties. He asks some of the men: what do they think of staying here? They tell him they joined up to fight Germans, and he agrees with them. He passes on the promotion. They will go overseas.

He rarely steps over the line in his discipline; Ted Reeve is there to let him know when he's going too far, and he listens to Reeve, a great former lacrosse and football man, at forty-one closer to Smythe in age than the rest of the men. Houle comes to conclude that if you tuck your tail between your legs when attacked by Smythe, you are finished. If you stand your ground, you have a chance of winning his respect. Lance-Bombardier Geoff Archer will recall how Smythe can come down on you like a ton of bricks, but that he also instils life into the battery, and that Smythe sometimes surprises him by showing a sense of humour. For Nick Hatten, who rises to become Smythe's battery sergeant-major, he is the greatest thing that has ever happened and will ever happen to him. He is a hard-nosed perfectionist who does not hesitate to dress you down in front of the rest of the battery. You can either sulk or do something about it, and if you do something about it, if you respond to one of his blasts by trying your best and working hard, he is a great man to have as your commander. He will reward you with public praise and confidence as soon as you have righted the wrong that elicited his wrath.

And this being an athletes' battery, there must be athletics, though Smythe never lets games interfere with basic duties. They are brilliant at baseball, at basketball, at hockey, at soccer—even at bridge. They win camp championships, army championships. The 30th and the rest of the 6th Regiment sail for England on October 27, 1942, and in 1943, the 6th Regiment squad, its lineup formed by 30th Battery men, is crowned the best softball team in the Canadian army in England. In February 1944, the 6th wins the II Canadian Corps hockey title.

The 30th is perhaps Conn Smythe's greatest team ever, as capable on the battlefield as on the sports field. He is unabashedly proud of them, and always will be. There is a purposefulness to them that the greatest professional hockey club can only hope to emulate. They have come to England of their own free will, to wait for their chance to fight, and if necessary to die, and some of them will.

After being kept off the ice at the brawling Canadiens scrimmage, Ted Kennedy attends a Royals practice. On hand is Maurice Richard. A right-winger like Kennedy, Richard moved up from the Verdun Juniors to the Senior Royals in 1940/41, but his season was put on ice by a broken ankle. The next season, a broken left wrist took him out of the lineup. In September 1942, he is destined for the ranks of the Canadiens, if he can keep his body in one piece. He marks the beginning of his latest run at a Canadiens starting position by marrying Lucille Nordet on September 12.

Kennedy carries away from the practice no impression of Richard, but he cannot forget goaltender Bill Durnan, a twenty-six-year-old veteran of Senior hockey who will move up to the Canadiens from the Royals in 1943/44 and win six Vezinas in seven seasons. Also on the ice is twenty-six-year-old Buddy O'Connor, who played thirty-six games with Montreal the previous season and is about to become a star playmaking centre with the Canadiens and later the Rangers. He also meets Glen Harmon, a very capable twenty-one-year-old defenceman who will play his first games in an eight-season career with the Canadiens in this new season. With him in the defence corps is Red Storey, who will become one of the more colourful and capable referees of the modern NHL era.

Richard does make the Canadiens, signing a two-year contract on October 29. Irvin combines the francophone Richard with the anglophone Lach and the bilingual Blake, thereby creating the offensive unit that will be known as the Punch Line in honour of its offensive impact. Richard's first game as a Canadien is also the first regular-season Canadiens game he has ever seen. He has played against the Canadiens when scrimmages have been held with the Royals, but he has never actually sat in a seat in the Forum and watched this team play. The myth that the Canadiens are skating and shooting symbols of French Canada is still evolving. When Richard joins the team, it is far more English than French. Dick Irvin doesn't speak any French, and general manager Tommy Gorman came over from the defunct Maroons, an avowedly anglophone Montreal team. English is the designated language of the Canadiens dressing room. Only when speaking to another French Canadian in the room does Richard use his French. Otherwise, he is limited to a basic vocabulary: "yes" and "no."

He scores his first NHL goal on November 8. But Richard's debut, and that of the Punch Line, quickly fizzles. After appearing in only sixteen games, and scoring five times, Richard breaks his ankle. Wrist and ankle fractures have now knocked him out of three straight seasons. He will one day tell a fellow NHL player that he was considered so brittle that the Canadian military declared him unfit for duty.[1]

Several young Junior Royals, French-Canadian kids, are also staying at the Queen's Hotel that September. In the evenings Ted Kennedy hooks up with them and heads uptown. Kennedy looks on as they converse among themselves in French, a language as foreign to him as Swahili. It is all very, very strange—the big city, the foreign tongue, living in a hotel, streetcar commuting. Ted decides he has had enough, and goes home to Humberstone.

A representative of the Royals organization follows him, pleading with him to come back and try again, which he does, for another week, before deciding that he and Montreal are incompatible. He enrols in school back home, his mind firmly set on following Joe King into the lecture halls of Western, and at the same time begins playing for the Port Colborne Sailors of the Ontario Senior League.

The Sailors are one of the league's traditionally stronger teams, playing in a small arena that makes them hard to beat at home. They are coached by Nels Stewart, an NHL star from 1925/26 to 1939/40 with the Montreal Maroons, Boston Bruins and New York Americans. In his rookie season, Stewart won the Hart Trophy, the league's most valuable player award, and the league scoring title, and while he never made the All-Star team he was a perennial top-ten scorer.

Kennedy is not a flashy skater, no dipsy-doodler, no Billy the Kid dazzler. He has a good shot, a scoring touch and exceptionally quick reflexes, but mostly he has a surfeit of courageous determination. He digs and chases and checks and presses until his knees are buckling from exhaustion. Under Stewart's tutelage, Kennedy hones his skills around the opposing net, where Stewart was so effective that his opponents honoured him with the nickname Old Poison. Stewart was an awful skater who in Leaf forward Bob Davidson's mind waddled down the ice. But he was also a big man, husky, standing six foot one, not an easy man to move off the goaltender's doorstep, and he was a master of the faceoff. When he retired in 1940 after fifteen seasons, the thirty-eight-year-old Stewart had 324 regular-season goals, more than anyone in the history of the NHL.

Kennedy is five foot eleven, leaner than Stewart, though well muscled; a suitable recipient of Stewart's hard-earned bag of tricks. Turning seventeen, Kennedy becomes an even more impressive talent as Stewart's guidance and his ice time with the Sailors expands his game. While the Sailors don't make the playoffs, Kennedy amasses twenty-three goals and twenty-nine assists by the end of Port Colborne's season in early 1943. Gus Ogilvy of the Montreal Royals reappears in Humberstone, trying to convince Kennedy to give his organization yet another try.

Ogilvy asks Kennedy if he is disappointed in the Royals organization, and Kennedy says, Gus, I couldn't have been treated better. I'm just not going back.

So, Ogilvy wonders, what are you going to do?

Kennedy tells him. He's going to finish high school and go to Western.

Soon after, Kennedy is sitting in class in high school in Port Colborne. It's about two o'clock in the afternoon, a day at the beginning of March. The principal calls him out of class. There's a long-distance call for him, from Toronto. He hands Kennedy the phone. Nels Stewart is on the line. Coach Nels, unbeknown to Kennedy, has taken it upon himself to do some career planning for him. He happens to be a good friend of Hap Day's, as the two had played together on the New York Americans at the end of their careers. Stewart tells Kennedy that the Leafs want to sign him. There's a train leaving Welland at four-thirty that gets into Toronto at six-thirty. Kennedy is to be on it, and Stewart will meet him when it arrives at Union Station.

He leaves the high school and speaks with his mother, who is deeply concerned about this turn of events, before heading to Welland to catch the train. Stewart delivers Kennedy to Maple Leaf Gardens, where he meets with Stewart, acting general manager Frank Selke and Day. Conn Smythe, the regular general manager, of course, is now overseas with the Canadian army, awaiting action in Europe. This is an imposing reception for a young man for whom the Leafs are the epitome of hockey. Kennedy had been up in the cheap seats of the Gardens in the spring of 1942, watching Hap Day execute one of the greatest reversals of fortune in Stanley Cup history as the Leafs rallied from a three-game-to-none deficit against Detroit to win the Cup for the first time in a decade.

Despite the persistent and persuasive overtures of these three impressive men, Ted Kennedy refuses to sign anything until he has spoken with his mother. He goes home, and he speaks with her. He is firm, and she is crestfallen. He knows all about the importance of education, but this—being a Toronto Maple Leaf—is what he now knows he wants to do. There is nothing she can do or say to change this seventeen-year-old's mind. He goes back to Toronto and plays in the last two games of the season, road games against New York and Boston. He earns an assist in each game, though the record books only grant him one of them. He does not appear in the play-offs, in which the third-place Leafs are eliminated in their semifinal series against the first-place Red Wings.

Kennedy does not know it, but he is the most important, and most controversial, Leaf acquisition of the war years. On Nels Stewart's advice, one month earlier, on February 10, Selke and Day took the gamble of dealing away one of Conn Smythe's most prized prospects, Frank Eddolls, to Montreal, just to secure the negotiating rights for Kennedy. If they had not been able to convince Kennedy to sign, the deal would have been a complete disaster; it might have put their jobs on the line. Even with a deal successfully completed, the news of it strikes Conn Smythe, in England with his battery, like a round from a Panzer. He is plunged into despair for months over the loss of his twenty-one-year-old defensive standout, currently playing hockey for the RCAF team in Montreal. The Canadiens, under the guidance of Dick Irvin, reach the semifinals that spring, though they are defeated by Boston. Now the Canadiens own Eddolls, and the Leafs have in return some kid Smythe has never seen named Kennedy.

"I am very worried about Hap & Selke having put Eddols [*sic*] off our list," Smythe writes the Leaf scout Squib Walker, an old compatriot, on April 20. They had played Junior hockey together at the start of the Great War—playing against Frank Selke's Berlin Union Jacks in the provincial finals—and enlisted together in 1915. "...This Eddols was the kind you only pick up every ten years. There isn't a defence man of his age around for many a mile. Also his class on & off the ice.... I still think I am the best judge of deals so you see [I] haven't got any smaller head. That's what breaks me down when I think of Eddols he was my ace in the hole to start my new soldier defence. Young Canada etc. so I've told him [Selke] to get the deal back again. Maybe you can help by swiping one of their prospects & then deal him back...."

It will be said that Smythe is angered by Day and Selke having traded a man currently serving his country, but there is no note of such umbrage in his letters to Walker. "Hap has been a great success & if I could only keep Frank's nose out of the hockey players end his (Hap's) job would be easier," Smythe writes to Walker on May 10. "You know, F. is for the experience he's had a very poor judge of hockey players. He has one or two success's but has overlooked or over sold dozens. The latest move in getting rid of Eddols contract is a heart breaker and I'm hoping in some way they can make up for it and get him back. He is of the Hap Day Joe P[rimeau] Syl Apps breed and you can only find one of these every five years & it took me ten years to land this kid."

On July 9, Hap Day sends to Smythe an accounting of all the prospects on the Leaf reserve list, with a grading of their potential. Very few rate an "A," assigned by Day to those he feels could play in the NHL. Eighteen-year-old Howie Meeker, who will make the Leafs in 1946, only rates a "B."

Kennedy is on the list, and Eddolls is not. Day and Selke have recognized in Kennedy the same inspiring qualities that Smythe has ascribed to Day, Primeau and Apps.

On the subject of the young Kennedy, Day makes this note for Smythe:

T. Kennedy—Right Wing—The Eddolls exchange. "enough said" (A)

Bob Carse returns for another season with the Blackhawks in the fall of 1942. At twenty-three, he comes into his own and produces thirty-two points in forty-seven games. In Toronto Billy Taylor blossoms with eighteen goals and forty-two assists to finish sixth in the scoring race, tied on points with fellow Leaf Lorne Carr. Chicago finds a pair of scoring stars in Doug and Max Bentley, who finish first and third in the scoring race, but the team as a whole flounders. While the team scores 179 goals, it allows 180. And though play in the league is exceptionally tight, with the Red Wings, the top team, winning just twenty-five of fifty games, by winning only seventeen games the Blackhawks slip to fifth behind the improving Montreal Canadiens and miss the playoffs.

At the moment he is hitting his stride as a professional hockey player, Bob Carse steps away from the game. Like his brother Bill before him, Bob Carse decides his services are more urgently needed by the Canadian army than by the Blackhawks, and goes active. Since entering the Edmonton Athletic Club system at age twelve and working up through its Midget, Juvenile and Junior ranks, he has been determined to play professional hockey. But he has also absorbed the team-focused culture the game instils in its best players. He will always talk in the language of teamwork, of all for one and one for all, of harmony among the players being the key to the success of a club. With the country at war, with many young men he knows from his amateur hockey days in Edmonton now in the armed services, it is only right and natural that he should now join them. On September 29, 1943, Bob Carse enlists in the Canadian Infantry in Calgary.

TO SERVE AND TO FIGHT

You just get established in a business like hockey and you have to give it all up. The — Japs bomb Pearl Harbor and a damned war comes along.

—Boston Bruins goaltender Frank Brimsek, an American citizen, grouses about the collateral damage caused by Pearl Harbor on December 7, 1941

May 27, 1943

BORN on January 13, 1924, Albert "Red" Tilson is nineteen and single when he volunteers for service with the Canadian army. He has a grade-eleven education; he gives his trade as apprentice electrician. Under "Business or Professional" on his service record, the army more accurately assigns him the category of "Hockey Player." Red Tilson is one of the star forwards of the Oshawa Generals. Like Billy Taylor before him, who at the same age led the Generals to a Memorial Cup over Bob Carse's Edmonton Roamers in 1939, Red Tilson's professional rights are held by the Toronto Maple Leafs.

Tilson enlists at a time when it is a challenge to draw much of a distinction between professional and military hockey. The 1942 national Senior championship, the Allan Cup, was won by the RCAF Flyers, which received intact for 1942/43 the Kraut Line of Woody Dumart, Milt Schmidt and Bobby Bauer of the Bruins. (Schmidt and Bauer then headed to England to serve as player–coaches with the Canadian Bomber Group.) Following the 1941/42 season, which saw Japan bring the United States into the war via Pearl Harbor, came serious doubt over whether the NHL would be able to play another season during hostilities. Manpower was one consideration for all sports, but another was restrictions on the consumption of strategic materials such as oil and rubber, which were being consumed by fans (in the form of gasoline and tires) driving to games. With gasoline in particular being rationed, sports teams whose fans can't get to the arena or stadium by streetcar are in trouble. The American Hockey League is on the ropes. It grew to ten teams in 1941/42 with the addition of the Washington Lions, but for 1942/43 the Philadelphia Ramblers folded and the Springfield Indians were forced to merge with the Buffalo Bisons when Springfield's arena was taken over by the U.S. military as a storage facility. On January 18, 1943, the New Haven Eagles withdrew from the league, leaving it with seven franchises. In 1943/44 the AHL is down to six teams as the Lions shut down for the duration of the war.

In anticipation of the NHL folding its tents before the start of the 1942/43 season, New York Rangers coach Frank Boucher approached Cecil Duncan of the Canadian Amateur Hockey Association and a friend in the civil service in Ottawa with the idea of creating an all-star army hockey team, which would be packed with enlistments from the NHL clubs. This team could make itself useful by entertaining the troops, war workers and the general public. Thus was created the Ottawa Commandos. Into the lineup came Neil and Mac Colville and Alex Shibicky, a line that helped win the 1940 Stanley Cup for New York; also in the lineup was Ranger goalie Jim Henry, who played for the Brandon Elks when Bob Carse's EAC Roamers defeated them in the Memorial Cup playdowns of 1939. The Commandos also had a first-class defence corps: Joe Cooper, a former Ranger and Blackhawk, Ken Reardon of the Canadiens (a substitute player with the 1939 Edmonton Roamers) and Maple Leaf Bingo Kampman. (The Colvilles, Reardon and Kampman all had Edmonton roots.) And Dick Irvin put in double shifts as coach of both the Canadiens and the Commandos.

As it turned out, the NHL continued to operate in 1942/43. It began the season with a blessing of sorts wrested from Elliott M. Little, director of Canada's selective service board. "Professional sport is of comparatively low labor priority," Little stated, but stitched a silver lining into this cloud. "Because it contributes something to the war effort by providing a degree of popular relaxation, it is permitted to continue, but only on the same basis as any other activity of low essentiality. Professional athletes, of course, receive no special consideration as far as military service is concerned. If a person is engaged in work of low priority for which he is particularly skilled, he may be given a permit to play professional sport." Using this rather tepid endorsement, professional hockey was able to present itself as an enterprise deemed essential to the nation's well-being. But in the fall of 1942 NHL teams were being denied the services of some players when the selective service administration would not allow them to quit jobs of high essentiality in war industries to accept positions with a team.

At the same time, though, professional hockey was able to exploit a loophole in an order-in-council that went into effect on October 20 setting restrictions on cross-border employment for Canadians. The order-in-council, PC 9011, stated that no person over age sixteen could take or seek employment outside Canada unless he had a valid exit permit. There were, however, exemptions spelled out, and PC 9011 prescribed that "members of dramatic, artistic, athletic or spectacular organizations departing from Canada temporarily for the purpose of giving public performances or exhibitions of an interesting or instructive character, are exempt from obtaining labor exit permits." Instead, they need only secure an exemption certificate from the selective service administration. That fall, the Winnipeg office of the selective service began issuing them to professional hockey players, evidently concluding that what these men did on the ice with a stick and puck was indeed interesting or instructive.

For the 1942/43 season, the Leafs produced a promotional piece showing thirteen "former Maple Leaf hockey players now in active service." They included Jack Fox, photographed in a Maple Leaf jersey and identified as "the first pro hockey player to make the supreme sacrifice in the present war." Fox, however, had never played a game as a Leaf. The rest of the players were a mix of Leaf starters and prospects, all of whom will come out of the war in one piece. Some have never played as a Maple Leaf, despite the uniforms they sported in the promotional piece, and never will. In addition to Fox there was Nick Knott, who had spent two seasons in the American League, during which he saw action for fourteen games with the Brooklyn Americans in the franchise's last NHL season. Knott entered the Canadian army in 1942; after his discharge in 1945, he will play with Tulsa of the U.S. league. Victor Grigg had spent a season in the American league before entering the army in 1942, and will go back to the American league in 1945. Buddy Hellyer, who went into the RCAF, similarly does not ever play for the Leafs.

Only one of these thirteen true and would-be Leafs, the unfortunate Jack Fox, enlisted before the summer of 1942. Thus, almost three years of war were witnessed before any Leaf property other than Fox entered the volunteer armed forces. Overall, the summer of 1942 was when the floodgates opened on enlistments by NHL players, and there seems to have been a link between the stepped-up enlistments and the NHL's desire to keep operating. With the league (particularly its American franchises after Pearl Harbor brought the United States into the war) feeling pressure to take a more active role in the war effort to justify its continued existence,

the most logical contribution it could make was to have those players who were subject to the NRMA draft actually enlist. Whether
players were counselled by their teams to volunteer or did so of
their own accord, the rush to join up was sudden and significant,
and it produced a pronounced side-effect: powerful military hockey
teams. Sometimes this seemed less a side-effect than part of the
agenda. The Commandos, of course, were created expressly for the
purpose of accommodating the enlistment of the game's stars. It
was as if the NHL was establishing a shadow league for its players
within the Canadian armed forces, a safe haven for those precious
talents who were given non-combat roles that insulated them
against any future Hong Kongs or Dieppes.

Armed forces teams created by the enlistment rush over the sum-
mer of 1942 completely dominated Senior hockey in Canada.
Victoria Army, led by eight-season Maple Leaf veteran Nick Metz
and Blackhawk Bill Carse, won the B.C. Senior Championship. In
Calgary the Currie Barracks army team was led by player–coach
Cowboy Anderson, who did his militia training with Bob and Bill
Carse in September 1940. Anderson won the Hart Trophy as the
most valuable player in the NHL in 1941/42 as a Brooklyn
American; when the Amerks folded, Anderson went into the army.
On his Currie team he has goaltender Frank McCool, who played
for the Calgary Knights of Columbus Juniors in 1937/38, and made
an unsuccessful appearance at the Chicago Blackhawks training
camp with the Carse brothers in 1939. In the spring of 1943, Currie
Barracks won the Alberta Senior title over the RCAF Mustangs of
Calgary. Victoria Army then eliminated Currie Army and the RCAF
Bombers of Winnipeg to win the western Allan Cup playdowns.
Back east, Allan Cup playdown contenders in the Maritimes
included Halifax RCAF, Halifax Navy and Cape Breton RCAF.
The RCAF Flyers all-star squad was playing in the Ottawa City
League playdowns, while in the Quebec Senior League, three of
four playdown participants were military teams: Ottawa
Commandos, Montreal Army and Cornwall Army, with the Quebec
Aces the only civilian squad.

In the Allan Cup finals that spring, it was Victoria Army against
the Ottawa Commandos in a five-game series played in Winnipeg,
Regina and Calgary. There was a yawning difference between teams
like Victoria Army, which had a few former pros going through their
basic training in the lineup, and the star-packed Commandos. The
Commandos won the series, and as Ken McConnell, a sports colum-

nist with the Vancouver *Daily Province*, would observe: "It was, to say the least, an uneven series on paper, but with [Bill] Carse spearheading the attack and Art Rice-Jones performing miracles in goal, the Victoria soldiers gave the Ottawas a terrific struggle before giving up. That was a series over which there was prolonged controversy. It was said the Commandos were receiving a lush salary to play hockey and their every wish was respected by the commanding officers. Victoria's Army club was lucky to get stale beer."

As Red Tilson enlists, Senior hockey is on its way to becoming even more dominated by military clubs, some of which are stocked with former professionals. The ongoing talent drain created by enlistments and the NRMA draft means that few civilian Senior clubs can continue to exist, particularly after Canadian troops enter combat full-time with the invasion of Sicily in the summer of 1943. For the 1943/44 season, the only Senior level hockey in Alberta is being played by the Services League, its four teams provided by training bases. Bob Carse, entering basic training, plays on a line with Max Bentley, who has also left the Blackhawks, and Alex Kaleta, who was with the Currie team in 1942/43 and played with the Lethbridge Maple Leafs when they won the Alberta Senior title of 1941. Elsewhere in the Alberta league, the Red Deer Army Wheelers have former Commandos Jim Henry in goal and Mac Colville as player–coach. Manitoba Senior League is also a military loop, with play between the RCAF Bombers, HMCS *Chippewa* and Winnipeg Army. Winnipeg has been a major recruitment centre for both the Maple Leafs and the New York Rangers, and the Bombers have in their lineup a group of local boys that includes Maple Leaf veterans Pete Langelle and Wally Stanowski, Joe Krol, who played twenty-four games with the Brooklyn Americans in 1941/42, New York Ranger Alf Pike and Rene Trudell, a Leaf property who will join the Rangers after the war.

Albert Tilson was born in Regina, raised in Regina and is still living in Regina, at 101 New Armour Block, when he enlists as an infantry reinforcement. It would make eminent sense that he volunteer right in Regina, home to the Regina Rifles Regiment. There is even a very good army hockey team right on hand, the Caps. The team has just won the Saskatchewan Senior championship; what is more, Albert's older brother Bill centred a line on the championship squad, between Maple Leaf Don Metz and former New York American Murray Armstrong. But Albert Tilson does not enlist in his home town. Instead, he goes all the way to the Military

District 3 depot in Kingston, Ontario.

Why Kingston? To answer that, one must answer why hockey players in general are volunteering in such large numbers. To say that there is a war on and that all able-bodied young men are needed doesn't go far enough. While prominent NHL figures like Frank Boucher have been actively reshaping the military hockey system as a haven for professional players, some players unquestionably are enlisting to do their part for the war effort. Others clearly are doing it because their professional careers are nearing an end and, even though they are (for now) exempt from the draft because they are married, going into uniform, even if only to coach or to play hockey, is a more dignified way to round out a career at a time of national crisis than to persist in playing in a struggling professional system. And it is by no means certain that professional hockey will continue to exist, now that the war is escalating. If the NHL is going to shut down, why not get on with serving your country forthwith? As well, there are concerns that the draft might be expanded to include married men, and those who do not want to end up Zombies decide over the summer of 1943 to enlist so that they can serve on their own terms.

For a young amateur hockey talent like Red Tilson, choosing to enlist specifically in Kingston is significant because it is home to the Kingston Frontenac Army club, which has just secured Red Hamill, the twenty-six-year-old veteran of the Boston Bruins and Chicago Blackhawks, as its player–coach. (Montreal Army secured former Red Wing and Bruins star Marty Barry as its coach for 1942/43.) Enlisting at Kingston also means being sent to Cornwall for basic training, and Cornwall is emerging as a military hockey powerhouse. On the base staff are two notable figures. The first is Punch Imlach, who played Junior hockey for the Young Rangers of Toronto and will coach the Maple Leafs to four Stanley Cups in the 1960s. Given the rank of lieutenant in 1942, he spends the entire war at the base as an instructor, as well as serving as player–coach with the base hockey team. The other is Torontonian Tommy Ivan, a former Senior league star who before coming into the army coached Junior hockey for five years. Holding the rank of sergeant, his formal military duty is instructing recruits in platoon weapons and chemical warfare. Immediately after the war, Ivan will become coach of the Omaha Knights of the United States Hockey League; he will coach the Indianapolis Capitols of the American Hockey League in 1946/47 and be named coach of the Detroit Red Wings

for 1947/48. Ivan will stay in the job until 1954, and under his tutelage the Red Wings will win three Stanley Cups. He will then
spend twenty-three years as general manager of the Chicago
Blackhawks, who will win a Stanley Cup for him in 1961.

With Imlach and Ivan on its instruction staff, Cornwall Army
cannot help but have a hockey program that is the envy of any military establishment. Among the soldiers who play some hockey here
are Aldege "Baz" Bastien, an outstanding goaltending prospect in
the Maple Leaf system, and Bud Poile from Thunder Bay, a star
rookie with the Maple Leafs in 1942/43. Cornwall Army was
strong enough to defeat the Montreal Canadiens 5–4 in an exhibition game on October 29, 1942. On June 17, 1943, Private Tilson is
transferred 120 miles down the St. Lawrence River to Cornwall for
basic training. On August 18, Red receives a promotion: he is made
an acting lance-corporal, with pay, which makes him a junior non-
commissioned officer.

Tilson never does play hockey for Imlach or Ivan. An infection in
his left leg waylays him for five days in Cornwall Military Hospital
at the end of August. After a few days' leave of absence following
his discharge from hospital, on September 10 Lance-Corporal
Tilson is transferred back to Kingston, to the Canadian Ordinance
Corps Training Centre at the Barriefield base for "all purposes"
weapons training. Canada has officially been at war for exactly
four years. A week before his arrival at Barriefield, Canadian
troops go ashore at Messina on the toe of the Italian boot.

In October he attends an Assistant Instructors Course at COTC in
Barriefield, a move that suggests he is destined, like Imlach and
Ivan, to play and organize military hockey while serving on the
staff of a training base. Tilson is in fact penned into the starting
lineup of Kingston Frontenac Army. Six teams are slated to com-
pete in OHA Senior competition in November: Kingston Frontenac
Army, Toronto RCAF Airmen, Toronto Army Daggers, Toronto
Navy Bulldogs (HMCS *York*) and two civilian clubs, the St.
Catharines Saints and Hamilton Majors.

The 1942/43 season was shot through with enough irregularities
to give pause to those who think military bases are supposed to be
training men to defeat Hitler, Mussolini and Tojo, not conspiring to
win hockey championships. Military teams that season were wont
to call in players stationed at bases at the other end of the country
to bolster their lineups. Players have managed to receive discharges
from one service branch and re-enlist in a different branch to play

hockey for a new club. Base teams have also been able to stack their rosters by having key players transfer there for a particular training course. Men in the military are also being allowed to play on local civilian Senior and Junior clubs; some civilians, for that matter, have been playing for military clubs.

The army has become sufficiently concerned by the professionalism of military hockey to issue a policy for the new season: "If a player is enlisted for general service and is up to the standard of overseas service, he will, on completion of his training, be dispatched overseas. There will be no interference with the ordinary program of hockey players through basic, advanced or trades training and no player may play hockey on a team representing a military station other than his own."

Military hockey is in trouble because it has become caught up in the murky machinations of Canadian amateur hockey, which is part and parcel of the professional system. Senior hockey in Canada is little more than another tier in the professional system, with many players under contract to professional clubs. A typical professional contract specifies three levels of pay: for playing with the parent NHL club, with an affiliated minor pro club in a league such as the American or United States leagues, and with a Senior club.

Amateur hockey is also big business for Conn Smythe and his fellow Maple Leaf Gardens shareholders. In 1937, the Gardens secured the exclusive right to host all Junior and Senior regular-season and playoff games in the Toronto area. The agreement was renewed for another five years in 1942. A November 1, 1943, year-end statement issued by Maple Leaf Gardens Ltd. indicates that 150 amateur games over the past year resulted in the sale of 275,861 tickets—a huge increase over the previous year-end, when 116 games generated 112,693 ticket sales.[1] At the beginning of the 1943/44 season, the Gardens has a lucrative lineup of amateur teams in place to keep the stands packed when the Leafs are not playing at home. The Gardens will be home ice to the Toronto Marlborough Juniors and St. Michael's College Majors and three Senior military clubs: Toronto Army Daggers, Toronto Navy Bulldogs and RCAF Airmen. The Bulldogs enjoy the services of Dudley "Red" Garrett, a former Leaf amateur prospect whom Toronto traded away to New York to get Babe Pratt. Garrett appeared in twenty-three games for the Rangers in 1942/43, then joined the navy on July 13, 1943—the day before his nineteenth birthday. The RCAF team is coached by Joe Primeau, star of the Leafs' Kid Line of the 1930s, and in goal is Red Wings star Johnny Mowers, fresh from winning the Stanley Cup last spring. The Marlboroughs, managed by Harold Ballard, are coached by Billy the Kid Taylor. A marquee Maple Leaf, Taylor enlisted in the army in June, and is in the lineup of the Daggers. So is Leaf captain Syl Apps, who broke his leg last January and enlisted in the army in September; and Hank Goldup, who played with Toronto and New York the past three seasons; and Gord Drillon, who played six seasons for Toronto before skating as a Canadien last season. Finally, there is Turk Broda, the Leafs' Vezina-winning goaltender.

Or perhaps there isn't Turk Broda. The Turk singlehandedly brings the whole military hockey system crashing down. The story will long be told of how he has until midnight on October 18 to report to his nearest depot and join the ranks. It's assumed that he will be inducted in Toronto and join Taylor, Apps, Goldup and Drillon in the Toronto Army Daggers lineup. Except that on the evening of the eighteenth he is on a train in the company of a staff sergeant from Montreal Military District, heading east.

At 11:18 p.m. the RCMP boards the train and takes Broda into custody on the grounds, it is said, that he is about to breach his draft notice, even though he is plainly in the company of an army NCO. The RCMP whisk Broda back to Toronto to have him sign up there.

Oh, the scandal that erupts. The Montreal *Gazette* charges that Broda has been kidnapped by the RCMP for the express purpose of making sure that Broda plays his military hockey for the Daggers and not Montreal Army. It says Broda was lured to Montreal by an offer of $2,400 above his normal military base pay. The rumour even arises that Conn Smythe personally arranged for the RCMP to snatch Broda back, although this is extremely unlikely, given that Smythe is far from the scene, training in England with his battery.

The scandal is real, and so, it seems, is the fact that Broda is found by the RCMP in the company of a Montreal army district NCO. But Turk Broda has never been in danger of violating a draft notice. On October 15, three days before he was arrested on a train bound for Montreal, Walter "Turk" Broda volunteered for service with the Royal Canadian Artillery at Toronto Military District 2 depot.

On October 16, Broda was interviewed by Major E.A. Macdonald. Broda's military records indicate a painfully gained grade-eight education that began in his native Manitoba at age six and was completed at age fifteen in Ontario after losing two years when he transferred from the separate to public school system. (The Brodas, Polish immigrants, are Roman Catholic.) His occupational background details eleven years of hockey—two amateur, nine professional. His summer employment is defined as "occasional," which includes working as a trucker/salesman for a brewery for eighteen months and on an assembly line for six months. His October 16 assessment by Major Macdonald describes him as

> a pleasant, responsive, rather stolid man of average height and husky build, (5' 8"—188lbs), who was co-operative during the interview. He states that he has always been of sound health.
>
> Married, (3 children), BRODA has lived a normal domestic life. The greater part of his occupational life has been devoted to active athletics, being employed as a professional hockey player for 9 years, and spending almost the remainder of his time in a semi-professional capacity, as well as being a member of organized baseball and school rugby teams during the summer months.
>
> He and his wife are interested in dancing, movies and bridge.
>
> His non-athletic work record has been briefly spasmodic and of a distinctively "labourer" calibre, reflecting—in part—his indicated low-average learning ability.

Major Macdonald recommends that Broda be assigned to the RCA Automotive Group as a Trade Trainee—in other words, Broda would best serve his country as a truck driver. Clearly this is not what Turk Broda has in mind for himself, so after the assessment he moves to accept a better offer from Montreal military district, failing to understand that in so doing the army could consider him AWOL and have him hauled back.

Broda's motivations for enlisting are not clear. He may have wanted to follow in Conn Smythe's footsteps, even join his battery, and for this reason chose to enlist as a gunner. His interview, on the other hand, may have given him a firm indication that he was not going to do any real artillery work or get near the 30th. It may also have given him an indication that heading to Petawawa for training would mean he could not play Senior hockey.*

---

*The exact circumstances of Broda's enlistment will never be entirely clear. His military record gives no indication of an arrest or any shenanigans in Montreal. The only hint is the fact that he is fingerprinted on October 19, the day he returned under RCMP escort to Toronto.

The Broda incident sets off a national firestorm of indignation over the tarnished state of military hockey. Men overseas and their families at home are indignant that players are having permanent staff positions on training bases arranged so that they can participate indefinitely in what should be a recreational distraction for men in training. All three branches of the armed services are now fully embroiled in the war—the navy in the Battle of the Atlantic, the air force in the bombing campaign against Germany, the army in the fighting in Italy. The utter lack of priorities shown by military hockey organizers is seen as a national disgrace. "It is an obvious fact that many prominent hockey players who enlisted one or two years ago are still in Canada and appear on the rosters of armed services teams," blasts the *Calgary Herald* on October 20.

It is not the first time that the Canadian military and professional sports have become entwined. During the Great War the 228th Battalion, also known as the Northern Fusiliers, iced a hockey team packed with star talent from Toronto and Northern Ontario.[2] It entered play in the professional National Hockey Association for the 1916/17 season, its players sporting khaki uniforms with the battalion crest. In its first game on December 27, it dispatched the Ottawa Senators 10–7.

The 228th was a magnet for controversy from its first faceoff. Eddie Oatman, a star with Portland of the Pacific Coast league, was allowed by the PCHA to play with the 228th in the NHA on the understanding that the 228th was participating in the league only temporarily before heading overseas. That appeared not to be the case, as the team had put up a $3,000 bond to cover the league's inconveniences should the team withdraw from competition before the season was over. The pullout came on February 10, when the 228th was leading the league in goal scoring by a wide margin. The country by then had suffered through five months of bloodshed in the Somme offensive, which ended in late November with almost 25,000 Canadians and Newfoundlanders as casualties. Volunteering was drying up—in a few months Borden would move to introduce conscription—and neither the army nor the public could justify having men in uniform playing games, never mind games in a professional league.

But in the process of trying to get the 228th overseas, a bona fide scandal overcame the battalion. Eddie Oatman's status as a legitimate soldier fell into question; already causing friction between the PCHA and the NHA over his transfer, he now asserted he had signed a $1,200 contract to play for the 228th, of which $500 was just for hockey. When he arrived in Saint John, New Brunswick, for embarkation, he was granted a discharge. Also discharged was Gord Meeking, who said he was promised a commission in the army in return for playing for the 228th. Meeking also understood that the gate receipts were to be split up among the players at the end of the season. "During the recruiting of the battalion he had worn an officer's uniform," *The Trail of the Stanley Cup*, the trophy's history published by the NHL, will state. "When the battalion entrained for [Saint] John he was ordered to put on a private's uniform. After being discharged as being medically unfit he returned as far as Montreal, not going to Toronto where he said he could not face those who had given him a sendoff."

A quarter century later, the armed forces have blundered into another hockey scandal. Reaction by the army to the Broda "kidnapping" and publicity is swift. On November 8, on the eve of a new season of Senior league play, Montreal Army pulls out of the Quebec league. Broda meanwhile has been shipped out on November 5 to Petawawa for basic training, far from the lineup of the Daggers. On November 10, the Daggers are pulled out of the OHA Senior league. Kingston Frontenac Army is permitted to stay in the Ontario league, as is Cornwall Army in the Quebec league. The Ottawa Commandos are having their Allan Cup–winning lineup broken up as players are posted to other bases for advanced training. (As noted, Jim Henry and Mac Colville moved on to the Red Deer Army Wheelers for 1943/44.)

Pronounces Toronto *Telegram* sports editor J.P. Fitzgerald on November 10, "The Army is training soldiers and the very best material should be young athletes. When they stay athletes and are not turned into efficient fighting soldiers in the least possible time, there is something wrong. And that should now read there 'was something wrong.' " The very next day, Red Tilson is transferred to Camp Borden's Canadian Infantry Training Corps for advance training.

Tilson is able to join the Kingston Army team for three games while stationed at Borden, but that is all. In December the Oshawa Generals attempt to secure Tilson's services for some games, but are turned down—not by the army, but by the Ontario Hockey Association, which rules him ineligible for Junior play since he has already played three Senior-level games this season with Kingston Army.

Concerns persist that military teams chasing Allan Cup glory are packing the fans into privately owned arenas. The air force is the first to put an end to the practice, telling its teams that they are finished as far as competing for the Allan Cup goes. On January 3, the Toronto Airmen play their final game of the 1943/44 OHA season, defeating the St. Catharines Saints 4–3 at Maple Leaf Gardens. That same night in Oshawa, the Generals of the OHA Junior league are stunned to see Lance-Corporal Red Tilson facing them in a Toronto Marlboroughs uniform. Tilson doesn't make much difference in the game, a 13–0 romp by the Generals, but his appearance results in Harold Ballard's being hauled over the carpet by the OHA for using an ineligible player.

The army quickly follows the air force's example as the adjutant general sends out the order that knocks the army out of Allan Cup contention.[3]

TELEGRAM
H.Q. 54-27-29-113 F.D. 4
(Adm.1)
OTTAWA, Ontario,
8 Jan 44

Mailing List "A"
              "B"

RANKS 7775
REFERENCE HOCKEY stop EFFECTIVE TENTH IN-STANT NO OFFICER OR SOLDIER OF THE ACTIVE ARMY MAY TAKE PART IN HOCKEY CONTESTS IN ANY ORGANIZED LEAGUES THE CHAMPIONSHIP OF WHICH WOULD QUALIFY THE TEAM TO PLAY OFF FOR THE ALLAN CUP OR MEMORIAL CUP stop ARMY HOCKEY TEAMS MAY PLAY IN INTERMUR-AL GAMES LOCAL GARRISON LEAGUES AND MAY ALSO PLAY EXHIBITION GAMES AGAINST TEAMS BELONGING TO THE OTHER ARMED SERVICES WHO ARE LOCATED WITHIN THE SAME GEO-GRAPHICAL BOUNDARIES AS THE COMMAND OR DISTRICT TO WHICH THE ARMY TEAM BELONGS stop SUCH EXHIBITION GAMES WILL NOT BE HELD MORE THAN ONCE EVERY TWO WEEKS stop

ENSURE ALL UNITS INFORMED stop ACKNOWL-
EDGE BY WIRE
(ARMY)   ADJUTANT-GENERAL

And on January 29, the following explanatory document is issued:

Annual Army Estimates, 1944-45
SECRET H.Q.S. 8215-71-5 Fd.1.

SUBJECT PARTICIPATION OF ARMY PERSONNEL IN
ORGANIZED ICE HOCKEY
Item 25

The idea behind the playing of Hockey and all other games
by Army teams has been the maintenance of morale and the
creation of an "esprit de corps" in the units, as long as the
interest created by such contests were of Service significance mainly, games and competitions in which teams composed of civilians were involved, were not discouraged.

As matters proceeded however, such competitions and the
service teams playing in them, were found to be in danger of
coming under the domination of civilian organizations who
were for commercial reasons using the teams for their own
purposes with the result that instead of the teams being organized in the interests of the service there was a possibility of
their becoming revenue earning units of commercial corporations.

When this trend was realized several meetings were held
by Officers of the Navy, Army and Air Force responsible for
the organization of sports in the Services. The situation was
explored in all details and as a result of these conferences it
was decided, in the best interests of the Service, to withdraw
all service teams from competitions in organized leagues.

Hockey is still played in garrison and camp leagues and
exhibition games are organized between teams of the three
branches of the Armed Services with very satisfactory results.

For your information please.
Prepared by the Directorate of Auxiliary Services.
E. A. Deacon, Colonel
Director of Auxiliary Services

The quasi-professional military hockey system, which was thriving when Red Tilson travelled all the way to Kingston to enlist, has been demobilized. The Quebec Aces will win the 1944 Allan Cup, and there will be no Allan Cup at all in 1945. Military teams will continue to exist, and will continue to have star players in their ranks—Currie Army will win the Alberta Services Senior championship of 1945 with Max and Reg Bentley in the lineup—but the days of high-profile clubs packing in the fans at Maple Leaf Gardens are over (although military teams will continue to play there). On January 13, Lance-Corporal Tilson turns twenty. On January 26, he is granted a furlough through to February 8.

It is entirely possible that the main reason teenage Red Tilson went all the way from Regina to the eastern end of Lake Ontario to join the army in May 1943 was to advance his emerging hockey career; and that he enlisted where he did because older, more experienced hands told him it was the thing to do. By then, almost anyone wanting to play Senior hockey had to be in the military. But there is no proof that his young mind was focused exclusively on continuing up the road of progress that would make him a Maple Leaf, that anyone from the organization told him to go to Kingston with the objective of starring with Kingston Frontenac Army or Cornwall Army. He must have wanted to play some Senior hockey with an army team in Ontario—otherwise his choice of Kingston as an enlistment site makes no sense. But he also may have wanted nothing more than to serve and fight, and hoped only to play some decent hockey in the course of his standard eight months of training. What is irrefutable is that by January 1944 there appears to be no other course open to Red Tilson than to become the fighting man he pledged he would when he enlisted. Because he has volunteered, if he is trained and fit he must go overseas and take his place in the line.

At some point in the new year, Albert Tilson is selected to go overseas. On March 7, the day after the OHA Senior league regular season ends with no military teams left in contention, his war takes a strange twist—he goes absent without leave and is missing for six hours, from six in the morning until noon, and is arrested as a result. The next day, he is admonished and has to forfeit a day's pay and allowances. On April 6, he is granted embarkation leave, then a two-week furlough on April 10. Back at Camp Borden, Tilson has an unelaborated note entered in his record on April 24: "Not qualified as tradesman." It suggests a final evaluation of how Private Tilson can best be employed within the army. If he showed any technical facility, he might have been channelled into some role other than that of a common rifleman. Whatever ambitions he may have shown as a teenager toward becoming an electrician, he does not know enough for the army to consider him as anything other than an infantry reinforcement. Red Tilson has hockey as his only trade, but the army no longer needs hockey players quite the way it did when the Commandos were winning a national Senior championship, or when Kingston Frontenac Army was building its own Allan Cup contender.

On September 3, 1943, the 6th Light Anti-Aircraft Regiment begins publishing its own weekly newsletter, *FLAK*, and for ninety issues culminating with the June 22, 1945, edition, the regiment of which 30th Battery is a part records its hopes, fears, irreverences and convictions. In all, it comes to convey a group of men fused by a remarkable conviction. Ideology is more important than empire for this new generation of warriors. Their enemies are not categorized as aggressors against the British empire, but are identified as the forces of fascism that threaten international peace. On March 31, 1944, *FLAK*'s editor suggests that, once the war is won, "we can turn to the job of making this, as one statesman put it: 'the Century of the common man.'" It has already proven, perversely, to be just that, with the communists of Stalin allying with the democrats of the western powers to confront the National Socialist German Workers' Party of Hitler. "There is only one thing that Russia looks for in us: sincerity in our professed fight for freedom," reports *FLAK* on September 29, 1944, quoting the Very Reverend Hewlett Johnson, Dean of Canterbury. Hindsight will call the admiring prose expended on the Russians, as Stalin's armies crush the Nazis from the east, sadly, though understandably, misplaced.

When elections come, *FLAK* counsels men to consider their votes carefully. Citizenship and its obligations are thrown into sharp relief by one's willingness to die for its underlying principles; it even makes one think more carefully about what those principles are, or could be. Being part of an army united in purpose, drawn together from different corners of an at times fractious nation, makes one wonder if the nation itself could not learn to function with the purposefulness of the army. "One of the lessons of war," *FLAK* observes on October 13, 1944, "is that under the stress of necessity and understanding, we can attain some degree of unity. Can we carry that same urgency of purpose over into peace, and place Canada on the road to progress?"

The 6th Regiment is not some strange enclave of civic policy specialists. On the basis of the thoughts of those who take the time to contribute to *FLAK*'s pages, they have a sense of purpose that goes beyond preserving an existing order. A not atypical young 30th Battery recruit is Geoff Archer, who was working in a munitions plant when the Japanese attacked Pearl Harbor (and who will become an ordained minister). He has a sister and a brother in the navy, a brother in the air force (who is shot down in the Mediterranean and taken prisoner) and another brother, an engineer, involved in the production of the Bren gun at the Inglis plant in Toronto. When the smoke cleared over the demolished American Pacific fleet, Archer made up his mind to enlist, quitting his job at the first opportunity. I guess they need me, was his simple rationale. In the best tradition of fighting men, the men of 30th Battery fight with a purpose.

🍁

When 30th Battery heads to England for further training and anti-aircraft duties, Smythe finds himself an ocean away from a tempestuous home front. His eldest son, Stafford, in the navy in Halifax, ignites a family catastrophe in 1942 by marrying a Catholic girl in a Catholic ceremony. The bookkeeper at C. Smythe Ltd. skips town with about $1,500—Smythe initially thinks the loss is $3,000, and that his other employees are walking away from their jobs. He was delighted almost beyond words when his Leafs, down three games to none to the Red Wings in the 1942 Stanley Cup, rallied to win the next four games and the championship. Hap Day, he tells Squib Walker in a letter, is the greatest coach in the world. But the club's fortunes take a downswing in 1942/43. The Leafs have endeavoured not to use any players who meet the military eligibility requirements set down by the federal draft policy, apparently adhering to Smythe's wishes that those who can be in the armed forces should be in the armed forces. The policy, though, is making it difficult to ice a team that will allow the Gardens to adhere to the marching orders Smythe left behind, calling for a winning product with no ticket price reduction. In January 1943, captain Syl Apps breaks his leg and is lost for the season. And while there is a positive note in nineteen-year-old Gaye Stewart being named rookie of the year, the 1942/43 campaign ends with the Leafs winning five fewer games than in 1941/42 and being eliminated in the semifinals by Detroit.

Smythe's constitution is further undermined by his own standing with the army. He senses initiatives afoot to be rid of him, mainly because of his age—he is forty-eight years old in 1943. The Canadian army in general has been under pressure, in particular from Field Marshal Bernard Montgomery, to do something about its poor training, a problem not surprisingly linked to the quality of its officers. A purging of old warriors begins, and Smythe becomes one of its targets. The army's game plan, he suspects, has been to have him form 30th Battery, then move him out of the way for a younger commanding officer. The grapevine holds that if you're over forty, you're not going over to Normandy.* Sackings are occurring right in the 30th—his battery sergeant-major, like Smythe a Great War veteran, is sent home, replaced by Nick Hatten. Smythe is sensitive to any hint that his role in creating a battle-ready battery is not recognized by the higher ranks. On November 28, 1943, he writes a heartfelt note to "Price"—Major-General Price Montague at Canadian Military Headquarters in London. The chattiness of the note illustrates just how well connected Smythe is with the army's senior command. "In spite of your information that all good men are recommended," he confesses, "my [Commanding Officer] HM Dow tells me, altho my battery has done well, at firing camps—manoeuvres—and raises enough hell to show their good, that no word has gone forth about their major."

The purge surely provides Smythe with an unsettling flashback. In 1926 he was hired by Colonel John Hammond to assemble the latest New York NHL franchise, the Rangers, and serve as general manager. But after doing a superb job of pulling together a lineup that would be good enough to win its division in its inaugural season and then take the 1928 Stanley Cup, Smythe was fired before the team's first game. His contract was bought out for $10,000 as the Rangers opted for the services of Lester Patrick, one of the founders of the just-folded professional western league.** Could this be happening to him again? Could karma be so cruel? Having

---

*In his memoirs, Air Minister Chubby Power recalled a meeting in October 1944 with senior military staff at which he was informed that "there was a regulation that no one over the age of thirty-eight would be allowed to serve in the army in the actual theatre of war. This surprised me and also [Navy Minister Angus] Macdonald, who I am sure was able to recall a large number of excellent soldiers in the front line in the previous war were well over forty."

** Why Smythe was fired is open to speculation. Certainly he did a brilliant job of lining up players. He got the team the superb forward line of Bill and Bun Cook and Frank Boucher, defencemen Ching Johnson and Taffy Abel, and goaltender Lorne Chabot. One theory holds that Colonel Hammond wanted a

gone to such lengths to assemble 30th Battery, high command appears to be on the verge of taking it away from him.

Smythe survives the purge, quite possibly through sheer merit, but also undoubtedly because of his reputation. Nick Hatten senses that his name helps keep him in place. He is a popular public figure, a good man for the army to have in the line of duty for publicity purposes. But Smythe's beloved General McNaughton—if he is still beloved to Smythe—does not survive the purge. McNaughton performs poorly in command of the First Canadian Army in the training manoeuvres known as Exercise Spartan in the first two weeks of March 1943. (Smythe's battery, for that matter, has two men killed accidentally during Spartan.) McNaughton is on his way out, with Harry Crerar moving in to fill his shoes.

Smythe is a long way from Tofino, where there wasn't a higher ranking officer for at least one hundred miles, where he also was in charge of the Lincoln and Welland Regiment. General Stuart, then Chief General Staff in Ottawa, once called on Smythe and his men in Tofino. Over in England, Stuart, having risen to Chief of Staff at Canadian Military Headquarters in London, makes another inspection of Smythe's boys. When he moves down the line of men and comes to Smythe himself, Stuart marvels, Well, well. If it isn't the King of Tofino.

Smythe now despises the army, chafing at what he sees as its counterproductive, self-serving, bureaucratic mindset; he is well aware that the disastrous assault on Dieppe, the planning for which on the Canadian front was largely by Crerar, was anything but glorious. In 1943 he writes furious notes to himself:

> The army is so constituted that the #1 priority is to have documentary evidence that ensures the protection of all concerned should there be any criticisms...90% time spent on seeing if this protection has been maintained and 10% on removing the causes for the problem.
>
> No I Priority: TO KILL GERMANS
>
> The rule to get things done and if possible to do them the

"name" general manager for his team, and so hired Patrick. Another proposes that Hammond simply couldn't stand Smythe. Smythe claimed he was fired by Hammond because he failed to secure the rights to right-winger Cecil "Babe" Dye, who had been playing for the St. Patricks and ended up a Blackhawk in 1926/27.

right way but nevertheless <u>get them done</u> is out. No initiative
allowed.

To support the reports is the Sylabus—resembles an annual
statement which does not state the true facts. No one audits
the statements it is as if you ordered a load of boxed lunches
& the lunches came with nice labels on & no one sees if the
boxes are filled or the lunch is fresh.

He funnels his rage at the "man in charge," who could be anyone
from Mackenzie King to Stuart to Montgomery, deciding he

has his head so far in the clouds that he can't see whether his
feet are planted on firm ground.... He shows every evidence
of believing the mgr wins the games not the players—the
jockey the race not the horse etc.
    Is the results of the Press which has either been sold the
idea or oversold itself or from fear of not getting the story
(The offensive) is writing straight advertising now called
propaganda to stay on the job.
    The true story of Dieppe is never told.
    The true story of Reserves is never told.
    The true story of Commands is never told.

Inconceivably, Conn Smythe is disillusioned with the waging of
war. He is miles from the Maple Leafs, miles from home, and miles
from any battlefield.

The professional game in 1943/44 is not as good as it once was, or
as it will be. Many of the players have no business wearing NHL
uniforms; some would be hard pressed to make the cut at an
American Hockey League training camp, were it not for the fact
that a war has drained the game of so many key players. The New
York Rangers, Stanley Cup champions of 1939/40, have lost virtually their entire starting lineup to military duty by the start of the
1943/44 season, and the 1940/41 champions, the Boston Bruins,
have been similarly decimated. The draft in Canada and the United
States is in high gear, relentlessly drawing away the able-bodied
men populating hockey teams, and other talents are enlisting voluntarily. The coup de grâce for the Bruins is the loss of their star goaltender, Frank Brimsek, to the U.S. Coast Guard. He plays a season

with their very capable amateur club, the Baltimore Clippers, then joins the crew of a supply ship in the South Pacific.

In the fall of 1943, as Ted Kennedy begins his first full professional season, the NHL and the Canadian amateur leagues unveil a new wrinkle: the two-line offside. Until now, players in their own end of the rink have not been allowed to make a pass across their own blueline. They've been forced to stickhandle the puck out, and the rules gave rise to a dump-and-chase offensive style in which the attacking team shot the puck into the opposing team's end and then flooded the defensive zone, hitting any player who tried to carry the puck out. The new rule has added a centre-ice line. Now a player can make a pass across his own blueline, provided the player receiving the pass is on his team's side of the centre-ice line. In one season, the game breaks wide open and assumes its modern form. In the war on ice, counterattacks are swift and dangerous. Defencemen not accustomed to these quick breakouts are burned by line rushes that turn into breakaways. Average team scoring, already climbing during the war years, jumps half a goal a game in this one season.

Ted Kennedy is still seventeen when the season begins. He is placed on a line with Mel "Sudden Death" Hill, a twenty-nine-year-old veteran acquired by Toronto the previous season after the collapse of the Americans franchise. But after seventeen games, Hill is injured and lost for the season. Hap Day moves Kennedy from right wing to centre to take Hill's spot. In this way, a star is born.

He has an astonishing rookie season: forty-nine points in forty-nine games, with twenty-six goals and twenty-three assists. Playing at a new position in an entirely new game, Kennedy not only salvages the Maple Leafs' present: he represents its future. He acquires under Day's direction an uncanny ability to win faceoffs. In the new breakneck game, winning faceoffs is one of the most underrated skills. The game is rarely at rest; when it is, whether it is in your own end or the other team's, gaining control of the puck in the first second of resumed play becomes a key ingredient in winning games. In 1943/44 Ted Kennedy is where he belongs: in a Maple Leaf uniform, at centre ice of Maple Leaf Gardens.

The Leafs finish the season in third place, winning twenty-three, losing twenty-three, tying four. Out—far, far out—in first place are the Canadiens. Bill Durnan has moved up from the Senior Royals to play goal, and he is one of the greatest netminding talents the game has ever seen. Montreal allows only 109 goals, 65 fewer than the next-best defensive effort, turned in by Toronto. The Canadiens score 234 goals, 11 more than the next-best offensive effort, turned in by Boston. Only one Canadien, Elmer Lach, makes the top-ten scorers list, but his Punch Line has found its form in the new game. Lach has seventy-two points on the season, Blake fifty-nine, and Richard fifty-four. Altogether, they produce eighty-two of Montreal's goals.

After suffering through three consecutive seasons in which fractures sidelined him, Richard, at twenty-two, at last manages a full effort, appearing in forty-six of fifty games. Picking up the pace as the season progresses, he scores thirty-two times, and assists on twenty-two other goals. Richard will attribute his success in part to the fact that he signed a two-year contract in October 1942; otherwise the Canadiens might not have been inclined to give this brittle talent another chance.

He is no two-way player, but then he doesn't have to be. He is so dangerous offensively that an opposing team must constantly assign a player to check him. He customarily circles on the right side of the rink in his own end, looking for a loose puck or a breakout pass from his defence, the consummate opportunist. When he gets the puck, he gets rid of it, exploiting the speed of the new offside rule. Typically he hits Lach with a clearing pass across their blueline, and then Richard charges for the opposing blueline to collect a return pass from Lach and drive for the goal. Give and go, head-manning; this is the new game of firewagon hockey as Montreal plays it. Richard can no longer be simply Maurice. Richard becomes first the Comet, and then the Rocket.

From the blueline in is where Richard comes alive. He is a capable skater, powerful rather than stylish. He has an almost superhuman drive that carries him to the goal, sometimes with opposing players draped across him, his eyes alight. He will suggest that his scoring prowess is due to taking as many shots as he can in a game—if he can get away eight or ten, then he has a much greater chance of scoring at least once. But Richard also has one of the most accurate shots in the game. Forehand or backhand, Richard can put the puck anywhere he wants.

Montreal wins thirty-eight games, ties seven and loses five. In the opening round of the playoffs, the Canadiens are matched with the Leafs. In the schedule created by the six-team league that came into being in 1942/43, the two clubs play each other ten times over the regular season. But in the entire history of the Maple Leaf franchise, the Leafs and the Canadiens have never before met in a playoff series. The Leafs and the old Maroons, yes, but never the Leafs and the Canadiens. Playoff pairings always took them in different directions, one or both eliminated before there could be a confrontation. At this time, Toronto's most bitter rival is Detroit. That is about to change. The inauguration of the post-season relationship between the Leafs and the Canadiens cannot be more explosive.

The country is still divided over Quebec's commitment to the war effort. The resentments are felt even in Britain, where in war-game manoeuvres between British and French-Canadian troops, the enmity is so volatile that deaths on both sides result. In the spring of 1944, the teams most closely allied with the two conflicting cultures come together to unavoidably exacerbate the tensions.

Toronto wins the opening game of the best-of-seven semifinal, but in game two, the Leafs are overwhelmed, generally by the Canadiens, specifically by Maurice Richard, who scores all of the Montreal goals in the 5–1 victory. When Montreal journalist Elmer Ferguson chooses the game's three stars, he intones: Richard, Richard, Richard. With four straight victories that culminate in an 11–0 drubbing, Montreal brushes aside Toronto and proceeds to win the Stanley Cup with another four straight victories, over Chicago.

Toronto coach Hap Day cannot contain his disgust with the loss. You can't expect kids to beat grown-ups, he complains. Kennedy, for one, was held to two points in five games. The implications are scarcely beneath the surface of Day's dejection. Look at those Canadiens: Richard, Lach, Blake. Men, not kids. Durnan in net, almost thirty. Butch Bouchard on defence, twenty-three. Who do the Leafs have? Two of our centres, Ted Kennedy and Gus Bodnar, who has just won the rookie award, are eighteen years old. Look at all our guys in the military, starters and prospects. Nick and Don Metz. Bud Poile. Turk Broda. Billy Taylor. Joe Klukay. Jackie Hamilton. Bob Goldham. Gaye Stewart, who was good for forty-seven points and was rookie of the year last season. Sweeney Schriner, a perennial top-ten scorer, a steady thirty-point man, in the navy. Our captain, Syl Apps, for Pete's sake, a father of three, a volunteer. Red Tilson, a future star, in the army.

And leading the rushes for Montreal is Lach, whom Smythe will flat-out call a deserter—not from the military, but from the Maple Leafs. He came east to play hockey at St. Michael's College in Toronto, a Leaf-sponsored team, and he agreed to sign with me, Smythe will complain, but he deserted, went back home without saying a word to play some Senior hockey, and then returned to star for Montreal.

It will long be proposed that the league has been kept alive during wartime to entertain on the home front, to avoid denying every privation to the families whose sons and daughters are part of the war effort, to the men and women toiling in essential industries and producing war materiel, to the children for whom a devotion to the exploits of sporting heroes is an essential pleasure of youth. But in a game in which rivalries are naturally generated between the cities represented, and in which those sporting rivalries can also give concrete dimensions to the antagonisms already alive in those cities, the continuation of play in the National Hockey League as war escalates has inevitable consequences. The citizens it means to entertain it also inflames. The Leafs and the Canadiens are not simply rivals. They are enemies. The Leafs, guardians of a glorious tradition, are on the defensive, the standard borne by a children's crusade. The Canadiens, ineffectual for more than a decade, have come alive in a new game of strength and speed, their finesse overwhelming the makeshift rosters of the rest of the league. The new rivalry between Toronto and Montreal does not help the fans, in particular the fans of the Maple Leafs, forget the war. It makes them brood on issues of duty and sacrifice. It makes their Maple Leafs seem part and parcel of the war effort, the rival Canadiens opportunists, veritable profiteers. It does not matter that military service for many hockey players is about playing more hockey, not fighting Nazis, that the actual role of athletes in military uniform is far from black and white. In the minds of fans, the Leafs are an organization solidly behind the war effort, making all necessary sacrifices as an English-Canadian institution in good standing. Montreal was a club on the verge of collapse when Conn Smythe suggested Dick Irvin be signed to rebuild it. Ironically, now that he has, their success is resented, and a largely anglophone institution manages to be seen as a symbol of francophone indifference to the cause of subduing the Axis powers.

"I went to the Somme in the First Great War," Conn Smythe will reflect at the end of his life. "The Van Doos were there, and they never gave an inch. Great fighting men, those fellows were, and every one of them was French [Canadian]. Then you have the Montreal Canadiens. When I was with the Maple Leafs, it seems like I battled with the Canadiens for a hundred years and it was tough all the way. Those French players were great but, remember, they always had to have some English on the team, Harvey and

Elmer Lach and this Ken Dryden fella today. Know why that is? Because the English may not be able to rise as high as the French, but they never sink as low either."

Sport cannot rise above resentments, not when its advocates are constantly imbuing it with deeper meaning, upholding its participants as role models of various stripes. The uniforms the players wear, in Montreal and Toronto if nowhere else in the league, embody the values their fans, and the fans of their rivals, perceive in them. When players converge and collide, an argument comes alive and rages.

Kids against grown-ups.

After seven weeks of training at Petawawa, Turk Broda is given an assessment interview. "Training progress is satisfactory," Captain H.O. Barrett notes on January 3, 1944. "Civilian experience suggests that he could be more useful as driver than as gunner.... Recommendation: Suitable for training as driver i/c." And so Gunner Broda receives his driver training, completing it on March 17, and is recommended for overseas service. He is taken on strength by the 2nd Canadian Artillery Reinforcement Unit in England on May 8. "Feels unduly tired," Captain F.H. Potts notes of him on May 11. "Clean conduct sheet."

Red Garrett, the former Leaf property who was traded to the Rangers and then entered the navy, passed muster with the Preliminary Officer Candidate Selection Board on August 11, 1943, before joining the lineup of the HMCS *York* Bulldogs. He serves as an ordinary seaman out of HMCS *York* until January 18, 1944, when he is transferred to HMCS *Cornwallis* in Halifax during the crackdown on Senior military hockey. On May 16, he fails to pass inspection before the Promotion Board. Not considered officer material, Garrett receives his able seaman rating; on June 12, not yet twenty years old, he joins the crew of the corvette HMCS *Shawinigan* in coastal patrol and escort duties.

Red Tilson receives another promotion on May 1, 1944, albeit a very temporary one: he is made an acting sergeant with pay to help with the transfer of a draft of fellow reinforcements to the base at Debert, Nova Scotia, the marshalling point for those soon to ship out. Such a promotion, even though temporary, indicates that the army considers Tilson a reliable young man. Arriving at Debert on May 2, he reverts to his permanent rank of private as he joins the training brigade group. On May 19, he is back to lance-corporal

with pay "for conducting purposes"; he has been given the junior
NCO rank for the forthcoming Atlantic crossing.

The fierce fighting from D-Day forward saps the ranks of the
invading armies. As the Canadian infantry struggles toward Caen in
the days following the June 6 landing, they suffer tragic losses at
the hand of crack German SS units. In the first six days of the invasion, the 3rd Canadian Division alone incurs almost three thousand
casualties, more than a third of them deaths, and 70 per cent of the
casualties fall among the infantry.

On June 17, Lance-Corporal Tilson ships out, arriving in England
on the twenty-fourth, and is promptly returned to the rank of private. A little more than a month after arriving in England, and fourteen months after the toast of Junior hockey walked into the army
depot in Kingston, Ontario, Private Tilson is in France, awaiting his
posting to a combat unit.

In Action

A badly wounded man looks pale and sweaty. Be prepared for this. Treat him like a child. Calm him. Calm the men in your post. This is First Aid.

—from the brochure "First Aid for Fighting Men" given to Canadian soldiers

June 6, 1944

D-DAY proceeds without him. Overlord, the largest amphibious assault in military history, unfolds this morning with Major Conn Smythe and his men of the 30th Sportsmen's Battery held in reserve with the rest of II Canadian Corps, which will be called into action once the 3rd Canadian Infantry Division, 2nd Canadian Armoured Brigade and their immediate reinforcements establish a toehold in the Norman countryside. The Canadians who do participate perform brilliantly. No D-Day force makes more progress on that first day than the Canadians. By the evening of June 6, Canadian troops have pressed five miles inland, nearly gaining the town of Carpiquet on the outskirts of the ancient city of Caen on the river Orne. But confronted by elite Panzer divisions, the advance of the Canadians, and of their British and Polish comrades under the ultimate command of Montgomery, bogs down in costly fighting. With their drive stalled at Caen, Normandy promises a return to the futile grappling of the Great War.

Smythe's battery remains on the sidelines for almost a month, assigned to anti-aircraft duties back in England, completely in the dark as to when it will be called upon to cross the English Channel. The 6th Light Anti-Aircraft Regiment, to which Smythe's battery is attached, is so confident no move is forthcoming that on July 3 its supplies and equipment are still unconcernedly scattered. At midnight comes the order to head out at 7:30 the very next morning.

Smythe almost doesn't make the trip. He has survived purge after purge of officers, the most recent wave coming when Guy Simonds, fresh from the Italian campaign, took command of II Canadian Corps in January and tore through the officers' ranks, dismissing men far senior to Smythe in an effort to build a competent command structure. At the same time, Montgomery, in preparing for D-Day, was replacing virtually the entire field command of the British army. Smythe emerged intact from this housecleaning only to have his command jeopardized by a freak accident. In a recreational softball game, a collision with a base-runner leaves the forty-nine-year-old Smythe with broken ribs.

Convinced that the injury will allow the army to leave him behind, Smythe refuses to be treated by a military doctor. Instead, he has his men take him to a civilian physician in the local town for repairs. But he cannot hide his injury. The regiment's commanding officer, Lieutenant-Colonel H.M. Dow, makes the unavoidable visit to Smythe's bedside to tell him he'll have to stay behind. As the men of 30th Battery, and Smythe himself, will later relate, the major responds to being struck off the invasion roll by removing his service revolver from its holster and pointing it at Dow. If I'm not going, he tells the lieutenant-colonel, you're not going.

It turns out Major Smythe is going. When the regiment gathers at Tilbury at the mouth of the Thames to board their ship, Smythe is still in charge of his battery, though his painful broken ribs so limit his mobility that his men have to go to ingenious lengths to bring him along. A swivel chair has been purchased from a second-hand shop and secured to the floor of the rear of the "tin can," the battery truck that serves as Smythe's mobile office. Smythe is then strapped into the chair and hoisted with the truck on board the liberty ship that will deliver him back to the battlefields of France after more than a quarter century.

The convoy lies off Southend on the night of July 6. On the afternoon of July 7, the channel crossing begins. That night, Bomber Command unleashes 450 aircraft on Caen to soften up the German forces in preparation for a fresh offensive on the city; Operation Charnwood begins the next morning. Overly careful not to strike their own troops, the bombers rain down munitions on the mediaeval core of the city, causing numerous deaths among the remaining civilians and few casualties among the Germans. Charnwood accomplishes little more. Two days of fierce fighting with Panzers result in the British and Canadian 3rd Divisions reaching the Orne and securing the northern half of the city, but the advance comes at the cost of heavy casualties, and the enemy pulls back largely unscathed and still very much in command of the terrain.

Charnwood is thrashing forward when the regiment's crossing concludes early on the evening of July 9 in the Bay of the Seine at the beaches of Valette, with warships firing broadsides deep inland at Caen. Most awe-inspiring are the salvos of the 35,000-ton battle-ship HMS *Rodney*, a veteran of the sinking of the *Bismarck*. The disembarkation, employing landing barges, is complicated by heavy seas. A miscue in the landing is almost disastrous; the front door of the barge drops open prematurely and an overeager jeep driver with a Scottish regiment roars out into ten feet of water and goes straight to the bottom. Several navy men go in after him and save him.

Their arrival, while complicated and even harrowing, cannot compare with the landing experienced on June 6 along this short section of the Norman coast by the men of the Royal Winnipeg Rifles and the Regina Rifle Regiment. The German defences next door to Valette at the fishing port of Courseulles-sur-Mer were the most daunting of the Canadian D-Day landing sector. They claimed forty-five members of the Regina regiment; only twenty-six members of the Royal Winnipeg Rifles avoided the casualty ranks. Royal Winnipeg's D Company had come ashore at Valette itself and opened a path at great sacrifice through the beach minefield. Valette became a major landing point for successive arrivals. Six days after the Royal Winnipegers secured this section of coast, Churchill, George VI, field marshals Montgomery and Smuts and Chief of the Imperial General Staff Sir Alan Brooke made their own Normandy appearances on this beach. Two days after this august party, de Gaulle also followed the Royal Winnipegers ashore.

A few miles to the east, Joe King and the Highland Light Infantry were scheduled to go ashore at Red Beach at St. Aubin-sur-Mer at eleven o'clock on D-Day morning. But when the time approached for them to disembark, there was still heavy fighting at St. Aubin; the preliminary naval shelling had left the German defences there untouched. The HLI were switched to "White" at Bernières-sur-Mer and landed without casualties, though they took some time clearing the beach. As a second-wave unit, the HLI were equipped with bicycles to speed their progress inland. These were quickly abandoned as they moved inland behind the 8th Canadian Infantry Brigade.

In Operation Charnwood, still unfolding as Smythe and his men come ashore at Valette, the HLI receive their first battle experience in the ferocious fighting around the town of Buron. More than half of the regiment's strength is lost in just one day in combat against well-dug-in defenders armed with mortars and light machine guns. The HLI take the town, but at the cost of almost every officer they have. As a result of the losses, Lieutenant King is made a captain and second-in-command of B Company.

The 6th moves a few miles inland and gathers itself around Banville, which bears scars of the D-Day invasion, though actual fighting here was light as a few snipers were cleared away. A regimental advance party moves on to Le Vey, wanting to waste no time engaging the enemy.

By now planning is well under way for a follow-up operation to Charnwood, known as Goodwood. Montgomery's strategy for this armoured breakthrough at Caen is finalized on July 12, the day after II Canadian Corps officially goes operational. Under the Goodwood battle plan, the Corps is expected to punch through the German defences from the centre of Caen and secure the rest of the city.

The 6th establishes itself near Cairon, which was on the front line as Smythe and his men departed England; Charnwood pressed the line about five miles southeast, through Buron and into the northern half of Caen. Dawn on July 14, Bastille Day, brings Smythe his first taste of battle since 1917, as his battery, along with the regiment's 1st Battery, fires on German aircraft and downs a Focke-Wulf 190 fighter; the kill is credited to the 1st. Smythe's opinion of 1941 that the war belongs in the iron age and not the machine age is about to be emphatically refuted. With his men already awed by the display of naval gunnery that accompanied their landing at Valette, the latest spectacle of modern mechanized war comes at 5:30 a.m. on July 18. Every medium and heavy bomber the Royal Air Force can put in the air, 1,056 Halifaxes and Lancasters in all, are joined by 1,021 medium and heavy bombers of the USAAF in one of the largest aerial assaults ever inflicted on enemy ground forces. For two and a half hours the men of the battery watch from their vantage point in an orchard as three sorties of aircraft drone overhead en route to pummelling Panzer Group West in preparation for the ground attack of Goodwood. The RAF alone drops 5,000 tons of bombs on the German armour.

The machines continue to tear each other apart, and with them thousands of men, as Goodwood turns into one of the costliest Allied actions of the war. A confused, ill-planned assault costs the British more than one-third of all their armoured strength in France—400 tanks in all, with 5,537 casualties to go with them. Eleventh Armoured alone loses 126 tanks on the first day of Goodwood, and then sixty-five more in taking just two villages. Operation Atlantic, the Canadian strike on the British flank, amasses 1,965 casualties.

Montgomery is quick to claim total success for the operation, but Caen is far from secure and the Allied losses are dreadful. The

Canadian forces must immediately prepare their own follow-up offensive, Operation Spring, just to meet its objectives for Goodwood.

On the eve of Spring, 30th Battery is established on the southern outskirts of Caen. Its three troops, each manning a half-dozen of the self-propelled Bofors guns, are dispersed over an area of two to three miles, with battery headquarters in the village of Faubourg-de-Vaucelles. The guns of the 30th, and the 6th LAA regiment, are part of a concentrated anti-aircraft umbrella around Caen, the staging area for Spring. There are plenty of munitions and supply dumps around, as well as bridges over the Orne that are essential to the Allied offensive. Buck Houle's troop, for example, is stationed far from battery headquarters, right beside a German-built concrete signal post and an Allied ammunition dump. Battery headquarters is in the abandoned house of a tradesman, a plumber probably, judging by the contents of the shed in the rear of the property. A wall runs around the property, and within the compound the battery has assembled its supply trucks. In the field, the men on the guns have little reason to come into HQ, its administrative and supply centre. Food, ammunition and other supplies are moved out to them as required, as well as orders by dispatch riders.

The Allies own the skies, at least by day, but it would not be inaccurate to say that Allied ground troops have suffered more casualties from miscalculated aerial bombardments by their own air forces than from German air attacks. So supreme is Allied control of air space over the combat area that 30th Battery's gunners are under orders not to shoot at anything during daylight, as the odds are overwhelming that they would be firing on one of their own. It is only after dark that the Luftwaffe dares show itself. And on the night of July 24–25, as Spring prepares to roll out under the cover of darkness, the Luftwaffe comes—first the pathfinders, dropping parachute flares, then the bombers.

It is a night of explosions, screams and chaos. The Bofors gun closest to battery HQ is being manned by lance-bombardiers Geoff Archer and Jimmy Sibthorpe. Archer is knocked off his gun twice by the percussion of bombs. After getting back on a third time, he is knocked off for good, and out of the war. Sibthorpe, who is wounded in the shoulder, will return to the unit after treatment. Archer, out of action, looks in the direction of battery headquarters and sees flames.

In the headquarters compound, Smythe is standing with his second-in-command, Captain Jim Boekh, and his battery sergeant-major, Nick Hatten. They are thirty feet from an ammunition truck whose tarpaulin has been set alight by a parachute flare. Men are attempting to remove the tarpaulin and put out the flames before they ignite the ammunition. A 40-mm Bofors fires 120 rounds of two-pound high-explosive shells a minute, and Smythe has eighteen guns to keep supplied. The compound is a tinderbox of anti-aircraft munitions. It is also completely defenceless against any sort of attack. The only weapons the men have are their own sidearms. The three officers are watching the firefighting efforts, discussing among themselves what should be done, when they hear the whistle of an antipersonnel bomb; the bombers have arrived, following the path of the flares. As one, the three men throw themselves to the ground.

Shrapnel flies in all directions. Hatten cannot get up. He puts his hand to his side and feels the ooze of blood. A piece of shrapnel has passed right through his pelvis.

What's the matter? Major Smythe asks Sergeant Hatten.

I've been hit, says Sergeant Hatten.

So have I, says Major Smythe.

Having been a corporal in the Great War, Adolf Hitler once summed up Germany's return to military conquest as *putting on the greatcoat*, the standard-issue outerwear of that conflict. Conn Smythe happens to be wearing a greatcoat, far too hot for the July weather, even in the middle of the night, and he will not be able to explain what impelled him to don it as he raced into the darkness, the flames and the confused shouting after the parachute flare fell among the ammunition trucks. It is the kind of coat he too wore in the Great War, and the act may have been instinctive, a gut reaction that twenty-six years cannot suppress. If it was instinct, it was a fortuitous one, as Smythe comes to believe that the coat saved his life. When a jagged piece of shrapnel buried itself in his back, the heavy cloth of the coat impeded it just enough to spare his life, though it pierced his bladder and colon.

The battery will never have a more catastrophic episode in the rest of the war. Two battery-men are killed and eight wounded; in all, the 6th has five men killed and fifteen wounded the night Spring rolls out.

Almost five years after determining to return to uniform, and little more than a fortnight after landing on French soil with his battery, the war is over for Major Smythe. In one respect his convictions of 1941 prove correct: this war will require a steady supply of men.

He is replaced on an interim basis by his second-in-command, Jim Boekh, and then permanently by H.Z. Palmer, a former adjutant of the regiment who also happens to be General Crerar's son-in-law. Smythe is one of about one thousand Canadians to have been wounded or taken prisoner in the havoc of Spring; the five dead batterymen of the 6th are near anonymous in the numbing loss of some 450 Canadian lives. Smythe returns to England to convalesce, and then home to Toronto, in time for the start of another hockey season and a fresh and spectacular round of public sparring with both government and military.

Can you hear that whirr of the bombers engines? Its [sic] after dark so they can't be ours. You can sense their drop in altitude. The medium gunners dive for cover, they have no part in this action, everyone who can get under is below ground. Now flares are dropping, and there is the dark silhouette of the Bofors' gunners manning their weapons and ready for action.

For a moment a tense silence, and then Hell let loose. Heavies and lights open up, the sky is full of tracer and searching sounding, there is the steep dive of the bomber, the fearful whistle of bombs, the shattering explosion, the rattle almost of a hundred A.P. bombs exploding, and still the guns. An ammunition dump has gone up, shells, large and small are exploding in all directions. There is fire, and bright blinding flares, and through it the whine of another dive bomber, and again tracer and the guns.

"I thought your job was pretty soft," says a medium gunner to one of our lads the other day, "but you can have it all boys: me, I like to be under cover when those devils are over."

And the raiders pass, and with them some of our boys into honoured memory. God Bless them.

—*item written by Captain S.E. Higgs in August 11 edition of* FLAK

To show how some people's minds run in a groove, we record the conversation that took place the morning after the fire at 30 BHQ.

As Herb Morton approached L/Bdr Doug Gillespie to enquire after the victims' welfare, Doug says: "They're fine, Herb, not a scratch on the lot."

Herb: "All six of them?"
Doug: "No, I mean the records I borrowed from you."
—FLAK, *July 28, 1944*

Judging by the clippings and the comments in the letters from home your misfortunes during the B.H.Q. shelling caused almost as big a sensation as though you had been stabbed in the back by Art Ross or winged in the corridor by Referee Bill Stewart.

Seriously, it must have been heartening to have so much sincere regret expressed by those who knew you best back home and believe me, the boys are all rooting hard for your complete recovery.

The truth is (even though it may still surprise you) we miss you very, very much. There is nothing wrong with the young fellow who took your place, of course, but just as the Gardens were your Maple Leaf Gardens this Battery was and is C. Smythe's battery and will be as long as the likes of Jonesy, Lawson, Alexander, King, Houle, Hewit, Gillespie, MacKenzie, Bennett, Rookie, Milne, Dixon, James, Williams, Rigby, Cox, Kyrcia and a hundred more of the good ones are part of it....

You were saying once how much sport would miss Powers and a few more who have gone since we left home. On guard the other night I was thinking of what a hell of a gap in sport and in the routine of us sport scribes there would be without you around. The Gardens would still be having their 13,742 paid on hand, but would nonetheless be rather empty as far as many of us were concerned.

So keep punching, as Dutton used to scream, and all the best for now from your faithful gunner, Edward Reeve.
—*Letter from E.H. Reeve, August 17, 1944*

I've been sitting here quite a while trying to figure out how I'm going to say what I want to say; it's a queer feeling writing as commander of the best bty yet to the fellow who made it that way—for me it's just about the proudest moment of my life, and yet at the same time I can guess just how you must feel to have been forced to give up the command. Originally, when I heard the news, I could hardly believe my luck, and now, after three weeks with the gang, I can honestly say I underestimated. You've done a great job; the bty's efficiency and keeness [sic] I know is second to none—and you can be assured I will do my best to ensure that the standard you and the bty have set will not be lowered, and that as usual the 30th will sct the pace. They think the world of you, "The Major"—in spirit the bty will always be yours—and will want you there at Union Station to march the boys back home again.

I have just read this over and remarked to Jim Boekh how difficult it is to write anything that sounds any more than the sort of thing anyone might write on taking over any command. I want you to realize how seriously I mean it. I can probably best explain by quoting from a letter I just got from my Mother yesterday: "I know how proud you'll be to get that bty, you were always a great admirer of C.S."...

[A]ll goes on as usual—Scotty is out there under the trees banging away at a tire, Yorkey is telling us how the Germans are all being masqueraded on the other side of the Seine, and Jim, I might add, is making excellent use of the folding chair he inherited from you. They, and the others, all join me in the very best wishes for a speedy 100% recovery, and good luck—

—*letter from H.Z. Palmer, August 30, 1944*

Dear Daddy
Welcome home. We are looking forward to having you home. Do you think you could play marbles with me. I am now in Grade four.
XXXXXX
OOOOOO
—*letter from daughter Patricia Smythe, September 14, 1944*

INCOMING

September 19, 1944

HE is raised on one elbow on a small bed, his pyjama top askew, his lower body hidden beneath the blankets. Conn Smythe is aboard a hospital train, "On the Road Back," as the heading above the photograph puts it when the item appears in the Montreal *Gazette* this Wednesday. The Canadian army took and released the photograph, a morale-builder with Smythe flashing an "OK" sign with his left hand and offering a tight smile. The train passed through Montreal last Sunday, arriving in Toronto to deliver Smythe to Chorley Park Military Hospital on Tuesday, the eighteenth. The *Gazette* is a conservative newspaper; its editorials have been pressing the Imperial doctrine as delegates have converged on Montreal to refine plans for a United Nations in the peacetime awaited by all.

Mackenzie King is making his own passage, moving back into the swamp of domestic politics from the international stage of the Quebec Conference with Churchill and Roosevelt, where Canada could pose as an equal partner in international affairs. The country seems more an artifice of law than a purposeful confederation, his own government a precarious construct. It is the war that is to blame—the war that attracted and mauled Conn Smythe, that has given King's Liberals a tentative command of the electorate. Compromise has served him well. No other national party has been able to strike a soapbox stance that can appeal to both English and French Canada. The CCF, on the left, is strong in the Prairies and gaining in popular appeal, but has no presence in Quebec and has been undermined in the rest of the country by a pacifist opposition to the war from which it is only beginning to turn away. The Progressive Conservatives, under national leader John Bracken and Ontario premier George Drew, have pursued a program of strident rhetoric: pro-war, pro-conscription, anti-Quebec; supportive of the

Imperial dogma, opposed to King's social programs. They have effectively written off Quebec as an electoral base. King is convinced the Conservatives have resolved that, by publicly despising Quebec, they can rally the support of voters in English Canada. It is a dangerous, inflammatory game he sees them playing, dividing to conquer. There might be nothing left to rule at the end of the day as Quebec goes its own way and the rest of the country goes the way of the United States.

Within his own cabinet, animosity is building. The country's military command and some of its cabinet supporters appear to have their own ambitions for the war. It will be a battle for King to wind down the country's efforts when powerful colleagues and officers want to fight on to the last German and Japanese. There are fresh notes of discord in his relationship with Defence Minister Ralston. The previous Friday night, the fourteenth, King addressed a private gathering of local Liberals at the Reform Club in Ottawa, an event closed to the press but attended by several cabinet ministers. Ralston was not among them, but when accounts of King's remarks are passed on to him, he is furious. On December 1, *Maclean's* magazine will offer its own ear-to-the-wall spin on King's address. "King asked rhetorically whether or not we'd had conscription, and when his audience of Quebecois cheerily answered 'No,' he said something to the effect that of course they hadn't had it, that he'd never intended they should have it, and furthermore they weren't going to have it."

Ralston went to King the day after the luncheon, demanding an explanation. Ralston told King he understood King had said that he would not stand for conscription or be at the head of a government that would. *[Ralston] said he had been one of the team and had wondered whether I was changing our policy. That it made a pretty hard time with him in dealing with his staff and others in trying to squeeze out the numbers that they needed for reserves. That there might be a holocaust when they try to get into Germany which we would have to be in a position to meet.* King told Ralston he had made no such statement. *That what I had said was that I had mentioned that conscription would not be resorted to unless it was necessary. That it was apparent the war was going to end soon and that it would be to the glory of the men overseas to be able to say they had enlisted voluntarily.* What he had said about there being no conscription to be feared, King explained, was that there certainly would not be any conscription for Canada's participation in the war against Japan. This, King reminded Ralston, had been agreed to by the war cabinet. King would not be the head of any government that sought conscription for the fight against Japan. According to King, Ralston admitted to him he had not thought of that difference. It was Charles Gavan "Chubby" Power, the air minister, who had asked King to make it clear that there would be no conscription, King explained; it was Power who felt that if King said this to the gathering, it would do more than anything else to solidify the Liberal family.*

Power has one of the more enigmatic résumés of any cabinet minister. In the first decade of the century, Power was one of the country's finest hockey players.[1] His brothers Joe and Rockett preceded him in entering the ranks of elite organized hockey, both playing for the Quebec City team in the Canadian Amateur Hockey League in 1903. After starring for the Loyola College team in 1906, Chubby played one game for the Quebec Nationals of the Eastern Canadian Amateur Hockey Association in 1907, then became a regular with his brothers in 1908. Joe and Chubby were high-scoring forwards; Rockett was back in the defence corps. In 1908 and 1909 Chubby Power was the top-scoring player on the Nationals, finishing fourth overall in the league scoring race in both seasons. His performances included a six-goal and a five-goal game in successive seasons. Chubby played at a time when professionalism was overtaking what had been nominally amateur competition, and he left the Nationals the season before a shakeout of rival leagues created the National Hockey Association, forerunner of the NHL. Hockey's loss became federal politics' gain as he followed his father, a senator, into public life.

King might as well have added in his explanation to Ralston that few ministers have a clearer picture than Power of what it takes to

---

*Power was skeptical of King's version of his address. In his memoirs, Power asserted that King "stated categorically that conscription would never be imposed as long as he was Prime Minister and that he had never intended to impose conscription under any circumstance. This statement was greeted by prolonged applause from the Liberal supporters who were present and I am led to believe, from what I heard at that time and since, that among others [Navy Minister] Angus Macdonald and [Finance Minister] J.L. Ilsley protested against it. There are also indications, though I have no personal knowledge of it, that Ralston also spoke to King about it. King is reported to have answered that he really meant that there would be no question of conscription for the Japanese war, which was neither the impression he left on his audience nor the one I am sure he intended to leave."

bind the Liberal family together. Irish Catholic by descent, he grew up in the cultural melting pot of the Quebec City suburb of Sillery. Chubby enlisted in 1915 with brothers Frank and Joe. Frank was killed in action; Chubby returned home after a German grenade knocked him out of the war in September 1916. After winning a seat for the Liberals in 1917, he has been successfully returned in every election since then. Entering cabinet as the minister of pensions and national health in 1935, Power was made postmaster general in 1939 at the outbreak of war, and air minister in May 1940; the additional title of associate minister of defence came in July 1940, when Ralston assumed the defence portfolio from the late Norman Rogers.

With Ralston mollified, another crisis passes, as King strives to get Canada's war in Europe over with and to minimize her involvement in the Pacific theatre. Provided all goes well, the entire conflict will be behind him, the Liberal party and the country by the time he has to call an election. If the flames of war can be suppressed, then so can the flames licking around the edges of his own government and at the very fabric of the nation.

He understands the antagonisms within his party and within his country, and he lets accommodation as much as conviction shape his actions. It is not within his power as a consummate stage-manager of political variables to direct or calculate every vector of influence. He has only slightly more knowledge of what the Allied high command has in store in the way of operations than he does of what the Axis powers plan in resistance and retaliation. As much as King has embraced the war as an exercise in Canada's emergence as a major player on the world stage, she is only a secondary partner in military activities, her forces ultimately under the direction of British and American commanders. The political and the operational are distinct realms, and this is one of the greatest conundrums facing him. Canada may have gone to war, but in so doing she has committed herself to an enterprise over which her government and her most senior officers have little fundamental control. Unable to hold much sway over operational activities through his political office, King strives to at least make the political consequences of operational activities understood by colleagues. Whenever you make a decision about the war, he might well sum up, you also make a decision about Canada.

With autumn approaching, the political and the operational are about to collide in a way no one in King's government has foreseen.

The smile is frozen, the OK is given; the photo is taken and distributed by the very army the subject is about to excoriate.

❧

On July 29, 1944—four days after his wounding at Caen—Conn Smythe was the subject of a profile by *Toronto Star* reporter Frederick Griffin. The writer recounted how, earlier in the year, he had had dinner with Smythe in London. "That evening the talk turned to the part played by professional athletes and especially by Canadian hockey players in the war. Connie was sad about it. He felt that many men had not played the part they should, that they had not lived up to their role of fitness and health. I shall not attempt to give his arguments, but he felt deeply that professional hockey had failed if the men in it had not the sense of duty that they should have to country and to society."

When Smythe returns to Toronto, suffering partial paralysis and surrounded by doubts that he will ever fully recover, it seems that the Maple Leafs, his treasured exercise in resurrecting the spirit of the soldiers of the Great War in the corpus of a professional hockey club, have failed in his own eyes. He led the charge, and almost no one followed. The response of professional hockey to the war by and large has been to avoid it, even to exploit it. Many players enlisting or being drafted have carried right on playing hockey while in uniform on powerhouse military teams at home and overseas. On the home front, league owners have worked every angle available to make sure their draft-eligible players steer clear of the despised Zombie ranks. If a player with some ailment or another can persuade a military medical examiner that his condition does not qualify him as A-1, then he can secure a draft deferral and continue playing hockey. The simplest method of securing such a deferral is to make sure the player has an off-ice job in an industry deemed essential to the war effort.

The league is still operating, but without any grand plan. Day-to-day survival has been its operating principle; since Frank Calder died in 1943 it has been under the stewardship of an interim president, Red Dutton, the former league star and coach and manager of the defunct New York Americans. Dutton is making it clear he does not want to carry on. At the meeting of the league's board of governors on September 8, the NHL resolved to offer Smythe the presidency. He has not yet turned down the offer as he makes his way to Chorley Park, saying that accepting the posting depends largely on the recovery of his health.

He has lived through the perilous exercise of revisiting and reviving his own youth, marrying the present with the past through combat and catastrophe. And the return of war has proved that the ice of Maple Leaf Gardens is no substitute for the battlefield. Being a Maple Leaf requires bravery, and commitment, and courage, and sacrifice, but not in the dimensions exhibited by their inspiration, the men of the Canadian Corps of the Great War. Smythe was instrumental in creating a team that had been embraced by the common man as an embodiment of those warrior values, but when it came time to answer the call to arms in this latest conflict, it was the common man, and not his heroes, who answered the call. The idol-worshipper has outshone the idols.

Which, perhaps, is how it was meant to be. Perhaps Smythe expected too much of an abstraction, which is what the Maple Leafs were. The public had responded to their exploits, and that was to the credit of the players who had donned the uniform. They had delivered as promised, and when war demanded more, it was proven irrefutably that their heroism was something that blazed for sixty minutes at a time in a rectangle two hundred feet long and eighty-five feet wide. In the theosophical conception of evolution of physical worlds, the rink could be seen as one plane removed from the battlefield, and it had disappointed Smythe that the players did not, in effect, make the leap from one to the other. The war had shown the two enterprises to be distinct; they had indeed carried on independently of one another, an athlete no more likely to volunteer for war than a bricklayer or a clerk or a farmer.

He does not accept the presidency of the league; he suspects that he was offered it at the instigation of Maple Leaf Gardens director Ed Bickle and acting general manager Frank Selke, to remove him completely from team affairs. In any event, hockey is the furthest thing from his mind when he arrives at Chorley Park Hospital. Training camp for the Maple Leafs is three weeks away. During his convalescence, which is approaching the end of its second month, Smythe's attentions have been focused on an altogether different campaign from the one normally preoccupying him at this time of year. As a veteran manager of sports teams, he understands one truth that can be applied beyond the rink: in a game, the first goal is critical. It carries with it momentum, and puts one's opponent on the defensive. As a gunner, he knows how to choose and sight a strategic target, and the importance of laying in plenty of ammunition before firing the first round. Once he fires, he will attract retaliatory strikes. It will be a war of attrition, and he will survive and prevail if he can inflict maximum damage with his opening salvo. On September 18, the day he arrives at Chorley Park, Major Smythe loads 273 words, aims carefully and fires.

*

Conn Smythe's release to the *Globe and Mail*, printed on September 19, reads as follows:

> The need for trained reinforcements in the Canadian Army is urgent.
>
> During my time in France and in the hospitals of France and England, I was able to discuss the reinforcement situation with officers of units representing every section of Canada. I talked to officers from far eastern Canada, French Canada, Ontario and all the Western Provinces. They agreed that the reinforcements received now are green[,] inexperienced and poorly trained. Besides this general statement, specific charges are that many have never thrown a hand grenade. Practically all have little or no knowledge of the Bren Gun and finally, most of them have never seen a Piat Anti-tank gun, let alone fired one.* These officers are unanimous in stating that large numbers of unnecessary casualties result from this greenness, both to the rookie and to the older soldiers who have the added task of trying to look after the newcomer as well as themselves.
>
> I give these true facts of the reinforcement situation in the hopes that
>
> (1) Col. Ralston, if he has other information, will know that his facts are out of date, or that he has been misinformed,
>
> (2) The taxpayer will insist that no more money be spent on well-trained soldiers in this country except to send them to the battle fronts,
>
> (3) the People, who voted these men should be used overseas when needed, should insist on the Government carrying out the will of the people, and
>
> (4) the relatives of the lads in the fighting zones should ensure no further casualties are caused to their own flesh and

---

*The Bren was a light machine gun designed in Czechoslovakia in 1936 that quickly became the standard weapon of its class for British Commonwealth troops. Manufacture of Brens began in Canada in 1938. The PIAT (Personal Infantry Anti-Tank) was a shoulder-fired tank killer.

blood by the failure to send overseas reinforcements now available in large numbers in Canada.

The statement's appearance is quickly brought to the attention of Ralston. From 10:45 a.m to 1:15 p.m. that day, he meets in his office to discuss the Smythe charges with an august group: the Chief General Staff in Ottawa, Lieutenant-General J.C. Murchie; Murchie's adjutant general, Harry Letson; and Brigadier Howard Graham, who had won the DSO in action in Italy and added a bar to it in action in Italy in command of first an infantry brigade and then a battalion. Graham is now in charge of training recruits in Canada.

Smythe's position can be distilled to two intertwined arguments. Canada is doing a disservice to its volunteers by rushing them into the battle line with poor training to meet a reinforcement crisis. The solution is to send overseas the fully trained NRMA men, the much-maligned Zombies of home defence. In other words, the time has come for full conscription. It is a dead ringer for the argument George Drew put to the nation after Canadian troops were overrun at Hong Kong: they were green, they were poorly trained and the Zombies should be in the fight, Drew had declared.

A two-page rebuttal is drafted, patiently outlining the training procedures volunteers undergo on all three weapons Smythe cited. But the draft is then boiled down to a one-page press release, issued under no one's signature, declining even to identify Smythe by name:

The Departments of National Defence issue the following respecting a statement in the morning newspapers regarding the training of reinforcements sent to France.

As far as training in Canada is concerned, the statement is simply not understood.

Canadian reinforcements are well trained in Canada. This training includes Grenades, Bren Gun and Piat training. This training is continued in the United Kingdom.

With regard to Overseas, special inquiries are being made, but no complaints whatever have been received from the General Officer Commanding-in-Chief of insufficiently trained reinforcements. The performance of the Canadian Forces, both in Italy and France, demonstrates their mastery of their weapons and their ability to handle them effectively.

It is deeply regretted that distress may have been caused in many thousands of homes in Canada by the suggestion that casualties have been increased on account of insufficiently trained reinforcements. There is nothing whatever which is known which would provide the slightest justification for that conclusion.

The Minister had planned for his regular visit to the operational theatres and the United Kingdom early in September, but was prevented by the Quebec Conference. He anticipates leaving in due course to discuss plans and check on all Army requirements.

Ralston, it appears, is not prepared to issue anything more detailed until he has collected his own ammunition. He wires General Stuart "top secret most immediate" at Canadian Military Headquarters in London:

DPR WIRING DPR CMHQ TONIGHT QUOTING STATEMENT ISSUED BY CONNIE SMYTH [sic] MAKING CHARGES REGARDING REINFORCEMENTS. WOULD LIKE STATEMENT FROM YOU IMMEDIATELY DEALING WITH EACH ALLEGATION. PLEASE TREAT AS URGENT

Stuart replies the next day, September 20, confidently shooting holes in Smythe's allegations. On the charge that reinforcements being received in the theatre of combat are green and inexperienced, Stuart replies, "You will appreciate that any [reinforcement] other than a returned [casualty] is of necessity lacking in battle experience on his arrival in theatre. Moreover rfts in general arrive as strangers in their [field] unit and unit is strange to them. Therefore it is inevitable that rfts on first joining fd unit are not as useful as men who have served in unit for some time. In short the only cure for inexperience is experience."

Stuart then dismisses Smythe's charges that the reinforcements are poorly trained, which he buttresses with the allegations that many had never thrown hand grenades, practically all of them had little or no knowledge of the Bren gun, and most had never even seen a PIAT anti-tank weapon or fired one.

Stuart presumes that the pertinent period of training was May through August 1944. "You are aware of the policy of TRG being carried out in Canada and of its effectiveness. All rfts received in UK have passed through the syllabus of trg in Canada and have been passed out as fit to go forward to UK. Any deficiencies are noted on man's documents and steps are taken to correct such immediately on arrival in UK."

Since before D-Day, notes Stuart, the training policy enforced in the U.K. has been to put every reinforcement arriving from Canada through a two-week refresher course. The course includes four periods on grenades, during which every man must throw at least one each of the No. 36, 69 and 77 grenades; six periods on the Bren plus one period on the anti-aircraft light machine gun, as well as five periods of Bren practice on the range, during which each man must fire at least fifty-five rounds; and two periods on the PIAT, during which each man must arm and fire at least one live round.

The onus is on the commanders of reinforcement units to satisfy themselves that every man is in fact trained and has passed his training syllabus before being dispatched to a field unit, Stuart points out, even if this involves having a man repeat a portion of the syllabus in the event of failure.

Stuart also provides Ralston with a summary of ammunition expended by Canadian reinforcement units from May through August, to give some idea of the amount of training that has actually been going on. This included 3,277,280 rounds for the small arms ammunition rifle, the .303 Lee-Enfield, and Bren light machine gun; 120,190 grenades; and 12,063 live PIAT rounds—a figure that does not take into account the "huge number" of practice PIAT rounds also expended.

"Therefore," sums up Stuart, "I can state with confidence that any sweeping allegations as to poor trg of rfts and in particular any general deficiency in respect of throwing grenades firing Brens and handling and firing Piat guns simply are not borne out by the facts.

"The proof is that these rfts have been absorbed in the fd units to the general satisfaction of comds in the fd. This does not imply that comds are not constantly alert to draw attention to what they regard as necessary improvements or modifications in our trg doctrines and syllabi. This process of criticism and modification goes on continuously."

What Stuart does not say is that few soldiers could be called competent with the PIAT owing to its own shortfalls. Smythe called it a gun in his release, which it isn't at all. It is in a different class altogether from infantry weapons like the Bren or .303 Lee-Enfield,

or the artillery's towed anti-tank guns. A recent addition to the
infantry's arsenal, the PIAT is a shoulder-fired hollow-charge anti-
tank weapon. It differs significantly from its American counterpart,
the rocket-propelled bazooka, in that it employs a spring-loaded
delivery system to lob its 2.5-pound bomb. Its short range (about
100 yards) makes it a life-threatening weapon to operate effectively
if its user takes the time to aim it properly within killing range of a
German Panther or Tiger. It is superior to the bazooka in that its
charge can actually damage a German tank, and it can double as a
crude mortar, but it is not a very good weapon. In short-range test-
ing in Britain, it has demonstrated only 57 per cent accuracy in hitting its target. Even a soldier fully trained in using a PIAT does not
look particularly skilled when wielding it.

Stuart's rebuttal is authoritative, but Ralston does nothing with it.
Ralston makes no effort to reply to Smythe's charges beyond the
September 20 press release. What is holding him back? Certainly
part of the reason is an unwillingness on the part of the King government to be drawn into a partisan scrap with someone they view
as a Conservative agitator. Let sleeping dogs lie is the order of the
day. Another factor may be that Ralston fears at this early stage of
their confrontation that there could be some truth in Smythe's allegations. Ralston greatly respects Stuart's opinion and ability, to the
extent that he will allow Stuart's views to shape his own, but whatever men like Stuart in London and the general staff people in
Ottawa might be telling Ralston is going on, the armed forces are a
grand bureaucracy in which there is plenty of room for activities
beyond the minister's control, whether by design or by incompetence. Certainly it is not the policy of Ralston or his government, or
the military, to throw untrained volunteers against the Wehrmacht.
That does not rule out the possibility that a small percentage of the
volunteers—enough of them to give at least some credence to
Smythe's sweeping allegations—are being mismanaged. After all,
Stuart's memo leaves open the possibility that the training of reinforcements was not being run according to the prescribed plan. The
onus, he has noted, is on the commanders of reinforcement units to
ensure that all reinforcements are properly trained before they
reach a field unit. Stuart has deftly provided his minister with the
heads that should roll if Smythe turns out to be right. The fact that
Ralston would not attach his name to a defence department rebuttal
suggests that he personally is not yet prepared to take a public
stand, for fear of being caught in the wrong. And the warning signs

that all may not be running according to plan in the reinforcement program are in the minister's mail, which begins to contain responses to the Smythe charges almost immediately. A woman in Petawawa writes, in a letter received by Ralston on September 20:

> Reading Major Smythe's accusation of older & younger untrained men being sent as reinforcements for the men overseas makes a person wonder <u>why</u> this has to be. We civilians in Petawawa know the true situation in this military camp, there is any number of young A.1. men wearing the Active Service badge who have been here for three and four years, surely they have had enough training in that time to equip them for overseas service & there's also a great number of returned men who are capable of taking over their jobs as instructors, etc. Why should young fellows who have never seen service be given promotions over returned men who have willingly fought for their country? My husband has four & a half years service in the last war & was honorably discharged as a Battery Sgt. Major, enlisted again in 1939, went overseas in 1941 as a confirmed B.S.M., after a year overseas was given compassionate leave, (my only son was taken prisoner in the Dieppe raid & the doctor in whose care I was placed thought it advisable he be sent home[)]. My husband dropped his Crown & reverted to a Sgt. with a letter of recommendation he be promoted to his own rank at the first opportunity, a great number of promotions have been given to younger men while he is still a Sgt. Surely a Colonel wouldn't send a letter of recommendation if the person hadn't the ability of holding that position. Those young men are what we need in France & Normandy. There are other mothers around here, who, like myself, have given their all & try & imagine our feelings when we hear the young fellows boast they have a "position" & won't be sent "over," it's surely time they were dug out of their holes & made use of if we expect to get this job over quickly. My son is in his fifth year away from home & it is time he was back, he means more to me than these cowards back here can ever mean to their people. So here's hoping to see a speedy "clean-out" of these young "positioned men."

Perhaps the letter is nothing more than the work of a wife resentful that her husband has not been getting the promotions and pay raises she would like him to have, a mother desperately missing her captured son. But there will be more letters like it—angry ones, heart-breaking ones. Smythe's well-aimed salvo at Ralston and the Liberal government produces collateral damage—young men afraid to enlist because they will be sent into battle with little or no training, relatives frightened for their loved ones in uniform, and widows who now hold the government, and not the Nazis, responsible for the death of their husbands.

A woman from Brantford, Ontario, writes to Ralston:

> Would like an explanation concerning my husband's death in France. He had exactly six months training and you send him right to France. You talk about Germany sending youths and old men into battle, but don't you think this country is as bad, sending half trained men into battle, right up the front, at least these people in Germany are trained, that's more than I can say for some of these boys of ours.
>
> My husband tried to enlist in the Navy and Airforce, they wouldn't take him. He had been in the Army once for three days and was discharged for a perforated eardrum. Sometime later he was called up and went to Toronto the end of Nov. he came to Brantford New Year's eve, and left here on Feb. 28th to go to Borden, he then left there June 14th, went to the coast a boat was waiting for them. They were in England for about two weeks, left for France was there four days and sent up to the front lines only to be killed. He was attached to the Calgary Highlanders in Eng or France.
>
> I think there is something rotten about this government. I have talked to boys in the Army since then some have been here in Canada training for 2 1/2 yrs. Boys in the Airforce some have been in 4 yrs and are still here, they aren't zombies they have the G.S. sign. I get a paper from the government saying I have been awarded a pension, do they think they are giving me something. I would rather have my husband than all the pensions you could give me. He would still be alive if you had given him any kind of break. Just before the war if he asked anyone for a job they would look and laugh as if you were crazy. They didn't care if he starved to death or what happened, but soon as the war comes he has to

go and fight for this wonderful country of his. When he did you couldn't even give him a chance to live. You sent him into battle half trained. I wouldn't have minded so much if he had been around for two yrs. and then sent over, because you expect things like that in war. What's wrong with some of these other boys, have they got friends in the Army or government or maybe a little more money than we have.

I have a son and I hope you won't be sending for him to fight in the next war. I shall tell him to stay a zombie. All my husband got was a rotten deal from this great land of ours.

Would like to hear your side of the story. He was killed July 25th.

PS   I see by the daily paper and radio per Major Connie Smyth [sic] that he has much the same idea as I have, he should know as he has been there and makes the same statement.

From a couple in Eden Grove, Ontario, comes this plaintive appeal, received by Ralston's office while he is overseas:

In regard to our two sons who are training in Camp Borden, we beg of you to leave them in Canada until they are properly trained, they were to have had eight months training here before leaving, so they were told when they enlisted and now two weeks more is the finish of advance training. They only enlisted about the middle of June 1944.

There are around 50,000 A-1 trained men [the Zombies] held in this country which we beg of you to send over at once. We have two boys overseas now and one has been in action for two years almost. We sincerely hope you will consider the dear boys lives which are over there fighting out in all kinds of weather and send trained help at once when it is here to send. If our boys are doing what is right by going active the Zombies are a disgrace to Canada.

Please grant our request.

And from Major George Williams, a former provincial cabinet minister, comes a disturbingly authoritative missive, written on September 20 and received by Ralston's office on September 25, as the minister is en route to Italy:

I noticed in this morning's Victoria newspaper that you are somewhat in a quandary to know what to do about Major Connie Smythe's statement re Canadian training of overseas reinforcements.

As a matter of fact Major Smythe is absolutely correct. As a matter of fact Canadian trained reinforcements in many cases had not only not been trained in grenade throwing and Bren gun but many had had very little target practice with a .303.

On one occasion while with ICORU [First Canadian Overseas Reinforcement Unit] I took a batch of Canadian reinforcements to the ranges and found many of them actually gun shy. They told me they had only been to the ranges once and had fired only 10 rounds.

You wonder why this information came from a junior officer rather than from your high ranking Staff Officers. The answer is obvious. The CRU Staff Officers and Brigadiers do not go to the ranges with the men. That is done by the Captains and the Majors in the units themselves. The CRU Staff Officers make plenty of inspections. But nearly always dress parades, schemes, and brief inspections of documents, kitchens, etc., which does not bring them in contact with the newly arrived Canadian reinforcement.

I think Major Smythe should be punished by being awarded a D.S.O. for he has certainly rendered a service to Canada if you will follow it up. Which I trust you will.

I am rapidly recovering from the heart attack I suffered in Regina. I am hoping that by staying quiet for 6 months I can resume my duties as Minister of Agriculture in Saskatchewan.

❧

Peace is within his grasp. If only the prime minister can get his defence ministers to stop waging all-out war.

King is becoming impatient with these men—Ralston in charge of defence overall, Power handling the air force, Macdonald the navy. King has been presented with manpower estimates for the three branches of the services, and he is incensed, in the case of the navy and air force, to find them so high. At a previous war cabinet meeting they discussed reducing the manpower of the navy by half as its role in the fighting wound down; the Battle of the Atlantic had turned in the Allies' favour in 1943. Now, on September 20, King has been presented with figures running far above the discussed target. The air force has also presented numbers higher than King feels are called for. *I decided to speak out very frankly and told the Cabinet that I wanted to make my position wholly clear. That I thought our duty was to save lives. That we were trustees of the people of Canada in the matter of saving lives of our young men and also the money of the people; that we were not justified in making vast expenditures which were only for the purposes of show but which could not help but to lead to probable considerable loss of life and certainly to great and unnecessary expenditure.*

The defence ministers and their staff have been at odds with King over Canada's role in the coming Pacific war. Britain pledged to help the U.S. in the Pacific once Germany was defeated, in exchange for the Americans agreeing to put off D-Day from 1943 until 1944 and invade Sicily and Italy in the meantime. Canada had joined in the Italian campaign at its own insistence, but was under no obligation to throw all of its armed might into the Pacific theatre once there was peace in Europe. At Octagon, Canada agreed to assemble a force of up to 30,000 men for the final assault against Japan, but King is adamant that Canada's Pacific role should not expand onto all fronts on land, sea and air. King points out in the meeting that the defence ministers and their staff have fought him on everything he has said about it not being necessary for Canada to fight in the southeast Pacific, in India, in Burma, in Singapore. They have fought him on his assertion that they are not expected to contribute any more than a token force to the theatre. I was shown at the Quebec Conference to be right on this, he emphasizes. His own ministers heard Churchill ask his air marshal, Sir Charles Portal, why he had put such a burden on Canada. He also notes that Roosevelt and Churchill together mentioned Canada's simply doing patrol duty in the north and helping drive the Japanese out of China. In the light of all this, it would be quite wrong for Canada to push its way into areas of combat where the country has nothing to gain and everything to lose. *I pointed out that the British had their possessions and interests in the Orient which they wished to recover; that the Americans had their possessions and interests; that Canada had not an acre of land or property in the Orient. That it was only because of our undertaking to be at the side of the U.S. and Britain that we were going to the extent that we could really be of some help.*

King works over the manpower figures, winning significant concessions. (As a result the government will decide to release up to 4,200 men from the air force. Those who do not agree to remuster in the army or navy become eligible for the draft and, ironically, end up as Zombies.) King then asks for the opinions of everyone present and receives varying degrees of support. His defence ministers, though, say nothing. King realizes his outburst put them on the spot. It is painful to have to disagree with colleagues, King says, and he knows they feel an obligation to support their officials in the service branches, but it is the duty of everyone to tell those officials what they could and should do. His conscience, he says, will not allow him to waste a single life for the sake of appearance. We are not justified in trying to put on a show in the Pacific on top of everything the country has done. It would be different if Canada had not entered the war several years before the Americans, if Canada had not helped so much financially and with mutual aid, with the United Nations Relief and Rehabilitation Administration.

The meeting is a clear rebuke to the ambitions of the defence ministers and the senior staff in the branches they represent. If they have imagined a glorious campaign in the Pacific, it will never happen so long as William Lyon Mackenzie King is prime minister.

As the Allied forces break out of Normandy in September, sweeping east toward Germany and the Low Countries, the Canadians are given the task of helping clear the Channel ports. Dieppe, which resonates with almost more emotion than words can express for Canadian fighting men, is retaken on September 7. On September 22, Canadian troops overcome determined resistance to wrest back Boulogne. At the German stronghold of Fort Albrech, the commanding officer, General Heim, is found among the prisoners. He is sent back to the headquarters of the 9th Infantry Brigade. A proud warrior, Heim refuses to surrender personally to a staff officer. It must be to someone in the field. The brigade HQ sends for Joe King of the Highland Light Infantry, who was promoted to acting major the day before. He will do fine. General Heim hands over to Ted Kennedy's half-brother his service revolver, his ceremonial sword and his typewriter.

The conservative press is primed for a scrap. *The Globe and Mail* and the *Ottawa Journal* move in lock step on September 20 with similar editorials in support of Conn Smythe—the *Globe*'s labelled "Major Smythe's Grave Charge," the *Journal*'s labelled "Grave Charge about 'Green' Troops."

In the *Journal*'s opinion,

> This cannot be dismissed as the complaint of an irresponsi-
> ble junior officer, unfamiliar with his subject. It is the con-
> sidered, written statement of a man who is well known to
> Canadians, who is a veteran of the last war, and who won
> the Military Cross for valor in this war [sic]....
>
> No official brush-off can dispose of these charges by
> Major Smythe. They are true or they are not true. If they are
> not true, the public has a right to expect of the Government
> that it prove they aren't true; to show where, why, and how
> they are false. If they are true, with the Government unable
> to produce facts to the contrary, then the country has a right
> to feel that our men overseas and the whole war effort are
> being betrayed, and to demand that those responsible for the
> betrayal be punished.
>
> The Canadian people, by an overwhelming majority [in
> the 1942 plebiscite], voted the Government a mandate to
> draft and send reinforcements overseas when they were
> needed. If it be true that the Government is flouting that
> mandate, refusing to send overseas the right reinforcements
> when the right reinforcements are vital, while keeping in
> Canada more than 50,000 trained men who refuse to go
> overseas voluntarily, then the position is disgraceful. So dis-
> graceful—if that be a strong enough word—that those
> responsible for it deserve severe condemnation.

After the Defence Department issues its non-response on September
20, the conservative press editorials erupt. As the *Journal* fumes on
September 21,

> What the public has been given, in a statement from the
> Defence Department, is an attempt at an official brush-off.
> That and nothing more.... Col. Ralston, who is a first-class
> lawyer, should inform some of his officers that the first duty
> of a statement, and especially of one which purports to give
> evidence, is to identify its subject. Also that assumed disdain
> in a matter of public right or interest is no part of their busi-
> ness....
>
> [T]he public is in no mood for official brush-offs....
> [T]hey want an answer, and a civil and specific one, and this

not from some anonymous and irresponsible official, but
from the Cabinet itself, or the War Committee of the
Cabinet, or from the responsible Defence Minister. They
want somebody—somebody in authority—to go between
quotation marks.

In the *Journal*'s opinion, the public specifically wants to know if
volunteers are receiving brief training as a result of a manpower
shortage while "50,000 well-trained 'Zombie' troops" sit at home.
Further, are volunteer troops being sent to fight in France as reinforcements with less training than the Zombies receive?

"There should be an answer to these questions; a clear, authoritative answer," thunders the *Journal*. "If the Government thinks it can
get away with anything less, and least of all with the sort of thing put
out by the Defence Department yesterday, it is profoundly mistaken."

That night, the Smythe controversy gains momentum. Premier
Drew comes out in public support of Smythe and his charges. Upon
hearing of it, Ralston's reaction is to call the director of censorship,
Wilfrid Eggleston, and demand a report on whether Drew has violated the security act. Ralston has Eggleston's report the next day.

Re: Statement on Reinforcements by Premier Drew
   Following your telephone call last night, I made some
inquiries about the above, and beg to report as follows:—
1. Premier Drew held a press conference at Toronto yesterday afternoon, and was asked by a reporter for comment on
the accuracy of a statement made by Major C. Smythe that
some Canadian troops went into action without training in
the use of grenades or Piat and Bren guns. Premier Drew is
quoted as having said: "I know that to be correct from my
own knowledge and contacts with the troops in France." He
was also quoted as saying: "I haven't seen Major Smythe's
statement, but knowing him I am sure he made no statement
that was not entirely correct. No man in the forces is held in
higher respect by the men he led into action."
2. The reporters present did not submit this statement to the
press censors, nor did any of the newspapers or press agen-
cies which carried it. The Chief Censors of Publications
advise me that had the statement been submitted, they would
have felt obliged to pass it as being covered not only by
39B(2), but in harmony with established precedents that

charges made by provincial premiers, unless they contain material divulging military secrets—and thus contrary to Regulation 16 of the Defence of Canada Regulations—are normally passed. (Use of a Dominion censorship board to suppress charges by provincial premiers or other political leaders has always been held to be a very delicate and difficult matter, inasmuch as it would almost inevitably lead to charges of "political censorship" by the Dominion Government).

3. It may be of interest that when Major Smythe made his original charges, which were printed in the Globe and Mail without submission to Censorship, the Chief Censors of Publications discussed with the security branches at Ottawa the question as to whether his statements constituted a violation of Section 16 of the Defence of Canada Regulations. It was the opinion of these officers that they did not. The Chief Censor of Publications also discussed among themselves the question as to whether Major Smythe's charges violated 39A, and reached the conclusion that while there might be a technical breach, it could easily be defended in court under the provisions of 39B(2).

4. The question whether Premier Drew committed a breach of Regulation 39 in making such a statement to a press conference (which in effect is a form of publication) is, we think, in the category of statements made at public meetings, and would be a matter for the decision of the Department of Justice.

Ralston circulates the report among his colleagues, inviting them to consider taking the matter further, but the King government decides not to have the premier of Ontario hauled up on charges of violating state security.

A few days after making his statement in the *Globe and Mail*, however, Smythe is visited in his room at Chorley Park by a staff officer, who tells him he is facing court martial. Smythe tells him it's the best news he's heard yet. He produces a list of officers he spoke with during nearly two months of fact-finding after his wounding. You court-martial me, he promises, and I'll publish every one of these names, the regiments they were with, the number of men they were short when they went into battle, and what it cost in casualties. He then orders the staff officer out of his room.

No court martial ensues. The staff officer returns a few days later and asks him what it is he wants. Two things, Smythe tells him. I've got men over there who trusted me. I want to get reinforcements to them. And I want to get the hell out of the army.[2]

❦

At the war cabinet meeting on September 22, demobilization is the main topic, one that inevitably raises the issue of the conscripts. Ralston is vocally determined that no Zombie should secure a peacetime job until the general service men at home and overseas first have a crack at them. King objects to Ralston's entire rationale: the position should be that the government's policies have been designed to create work, and there will be work for everyone. Justice Minister Louis St. Laurent rounds on Ralston as well: if the government tries to keep the NRMA men on for an indefinite period just to ensure the volunteer army gets to the job market first, there are sure to be objections from the provinces and from a constitutional standpoint.

King emphasizes that the government has no right to penalize anyone—the NRMA men are doing the duties required of them by the state, a fact that must be recognized. While he agrees that they should carry out a policy of making sure general service men should not lose out on jobs to men who have stayed at home, they should also demobilize the NRMA men as rapidly as possible.

C.D. Howe is sick of the NRMA. Men are needed today in industry, argues the cabinet minister charged with overseeing the NRMA legislation and directing the postwar economy. We are holding back industries by maintaining a standing army that is useless, that is doing nothing in the way of real military service. The sooner they are disbanded and the whole business forgotten, he says, the better. King is in accord. *I think his view was entirely right and sensible.* But King also knows it is important to consider the views of the fighting men, of how they might feel if they suddenly saw all the jobs going to NRMA men, were they to follow Howe's advice and immediately disband the conscript force while the war was still being fought. In any event, Ralston will not stand for turning the Zombies loose. *Ralston is quite determined to keep these men until he is sure we do not have to use conscription which means, in his mind, practically until the war is over.*

It is one of the most interesting meetings of the war cabinet King has ever presided over. He sees it as a test of endurance between himself and Ralston, to see who can hold out longest. King is now quite conscious of how the war cabinet may be dividing. He puts on his side of the ledger his minister of mines and resources, Thomas Crerar, C.D. Howe, Labour Minister Humphrey Mitchell, St. Laurent and, to some extent, Ilsley and Macdonald. Ralston appeared isolated in the meeting, but King feels Ilsley and Macdonald were ready to join Ralston at any point at which they could come to an agreement with him. King also senses a slight possibility that other cabinet members could be swung to Ralston's side.

Ralston is leaving for Europe tomorrow for his tour of the battlefields. He and King speak on the matter of General McNaughton, who has been on leave since being relieved of command of the First Canadian Army nearly a year before. Yesterday Ralston and McNaughton met in Ralston's office for three hours, and King is scheduled to meet with McNaughton tomorrow.

McNaughton is said to be interested in resuming the presidency of the National Research Council, but this, King notes, is not possible. In speaking with Ralston, King mentions that he might offer McNaughton a Senate seat. Ralston says he doubts that McNaughton would be interested, but he also hears in Ralston's demurral a fear of having McNaughton in Parliament. Are you opposed to that? King asks. Ralston tells him that, as far as he is concerned, King is free to offer McNaughton the position.

At 10:10 a.m. on September 23, a Saturday, General McNaughton calls on Prime Minister King at his office in Laurier House. King hasn't seen him in months. *He was looking very well and quite self possessed. Was quite happy and friendly in his attitude toward myself.* King apologizes for not having seen him for so long; it was the day-to-day pressure. I understand, says McNaughton, and King mentions how much better McNaughton looks. The teeth, McNaughton explains. He'd had them all out, and was now feeling quite strong again.

The two men trade compliments. McNaughton observes how very good the government has been to him in granting such an extended leave. It is a leave that is coming to an end, as a three-month extension granted to McNaughton by Ralston on June 27 expires in four days. King tells him that the success the Canadian army has been having on the continent is due to the splendid training he gave them. It is kind of you to speak that way, McNaughton says. McNaughton cannot help wading back through the essential elements of his downfall. *It was a terrible thing having the Army divided, he says. He said he believed in the doctrine*

*of "whole-ism." That the whole was greater than the sum of its
parts, which meant that an army as a whole can do more than an
army broken into parts. However he was prepared to view the matter of strategy in a different light once the Americans had come in
but he said if they had to go to the continent with only part of an
army with conditions as they were, when the question first came up,
there would have been complete destruction.*

King moves to clear the air on McNaughton's dismissal. He reiterates he was right in what he had said before to him about Ralston
not having in any way conspired against him. Ralston had simply
been repeating what had been said to him in Washington; both
Ralston and Stuart felt that if things were being said at the highest
command level about McNaughton not being the man to lead the
Canadian forces overseas, then this should be made known to King
at once. It is a charming effort by King to smooth over an impressive
ambush. The actual unravelling of McNaughton's command came at
a White House gathering in June 1943, at which British field marshal Sir Alan Brooke mentioned concerns about McNaughton's ability to Stuart, then Chief General Staff in Ottawa. One by one over
the next two months, Harry Crerar, commander of I Canadian Corps,
Stuart and Ralston all called on Brooke and let him know their dissatisfaction with McNaughton; both Ralston and Stuart also made
their doubts known to King. I Corps' First Canadian Infantry
Division and a tank brigade had already been pressed upon the
British for use in the upcoming Sicily invasion, Operation Husky,
over McNaughton's objections, in April 1943. When Stuart and
Ralston arranged to have all of I Corps and its headquarters committed to the Italian campaign in August, McNaughton exploded, telling
Ralston he was no friend of the army. His removal as head of the
First Canadian Army followed, his place taken by Crerar, with his
once-close friend Stuart moving into the newly created position of
Chief of Staff at Canadian Military Headquarters in London.[3] Today,
as King attempts to put the best face on the most crushing reversal
of his military career, McNaughton is magnanimous; all that, he
says to King, is in the past.

King steers the conversation out of McNaughton's troubled past
and toward his future. He tells McNaughton he has in mind for him
some kind of appointment in external affairs. There are legations
and high commissionerships he could be considered for, or work in
connection with the UNRRA. But King says he has gathered from
Norman Robertson, under-secretary of state for external affairs,

who had already felt out McNaughton on his ambitions, that he is not anxious to leave Canada; that he wants to stay and work in this country, for this country.

They ponder and dismiss the possibility of McNaughton resuming the presidency of the National Research Council. McNaughton then reveals to King that he has been approached to become involved in politics. For obvious reasons, he says, he cannot name names. King says he fully understands—he would be surprised if other political parties were not placing tremendous pressure on him to enter public life. King himself would like nothing more than to have McNaughton in his cabinet, as minister of veterans affairs, or reconstruction, or a deputy minister of either one. But King knows that Ralston will not stand to have McNaughton in cabinet with him, and so King's only hope to bring McNaughton into the government's ranks is through the Senate.

King suggests that a man like McNaughton who is interested in social issues would be interested in a Senate posting. But Ralston was right. McNaughton is not interested. To McNaughton, a Senate posting is a sign of atrophy. He can, however, think of one high executive office of which King had spoken to him, one in which he might interest himself and for which he would be glad to be considered.

And which is that?

Andy McNaughton would like to be the Governor General.

It is a bolt from the blue for the prime minister. McNaughton recounts for him a meeting they had in England in 1941. King told him that when McNaughton returned to Canada after a victorious war, any position in Canada would be open to him, up to and including that of Governor General. King is surprised that McNaughton has remembered this. When McNaughton feels out the opportunity, having returned not at all a victorious general, King hesitates, telling him he will have to confer with the King concerning the appointment of his representative, and that he will have to discuss it with his colleagues as well.

But King is by no means immune to the idea. Despite his dismissal as army commander, McNaughton remains popular with the public and the troops—his removal was explained to the press as having been due to a health problem. His popularity, as much as King's basic respect for his abilities, is assuredly why King wants him in his government before he becomes allied with a rival party. And for some time King has been mulling over the idea that the governor generalship should, finally, be held by a Canadian citizen, as a symbol of Canada being a true nation. So why not McNaughton?

King tells McNaughton he is glad to hear him say he would want the position, that he feels he could fill it. McNaughton expresses his interest in constitutional questions, the relationships between different parts of the Empire. King is excited by this: *I said to him I thought no two men shared more in common than he and I did in the constitutional position and relationship. He said he agreed with that.*

King's concern with the governor generalship is that the position isn't even available until the spring. What will McNaughton do in the meantime? Will he consider writing of his experiences? King cannot endure a public airing of McNaughton's fall from grace at the hands of Stuart and Ralston. McNaughton sets his mind at ease. He has no intention of writing anything. He intends to turn his personal records over to the state, having no desire to spark a controversy. Whether the army should or should not have been divided will be fought over and over again through the years, he tells King. It is something that can look after itself.

When they are finished discussing the governor generalship, King moves to wrap up the conversation, wanting to join the war cabinet meeting that began at 10:30. His last item of business with McNaughton is to make him a full general. Still striving to mend fences, King tells him Ralston was the one who suggested the promotion. McNaughton then observes that he feels he should no longer take advantage of the long leave he has been granted. It was time for him to sever his connection with the army, as he could not see any place he could fit in or was needed. It should be done right away.

King is anxious about this, about a resignation in any way appearing to have been imposed on him. I've already told Ralston I want to resign, McNaughton replies, and would be glad to write to him to that effect.

King is pleased. Do that, and it would relieve Ralston's mind and mine. Can I say to Ralston that you will be writing to him saying you would like to retire, and then let him proceed accordingly?

Certainly, says McNaughton as he is moving out the door; do that. Then he returns to the subject of the governor generalship. I will have to make a decision pretty soon, he tells King, *either settle on this or throw my hat into the ring.* McNaughton does not specifically mention politics, but King surmises that it can only mean a position in opposition to him.

King asks that he and McNaughton talk in the coming week, which suits the general. He will be in town at the end of the week, after which he has a few university addresses to deliver. They part on the best possible terms.

King summons Ralston from the war cabinet meeting, to tell him what has happened. *When I began to speak, not knowing what was coming, his face was ashen pale and motionless, like that of a man who...was having his own fate decided. As I went on with the discussion, his calmness came back a little, and when I mentioned the Governor Generalship he was at once immensely relieved. When I told him about McNaughton having agreed to write him himself, his countenance completely changed, he stood up and said that there again I had shown my remarkable skill in doing a splendid bit of work. He was so immensely relieved and pleased.... He made it quite clear he would like to see McNaughton in the position of G.G....*

Ralston later speaks with McNaughton for forty-five minutes, his last meeting before leaving for Rockliffe Airport and beginning his overseas tour. When the meeting is over, Ralston reports back to King, pleased with the result. It was very pleasant; McNaughton would be writing to him at once announcing his retirement, Ralston was writing a reply, and both would be dated today. Ralston has already arranged for McNaughton's appointment as a full general, so that he will retire with that rank.

They also discussed the Governor General's posting, and, most important, the two antagonists broached the subject of their enmity. *Ralston said that McNaughton had spoken to him about past relations and said we had all been working in our directions but all of that was now passed and they apparently parted the best of good friends.*

I have always been a believer in Providence, King tells Ralston. I hope He protects you in your journey and grants you a safe return. *I then extended good wishes to him for his birthday, which comes in a couple of days from now, and he left with the lightest heart that I think he has had for many a day.*

That night, King ponders the suitability of McNaughton and his wife for the governor generalship. King has also considered two other Canadians for the role: Georges Vanier, a Great War veteran of the Van Doos who is serving as Canada's ambassador to all Allied governments in exile in London; and Vincent Massey, Canada's high commissioner to Britain. *Of the three I really believe McNaughton would be the best and it would be a fine recognition of his services as a General at the beginning of the war. Churchill has said to me he would be prepared, if he were in England, to offer him a peerage.*

Lord McNaughton. That won't do. Having brought McNaughton back from England against his will, King is resolved to make the most of his talents on the home front.

Ralston's flight left Ottawa for New York at four o'clock in the afternoon. On Monday he is in Terceira in the Azores, awaiting the next leg of his journey to Naples, where he will embark on a tour of the Canadian forces in Italy before moving on to Holland. The news of the fighting in Holland fills King with *considerable anxiety*. The German resistance is fierce, the Canadian losses heavy. *A hard struggle there.*

Dick Irvin (left) and Conn Smythe
converse at a Toronto Maple Leafs
training camp in the 1930s.

Bob Carse (kneeling) appears
next to goaltender Frank
McCool at the 1939 Chicago
Blackhawks training camp.

Conn Smythe merges the uniforms of sport and war in September 1940 during militia training with the Toronto Scottish Regiment, attended by 25 members of the Toronto Maple Leaf organization.

The Boston Bruins "Kraut" line of Milt Schmidt, Woody Dumart and Bobby Bauer brought celebrity and scoring punch to the RCAF Flyers team in 1942.

Military hockey put athletes in uniform—and into Senior league play. Former Boston Bruins defenceman Des Smith examines a skate held by Norm Burns, who had played 11 games for the New York Rangers in 1941/42, in this publicity photo published on December 12, 1942 before a game at the Montreal Forum.

JOE COOPER   KENNY REARDON

OTTAWA COMMANDO'S - 1944 ALLAN CUP CHAMPS

The Ottawa Commandos army all-star team won the 1942/43 Allan Cup (the photo is incorrectly dated as 1944) with Chicago Blackhawk Joe Cooper and Montreal Canadien Ken Reardon.

Albert "Red" Tilson stands next to goaltender Harvey Bennett in the lineup of the Oshawa Generals, circa 1943.

Major Conn Smythe of the 30th Sportsmen's Battery personally swears in recruit Ted Reeve, Toronto Telegram sports columnist.

Major Smythe leads the men of the 30th Battery on parade.

Imperial Oil–Turofsky/Hockey Hall of Fame

Two Smythes at war: son Stafford, in the Royal Canadian Navy, and father Conn, in the Canadian army.

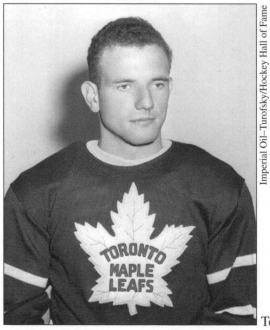

Imperial Oil–Turofsky/Hockey Hall of Fame

Ted Kennedy

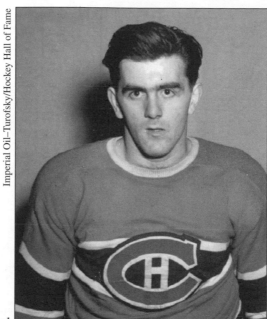

Maurice Richard

Leafs in service: Billy Taylor, Gaye Stewart, Syl Apps, Bud Poile.

RED GARRETT

Dudley "Red" Garrett

Star Maple Leaf goaltender Turk Broda's stint as a sporting ringer in the Canadian military took him all the way to eastern Europe, playing with and against the locals.

Conn Smythe's attack on the conscription policy of
the Mackenzie King government was vigorously
supported by the Toronto Globe and Mail, as this
September 22, 1944 Jack Boothe cartoon illustrates.
The item was clipped by the Armed Forces Press
Index Section and saved by its object of ridicule,
Defence Minister J.L. Ralston.

The 1944/45 Toronto Maple Leafs.
L–R, front row: Mel Hill, Nick Metz, Frank Selke, Conn Smythe,
Hap Day, Bob Davidson, E.W. Bickle, W.A.H. MacBrien,
Sweeney Schriner, Lorne Carr.
Middle row: Archie Campbell, John McCreedy, Tommy O'Neill,
Ted Kennedy, Walter "Babe" Pratt, Gus Bodnar, Art Jackson,
Jackie McLean, Tommy Daly.
Back row: Don Metz, Frank McCool, Wally Stanowski,
Ross Johnstone, Pete Backor, Reg Hamilton, Elwyn Morris

FIREFIGHT

September 26, 1944

JAMES Layton Ralston arrives in Naples, via New York, the Azores and Algiers, delivered by American military transport to the heart of the Canadian war experience. Fourteen months have passed since Canadian troops came ashore at Sicily and then Italy. The self-contained Canadian fighting force, the force greater than the sum of its parts, as General McNaughton imagined, was thus lost when I Canadian Corps, with its armoured and infantry battalions and tank corps, was placed under the command of Britain's Eighth Army. McNaughton of course was lost too, his objections to the move helping speed his removal from command of the First Canadian Army.

Canadians have been fighting in a campaign that is essentially diversionary. In 1942 the Americans formulated a plan calling for a British–American invasion of Normandy, codenamed Roundup, for April 1943. The British balked; at the Casablanca conference in January 1943, General (in 1944 Field Marshal) Sir Alan Brooke, Chief of the Imperial General Staff, was able to convince the American Chief of Staff, General George Marshall, that the invasion of northern France should wait until 1944; in the meantime, the Allies would invade Sicily and then Italy to eliminate a German ally and draw away some of the divisions that gave the Nazis a numerical advantage in Normandy. Britain, in turn, promised to join America in the Pacific war as soon as Germany was defeated. Ralston was successful in having his government lobby while detailed planning was under way in April 1943 to have Canadians take part in the Sicilian invasion, codenamed Husky. So it was that Canadians went ashore on July 10 as part of a greater Allied force of 160,000 men and 600 tanks.

It was a plan of action that echoed the diversionary strategy of the Great War: when British military planners were confronted with a bloody stalemate in the trenches of northern Europe, their solution was to distract Germany with a Mediterranean assault, on the Dardanelles, in 1915. The idea was to open up a new front in this critical Turkish territory on the Austro-Hungarian flank, take Turkey out of the conflict, and not least grasp for the Empire a strategic piece of landscape that would come in handy if a negotiated peace with Germany followed. The plan was vigorously supported by imperialists like Churchill, but it failed spectacularly. Some 130,000 soldiers of the Empire, one-third of them Australians and New Zealanders, began going ashore on the Gallipoli peninsula in the spring of 1915; by December the survivors were gone, the Empire having suffered a humiliating defeat at the hands of the heathen Turks.

The Second World War has provided an opportunity essentially to repeat the exercise. Some who watch Churchill as prime minister and defence minister commit troops with disastrous results to the defence of Greece and Crete in 1941 cannot help but see an unrequited imperialist obsessed with the strategic importance of the Mediterranean, a priority of the British since the early eighteenth century. In the Great War, strategists were divided into "westerner" and "easterner" camps, the westerners wanting to concentrate on fighting in northwestern Europe, the easterners bent on the Dardanelles. There is an echo of this division in the tactical schism between McNaughton and Ralston (and Stuart, who backed Ralston on the Italian initiative), all of them Great War veterans, although it has far more to do with contrary visions of how to make the best use of Canadian troops than any overarching strategy for the European theatre. From the Canadian perspective, the Italian campaign serves more of a political than a military purpose. It has allowed Ralston to commit to combat more than two divisions of volunteers accumulating in camps in England since December 1939. Canada passed on North Africa; McNaughton was rebuffed by his government after he unilaterally offered Canadian troops to fight in Norway in the spring of 1940. Until Italy, Canada's war on land was limited to quick and mostly devastating reversals: France in 1940, Hong Kong in 1941, Dieppe in 1942. The Italian campaign has put Canada in the fight, and in a winning way.

The invasion of Sicily, and then Italy, which began by crossing the Strait of Messina at the toe of the Italian boot before dawn on September 3, 1943, unfolds with immeasurably greater success than the Gallipoli debacle of the Great War, or the reversals suffered by the British in Greece and Crete two years earlier. But its strategic contribution to the overall Allied effort in Europe will be debated. While the Sicilian invasion drove Mussolini from power and defending Italy and the Balkans forces Germany to reallocate about 50 of its 300 divisions, in hindsight, it will be argued that the Italian campaign has only minimal effect on Germany's combat strength in France and the Low Countries.[1] And once the Normandy invasion begins, public attention turns to the successes and sacrifices there, to the campaign recognized as the critical one, the one everyone has been waiting for to end the war, the one McNaughton wanted to wait for before sending his soldiers onto the continent en masse. Meanwhile, the Italian campaign has carried forward a difficult struggle up the boot and around the Apennines range. Casualties are accumulating. The Canadian decision to join the Italian campaign, a decision rooted in politics, invites political consequences.

Even before troops were committed to Operation Husky, there were concerns about the country's ability to fight without conscription. It is not enough to raise and train an army; you must also keep a steady flow of volunteers in the pipeline as reinforcements to replace men lost as casualties. For Canadian military planners, this has been a considerable task. Unlike their American, British and Russian allies—or their enemies, for that matter—they do not have the luxury of creating and maintaining an army with draftees. They are dependent on volunteers until the day someone realizes the monumental task of changing the prime minister's mind. They must create an army with sufficient presence to give the country stature in the field, rather than having individual regiments swallowed up by British corps, but they must not create an army so large that only conscripts can keep up its numbers. This was the country's undoing in the Great War: committing so many volunteers to the killing fields that when the casualties mounted, conscription was the only answer to keeping units up to strength. In moving to avoid disaster on the battlefield, Prime Minister Borden nearly brought about disaster on the home front. Mackenzie King has been acutely aware of the danger of history repeating itself since the fall of 1939, and he has assented warily to successive increases in the size of the volunteer army.

Ralston arrives in Naples as evidence is mounting that the volunteer system is breaking down. Heavy fighting since the Normandy invasion, to free Caen and close the Falaise gap, to drive the Nazis from the Scheldt pocket in the Low Countries and open the port of

Antwerp, has produced heavy losses for Canadian troops in northern Europe. And in Italy, the casualties in I Canadian Corps are placing their own demands on reinforcements. In recent weeks, I Corps has led the Eighth Army's charge on the east end of Germany's Gothic line of defence in northern Italy. The day before Ralston arrives on the peninsula, the Allies establish an unbroken position stretching from Pisa in the west to Rimini on the Adriatic. But in so doing, the Canadians have paid with more than 2,500 casualties.

Ralston has left behind him the brewing controversy over reinforcements. As the minister leaves Canada for Italy, Smythe's original 273-word statement is inspiring a torrent of debate, serving as a national cause for those who loathe the Zombies and are looking for any reason to demand their commitment to combat. Ralston, ironically, might well be one of them. Tactically, the Smythe salvo could not have chosen a better target. Ralston has striven since 1942 to ensure that King will send in the conscripts if necessary, consulting him immediately whenever he suspects the prime minister of backpedalling on the government's position. That is, if anyone can agree what the government's position is. In Ralston's mind, the conscripts are to be sent in if it is a matter of keeping the army up to strength. In King's mind, conscripts will be sent in only if it is a question of defeating Germany.

No sooner is Ralston in Italy than he is in the midst of Smythe's charges, though the allegations were restricted to the fighting in France. On September 27, Ralston tours No. 15 Canadian General Hospital north of Naples at Caserta, after which Brigadier E.W. Haldenby, commander of No. 1 Canadian Base Reinforcement Group in Italy, tells him casualties have been running at 110 per day "all arms" for the last few days.[2] During intense periods of fighting, reported casualties have averaged 380 per day for both Canadian divisions. Ralston is told that another month or less of fighting will drain I Canadian Corps of reinforcements, and that officer casualties are particularly heavy. Haldenby says the reinforcements have been fine soldiers, though some have in fact arrived poorly trained because they were employed as cooks and the like before being converted to fighting roles.

In the afternoon, Ralston and his group fly to Ancona, about forty miles down the Adriatic coast from Rimini, and drive to nearby Iesi to meet with the reinforcements of the 4th Battalion. It is Ralston's first opportunity to hear the regular enlisted man in Italy speak his mind. The men of the 4th asked him about the prospect of having to fight in Burma, plans for an army of occupation in Europe, issues on rehabilitation once fighting is over, as well as other matters close to their hearts—the slow delivery of cigarettes and shortfalls in their half-bottle-per-week ration of Canadian beer (which sometimes, because of pooling, turns out to be despised British beer). And they also want to know about the government's plan for the Zombies.

On Friday he visits with men of the 48th Highlanders, the regiment Brigadier Haldenby joined in June 1915 and with which he served for twenty-five years before being given command of the 9th Canadian Infantry Brigade in August 1940. The 48th is also the regiment whose band played at the opening of Maple Leaf Gardens in 1931. (In 1943 Haldenby moved to reinforcement duties.) Accompanied by Haldenby, Ralston invites the 48th to air any complaints they might have. Ralston is confronted by an alarming one from no less than the regiment's sergeant-major: that in a recent group of seventy-two reinforcements who joined the battalion, only seven were found to be fully trained. Most of them did not know how to throw a grenade.[3] This is a serious allegation, dovetailing precisely with Smythe's public charges. The sergeant-major is questioned by Ralston and Brigadier E.G. Weeks, who is in charge of all Canadian reinforcements in the Italian theatre. The sergeant-major is ordered to submit a report to Weeks giving the name of each soldier he alleges to have been untrained. Weeks, in turn, asks for Haldenby's comments on the complaint.

On investigation, the quality of reinforcements does not seem so dire. The sergeant-major can only bring forward thirty-two names, and of those, most seem adequately trained. But there are irregularities. In the case of one private who was said to have no grenade training, for example, the complaint is legitimate. He had no experience with grenades when he was told to clean one. After he mistakenly pulled the pin, the explosion wounded three men. Haldenby concludes, "if this man had been properly trained this accident would never have happened…. This man should never have been allowed to clean a grenade with a detonator in it."

Haldenby emphasizes in a memo that his reinforcement group is not a training organization; rather, it is designed for holding reinforcements and keeping them fit. That said, he notes, "It has been found necessary to do considerable refresher [training] in this theatre to augment the [training] received in UK and in Canada due to the fact that some [reinforcements] have missed some part of their [training], and we have endeavoured to fill this gap. Every man is tested as soon as he arrives, and, if he needs extra instr[uction] he receives it. In any event he must fire all his weapons and throw grenades."

Though it is clear from Haldenby's memo that troops are indeed departing Britain for the front with incomplete training, there appears to be no complaint from senior command about the quality of reinforcements, no concurrence in Italy with Smythe's allegations about troops in action in France that green, untrained recruits are being thrown into battle. The Commander of I Corps, Lieutenant-General E.L.M. Burns, observes that he has had no complaints from any of his commanders regarding the lack of training of reinforcements, although he appreciates that there might be the odd man who slipped through the system of training checks and arrived at a unit without a satisfactory knowledge of weapons. Ralston seems most concerned about damage control. In demanding that the sergeant-major's complaint be fully examined, he also says he well understands that any commanding officer naturally considers the training his men receive with the unit is far better than any done back in Canada or England. Pride of combat experience makes it inevitable that an NCO will think his fresh recruits are not up to snuff.

But it is not an issue Ralston ever wants to have to revisit. A policy is developed wherein Weeks and Haldenby are (according to Weeks' diary) "responsible for ensuring that no reinforcements went forward to field units unless Brig Haldenby was personally satisfied that they were fully trained in every respect. Further, it was agreed that a detailed record would be kept of the training given at the Base to each Canadian officer and soldier so that in future if enquiries were raised it would be possible to explain just what training each individual had."

In Italy at least, Conn Smythe's complaint over the quality of reinforcements is not a serious issue. But there remains the fundamental charge that volunteers are being placed under undue strain because of King's refusal to relieve them with Zombies. Ralston must constantly answer questions from the enlisted men about the government's plans for the Zombies. In conversation with men of the Hastings and Prince Edward Regiment, Ralston is told that there simply aren't enough reinforcements. Many men have been sent up to the line five or six times after being wounded. They want to know if the Zombies are going to be sent over. And the men of the 48th want to know if the Zombies are going to be demobilized to good civilian jobs before those overseas get a chance to secure them.

Whenever Ralston is asked about the government's plans for the NRMA men, he sticks to a basic statement. It is the government's policy to maintain a volunteer army overseas, Weeks hears him say. As long as there is a sufficient flow of enlistments in the Canadian army to meet the losses from casualties and sickness, NRMA personnel will not be sent to theatres of operations. But Weeks also hears Ralston promise that if the military commanders are not satisfied with the reinforcement situation, the government is prepared to give the matter of sending NRMA personnel overseas "the most careful consideration."

While Ralston is in Italy, the Allies blunder into one of the greatest setbacks of the war. Three British and American airborne divisions, 35,000 men in all, land behind German lines in Holland on September 17 in an attempt to secure a series of bridges culminating in the one spanning the Rhine at Arnhem. The attack fails horribly, with British paratroopers becoming trapped on the wrong side of the Rhine. Of the ten thousand British soldiers involved in Operation Market Garden, about one thousand are killed and another six thousand taken prisoner when they are forced to surrender on September 26. King is thoroughly traumatized by the disaster.

I have felt greatly pained at the terrible loss of life at Arnhem, he records in his diary.... *The disaster shows how wise I have been in not permitting any dissolution of parliament and an election at this time. We would have been anethmatized [sic], at a time when men are losing their lives, for precipitating a political conflict if it could have been avoided. The mention now of a winter campaign bears out my judgment as to having an alternative course for the preparation of a campaign this year or one for coming on next year.*

His mood is not improved by learning that Queen Wilhelmina of the Netherlands has been given the Order of the Garter by Britain's own royalty. The timing of the honour incenses him, sovereigns bestowing honours upon sovereigns on the eve of the terrible tragedy of Arnhem. To what does she owe the honour? When her country was overrun, she was given a home in England; Princess Juliana was given a home in Canada. And while they have lived in comfort and security in exile, our men have been giving their lives to give them back their country. *It all shows how absolutely wrong some of these customs are and how the institution of monarchy helps to raise enemies against itself which, in the end, will lead to its destruction. There was no chance in this coincidence.*

The next day, September 28, the war cabinet in the absence of Ralston spends about an hour on the issue of Canadian forces to be used against Japan. King begins by telling his assembled ministers that the real question before them is to decide whether Canada from now on is going to seek to return to the state of an industrial country, eager to further the arts of peace, or if it is going to regard itself, as the countries of Europe have for so many years, as a nation under steady preparation for war, supporting large armed forces. King seems to be getting nowhere with his navy minister, Angus Macdonald, and his ambitions to have Canada fight a broader Pacific war. Macdonald still challenges the idea that it has been decided the navy will be deployed only in the North Pacific.

He is a formidable cabinet opponent, Macdonald. The native of Inverness County, Nova Scotia, came into the Great War at its end as a lieutenant with the 25th Battalion, and was promoted to captain with the 185th. Graduating in law from Harvard, Macdonald became a professor of law at Dalhousie in Halifax. He failed in his first federal election bid in 1930, but in 1933 became the province's premier when he was elected in Halifax South. Macdonald resigned his premiership in 1940 to accept King's invitation to join the federal cabinet as navy minister.

As a result of Macdonald's obstinacy over the navy's role in the Pacific war, King produces the minutes of meetings at Quebec with Churchill and reviews them in their entirety for his assembled ministers. He also reiterates that the air force is being kept at much too great strength. He asks his air minister, Chubby Power, to make it clear that Canada has no intention of sending forces to Australia.

He finds it strange to have to fight in a Liberal administration to limit expenditures on war, when his government, he reflects to himself, has been informed by both Britain and the U.S. that they can manage the situation themselves and that Canada is not really wanted, except where it is necessary for Canada to take part in at least a token way against Japan. *I took very strong exception to the attitude of the three Defence Departments in seeking to retain so many men under arms and with heavy cost to the taxpayers. I told the Cabinet that I had responsibility of leading the country into war and it was the heaviest responsibility any man could have and that I did not intend to allow a single life to be sacrificed unnecessarily, or the taxpayers burdened any further than was absolutely necessary on war account. What was needed to win the war I would help to further, but I would not agree to anything that was expended merely that the services might qualify themselves or extend their activities.... The discussion I know will make the Defence Ministers more antagonistic towards myself, but I feel certain I have again helped to clear the air on the real position. It is all part of the conscriptionists versus the others.*

After the meeting, he reads a speech by Churchill. In the shadow of the disaster at Arnhem, confidence in a quick end to the war in Europe is wavering. Churchill has intimated that it may last until the spring.

🍁

On October 3, Ralston delivers a speech from Italy carried across Canada on the CBC. In it he makes his first public attack on Smythe's charges, pronouncing the allegations of improperly trained volunteer reinforcements to be groundless and motivated by politics.

That evening, Smythe returns fire from his bed in Chorley Park Hospital, releasing a rebuttal to the news media. According to the Toronto *Telegram*, "he had received letters from all over Canada, and overseas, urging him to continue his demands for a correction of a condition which permitted trained conscript forces to remain in Canada while inadequately trained forces went into action. Most of the letters came from parents or wives of men overseas, providing a formidable list of men whose dates of enlistment indicated corroboration of his charges." Smythe's statement reads:

> To suggest that there are political motives in my statements is untrue. My statement of September 19th is correct.
>
> To make up the pool of reinforcements prior to and after "D" Day required for the Infantry, thousands of men were needed. These were practically all obtained from two sources:
> (1) Large numbers of young lads just overseas who a few months ago were civilians, and
> (2) Thousands of men from other arms such as the Artillery, Armoured Corps., etc., with varying lengths of service.
>
> Anyone anywhere in Canada checking the casualty lists and noting the dates of enlistment can prove for themselves the truth of Item 1. Col. Ralston, by releasing the figures showing the number of other arms transferred to the Infantry

in the last few months will prove Item 2.

The officers who stated to me that the reinforcements were untrained were all of a company commander level or lower—the officers who actually lead the men into battle. They came from the following battalions:

>North Nova Scotians 3rd Div.
>North Shore Regiment, N.B. 3rd Div.
>Reg. de Maisonneuve, Que. 2nd Div.
>Reg. de Chaudiere, Que. 3rd Div.
>Royal Regiment of Canada, Ont. 2nd Div.
>Queens Own Rifles, Ont. 3rd Div.
>Essex Scottish, Ont. 2nd Div.
>Royal Winnipeg Rifles, Man. 3rd Div.
>South Saskatchewan Rifles, Sask. 2nd Div.
>Calgary Highlanders, Alberta 2nd Div.
>Canadian Scottish, B.C. 3rd Div.

On the home front, the Smythe campaign has encountered some opposition outside the ranks of government. Already on September 22, the *Ottawa Citizen* has published a letter attacking Smythe written by John Matheson, a discharged gunner convalescing in hospital in Kingston:

Many gunners were proud that Connie Smythe chose the artillery in which to serve. They felt that he was a man of sufficient stature to take orders as well as give them, broad enough to understand and live up to the written and implied responsibilities of his commission. And yet, sir, this field officer chooses to disobey the most basic law of soldiering. For perhaps greater personal publicity or more insidious reasons, he has taken this cheap and offensive way of making himself heard on his return.

The informed public knows that these statements are lies. Even were they not, Smythe has proved himself an offender against the military law which he has been entrusted to enforce on others. A lance-bombardier is familiar with the correct channels through which he is able to forward information and opinions to the top.

Although he is not brought before court martial and cashiered, this contemptible action on his part against this country will not be forgotten by men on active service.

While Ralston is overseas, his office receives a dissenting letter from CBC sportscaster Clary Settell, who proposes,

> I know nothing of the merits or demerits of Major Conny Smythe's charges, but a good way to test his sincerity would be this:
>
> For the years of the war before he went overseas or even organized a regiment and up to the present time, the Maple Leaf Gardens in Toronto has shown probably the blackest record of co-operation in war charities of any comparable sports organization in America. They have never lowered the price or admitted one single member of the thousands of eager servicemen now on their way to kill Germans or be killed themselves, as many of them have. All this under the same Smythe, the Managing Director of the institution.
>
> My suggestion is this—write to each of the other teams in the National Hockey League, or have a representative contact them personally, and obtain the number of members of the Armed Services who have been admitted free to their games over the years, as well as their contributions to all war charities. The record when placed alongside that of Maple Leaf Gardens will be all the argument you'll need. It will amaze you. I do not include the purchase of Victory bonds.[4] That is simply a good business transaction, but <u>out and out gifts for war causes</u>.

The most publicized opposition is provided by Edna Blois, who lost her husband Kenneth in combat in France only a few weeks ago. Lieutenant Blois was from good military stock—his father was a colonel in the Great War—and his widow is incensed by Smythe's behaviour. On the evening of October 3, as Smythe is releasing his rebuttal to Ralston, she delivers a speech on Toronto radio station CKEY, the text of which is reprinted by the *Toronto Daily Star*, a Liberal paper, the next day.

"Frankly, my first reaction to Maj. Smythe's charges was one of momentary alarm," she says, explaining,

> He is a Canadian sportsman who has public standing. And then I asked myself, "Why did Maj. Smythe as an army officer see fit to make these charges public before taking them up with his superior officers?" Could it be that the

charges flowed from some political motive?

These questions became more pointed in my mind when a short time later Premier Drew returned from England and immediately issued a statement corroborating Maj. Smythe's charges. I was struck by the fact that Premier Drew declared that he had not read Maj. Smythe's statement but he went on from there to repeat it almost word for word. I then remembered that our press had reported that Premier Drew had interviewed Maj. Smythe shortly before the latter returned to Canada and so I came to the conclusion that Premier Drew himself must have been the author and inspirer of the Maj. Smythe charge. This would not be the first occasion on which Col. Drew for purely partisan reason has gone out of his way to harry the feelings of the people over alleged military inefficiencies.

After thinking the matter over, I examined Maj. Smythe's charges more carefully and I invite you to examine them more carefully. Here is an officer of the Canadian Army who was in France. He charges that "green," "inexperienced" and "untrained" troops were sent into action with the result that many of them were needlessly killed or wounded. We are to suppose that he learned of this while in France. Then, why did Maj. Smythe not protest to the army high command when he supposedly learnt of this happening? Why did he not tell the reporters who interviewed him in France about this alleged crime? Why did he remain silent about this supposed outrage of all military common sense for many weeks and months? No man can throw out such grave charges without stating when and where he is supposed to have learned for the first time of this alleged crime.

Mrs. Blois wonders where Smythe's facts are—she, for one, can't detect any. "Is it possible that a responsible man can make charges of this sort without offering even one fact to support them?" On what date were the "green" troops thrown into action? In what sector of the front were they used? In what regiments and battalions were they? (She cannot have seen Smythe's list of regiments at the time of her speech.) Again, notes Mrs. Blois, he does not say.

"When you begin to examine Maj. Smythe's charges in this way," she argues, you begin to understand what a terrible thing he has done. He has made charges which cast the most damaging suspicion upon those who are responsible for the conduct of Canada's military effort without offering one single fact. He has charged the most serious crimes against the responsible men who are leading our forces against the enemy without committing himself to a single piece of evidence.

You cannot go about Toronto charging anyone you don't like with vague but horrible crimes. Everyone, including the officers of the law, would recognize that you were merely trying to damage another's character and you would be dealt with accordingly. Maj. Smythe is doing something much more serious. He is casting suspicion upon our military command; he is undermining public confidence in our military and war leaders by charges unsupported by a single fact that he is prepared to vouch for. And he is doing this from the hospital bed of a wounded officer, thus placing those against whom he makes the charge in a most unfair position.

She relates that her husband, while in England waiting to see action in France, wrote to her many times of meeting officers returning from the Italian campaign who would proudly state "that there were no better trained, equipped or braver fighters anywhere than those Canadian boys fighting in Italy."

"Shortly before his death my husband wrote from France of his genuine confidence in an early victory. I quote, 'There is no doubt we have one of the finest trained armies in the world. To see our men in action—our soldiers and airmen, convinces me it won't be long before we will call the tune of peace.' "

Mrs. Blois also offers up quotes by returned soldiers not impressed by Smythe's campaign. A lieutenant from Vancouver says: "The officers on board ship coming back felt very warm about the statements made by Major Connie Smythe that reinforcements were 'green' and 'poorly trained.' I don't think that Major Smythe has the authority to quote the boys as to whether they were well trained. He wasn't in England very long and he wasn't in France very long. He didn't fight with the infantry or with the paratroops. If they were 'green' they put on a very good show and are continuing to do so. Reinforcements may have lacked battle experience but I was in the army five years and all I lacked was battle experience. There is only one way to get it and that is in the field. The reinforcements were good fighters—the results are proving that."

In short, Mrs. Blois is not amused. She suggests court martial would be appropriate for Smythe. Pleased with the response to her speech, she sends along a copy to Ralston, and she is asked to give a talk to a meeting of the Labour Progressive Party in Toronto. "If Major Smythe's statements that untrained men are being thrown into action are true, and I believe they are not," she tells the socialist organization, "then the responsibility does not lie with the government but with the Military Command, and Generals Crerar and Stuart should be removed."

But Mrs. Blois and Gunner Matheson are lone voices in the wilderness. The conservative press stands staunchly by Smythe, whose charges continue to be amplified by Drew and national Progressive Conservative leader John Bracken. Within the Liberal party, support for the policy of turning the other cheek is eroding as it becomes evident that the Smythe campaign is becoming a political rather than a military hot potato. On September 30, Drew writes to King:

> When I returned [from overseas] a week ago, the statement made by Major Smythe and the reply of the Department of National Defence were brought to my attention. Knowing that the facts disclosed in his statement regarding reinforcements were correct, I expected that some appropriate action would result from inquiry into the facts by members of the Government, which I assumed would naturally follow public disclosure of a situation which is a matter of widespread concern amongst all Canadians overseas.
>
> As Ontario has contributed such a large proportion of our armed forces, the Government of Ontario should be informed as to what will be done to meet a situation which has so direct a bearing on many of our own responsibilities. I would therefore be pleased to know at your earliest convenience what action the Dominion Government intends to take in dealing with the urgent need for trained reinforcements.

The prime minister won't take the bait. He refuses to be drawn into a scrap with Drew. Instead, in Ralston's absence King hands the letter over to Chubby Power, his air minister and associate minister of defence, telling him to draft a reply and show it to King first.

Power's draft states:

> While the interest of the Government of Ontario in the well
> being of the Canadian Forces overseas is fully appreciated,
> the maintenance and reinforcement of the Canadian Army
> falls within the sphere of responsibility of the Dominion
> Government and this Government has accepted and will
> continue to accept that responsibility.
>
> The question of reinforcements has been considered on a
> number of occasions in the House of Commons and the pol-
> icy has been fully stated from time to time.
>
> You may be assured that the situation is receiving the clos-
> est attention of the Dominion Government and that any fur-
> ther statement that is considered necessary will be made at
> the appropriate time.

King doesn't like it. The less explaining, the better. Power ends up
signing a response that basically says nothing. As the main body of
the letter opines:

> It is the responsibility of the Government of Canada,
> through the Departments of National Defence, to maintain
> the Armed Services at their full efficiency. That duty the
> Government has discharged and will continue to discharge
> in the light of its responsibility to Parliament and to the
> Canadian people.

Meanwhile, a third rebellious front has been opened by the
Conservatives. John Bracken is in his native Manitoba, campaigning in Neepawa to secure the Conservative nomination for the local
federal riding, as he has not been able to secure a seat in Parliament
since winning the party leadership in 1942 after serving as
Manitoba's premier for twenty years. (Eleven seats are currently
empty in the House, but King has refused to allow any by-elec-
tions, preferring to hold off having them filled until the next general election.) Bracken's trumpeting of the Smythe charges is too
much for a local Liberal party member, S. James Dempsey. On
October 4, he writes to the national party headquarters:

> During the past few days John Bracken and his organizer Mr.
> Arthur Ross, M.P., have been very busy in this constituency.

In conversation with Mr. Ross the chief criticism the Tory party has to make is in connection with the manpower situation particularly with respect to volunteers and draftees—the so-called Zombie Army. This of course will have little influence upon thinking people but unfortunately in this part of the country as elsewhere we have a large number who never read and who do not think, but unfortunately have votes.

Could you let me have the latest figures covering the manpower situation—if this is not a military secret. If possible, I should like to know the number of volunteers, the number of draftees and the number of fully trained men ready for reinforcements in order to be in a position to meet this propaganda. Personally, I think the Tory party is utterly bankrupt in every way if this is the only criticism they have and rather than argue with them would prefer to see Connie Smythe and a few more prosecuted for subversive tactics. It is possible that Bracken, Ross, et al know that it would be giving comfort to the enemy to disclose exact details of our armed forces and knowing this use these tactics deliberately.

As to Connie Smythe—could you advise whether there is anything in military law which would apply. Could you also advise whether or not it has been ascertained if George Drew visited Smythe in England prior to Smythe's return to Canada….

Smythe was in fact visited by Drew in hospital in England. What's more, on the very day of his arrival at Chorley Park, he was visited by the *Globe*'s George McCullagh. The two men are old cohorts, though they have only lately come to rest on the same side of the political fence. Both have bred Queen's Plate–winning thoroughbreds, and both have invested in northern Ontario mining stocks, in McCullagh's case shrewdly enough to have apparently amassed a fortune in the 1930s. McCullagh was a devoted promoter and confidant of Liberal premier Mitchell Hepburn and a supporter of Mackenzie King. In 1942, though, in the face of Bill 80, McCullagh broke with the Liberals and threw the weight of his newspaper behind the Conservatives, where it would remain ever after.

In his memoirs, Smythe will make no mention of his visit from Drew in England, but he will reveal that McCullagh came to see him, and assert that, after he complained about the reinforcement problems, McCullagh said, "If you're sure, that should be published.

I'll publish every word you say." Smythe must have had his statement ready in a flash, to make the next morning's edition of the *Globe*.

Dempsey's letter is forwarded by Allan McLean to James Wells, Ralston's staff secretary, on October 6, with McLean asking, "Will you please get me all the figures possible for him and also a statement with respect to Connie Smythe."

Wells is moved to send a confidential communiqué to Colonel H.A. Dyde, who is travelling with Ralston, care of the personal assistant to Major-General Price Montague at Canadian Military Headquarters in London; at the time of writing, Ralston is still in Italy.

"Dear Sandy," he writes to Dyde,

> I am very disturbed about the failure everyone is making here to give any answer to the Connie Smythe charges.
>
> The Minister left instructions that [Navy Minister] Willie Macdonald was to handle the correspondence, but he went off to Halifax almost at once. The draft letter he left simply thanks the person for writing and says it will be brought to the Minister's attention upon his return. A fine help!
>
> It has been impossible to reach Mr. Power for the last week and no one seems to know for sure when he will be back. Naturally the C.G.S. [Lieutenant-General Murchie] is not in a position to take any action himself.
>
> The National Liberal Federation phone me almost every day wanting to know what we are doing and I am enclosing [a] copy of a letter I had from Allan McLean this morning with a letter which he enclosed [from Dempsey]. This speaks for itself. I can just add that I know from the newspaper reports that Bracken is campaigning all over the West, using the Smythe charges for his main platform.
>
> I am also enclosing an editorial and cartoon from today's "Globe and Mail."* This is a sample of the stuff all the opposition press are carrying. As a matter of fact the only

---

*The editorial cartoon shows Ralston reading a statement: "I regret that distress might be caused by statements regarding the inadequate training of reinforcements." Beside him, penned up like cattle, is a horde of NRMA men labelled "80,000 trained home army." In the foreground of the cartoon, grappling with a German soldier, is a Canadian infantryman who is shouting back, "It would cause *me* less distress if you could send some trained reinforcements!"

defence that is being put up is by the Communists in Toronto who are doing a fairly good job. The Liberal papers are doing little or nothing.

The whole trouble is that the Minister's original statement [on September 20], from the point of view of providing ammunition to defend us, was entirely inadequate. Perhaps originally there was no cause to worry a great deal about it, but since no real defence has been made, and no action has been taken against Smythe, the thing is building up bigger and bigger and I believe will shortly reach a stage where no amount of counter action will overcome the harm that has been done. It seems to be growing like a snoball [*sic*].

In case you did not get it, I am enclosing a clipping which gives a list of the Regiments named by Smythe as being reinforced with green men.

In my opinion the Minister ought to issue a statement at once which would give sufficient facts and figures to enable an adequate defence to be put up by those who wish to defend.

I wish you would discuss the matter with the Minister, or if you like give him this letter.

The momentum of the Smythe campaign has been maintained by Premier Drew with a speech to the highly receptive Canadian Corps Association in Toronto on the evening of October 5. The address prompts Lieutenant-General Murchie at General Staff Headquarters in Ottawa to wire General Stuart in London a top-secret summary of Drew's charges the next day:

After referring to Smythe statements and department statement of 20 Sep Drew referred to letter written by him to Prime Minister on 30 Sep asking on behalf of the Government of Ontario what action Dominion Government intended to take in dealing with urgent need for reinforcements and Mr. Power's reply dated 3 October....

After acknowledging that Canadian divisions which went to France on D Day were magnificently trained and fully equipped Drew made the following charges:

(a) Quote As a result of the heavy fighting desperate efforts were made to provide reinforcements for the infantry men who had been chopping trees with the Forestry Corps in

Scotland gunners from the artillery training centres men from the armoured units and so on were asked to volunteer as infantry and naturally they did so in large numbers. Most of them went into action with little or no real infantry training unquote.

(b) Quote reinforcements from Canada were also rushed overseas without the required training in Britain before they reached the front unquote.

(c) quote Many men have gone into action during the last two months who had never thrown a live grenade and never fired a Piat gun a Bren gun or a mortar before going into action unquote.

(d) quote Tank units received tank gunners who had been trained only with six pounders and they went into action on 75 mm guns although they had never operated a 75 mm gun before. Tank units also received tank drivers at the front who had been trained in ram tanks and had never been in a Sherman tank until they went into action unquote.

(e) quote not only are men going into action untrained with weapons they must use but they have gone into action with practically no training at all in field craft. Many of the reinforcements have been lost for lack of this training unquote.

Drew then alleged that in spite of these efforts there was still a serious shortage of reinforcements and urged that trained NRMA personnel in Canada be despatched at once.

He concluded by reading extracts from three letters from personnel overseas since killed in which complaints are [mainly] lack of training and shortage of reinforcements.

The Drew speech report prompts a twenty-four-point memo from Stuart's CMHQ. "Reduced to their essence," it begins, "the various statements recently made by Premier George Drew and Major Connie Smythe are obviously intended to give the Canadian public impression that the Canadian Army Overseas has suffered from a general shortage of reinforcements ever since D-day, and that, in trying to overcome this, especially in the Infantry, numbers of men have been sent to the front without proper training.... The truth is that, up to date, there has been no overall deficiency of reinforcements. The Army went into battle with its full quota behind it. It still has reinforcements behind it. On 23 Sep 44, the Army in the field, taking in both theatres, stood at 94.91% of its full authorized

War Establishment. On that day there were, immediately behind the Army, in the theatres of war, and excluding everybody in the United Kingdom and Canada, reinforcements amounting to 6% of the War Establishment." These figures, explain this secret memo, refer only to fit men ready for battle, and do not include anyone in the hospital or not otherwise ready to fight. "And the above was the situation after the Army in Italy had been fighting almost continuously for over a year, and the Army in France had been engaged in some of the fiercest and most important battles of the entire war for some 3½ months, the operations being of an intense nature practically throughout. It is extremely doubtful if there is any other Army anywhere that is in a position to better these figures."

As to the statements that volunteers were being rushed into the fighting line only a matter of weeks after they shed civilian clothing, the memo presents tables of analysis of service periods, one of which shows that 85 per cent of volunteers of all ranks recently sent to France (based on an analysis of three drafts selected at random) had one to three years' service. Of the 2,869 records analysed, only nine revealed service in the shortest period, and that was for five to six months.

CMHQ has no truck with the idea that recruits and men converted to infantry from other service arms or duties don't know how to use their weapons. "The allegation that the men we have transferred to the Infantry were sent to fight without proper training is not true. When these men were transferred they were not raw recruits. They had taken, in Canada, the basic training which is common to all arms. This covered such personal weapons as the rifle, the Bren, the Grenade, the machine carbine, and the PIAT, or its predecessor the Anti-tank rifle, and included range-firing practices." In addition, every man remustered to the infantry in the U.K. has been put through a special refresher training course on weapons, which also makes him competent at handling and firing such weapons as the mortar, a device peculiar to the infantry. The conversion training, the memo elaborates, also teaches the remustered enlistee infantry organization, field craft and minor tactics before he is sent to a field unit.

As for Drew's charge that armoured corps reinforcements have been going into action in Sherman tanks when they had only been trained on the Ram tank, it is misleading, according to the memo. "It is true that before D-Day some reinforcements were sent to Armoured units who had not received training on the Sherman tank. There was nothing wrong with this, because they could be, and were, trained in the unit before they went into battle. In spite of the difficulties of getting Sherman tanks, which have been in urgent demand for operations, we have not, since D-Day, sent Armoured Corps reinforcements forward without giving them conversion training on the Sherman tank, fitted with the 75 mm gun which they have to use in action.... It remains true that, because we have numbers of Ram tanks, the greater part of the training in Canada and in the United Kingdom is still carried out on this type. Nevertheless, drivers and gunners all get a minimum of one week's conversion training to teach them how to handle the Sherman before they proceed to the front."*

The legitimacy of the complaint about problems adapting armoured reinforcements trained on the Ram to the Sherman appears doubtful. Major R.D. Grant of the Fort Garry Light Horse, who went ashore on D-Day in an amphibious Sherman and was wounded at Carpiquet in the fighting around Caen, will not be able to recall any complaints about reinforcements having trouble adjusting to the Sherman—and in any event, as the Canadians lost their Shermans, they received the better-armed Firefly.[5]

"Even Premier Drew has stated publicly that the Canadian Army which went into action on D-day was magnificently trained and equipped," the memo observes, and concludes, "It is notable and

---

*The Ram, an exclusively Canadian medium tank based on the American M3 tank chassis, was developed in 1941 and built by the Montreal Locomotive Works. It was equipped with a two-pounder, then a six-pounder gun (known as the Mark 2), wholly inadequate for combat against Germany's new tanks, developed in response to the might of the Russian T-34. The 55-ton Tiger, which went into production in August 1942, had an 88-mm gun; the 43-ton Panther, which went into production in November 1942, had a 75-mm gun. These were joined beginning in February 1944 in limited numbers by the King Tiger, a 70-ton nightmare with an 88-mm (and then a 128-mm) gun. Sending Canadians into combat in Normandy against these killing machines with the undergunned Ram would have been suicidal, and because the Ram could not be upgraded with a 75-mm gun it was decided to end production in July 1943 and switch to the American M4. There were actually seven versions of the basic 33-ton M4, collectively known to Commonwealth forces as the Sherman. The Canadians built a Sherman variation on the original A1 design, called the A5, which was equipped with a short-barrelled 75-mm gun. All Canadian armoured regiments were re-equipped with the new machine before D-Day. The British employed a superior configuration, known as the Firefly, which carried a much more effective 17-pounder gun, which had a muzzle velocity almost 50 per cent higher than the 75-mm. Whatever the configuration, the Shermans were still badly outclassed by the German Tigers and Panthers.

significant that neither Major Smythe nor Premier Drew have ever made these charges, either verbally or in writing, to any responsible Commander or Staff Officer of the Canadian Army Overseas before making them in public. Major Smythe might have done this at any time through ordinary military channels. During his recent visit to England, Premier Drew had interviews with the Chief of Staff and the Major-General in charge of Administration. On these occasions he expressed nothing but admiration and praise for what he had seen, and at no time did he put forward to these officers the representations which he has now seen fit to make public."

The problem with reinforcements, the defence department memo concedes, is not the total number; it is the fact that not enough of them are infantry. Transfers from other arms—the air force and the navy—have been necessary, and with them the necessary retraining outlined above. "It is a fact that, in the process of readjustment, shortages developed in the Infantry Arm. It is even probable that such shortages will recur until the period of readjustment is over. They have never reached proportions endangering the overall ability of the Army to wage battle."

As confident as the memo might be, the Canadian military has grossly misjudged its manpower needs, a failing suffered by other Allied forces as well. At this stage of the war Canada has too many airmen and sailors and not nearly enough infantry. The problem has been an overly optimistic projection of infantry casualties. The Canadian army has based its recruitment and management of manpower on "wastage rates" borrowed from the British army. While the memo states that its forecasts of manpower needs "represented the careful and laborious work of a large body of statisticians and were based on the best available data that could be obtained, from every theatre since the start of the war," the wastage rates are fundamentally drawn from Britain's experience in desert warfare in 1941–42. Those tangles with Rommel led to the establishment of a wastage rate for the Normandy invasion that called for 63 per cent of all reinforcements to be infantry. But as of July 15, Canadian infantry have accounted for 78 per cent of the army's losses. And defence department analysis of Canadian casualties in August and September will reveal losses to be concentrated overwhelmingly among army personnel. Of 19,265 casualties suffered by all service arms in those two months, 17,783 are in the army—more than 90 per cent of total losses. In contrast, the air force accounts for 6.2 per cent of losses, the navy 1.5 per cent. The wastage rates borrowed from the British also assume that more than half of wounded infantry will be able to return to battle.[6] At No. 15 General Hospital at Ancona, Ralston is informed that only 12 per cent of patients are returning to their units every month.

Despite the confidence expressed by the memo, the picture in the field is far more dire. While in Italy, Ralston and Weeks meet with General Sir Oliver Leese, commander of the Eighth Army.[7] Montgomery made Leese commander of 30th Corps for the Battle of Alamein, the great desert victory over Rommel in October 1942, and he took over command of the Eighth Army from Montgomery when his mentor returned to England in January 1944 to serve as ground commander under Eisenhower for the Normandy invasion. The charismatic forty-nine-year-old Brit, who will be off to serve as the commander of Allied land forces in Southeast Asia in early November, is full of praise for the Canadian soldiers. Leese lays out his objective: to contain in Italy as many Germans as possible and to kill or destroy the enemy opposing him. German morale, he notes, is extremely high. The enemy is fighting very well. To mount a successful assault, Leese requires a three-to-one advantage.

Conscious of the demands Leese's battle plans will impose on the Canadian reinforcement pipeline, Weeks asks him if he envisions using the 1st Canadian Infantry Division in any action in the near future. Leese says he does; as a matter of fact, he intends to commit them to an attack within the next few days.

Weeks describes for Ralston a reinforcement shortfall approaching the calamitous. He tells Ralston that there is a constant daily return to action from the Canadian Convalescent Depot and the forward medical installations of sixty to one hundred men of all ranks, all fit and trained reinforcements. But the actual battle casualties during intense fighting—those killed, wounded and missing—amount to 250 to 300 daily, and then there are sick and injured in equal number to actual battle casualties. Thus, to keep the units of I Corps up to strength during intense fighting, 500 to 600 reinforcements are required daily. In Weeks' opinion, if I Corps continues to be actively engaged in operations, by about October 10 all general-duty infantry reinforcements will have been committed and there will be no reserves. Infantry units of I Corps will have to fight slightly below battle strength. Ralston surely understands the implications. Units not up to strength, asked to accomplish the objectives of full units, will be under even greater strain, prone to even greater casualties. Greater casualties will mean an even more desperate reinforcement situation.

Ralston's visit to the European theatre also coincides with the release by Eisenhower to all American combat units on October 4 of a report by the Office of the United States surgeon general warning about the dangers of battle fatigue.[8] The American forces in Italy have estimated that an infantry man can put up with about two hundred regimental combat days; the British, under whose command the Canadian troops fall, are supposed to be following a regimen of twelve days of combat, relieved by four days of rest, with a maximum fighting period of four hundred days. In Normandy, some Canadian troops were kept in constant combat for more than fifty days. Whether or not Ralston sees the American report, he instinctively sympathizes with its basic message: you cannot keep a man in the fighting line indefinitely, without relief.

Conn Smythe's recovery proceeds slowly. Because of the shrapnel puncture in his bladder and bowel, he will require a daily enema for the rest of his life. He is particularly affected by the cold, and must bundle himself against chills, which exacerbate the pain. On October 5, he is able to take a short stroll at Chorley Park, but the next day he suffers a relapse, attributed to the deluge of visitors occupying his waking hours. As *Globe and Mail* sports columnist Jim Coleman tells his readers, "although his condition is far from critical his doctors have insisted that the 'No Visitors' sign be placed on his door.... The man will be up and around soon enough if his friends give him a decent chance."

A letter in the *Globe* of October 6 must give him cheer. "Colonel Ralston, in a recent broadcast, said there was not a word of truth in Major Conn Smythe's statements," writes Tom Reid of Toronto, who was with the 16th Machine Gun Company at Vimy Ridge. "My oldest boy was in the Royal Regiment, recruited on Danforth Ave. two months before the Battle of Dieppe. I don't believe he had two weeks solid fighting experience—like Major Smythe would have to put his hockey team in shape for a contest with Montreal or any other team. My boy Tom was one of the luckiest bunch that crossed the English Channel to Dieppe. He was as green as any plowboy."

While Smythe convalesces in peace, his fight is carried on by others. Drew follows up his speech to the Canadian Corps Association with an address to the local Progressive Conservatives in Hamilton on October 6. Lashing out at King for his alleged failure to provide the army overseas with adequate reinforcements, he assures his audience that King had reports of "the terrible need for reinforcements" and that there was no reason for Ralston to have gone overseas to find out. He criticizes the CBC for presenting only the government's side of the reinforcement debate by broad-casting Ralston's address from Italy. (The *Globe and Mail* doesn't report a single word of the speech.) Charles P. McTague, national party chairman, also addresses the group, telling them he knows Smythe, "and I know that anything he said was prompted by the dictates of his conscience. I can't accept the things that have been said against him; neither can I accept the explanation of the govern-ment spokesman about army reinforcements."

At the October 5 war cabinet meeting, King continues to meet with frustration in making the departments of navy and air under-stand that Canada will not be waging an extensive campaign in the Pacific. The situation has been exacerbated by the drinking prob-lem of Chubby Power, which has essentially incapacitated him for a critical week when the Smythe controversy is boiling and Ralston is overseas. That morning, a drunken Power gave well-oiled inter-views to the press, and *obviously went so far that all could see that he was the worst for liquor and efforts had to be made with the press men to hold back some of the things he had said.* Without Ralston around, the situation is very embarrassing. On top of this, King finds himself learning of the navy's plans through alternative channels—that the British government is proceeding with plans for the South Pacific under the assumption that Canadian ships would be available. Had he not learned through cabinet secretary Arnold Heeney that approval had already been given by Vice-Admiral Percy Nelles, chief of the Canadian naval mission in London, King would not have been able to question the department, through Macdonald, on the very issue.

King at least finds C.D. Howe solidly on his side. *Ilsley professed to be equally so on matters of cutting down expenditures, but later when I spoke of both lives and expenditures being involved, he said the additional expenditures would not amount to much. He is not a good Minister of Finance. What irritated me most of all was Ilsley's argument he wanted to fight the ships anywhere and be at it at once, and made a long screed of not being willing to have the navy kept idle, month after month, year after year.*

King is benefited in his arguments by the presence of his new military secretary to the war cabinet, Lieutenant-General Maurice Pope. Ralston placed him in his new role in late August, recalling him from Washington, where he had been in charge of the Canadian military mission, liaising at a high level with British and American members of the Joint Chiefs of Staff. In his new role, Pope is also King's military staff officer and a member of the Chiefs of Staff Committee. King wants Pope to serve as someone he can seek advice from on military matters, as by his own admission to Pope in a meeting on August 30, he doesn't know anything about them. On policy and philosophy, they are a perfect match. Pope cannot see any sense in pursuing conscription, and he feels Canada's involvement in, or absence from, the Allied effort in the Pacific will make no difference in the outcome of the fighting in that theatre. In this meeting he supports King's position on the Pacific war completely and, as King notes admiringly, lucidly. To no avail. *But Ilsley would pay no attention. Macdonald would not concede that the policy was settled.* King finds their behaviour unpardonable. He finally leaves the council chamber rather than argue with these cabinet members.

King's control of the policy agenda is becoming precarious. He now sees a navy striving to fight the war the way it wants to, with or without his approval. There is little he can do about setting figures for the air force with Power laid out by drink. And Ralston is overseas, hounded by Drew, Smythe and Bracken and the conscriptionist cause, which is vigorously promoted by the conservative press. Typical is the editorial supporting the charges of Smythe and Drew published by the *Globe and Mail* on October 7, which offers an unqualified salute to the genius of George Drew. The premier, the *Globe* explains, has made a close study of military matters, prior to his service in the Great War and since then. "He is generally considered to be one of the best informed civilians on Canada's army."

The tub thumping of Drew prompts the return to the front lines of politics of former Ontario premier Mitchell Hepburn. Speaking at the annual dinner of the Aberdeen Angus Breeders Association in London, Ontario, on October 6, the Liberal leader who resigned as premier in October 1942 voices his fear of a growing racial hatred in the country as English Canada sours on Quebec. "I hold no issue with the Liberal government in Ottawa," he tells the cattle people. "My grievance is with the Drew government in Toronto which I believe is attempting to breed racial disunity in Canada." He admits he often criticized the policies of the King government while premier, "which I believe to be the privilege and duty of every Canadian citizen," but he had hesitated to re-enter politics until he heard the "uncompromising, arbitrary attitude of Premier Drew" toward the people of Quebec in the debates over King's family allowance policy.

Therein lies the possibility that the conscription crisis is about far more than conscription. As an issue, it could merely be serving as a Trojan Horse in a right-wing political campaign. People will support the Conservatives on the conscription issue and help defeat the Liberals in the process. Once they have gained power, the Conservatives can move against their true target, the Liberal social reforms.

On October 8, Defence Minister Ralston flies to Brussels, at his back the incessant public harangue of the conscriptionists and the promise of disaster in the Canadian volunteer army.

INTO THE BREACH

October 6, 1944

MONTGOMERY has gambled and lost. Having secured Brussels and then Antwerp on September 3 and 4, the Allied ground commander had Germany's Fifteenth Army on the run, in full retreat. Antwerp, the massive Belgian port forty miles from the North Sea, was taken so quickly by Montgomery's forces that the Germans didn't have the chance to sabotage the enormous dock facilities and lock systems. It is an invaluable asset for moving men and supplies to the advancing Allied armies, but it can only be used if the Germans are cleared from both banks of its link to the sea, the West Scheldt, which flows westward through the mud and reclaimed farms of Zeeland to the North Sea.

Prudence would dictate that Montgomery turn his forces west and clear the Scheldt, but instead he conceives a more audacious plan—to advance instead in one fell swoop northeast to Arnhem, using British and American paratroopers to leapfrog ahead and secure bridgeheads over the Maas, the Waal and the Rhine. In one strike, he can cut off German access to the North Sea. He can seal off the Rhine, the main artery of the Ruhr Valley and of such great German cities as Cologne and Dusseldorf. It is a master stroke that could accelerate the end of the war in Europe, perhaps even avoid a winter campaign, and Eisenhower accedes to Montgomery's vision.

When Montgomery's grand scheme known as Market Garden fails, when ten thousand men are killed, wounded or captured, not having dealt with the Scheldt at the first opportunity is proved to have been an enormous blunder. The optimism expressed at Octagon that victory was imminent has proved groundless, mainly because the Allies have tried to rely on a supply line fed from the Normandy beaches rather than from a major port. There simply hasn't been enough fuel to keep the Allied armies moving forward.

As Channel ports are wrested back from the Germans, some relief is provided. Ostend, captured on September 9, becomes operational September 28, but it is hardly enough to feed an army. Boulogne, captured on September 23, will not become operational until October 12. Calais, retaken on September 30, will not be operational until October 21.

As Montgomery passed on the opportunity to chase the retreating Germans from the Zeeland, and Market Garden misfired, the Germans were able to regroup and re-establish their fortified western front of 1940, the Siegfried Line, and in the process dig in around the Scheldt with hardened troops from the eastern front. Now desperate to open sea access to Antwerp, the port he needs to keep the offensive rolling, Montgomery must clear a Scheldt fortified by an entrenched German army, not a German army dazed and in flight. To do so, he must drive the Germans from the islands of Walcheren and South Beveland, which control the north shore of the West Scheldt, and from the Breskens pocket, the sprawl of water, mud, dykes, canals and reclaimed farmland all along the south bank known to the Germans as Scheldt Fortress South. And to achieve that objective, Montgomery looks to the men of the First Canadian Army.

The Scheldt estuary is as forbidding a terrain as any invading force has encountered. It will be a costly battle all round. On October 3, as a prelude to the Canadian assault, bombers breach more than 100 yards of dykes on the main island of Walcheren; the flooding kills 125 residents. For the next month, Allied aircraft will drop more than eight thousand tons of bombs on Walcheren.

The 3rd Canadian Infantry Division is given the south bank assignment, known as Operation Switchback. It opens on October 6 with the 7th Canadian Infantry Brigade moving north across the Belgian–Dutch border from Maldegem to secure a bridgehead over the Leopold Canal. On October 9, Major Joe King and the rest of the Highland Light Infantry join the other regiments of the 9th Canadian Infantry—the Stormont, Dundas and Glengarry Highlanders of eastern Ontario and the North Nova Scotia Highlanders—in an amphibious assault on the south bank of the West Scheldt between Terneuzen and Breskens, opposite Walcheren. The HLI hold a sector of the beachhead perimeter for several days, repulsing a German counterattack, and then press on to take the town of Schoondijke, which occupies an important lateral road south of Breskens. They then lead the charge on a coastal fort further east.

Making their way over dunes to within 150 yards of the German stronghold, the HLI bring up self-propelled guns and flame throwers to drive off the defenders.

To the north on October 6, the 2nd Canadian Infantry Division begins Operation Vitality, its assault on South Beveland, which stands between Walcheren and the mainland. The island delivers some of the bleakest moments of the war for Canadians. On October 13, a day thereafter known as Black Friday, the Black Watch, aka the Royal Highland Regiment of Montreal, sees every company commander killed or wounded in a daylight assault across 1,200 yards of beet fields. (Back on July 25, when Conn Smythe was wounded in the opening hours of Operation Spring, the Black Watch was virtually annihilated, suffering 307 casualties among its 325 men in an assault on Verrières south of Caen. For the second time since D-Day, the Black Watch has essentially ceased to exist as a fighting unit.) Losses are heavy as well for Toronto's Royal Regiment of Canada, the Royal Hamilton Light Infantry, the Calgary Highlanders and Les Fusiliers Mont-Royal. Not until October 24 has the isthmus linking South Beveland and, by extension, Walcheren, with the mainland been secured. The final assault on Walcheren remains, and there is still more than a week of fighting to come before the 3rd Canadian Infantry Division meets the objectives of Switchback.

In October, all across Canada, hockey players are engaging in their annual ritual of fighting for a job known as training camp. The buildup to the new NHL season is remarkably quick by the standards of the eighty-plus-game campaigns that will come. The playoffs ended last April and in the intervening months the newspapers have concerned themselves with other athletic pursuits. Professional baseball is wrapping up another precarious wartime season, its player supply greatly depleted by men either volunteering or being drafted as the United States fights a war in two theatres, Europe and the Pacific. There is no distinction between home defence and combat duty with the American draft, no equivalent of Canada's maligned Zombies. But with some 40 per cent of professional baseball players continuing to shag flies and hit grounders through medical deferrals, a scandal is lying in wait for American sport as their country sends its soldiers, airmen and sailors into a series of bloody campaigns over the winter of 1944/45.

With training camps opening, in a little more than two efficient weeks the NHL teams will hone starting lineups and begin their fifty-game schedules, which will wrap up in late March. The Leafs, Canadiens, Blackhawks, Red Wings, Rangers and Bruins will be rotating among each other's arenas in a parade of railway cars and one night stands, often sharing the same train, sometimes playing back-to-back home-and-away matches—Toronto in Detroit one night, Detroit in Toronto the next.

Wartime train scheduling meant that regular-season overtime was dropped on November 21, 1942. Quality players became so hard to come by that season for some franchises that the rule calling for a team to dress a minimum of twelve players for a game was dropped, and the dressed-to-play maximum (exclusive of goaltenders) was reduced from fifteen to fourteen players. To run the NHL in 1944/45, the six teams collectively need to be able to ice about ninety players, less if teams feel particularly hard pressed. Before 1942/43, when the player limit had not been reduced and the Americans franchise was still alive, at least 112 men appeared in NHL rinks.

Conn Smythe's Toronto Maple Leafs have as much depth of talent as any NHL club during wartime, but when they open their training camp for the new season in Owen Sound, Ontario, on October 10, they are without a major-league goaltender. Turk Broda is playing hockey and softball with Canadian army teams in England; last season the Leafs had the services of Paul Bibeault, on loan from the Canadiens, but this year Montreal, which also opens its training camp today, is unwilling to make a deal for him without hefty concessions from Toronto. Bibeault made the second All-Star team, and for this season Dick Irvin allows that he wants two outstanding Leaf properties in return, Bob Goldham and Gaye Stewart, both currently playing with fellow Leafs Joe Klukay and Jackie Hamilton (who was with the Leafs in 1943/44) on the HMCS *Cornwallis* team in the Halifax defence league. The price is too high. Leaf acting general manager Frank Selke gibes, "We might match Dick's bidding by offering to trade one of our stick boys for Maurice Richard." Leaf coach Hap Day is not enthusiastic about the proposal—his youngest son Kerry is the current stick boy.

In a telegram to *Globe* columnist Jim Coleman, published on October 10, Canadiens general manager Tommy Gorman whimsically attempts to project a state of chaos on the Montreal lineup as training camp opens. "Probable personnel of Canadiens as follows: Goal, the Lone Ranger; defense, Jesse James and the Green

Hornet; forwards, the Angel, Trigger, Silver, Gen. Custer, Buffalo Bill, Sherlock Holmes, Foxie Quiller, Steve Brodie and Luke McLuke, the man who stole second base with the bases filled."

But the scramble for players is not nearly as desperate as Gorman would like people to think. The Canadiens are able to ice virtually the same lineup in 1944/45 that won them the Stanley Cup last spring. And in the midst of an apparent crisis in military manpower, the National Hockey League overall benefits from the return to play of former Canadian military personnel whose services are no longer judged necessary. Many of these are returning as the navy and air force make their cuts. Nick Metz, who played with Victoria Army in the 1943 Allan Cup finals against the Ottawa Commandos, has received an honourable discharge after two years of service and will be back in the Leaf lineup; before the season is out the Leafs will also re-acquire Wally Stanowski, who starred with the Winnipeg Bombers RCAF team. The most important return to active duty for the Leafs is veteran star centre Sweeney Schriner. When he went back to Calgary after the 1942/43 season, he explains, he encountered rumours that married men up to age thirty-five were about to be drafted under the NRMA. Rather than end up a Zombie, and already inclined to retire from hockey because of a family illness and income tax burdens, he volunteered for service with the navy. The call-up of married men he feared did not come until after D-Day, and has been limited to men age 31 or less. After a winter of playing hockey for the navy in Calgary in the Alberta Services Senior League, and with Prime Minister King cutting back the navy's size, Schriner was discharged.

One player not returning to the Toronto lineup is Syl Apps, a man who has come to symbolize everything that is good and decent and courageous and inspiring about the Maple Leafs. The very first story about Syl Apps and Conn Smythe is set some time in the mid-1930s, probably the autumn of 1935, when Ted Kennedy was nine and Charlie Conacher was the young Kennedy's god and in his prime. It was a sobering time for Smythe. The country was deep in the Depression. That August, Smythe's party, the Conservatives of R.B. Bennett, were swept from office in Ottawa by the Liberals of that despised pragmatist William Lyon Mackenzie King. At Queen's Park, the Liberals of Mitchell Hepburn held sway over the province, having come to power in 1934 with promises of taking on the "big shots."

The Depression was hard on hockey. There were ten teams in the

National Hockey League in 1929. Philadelphia came and went, and in the previous season the venerable Ottawa Senators were finally lost for good after their one-year reincarnation as the St. Louis Eagles. The New York Americans hadn't made the playoffs in five seasons, and were about to be taken over by the league as a charity case in an effort to stave off their inevitable collapse. The Montreal Maroons were in such bad shape that they would be gone after three more seasons. The Canadiens were slipping badly. They would win only eleven of their forty-eight games that season, moving the league to give them first right of refusal on the services of French-Canadian players for the next three seasons.

The Maple Leaf team was a frustrating underachiever. It produced All-Stars and scoring champions and finished regularly on top of its division, but in the playoffs it either made an early exit or wilted in the finals. Smythe's frustration with some of his players was building; perhaps his confidence in coach Dick Irvin began to waver. He came to dislike his scoring stars, Busher Jackson and Charlie Conacher. Their playmaking centre, Joe Primeau, was about to retire to concentrate on his cement block company as well as to coach. Smythe would later pronounce Jackson and Conacher overrated and lazy, content to let Primeau do all the work. The word on Jackson was that if he didn't score early in the game, he wasn't much use for the rest of it. In the autumn of 1935, Smythe still must have thought well of the irascible Conacher, a hard-living charismatic star who would serve as team captain in 1938/39. But Smythe would come to avow that the Leafs, in this long and fruitless period, were cursed by some players who were inclined to base their careers on collecting their bonus money on regular-season performances, who did not have the intestinal fortitude to then bring the club a championship. He will do everything in his power to keep Conacher and Jackson out of the Hall of Fame. They will finally make it, but in Jackson's case not until five years after he has died, drunk and dissolute.

Smythe's stalwarts were coming to the end of the line. His great defenceman, King Clancy, thirty-two, had little more than one season left in him. His captain, left-winger Hap Day, was fast running out of steam; he was thirty-four years old that autumn. Day's last great season was 1933/34, and in his final 180 games in the league, as he shifted to defensive duties, he scored six times. Smythe indicated to him that it was time to retire by dealing him to the ghastly Americans in 1937. His goaltender, George Hainsworth, who didn't even turn pro until he was twenty-nine, was forty years old and about to play his last full season.

The new season may have been under way when Conn Smythe came to Varsity Stadium to watch the rugby players of his alma mater, the University of Toronto, take on their counterparts from McMaster University. At the time McMaster, located forty miles away in the steel town of Hamilton, was a Baptist institution. One could not imagine a cleaner living bunch of young men slugging it out on the pitch. Smythe was impressed with the performance of one McMaster player, who was kicking, passing, running almost at will through the double blue. I wonder, Conn Smythe said to his wife in this story, if that boy can play hockey.

Here is another story about Syl Apps and Conn Smythe. When he asked around and discovered the young man's identity, Smythe quipped: Nobody named Sylvanus can play hockey.

Well, of course, he could play hockey. He had played three years of Intermediate hockey at McMaster, and that very season made his Senior league debut with the Hamilton Tigers. There was nothing he could not do with the puck. He could score, skate and make plays. He could also lead by inspiration and example. He just didn't fight, fighting being an unseemly vice. He was a Hap Day reborn. Apps was a lean six-footer, about 175 pounds, exquisitely built, powerful, one of those almost effortlessly gifted people like Joe King who need only select a sport to excel in it. In 1934, at the age of nineteen, he won the British Commonwealth pole vaulting title, and he would represent Canada in the event at the 1936 Olympics in Berlin. Conn Smythe sought out Syl Apps, proposing that he become a Maple Leaf.

Syl Apps's life offered two paradoxical avenues of employment: as a Baptist preacher, or as a professional hockey player. The ties between God and goal-scoring were not so obscure or absurd: there is nothing necessarily contradictory about faith and athletics, especially not on a hockey team run by Conn Smythe. Apps is the antithesis of Conacher and Jackson. He never smokes or drinks, and he certainly does not curse—not even so much as a damn. "Gollygosh" and "By hum" are Appsian outbursts. He is Smythe's Gordon of Khartoum, who was idealized and exalted among the boys of the Empire when Smythe was growing up—the warrior leader whose brilliance in combat is rooted in his Christian devotion as he smites the heathen enemy. But Apps is neither above nor apart from the rest of the team. He enjoys its camaraderie, its tomfoolery, the jokes (when they are clean ones); he laughs readily, and sits in on the card games (when the game is rummy, not poker). On a visit to the Empire State Building, Conacher grabs the fedora of his captain and flings it off the observation deck in an impetuous attempt to make a dent in Apps's perfection. He is so clean-living, so morally upstanding, that he can intimidate even Smythe. He didn't register a single penalty minute in 1941/42, and only one minor penalty in 1942/43. After breaking his leg in a game in January 1943 and missing the rest of the season, Apps went to Smythe and tried to give back $1,000 of his salary. Smythe turned him down, reasoning that anyone so principled and dedicated would make up the lost wages in effort when he returns to the ice.

Syl Apps's faith is divorced from mortal power and authority. Baptism is not anarchic, merely pledged to be unbeholden. Church and state have nothing to do with one another. With war declared in 1939, Baptists responded to the conflagration as a moral crusade, not one of politics or empire. When Conn Smythe veritably ordered his players to join the local militia in September 1940, in part for them to avoid being called up in mid-season under the NRMA, in part as a show of solidarity with the perils faced by the British empire, Syl Apps, as captain of the team, would have enlisted with a private sense of obligation—perhaps in some part to Smythe and the team, but in greater part to the defence of decency and goodness. Syl Apps would have heard the same call to arms that Conn Smythe heard, but it must have played different notes to him.

Defence Minister Ralston, who sits on the board of McMaster University, played such notes in an address to a Baptist convention in Hamilton on June 9, 1942. He began by reflecting on his own Baptist roots: 104 years earlier, his ancestor William Ralston walked seventy-five miles from Westchester to Chester in Nova Scotia to attend such a convention. "I cannot help thinking of what a Baptist Convention would be like in Germany or what a Baptist Convention in Canada would be like if Hitler were in charge," he told the assembled faithful. "Here we have the zest of free association and the stimulation of exchanging views and ideas, without let or hindrance. We have the assurance that, within the law, and that law is made by ourselves, we may think and speak and act, none daring to make us afraid. We have been taking those privileges for granted and I want to tell you, my friends, and I think you know without any telling that we can't take them for granted any longer.... Baptists must be in the forefront in every activity of this fight to save the world from slavery."

Apps was having what was likely the greatest season of his career, with forty points in only twenty-nine games, when he broke his leg. He considered that his professional career, after seven seasons and a Stanley Cup in 1942, might be over. In any event the days of the warrior athlete were over, now that there was de facto war. In 1942 Toronto sportswriters shelved for the remainder of the war the annual conferral of its Lou Marsh Trophy, bestowed upon the Canadian athlete of the year. In September 1943, Syl Apps suspended his term as captain of the Leafs, and at twenty-eight, a husband and father of three, volunteered for active duty in the Canadian army.

He was penned into the lineup of the Toronto Army Daggers. Then came the Broda scandal and the decision to pull the Daggers from OHA Senior competition before the season had even started. Sylvanus Apps did not simply attach himself to another army hockey team. Instead, he completed basic training, played a bit of hockey along the way, and headed to Officers' Training Corps in Brockville, to effect the transformation from warrior in spirit to warrior in fact that Smythe had desired of his Maple Leafs.

FLAK has not shied away from addressing the Zombie issue. Editor S.E. Higgs took great umbrage in the August 18 issue at a Canadian Press item stating: "The Canadian Army which has remained inactive in Britain for a lengthy period before entering the European campaign, may be the first of the three Dominion services to see large-scale southwest Pacific action." The idea that the active army could have been considered "inactive" during its time in camps in England offended Higgs, and it begged a comparison with the contribution made to the war effort by the NRMA men during the same years.

"We may be dumb," Captain Higgs responded, "but frankly we don't see the point. What is the difference in being entirely inactive in Canada for five years, and being inactive in Britain? To us here a hell-uv-a-lot, with the comparison no credit to the Zombies. Inactive my foot! Ever counted the homes and next-of-kin struck off strength due to our too long absence from home? Ever seen the Canadian graves due to the Battle of Britain? And what of the Canadians in Sicily who helped crack the door to Hitler's Europe.

"Canada in our generation is grievously divided—the broad cleavage is between the privileged conscript and the penalized volunteer. The wound may yet prove mortal to the future of our country.

"The remedy is clear. When Germany is defeated, bring Canada's five fighting divs home and send the Zombies to the Pacific to fight for the country they love so much and are, it seems, reluctant to leave."

But *FLAK* is all but silent on the subject of Major Smythe's public outburst over reinforcements and Zombies. The only recognition of Smythe's campaign comes in an aside in a piece penned by Lance-Bombardier Peter White, Jr. in the October 8 edition, which appears on a Sunday morning in Belgium on the eve of the 9th Infantry Brigade's amphibious assault on the south bank of the West Scheldt. "I'm not sure whether it has been prompted by the dynamite publicly and recently exploded by a member of the Regiment [ie. Smythe], or by the thoughtful and thought-provoking words of the Padre this morning on civic consciousness and responsibility, or his suggestion to address to *FLAK*, thoughts on what may be termed the Battle of Canada—a subject vitally concerning each of us, and certainly capable of withstanding fresh ideas, whatever their origin. Here, at any rate, are mine.

"This spate of verbiage I'll admit quite frankly, is selfishly intended to conduct into channels useful to Canada, both as a country and a nation, the best parts of the lessons our Service has taught us. Some, indeed many, doubt that such Service has taught us anything.

"For these, to state my case only partially, attention need only be called to the unfamiliar parts and peoples of Canada, as well as other portions of the globe, to which service has brought us. Think of the ideas exchanged, the friendships now formed, the customs and manners of life observed—none of which would have been possible for many of us, apart from such Service.

"For me, the greatest experience has been to see and hear Canadians from the West, the East, the centre, from farm and city, from all walks of life, getting along with the job together, sharing troubles and what minor triumphs have come our way.

"This leads me to believe, more vividly than ever before, in the future of Canada as a nation, progressive and united. I believe too, in the ability of Canadians to overcome the difficulties of prejudice, be it sectional, religious, lingual or racial—providing that the proviso looms large, the lessons of army life have been well learned and are properly applied.

"Earlier, I used the word 'selfishly,' and I mean just that. It seems to me that not only the negative side of public consciousness should be stirred, so that no crime, vagrancy, V.D. or other public liabilities should be imported to our Canada, but its positive side as well. The assets of army life, lessons briefly touched on previously, should be introduced into Canadian life. The active participation in public life, be it civic, provincial or federal, of soldiers long after service has ended, is the only way these lessons can be permanently applied. This will result inevitably in a better life for all of us, hence it may be called 'selfish' from that point of view.

"We must, however, not lose sight of the fact that we have been away from Canada for some time, and are not quite up to date on all Canadian problems and opinion. Nor must we forget that we are but a small part of our nation, some of whom, to be fair, have had to stay home not entirely from choice. They too will have something to contribute to the successful conclusion of the Battle of Canada...."

Bombardier Geoff Archer, wounded along with Smythe on the night of July 24–25, is still in hospital in England when his major's campaign against the government and the Zombies begins making headlines. His family sends him newspapers, and by nature he is inclined to read the editorial page before the sports page. Smythe's outburst surprises him not at all. Archer knows he is a powerful man, that people will listen to him and that others, influential, will back him. The dislike of the Zombies is deep-seated and longstanding in the volunteer ranks. Even in the battery's earliest days, when the men were sent to Brantford for basic training alongside the NRMA conscripts, the Zombies were marked men. In a scene repeated at training bases all across the country, volunteers would be told that they could have a weekend off if they could persuade the conscripts training alongside them to go active. Naturally the persuasion sometimes turned physical. That was the way it was. By the time the active army gets into combat, and the volunteers see friends killed or wounded, units drop below strength, and cooks and clerks turn into combat troops with all possible speed, their exasperation with the conscripts is well honed. As Archer will recall, the general feeling is: What are we over here fighting for? Is it for those guys?

There is a sense of unreality creeping into their circumstances. Archer hears Mackenzie King deliver a radio speech in which he assures listeners that Canadians are in no danger from the German buzz bombs, and at the very moment King is talking, he can hear a buzz bomb through the hospital window. During one such attack, a few fellow patients gathered at his bed playing hearts run for cover. As the only one in the ward who cannot get out of bed, Archer is left by himself to be cut by flying glass as a window explodes.

Regret is the first thing Prime Minister William Lyon Mackenzie King expresses to Defence Minister James Layton Ralston; regret that he must trouble him with the matter referred to in the accompanying telegram, but he knows Ralston will understand the unfortunate reasons making it impossible for the acting minister, C.G. Power, to deal with it. Poor Chubby: waylaid by drink again. King doesn't even have to breathe a word of the mitigating circumstances: *unfortunate reasons* covers it nicely.

Ralston is on his way from Brussels to Antwerp by motor car to visit the First Canadian Army there when King's message, sent on October 9, is received on October 10. And therewith King deposits the nasty mess of Conn Smythe, George Drew and John Bracken in Ralston's lap. "I think it would be unwise for me to be drawn into any controversy so completely within the purview of the Defence Department," King explains. What he does not say is that said department to date has made a hash of dealing with Smythe's charges. Ever since Ralston approved the bland and unsigned response of September 20, the Smythe charges have indeed, as Ralston's staff secretary James Wells suggested on October 7, snowballed. They might be approaching the proportions of an avalanche that could bury King and his government. It is time for Ralston to take responsibility for damage control.

King reviews the situation for his defence minister. "As you have probably heard the Premier of Ontario, on his return from overseas, at once endorsed the charges by Major Smythe that untrained men were being sent as reinforcements to the Army. Mr. Drew wrote to me last week stating that he knew the facts disclosed in Smythe's statement were correct and asking what action the Dominion Government intended to take in dealing with the urgent need for trained reinforcements. The letter was acknowledged and passed on to Power for reply. In his reply Power stated that it was the responsibility of the Government of Canada through the Departments of National Defence to maintain the Armed Services at their full efficiency and added that the Government had discharged and would continue to discharge that duty in the light of its responsibility to Parliament and to the Canadian people. He refrained from making any statement bearing more directly on the point."

King then quotes from Drew's speech made in Hamilton: "I was visited to-day by a number of young officers and men who are determined to tell their own story of the ghastly need for reinforcements.

If Mr. King wants to know where I got my information I can tell him. It was from officers and men of the Royal Hamilton Light Infantry and other units. I can give the names of the units and the places where they were short. But Mr. King knows the terrible need for reinforcements in France and Italy. He has had reports and I know it.

"James Layton Ralston didn't need to go to Italy to find it out. And the Canadian Broadcasting Corporation didn't need to play its constant game of presenting the Government's side by broadcasting a speech by Ralston from Italy to the whole of Canada aimed at showing there was no need of reinforcements. By all means let there be an investigation but let there be no delay in sending reinforcements to the fronts. They need them now and they need them badly, not only as to numbers, but as to trained men. And it doesn't have to wait for Mr. Ralston's return."

King also provides for Ralston a quote from Drew's speech to the Canadian Corps Association—which, that very day, is rallying to the cause of its member Major Smythe by passing a resolution demanding that the government make effective immediately the plebiscite mandate of 1942 and send the Zombies overseas. "The man who bears the heaviest load of guilt for this shameful situation," Drew told the CCA gathering, "is James Layton Ralston. His word has been accepted because of his record in the last war. He was a very gallant soldier who did not hesitate to express his belief in those days that men who were fit to fight should be compelled to bear arms in battle. Because of his bravery in action and because of the stand he took at that time he has been trusted. He has betrayed that trust."

Smythe, King notes, has repeated his charges and provided a list of units to which untrained reinforcements were sent, a list King encloses. He explains, "An effective reply to these charges was made by a private individual named Mrs. Kenneth Blois, whose husband was recently killed in France, but this is the only reply I have seen which has been accorded any real publicity." King provides a few quotes for Ralston's edification, among which is

> Major Smythe's charges...raise only one issue, namely, should Generals Stuart and Crerar be removed. Are they guilty of the crime of throwing unprepared troops into action? Are they incompetent Commanders? Is the Canadian public to believe that our Army is led by irresponsible and utterly untrustworthy men? That is the question and there is

no getting away from it. It is either General Stuart and General Crerar and the other responsible general officers of the Canadian Army or Major Smythe.

As a test of confidence Major Smythe's charges are not an issue of politics. It is not a case of Major Smythe versus the Government. The Government comes into the matter only indirectly, to remove the Commanders if Major Smythe's charges are true. The test of confidence is between Major Smythe and General Crerar who commands the Canadian Army, and who decides what, when and where our troops go into action.

I regard as contemptible and despicable the spreading of terrible charges against the men leading our Army in battle by one who does not give a single fact to support such charges.

If political protection can make it possible to attack the Army Command with impunity then military discipline will cease to exist in the Canadian Army. I think this can be the only result of the partisan campaign around Major Smythe's charges.

King notes that "in the light of what Mrs. Blois has said would it not be wise to have a statement come from Stuart and Crerar."

"For obvious reasons I have refrained from entering into controversy with Drew. Unfortunately there is no one else who can reply with sufficient authority except yourself.

"The impression Drew is seeking to create is that untrained reinforcements have to be sent into action because there is a shortage of men overseas with adequate training while adequately trained men are being kept in Canada because they have not volunteered for general service. To meet Drew's point I believe the public must be assured that reinforcements are available in adequate numbers and have been available long enough to have time to receive proper training. Any apprehension as to the effect of such a statement on recruiting can surely be allayed by pointing out that recruits who enlist now are required to make sure there is no shortage some months hence if hostilities should be prolonged and that the need for recruits has obviously no bearing on the present position as to reinforcements.

"It is, I believe, of the greatest urgency that the present campaign should not continue unchecked and that you should take the earliest opportunity to make an authoritative statement."

Ralston has been handed the most forbidding assignment. King has made it clear, by quoting Drew, that the time has come for Ralston to defend his own reputation, and he expects him in the process to restore the reputation of his government. To do so, he must refute all of Smythe's and Drew's allegations—that reinforcements are green and inexperienced, and that the conscripts must be sent in. But surely by now, his experiences in Italy fresh and haunting, Ralston believes that the Zombies are precisely what are needed. And in the battle raging in the Scheldt, evidence is mounting that the reinforcements aren't up to the job. Joe King's Highland Light Infantry has its commanding officer pulled out of the fight and sent to England to help with reinforcement training. The Regina Rifles, fighting to hold the bridgehead across the Leopold Canal, suffer heavy losses and are discouraged by the quality of the men sent from reinforcement camps. "All through October 9 and 10 it was the same heartbreaking story," the regiment's history will relate. "The reinforcements that arrived, through no fault of their own, were inexperienced and had been quickly trained. Many of them had been clerks, drivers and gunners. It should be said to their credit that they did a magnificent job under a serious handicap." The days of relying on volunteer reinforcements, it would seem, are over.

The war has been a political challenge for the CCF, which began the war under longstanding leader J.S. Woodsworth in a strictly pacifist mood, opposed to conscription, unhappy in general with the country going to war. Woodsworth's resignation after the 1940 election brought in M.J. Coldwell as leader, and the party began to tone down its anti-capitalist rhetoric. Equally important to its political survival, as the war has progressed and proved, if not popular, then at least right and necessary with the vast majority of English Canada, the CCF has striven to appear supportive of the men overseas without wavering on its opposition to conscription, no matter how keen the public seems to be to send in the Zombies.

Electorally, the country's only socialist-minded party has done well in the war years. In the Ontario election of August 1943, the CCF finished ahead of the Liberals, winning thirty-four of eighty-seven seats as George Drew's Conservatives came to power with a minority government supported by the Liberals. Although the CCF only won eight seats in the 1940 federal election, one month after its breakthrough in the Ontario election of 1943 the CCF finished one point ahead of the Liberals and Conservatives in national popularity in a Gallup poll that indicated a virtual dead heat in the voter appeal of the leading parties. On June 11, 1944, the CCF gained power in Saskatchewan, its first provincial success. The Saskatchewan result prompted Mackenzie King to almost immediately introduce his family allowance program so as to position his Liberals as a reassuring alternative to voters who are debating supporting a full-blown left-wing party in the next federal election. The initiative backed the Progressive Conservatives into a strategic corner. Already hampered by the fact that their lacklustre party leader, John Bracken, was still without a seat in Parliament after gaining control of the party in 1942, the Conservatives had to choose between supporting a popular initiative, which would guarantee a continuation of King's Liberal dynasty in the next election, and standing opposed, which would alienate its supporters in the middle of the political spectrum.

To its critics, the Conservatives have chosen the most cynical possible path—demonizing Quebec to curry favour with reactionaries in English Canada. Toronto Conservative Herbert Bruce has portrayed the family allowance plan, given Quebec's high birthrate and importance as a wellspring of Liberal power, as "bonusing families who have been unwilling to defend their country." With one statement, Bruce managed to transmogrify Conservative opposition to social programs into a patriotic stance against the anti-conscriptionists of Quebec. The Conservative strategy, if it can be called that, is well timed—the family allowance plan came before Parliament on July 25 at the height of the fighting around Caen, just when Conn Smythe was wounded. Canadian soldiers are dying, and English Canada is warming to the idea of sending in the conscripts. The Conservatives are happy to make political mileage out of the issue, as they have virtually no standing in Quebec and no intention of establishing one in the next election.

The CCF is equally prepared to make an issue of conscription, in their case striving to oppose it. The party's grass roots in the Canadian prairies draws on an oft-overlooked anti-conscription sentiment at times as vigorous as that of Quebec. If French Canadians felt betrayed by Borden's introduction of conscription in 1917, prairie farmers felt doubly so. Conservatives had promised them they would not in introducing conscription take away their sons and young hands who were critical to bringing in the harvest, but once they brought in conscription and won the December 1917 election, they did just that, passing an order-in-council that erased all court-supported exemptions in the spring of 1918. Twenty-six years later, the CCF has been able to maintain an anti-conscription policy based in part on those long memories, although by the fall of 1944 the party is no longer categorically opposed to the use of conscripts. It comes up with a conscription policy based on "equality of sacrifice," which holds that if young men are to be compelled to participate in the war effort, then private wealth and industry should also be subject to compulsion. This, as it happens, was precisely the position put forward to King by the Canadian Corps Association on August 25, 1939.

The Quebec City newspaper *Le Soleil* finds great merit in the CCF's stance. "There cannot be equality of sacrifice if total conscription is imposed on young Canadians while rich men are free to do what they like with their wealth," it argues. "It is not known if a single big capitalist has pushed his patriotic devotion to the point of handing over all his fortune and his business undertakings so as to equal, as much as possible, the sacrifice of young Canadians who offered their lives for the cause of their country and its Allies. There has, therefore, been no equality of sacrifice in the voluntary system, and those who accept such a formula must begin by...ridding themselves of their material wealth, when they are not of an age to bear arms. What does Colonel Drew think of this idea?" There would appear to be little enthusiasm for this concept among Maple Leaf Gardens shareholders, for one. Gardens management has responded to the war by maintaining ticket prices, refusing special discounts, and even assembling a stable of military Senior clubs in 1942/43 and 1943/44 to put yet more paying customers in Gardens seats. There have been no financial sacrifices made by the men who own and run Major Smythe's garrison. In fact, business has never been better. Conn Smythe does not rush to *The Globe and Mail* a statement of congratulations to the CCF for adopting the Canadian Corps Association's conscription policy set down at the beginning of the war, which he personally reiterated in his telegram to King on June 18, 1940.

M.J. Coldwell makes his own tour of the battle front at the same time as J.L. Ralston. At a press conference on October 10 following his return to Ottawa, he professes not to have heard of Smythe's charges until he was home late the previous day. He had discussed manpower at II Canadian Corps headquarters in Belgium with its commander, Lieutenant-General Guy Simonds, the mastermind of the Scheldt offensive. "The corps commander said supplies were of excellent quality and that reinforcements were satisfactory. I never heard any complaints about reinforcements. We heard the usual queries about the fellows at home: When are they going to get over?" Coldwell's answer was in lock step with the position of King: "whenever it was necessary to win the war, we will send support."

It is as if Canada is fighting two different wars: one in which the volunteer system is working perfectly, another in which it is about to collapse.

❦

On October 11, the *Globe and Mail* letters page contains an item headed "Smythe's Mail Bag," which offers a letter of support for the major from a sergeant in hospital who was wounded at Falaise:

> This lad ankles up to us one day after climbing out of the truck from [Canadian Base Reinforcement Group] (this was before the attack at Falaise). Anyway, he comes up to the carrier and lolls around talking and asking questions. He pointed at a Bren and asked what kind of gun it was. Well, after I found out he wasn't kidding and I recovered myself, I showed him all I had learned about the weapons we handle. The next time I saw him he was in this same hospital as me with one arm off at the elbow. His story was, and he laughed as he told it, he meets a couple of Jerries in the town who were walking along armed. He was also armed with the Bren but when he went to fire on them the weapon was at 'safe' and before he had a chance to change it they saw him. Well, sir, I thought that pretty grim and you know, sir, as much about this sort of thing as I do. That's why you made that statement.

That evening, Ontario Liberal leader Harry Nixon announces in a thirty-minute CBC broadcast that his party has terminated its "political truce" with Drew. He criticizes what he calls Drew's effort to "pit race against race and Province against Province." Elsewhere that night, representatives of eighty-six labour unions in the Toronto area call upon the Liberals, CCF and Labour Progressives to call a special session of the legislature at once and defeat the minority Drew government. "Instead of the great forward-looking Ontario program of reconstruction we need," says M.R. Murdoch, president of Local 382 of the UAW (CIO),

"Premier Drew gives us a partisan campaign of hostility against our neighbours of Quebec, opposition to family allowances and health insurance, the stirring up of national and racial discord."

❧

Private Red Tilson, Oshawa Generals star of 1942/43 and Maple Leaf property, arrived in France on July 23. Two days later, he was awaiting assignment as Operation Spring began and Conn Smythe began his return to Canada as a casualty of the Luftwaffe.

Tilson was then spoken for by the Queen's Own Rifles of the 3rd Canadian Infantry Division's 8th Brigade. The QOR had been involved in uninterrupted and costly fighting since coming ashore at Bernières-sur-Mer in the first wave of invaders on June 6. Their Goodwood advance on July 18 resulted in hand-to-hand combat in Colombelles, in the industrial suburbs southeast of Caen across the Orne. They then fought their way into the town of Giberville; in all, Goodwood cost the QOR twenty-three killed and sixty-eight wounded. On July 21, they were ordered to the village of Grentheville to relieve the British armoured regiment that had taken it. They were patrolling there and taking cover from German shells when Tilson joined them on July 26.

That same day, the Queen's Own were relieved by the North Shore regiment; they began leaving Grentheville at midnight to take up a new position on Bourguébus Ridge. Their job was to hold it in advance of the assault at Falais, and in their five days in the position, the QOR had one rifleman killed and another ten wounded under shelling.

The 4th Canadian Armoured showed up on July 31, and the QOR were relieved by the Lincoln and Welland regiment—the regiment that had been under Smythe's command in Tofino in 1942. For the first time in fifty-six days, the Queen's Own were taken out of the fighting line, sent back north of Caen to a rest camp at Fontaine Henry.

Then came Operation Totalize on August 7. The QOR were moving back through Caen to the front when short bombing by the USAAF rained down on Canadians in the city; among the wounded were Major-General R.F.L. Keller, commander of the 3rd Canadian Infantry Division (wounded seriously enough to end his war), and two members of the Queen's Own. (The Chaudières had twenty men killed by this not infrequent instance of friendly fire; the incident caused about three hundred total casualties in Canadian and Polish ranks.)[1] On August 9, the QOR were ordered to take

Quesnay Woods, to clear the path for an assault by the 1st Polish Armoured Division attached to the First Canadian Army. It was the first truly calamitous action in which Private Tilson was involved. On the night of August 10–11, the Queen's Own had twenty-two men killed and sixty-eight wounded as they were driven back from their objective. In all, the Queen's Own and the North Shore suffered about two hundred casualties, many of the North Shore losses attributed to friendly fire from Canadian artillery.[2]

Tilson emerged from this action unscathed, and came through the battles to close the Falaise Gap on the retreating Germans and then to clear the French channel ports of Calais and Boulogne in September. He was a lance-corporal again, having received his promotion on August 28, before the port actions in September.

With the Germans driven from Calais and Boulogne, the Queen's Own were part of a convoy moving to Le Beau Marais, about four miles west of Calais, on October 2. As the convoy rolled, Lance-Corporal Tilson was attached to the headquarters of the 8th rather than the QOR specifically. The QOR moved to Kruipiut in Belgium on October 4, where they receive fresh orders: they are now to participate in Operation Switchback, clearing the south shore of the West Scheldt.

Joining Lance-Corporal Tilson and the thousands of other Canadian troops preparing for the Scheldt offensive is Rifleman Bob Carse. Having given up his hockey stick for a Bren gun in September 1943, the former Chicago Blackhawk arrived in France on September 25 and was taken on strength as a reinforcement by the Royal Winnipeg Rifles on October 2.

Carse was one of the most impressive volunteers to march through Calgary's Currie Barracks. On enlistment he was immediately considered "overseas material," possessing a host of desirable attributes. Having driven a truck for Edmonton's Canadian Bakeries for six months after graduating from high school, and having managed an Edmonton service station in his summers away from professional hockey, he was given training as a truck driver in addition to basic and advanced infantry training. "Youth has good physique and is a professional hockey player," read his assessment of March 13, 1944. "He is taking Basic at present and playing in Senior hockey team representing this centre. Of high learning ability." Because of his age and high physical and mental aptitude scores, Carse was recommended as a general reinforcement.

When his advanced training was completed on August 3, his

superiors were greatly impressed. "He has been highly commended by the O.C. of 'C' Company as being much interested in his training, cheerful, responsive and dependable. Evinces a good attitude to Service...." Carse was slated to go overseas in the next draft of reinforcements, but his superiors saw him as a future officer. His training reports were peppered with complimentary notes: "Good N.C.O. material"—"well liked, works hard"—"Outstanding attributes"—"Smart appearance. Sure of himself"—"A good leader"—"Stands up well"—"Shows intelligence"—"Conscientious"—"Robust and in good condition"—"Shows endurance". He had already begun an instructor's training course, and as such was a potential candidate for Officers Training Corps. "O.C. of 'C' company has designated [Carse] has leadership qualities and has been one of the best trainees in this Company." But the official interventions were disregarded in an army steadily drained of fighting men since going ashore at Juno Beach on June 6. Bren gunner Carse was shipped overseas on August 30.

In the second week of October, Red Tilson's Queen's Own Rifles and the other regiments of the 8th move up to the shore of the West Scheldt to the east of the fighting. Bob Carse's Royal Winnipeg Rifles, Regina Rifles and Canadian Scottish of the 7th have already been fighting for five costly days to secure a bridgehead from the south, across the Leopold Canal. After being relieved by a British division, the 7th moves around to the north and east, to the right flank of the Scheldt pocket, to cross the Braakman inlet ahead of the 8th. Before dawn on October 12, a platoon of nine men from the Winnipeg Rifles moves out ahead of the advance to secure a key crossroad west of the Braakman and await the arrival of reinforcements. Among the men is Rifleman Carse. At the end of the day, there is no sight or sound of Carse and his eight comrades. The entire platoon has disappeared into the mud and rain of the Scheldt.

J.L. Ralston visits his son Stuart, who is serving with the Canadian artillery in Belgium, then stops in a small cemetery at Caix on October 12 to visit the grave of his brother Ivan, who was killed in August 1918 as the Allies launched the final offensive that brought about the armistice that November. Afterward he flies to London with Colonel Dyde, where they are met by General Stuart. Ralston may well reflect on his pilgrimage to Caix, for General Stuart too lost a brother in that war—lost him utterly, for he could not find a stitch of him after searching the battlefield for days. Ralston takes dinner in his room, after which he, Stuart and Dyde have a conference, a main issue plainly the reinforcement situation. Dyde then walks home with Stuart, and as Dyde notes in his diary, "we had a chat about the reinforcement situation. I felt that when I left Gen. Stuart he had not fully made up his mind what recommendation he was going to make."

In the *Globe and Mail* that day, a letter in support of Smythe by Major John Spotton is published. Spotton returned to Canadian defence headquarters in 1943 as a technical staff officer, having commanded a battery of field artillery and then served as second-in-command of a field regiment overseas. Spotton tells *Globe* readers that poorly trained men are the issue:

> It is to be noted that the critics of Major Smythe are of the Canadian Home War Establishment (HWE), an organization that thinks, works and acts in an entirely different manner from the Army Overseas. In the Army Overseas "politics" does not exist—there is only a desire to get on with the war and get it over with. Such an attitude of mind simply would not be understood by the HWE where from my personal observation no action is ever taken or any decision made without full consideration of the "political" aspect of the situation, and where the war itself is treated as a secondary matter.
>
> The important point is that the Canadian Army Overseas has suffered and is suffering severe casualties. If these splendid men are not provided with proper reinforcements when they are known to be available and needless lives [*sic*] are sacrificed as a result there will be many, many people all across Canada who will not regard it in the light of "politics." The friends and relatives of the Army Overseas as well as the personnel of that Army itself will regard it as criminal negligence on the part of those responsible.

The idea of criminality takes hold with Conservative politicians, as two days later, on Saturday the fourteenth, Bracken, speaking in Alliston, Ontario, describes the alleged government policy of sending untrained men into action as "criminal folly." Chimes the *Globe* that day: "This is what it is."

The rhetoric on the pro-conscription side approaches a fever pitch. On Friday the *Globe and Mail* pronounces Drew to be "the most outstanding, most honest public man now holding office in Canada. He has the courage of his convictions, and has become the victim of violent, bitter and tarnished attacks by his political enemies…. His opposition to the King Government is specific. He has stated his position clearly about Quebec, the tail that wags the Canadian dog, and for this reason is the target of the forces combining against him."

The same edition of the newspaper contains a far more vitriolic attack on Quebec. A letter writer alleges that King "recruiting agents" have "invaded our secondary schools and snatched young boys from the cradle of learning" to "consign them to the graves of war in order to continue to appease the politically prostituted patriotism of Quebec's anti-British agitators and duty-dodgers…." This practice, he proclaims, "is a barefaced example of how so-called 'good intentions' can be used to camouflage the incompetence of power-crazed politicians.

"These anti-British slackers and separatists have, for much too long for the nation's good, been pampered and fattened upon the nitwit, hush-hush policy of political appeasers whose misleading slogan has been: 'Peace at Any Price on Behalf of Unity.'… Thank God for Major Conn Smythe and his fighting comrades, who by word and deed have said: 'The brave and willing may sacrifice and die, but the cowards and unwilling shall not inherit the earth…. It is the politically prostituted patriotism of the King Government and its Quebec-inspired Zombie army, and not Major Conn Smythe and his comrades of the active army, who menace both the moral and the physical well-being of our country and needlessly endanger the lives of our fighting men."

On Saturday, Drew further fuels the growing discord in central Canada. Having been criticized by Adelard Godbout, the former Liberal premier of Quebec, for his recent attacks on his province, Drew is anything but repentant. "If the rest of Canada is to bear a disproportionate share of winning the war, then at least the voice of the rest of Canada should be heard when Canadian units locked in mortal combat in the field of battle are without reinforcements because 80,000 trained men are held here in Canada by the will of one Province." Drew notes that in April Godbout's legislature unanimously voiced its "unyielding disapproval" of sending conscripts overseas. "I paid full tribute to the gallantry of those men from Quebec who have fought so magnificently in the army, the navy and the air force," Drew elaborates. "But all their gallantry only emphasizes the fact that the number of men from Quebec in the fighting services is pitifully small in proportion to their population."

Over in England, the crisis Mackenzie King has long feared gains momentum. If Colonel Dyde was unsure of General Stuart's position on using the conscripts last night, there is no doubt about it today. Before going into a cabinet meeting in the afternoon, King receives a telegram from Ralston *which has occasioned me great concern. It was in part a reply to my long message to him regarding Drew's statement. In part, an intimation that he was coming back with the intention of making proposals which may involve the whole question of conscription.* Ralston's telegram proposes he leave London on Sunday and bring Stuart with him; he asks for an early meeting of the cabinet, and notes that in the interim he will meet with General Crerar. King has a very good idea of what is coming. Ralston is prepared to argue before cabinet that the reinforcement situation is much more serious than thought, and that drastic steps will have to be taken to secure the necessary trained men. The number of available reinforcements will not be the issue—it will be the number of trained ones. *All of this of course will be an effort to have the NRMA men serve overseas.* King is not surprised. Ilsley has already said in cabinet that Ralston might be returning with some such suggestion. King suspects that the pro-conscriptionists in his government are still working together, in particular Macdonald and Ralston; perhaps Ilsley too, who in any case King feels is pretty certain to support anything Ralston suggests.

King sends for his Quebec lieutenant, Justice Minister Louis St. Laurent, and reads him Ralston's message. St. Laurent agrees the message is a cause for concern. Bringing in conscription now, King concludes, *would be a criminal thing, and would destroy the entire war record, as well as help to dismember the Empire, for I am certain that its after effects would be all in the direction of demand for complete independence [for Canada], if not annexation with the U.S. Anything to be separated from being involved in wars because of Britain's connection with them. I want to see the Empire endure. It can only endure by there being complete national unity in Canada. This is going to be a trying experience for me. Indeed, Ralston has been a thorn in my flesh right along. However, I have stood firm before and shall do so again.*

The Low Countries still have to be liberated; Antwerp is subjected to a new level of terror on October 13 as the first of a series of V1 flying bombs and V2 rockets begin raining down, killing forty-six civilians. The Americans are moving forcefully on Aachen, the first German city to face siege by Allied ground forces. That evening in London, Ralston, Stuart, Dyde and Brigadier W.H.S. Macklin work together on a draft statement responding to the Smythe–Drew allegations about the training of reinforcements. Its twenty-one-point counter-argument begins: "I have just returned from France and find another statement by the Premier of Ontario on the training of reinforcements, with a vicious attack on myself."

On the morning of the fourteenth, King wires Ralston back, telling him not to bother forwarding a draft of his statement since he is coming back sooner than planned. The urgency King expressed on October 9 for Ralston to reply promptly has faded; the reply he has drafted, as it happens, will never be made publicly. Ralston, effectively, has become for King a far more serious worry than Conn Smythe and George Drew. King's political skin has thickened against attacks from enemies. It is a revolution from within he cannot withstand. As King is steeling himself for Ralston's return, two German generals are handing Rommel a cyanide solution.

There is one note of good news for King on Saturday, the fourteenth. General McNaughton has written back to King, making himself "available to undertake the office you suggested." King is delighted. Canada can now look forward to having as her representative to the King one of her own citizens, *and he, one of the most distinguished in Canada's history*. King knows the appointment will create a sensation, here and in Britain, but he is sure it will be overwhelmingly approved at home. The days are over when Canada should have as its King's representative a member of the English nobility, *as if from among our own citizens, men of equal distinction and ability could not be found and trusted.*

Sunday brings snow, the news of Rommel's death, and within King a resolve to resist all efforts to introduce conscription. The tragedy of Arnhem is behind him; the suggestion in Churchill's speech that the war might last until the spring is ignored, as is the new terror campaign the Germans have launched against Antwerp. But there is promise in the American assault on Aachen, and there is now reason to look forward at least to a far shorter period of war in the Pacific. Churchill, meeting with Stalin in Moscow, has elicited a promise from the Soviet leader to join in the war against Japan once Germany is defeated.

King has convinced himself that the fighting is all but over. The latest appointments to his cabinet, designed for postwar concerns, were announced on Friday. He is going to see the Governor General tomorrow and take a great step toward creating a new, self-confident Canada in the era of peace that is surely about to dawn.

When King meets with the Governor General on Monday evening, the sixteenth, he is interested to see how the Earl of Athlone will react to his proposal that McNaughton serve as his successor. The standing of the general in the British corridors of power is ambiguous; many key individuals remain wary of him, disappointed by his performance as a military leader. King detects a moment of surprise in the earl when he hears his name.

The G.G. cannot help inquire: is McNaughton a Roman Catholic? King says he does not know, but allows that *Who's Who* lists him as an Anglican, and that he knows Mrs. McNaughton and their children are Catholics. Someone, presses the G.G., had said he had joined them. That might be so, says King, but it wouldn't make any difference; we have no state church in Canada and everyone is free to belong to any church they please. Yes, that is so, the G.G. agrees; he was only wondering about the truth of what he had heard. Lord Reading is a Jew and that made no difference to his being Viceroy of India. He was not raising any question, he stresses. Just a matter of simple curiosity.

King could see that for a while the earl was wondering if McNaughton might be bringing further headaches. *It became conventional for awhile for mention to be made in higher quarters of the trouble that McNaughton was occasioning.* But the G.G. raises no serious objection, agreeing with King on McNaughton's fine character and suitability for the position. Not a word about the break in tradition made by appointing a Canadian. And his wife is a fine woman.

Barring an objection from the King himself, the Prime Minister has his Canadian Governor General. He now must prepare for Ralston's return, to fight the initiative that would surely cost him an election and deny him the pleasure of actually seeing McNaughton confirmed.

❧

King is admiring the first snowfall of the season and pondering the death of Rommel when his defence minister visits No. 19 Canadian General Hospital at Marston Green. There he is confronted by about seven hundred casualties, most of them from Italy. He then visits No. 23 Canadian General Hospital in Leavesden, where 1,100 of its 1,157 occupied beds are casualties from northern

Europe.[3] The visits are a sobering parting glance at the sacrifices being made by Canada's volunteers.

His transatlantic journey concludes at Rockcliffe airport on Wednesday, October 18, at 9:30 a.m.; he then spends from 11:15 to 2:10 with Generals Stuart and Murchie—his Chief of Staff of Canadian Military Headquarters in London, and his Chief General Staff in Ottawa. At 3:30 he joins King at Laurier House, and the two men confer for the next three hours.

Ralston has a cold, and he seems to King to have aged considerably. They restrict the conversation to generalities at first. When King asks him how long he thinks the war will last, Ralston says he now feels it will go on until the spring. Montgomery, so recently rocked by the tragedy of Arnhem, has changed his mind about a quick finish. Eisenhower has told Ralston that he thinks it will take until the spring to defeat Germany, but that means fighting on regardless of the weather.

Ralston pauses, then says: Mr. King, I want to speak of the question of reinforcements, which is a serious one.

Fighting has been more intense and men have been kept longer in active combat than expected, he tells King. Reinforcements are considerably lower than had been anticipated when estimates were originally made. The situation is true for Italy, Belgium and Holland—everywhere Canadians are fighting. Ralston is particularly affected by the plight of some of the men in Italy, who have been away from home for five years. They will have to be allowed to come home, he says. He reports how some of the men feel about the NRMA men doing nothing in Canada when they are going begging for reinforcements. Their fighting morale, Ralston proposes, would be increased if there were more reinforcements.

The trip has deeply touched Ralston. He has seen men in hospital who were in the fighting line only hours earlier. Wastage is not just a term or a percentage. Bodies maimed or obliterated. Loved ones lost. Mr. Ralston, my husband would still be alive if you had given him any kind of break. Ralston recounts his visits to the hospitals, the wounded coming there to heal and then returning to the fighting line. I do not wish to be emotional, he says, but these visits have affected my feelings as to the necessity of easing the situation.

King strives to be cool in the face of Ralston's emotional appeal. He reminds him how, at each stage the government permitted an increase in the size of the army, the military assured them conscription would not be necessary. And the military question is only half of the issue. There is the effect on the domestic situation—the effect of attempting to introduce it at this stage of the war, in light of the intelligence information King has received, which, he tells Ralston, is more or less public knowledge. Whatever Ralston is reporting Montgomery and Eisenhower to have said, King is expecting a speedy conclusion to the war. He asks: have you read the dispatch dated October 14, which gives a summary of appreciation dated September 27 by British military advisers on weaknesses in Germany's capacity to resist?

No, says Ralston, I have not seen it.

King produces it and reads it through aloud, and notes that the report of the intelligence department in Britain contains a similar statement. The department has also intercepted telegrams bearing out the probable early defeat of Germany. It must be apparent, King lectures, with one country after another being liberated, with Germany losing, with the Allies gaining the support of these liberated countries, their resources and manpower, with the ring being drawn steadily tighter around Germany itself, with the Russian invasion against Prussia beginning on the scale it is, and with the breakthroughs at different places into Germany—with all of this it must be apparent that the Canadian people will hardly understand why we should resort to conscription at this time. To do so will create confusion, will undo much of the good our war effort to date has effected.

King evokes the memory of Borden returning from his overseas tour in 1917 and demanding conscription; he promises that it will be even worse this time if conscription is imposed. He tells Ralston we *have to think of the future of Canada as well as the present; that conscription after the last war had left a scar which had not been healed and was responsible for most of the trouble we had had in the present war. That all of this would have to be considered very carefully.* They must weigh the probable moral advantage that might result from sending some of the NRMA men overseas against *the very grave situation to which that would give rise.*

And there are the partisan consequences of conscription to consider. You know I myself am perfectly indifferent to power or to continuing in office, he tells Ralston, but I do not think it would be in Canada's interests *to hand the country over to the CCF, which would certainly be the result of any move by the government in the direction of conscription.*

Ralston is sanguine about the political repercussions. There are soldiers' families scattered throughout the country, and they would all support sending the NRMA over. The result would be a realignment in the party's constituency. In other words: stop worrying about Quebec. King counterattacks: *I indicated I did not see just how one COULD JUSTIFY any action of the kind in the light of what I had read as to the weakness of Germany's position.* Clearly the Allies don't need us to win the war, King argues. Personally, if saving lives is to be considered, it would be much better to have the war last a little longer and bring Germany to her knees that way than to sacrifice more lives through haste.

As his final argument, King says they have to consider if it is even possible to attempt conscription after five years of war in Europe while preparing for a year and a half of war in Asia. There is the probability, if not the certainty, of civil war if conscription is brought in. King says he can understand, for reasons of pride, the desire of the army to be kept up to full strength to the last. It has been admitted that they have more than the necessary number of reserves for the artillery and other service branches. It is only the infantry that it is difficult to keep up.

Ralston notes that the French-Canadian regiments in particular are considered to be well below standard for reinforcements. If they do not have enough volunteer reinforcements to maintain the size of the army, King proposes, then they should just reduce its size. After all, Canada has been in the war for five years, the Americans for less than three. And our war effort, he says, has been proportionately larger than that of any other country. King cannot imagine any of their allies expecting Canada at this stage to attempt to increase her effort through conscription.

Ralston defends his decision to divide the army and send part of it to Italy, *saying we had done honour to our country in giving it a place in world affairs by doing this or some such expression. I imagine he begins to see that McNaughton and Churchill were not unwise in wishing to keep the Canadian army intact for final operations in Germany.* Reducing the size of the army, Ralston says, would create very serious complications in the army itself. Breaking up units would be resented. Ralston agrees that conscription will create political difficulties, but he cannot ignore the fact that the situation presents very real problems from the perspective of the war itself. King sees Ralston *seeking to draw a line between military necessity and what might be regarded as political considerations.* In rebuttal, King notes that the dispatch he read predicting a quick defeat of Germany was prepared by military advisers, not political ones.

After three hours, they conclude their discussion with an agreement that they will convene the war cabinet first before taking the issue to cabinet as a whole. Though King has been steadfast in refusing to grant conscription, he sees Ralston leaving in a happy mood. *He said to me that he was sorry to add these burdens to others I have. I told him I was deeply sorry he had the load which he had to carry that we must seek to find the right way out.* Concerned about Ralston's health, King tells him that it would be wise for him to take a real rest.

It is a tragedy, King reflects to himself, to have to face this crisis, just when the fortunes of the Liberal party are on the rise. And to have this to happen when the country, he feels, is *in a mood to see the war through in a noble way. To me it is about as heavy a task as could be given to a man to bear; for whatever decision is made I shall be the one that will be pilloried on the one side by the Army and its friends, if I do not yield to what in the long run would not be in its interests and certainly at no time in the interests of Canada, and on the other hand by the great majority of the people of Canada itself if, after the stand I have taken right along and with such success, I should permit a situation to develop that will help to destroy the unity of Canada for years to come and that to no avail so far as the winning of the war is concerned.*

It is important to King that Ralston conceded to him that winning the war is not at stake. *To my mind that is the only stake on which we are justified in sacrificing more lives than may be absolutely necessary.* Despite the scale of the calamity he foresees, King draws on a reservoir of confidence that has seen him through many crises in his political career. *I believe that we shall get through without conscription*, he determines. And he will do so, he concludes, with the guidance of the same supernatural powers that have come to his aid before. The past shall pilot William Lyon Mackenzie King safely into the future.

CURRAGH, HURRAH

October 16, 1944

WITH less than two weeks to go to the start of the 1944/45 NHL season, teams are scrambling in their training camps to find, not a winning lineup, but any kind of lineup at all. The league has forbidden teams to use players who have held draft deferrals because of vital war work—deferrals secured through off-season jobs, even in-season jobs. The new regulation reads: "No person shall be eligible to play in the N.H.L. whose induction into the Armed Forces has been deferred for other than physical reasons. This restriction shall not apply to a student at school or college or one whose induction has been deferred as a farmer." In other words, in most cases only a medical examination ruling a player unfit for military service will allow him into the league; the strategy of holding down a vital war production job won't be permitted any more.

The new league regulations have left the league's coaches and general managers groping in the dark in assembling their rosters. A player's military status is a private matter between himself and the armed forces, although there is no question that individual teams have played an active role in arranging deferrals for many players. Still, managers are reluctant to sign or trade for players if they think they might be drafted before the season is out.

It is widely suspected that the Maple Leafs were behind the change in the league constitution—stung by their semifinal loss to Montreal last spring, convinced the Canadiens are packed with players holding vital-industry deferrals. Dick Irvin complained openly in the press in January 1944 about the merry-go-round of lineup juggling he was compelled to endure in mid-season, sending players home in the middle of a road trip so they could work for a spell at other jobs. These jobs were obviously arranged to allow the players to qualify for the vital-work deferral provisions of the

NRMA. And in the summer following their Stanley Cup win last spring, the Canadiens trooped into war-industry jobs. Richard has been working in a munitions plant, Lach and a number of team-mates in an aircraft factory, Blake in a shipyard.

To the Canadiens' detractors, off-ice industry jobs are just a man-power tactic designed to keep the club at championship strength. But to the Canadiens' supporters, having players pull their weight in war-industry assignments when off the ice is a practical patriotic gesture that deserves to be applauded, not derided. (And the Canadiens are by no means the only team with players who hold war-worker draft deferrals. At the beginning of this season, a news release from the Red Wings records that just about every Detroit player boasts some kind of technical trade as his profession, a con-venient assembly of skills for Motor City, which is turning out a substantial proportion of the Allied effort's war machinery.) Why should this be condemned when Maple Leaf Gardens' response to wartime is to funnel players into military hockey teams, which make no practical contribution to the war effort—and, in the view of the military in January 1944, were turning a buck for commercial interests like the Gardens? Why not keep the players in the league, entertaining the public and the troops via game broadcasts and help-ing make bombs, ships, tanks, guns and aircraft on the side?

But in a clash of front-office war strategies, the Leafs have won. The league has decided that it is better for players to be going into the military and playing hockey there than it is for players to stay in the league playing hockey and working in wartime industries in their off hours. And however much one can argue that the Canadiens' strategy is the more productive one from the war's point of view (provided such jobs are legitimately held), it is the least tol-erable one from the Leafs' point of view because it has made the Canadiens a powerhouse. The Leafs, with the military heritage and inclination of Conn Smythe, opted for a military solution to its obligations to the war effort. In the process, Maple Leaf Gardens helped create a military hockey system that kept many enlisted players far from combat and helped make the Gardens money when quasi-professional services clubs called the Gardens home ice.

The fact that the league has decided to outlaw the vital-industry deferral strategy in no way makes that strategy dishonourable. Professional hockey's reputation might be very different in the fall of 1944 if a Canadiens– or Red Wings–style, and not a Leafs–style, war strategy had been adopted by the league as a whole. Even if it meant implementing a shorter season or rotating more players through the lineups, the practice of combining ice time with war work would have served the country and the game far more productively than having so many of the league's marquee players vanish into non-combat military roles to play hockey, under the pretext that professional hockey was marching into the fighting line with every other Joe. Such a war-industries strategy would also have served to boost morale among those working in the shipyards, munitions plants and aircraft factories, reaffirming the vital contribution they have been making to the Allied effort.

But pumping rivets into a ship's frame is not nearly as glamorous as posing in basic training with a Bren, and the public themselves undoubtedly have expected athletes in the latter rather than the former role. Unfortunately, the public, once their own friends and family began to die in combat, have ceased to be uplifted by publicity photos of celebrity athletes playing military hockey, rather than struggling up the Italian peninsula, flying missions over Germany or hunting U-boats on the North Atlantic. The bitter letters from families of men killed in action published in daily newspapers is evidence enough that the strategy that helped create the military hockey morass has done more harm than good for public morale.

Hockey's wartime experience is a lens through which the country's war effort as a whole can be appreciated. The fact that so many hockey players who go into the services do not end up in the fighting line is not just a symptom of bases building championship clubs. It also reflects the fact that most Canadians who go into the army do not end up in combat. The majority of the army is serving in an indefatigable hierarchy of support roles, many necessary for maintaining an army in the field, but compared to its American counterpart the Canadian army is top-heavy with these non-combat positions.[1] And the number of hockey players being exempted from the draft for medical reasons, or being discharged from the service on medical grounds, is not so difficult to understand when one also realizes that the military has been maintaining particularly high standards of fitness—probably too high, considering the enormous number of rejections among the general population on medical grounds. As of November 25, 1944, an exacting (or compliant) Montreal military district alone will have rejected 157,450 potential soldiers on medical grounds; Toronto military district will have rejected 89,205. Quebec City will have rejected almost as many as

Toronto—73,923. Ironically, it is as if NHL clubs have more determination than the army to put a man in uniform. While the army is passing on fit young men because their eyesight isn't perfect, hockey clubs are taking into their lineups the most bruised and battered of old warriors to keep the game alive, as well as men the military has deemed too feeble.

"Canadiens still resent that war workers clause put in the NHL constitution and are trying to hand some of the other clubs a dose of worrying before cutting loose with any players," the Toronto *Telegram* asserts on October 16. Three Montreal players whose status is uncertain are goaltenders Bill Durnan and Paul Bibeault and right-winger Phil Watson. Watson was on loan from the Rangers to Montreal for 1943/44, and the eight-season veteran of New York has made it known he wants to return to his old team. The Leafs' Frank Selke notes he understands Watson has been playing on a war-worker deferral and won't be available to the Rangers or the Canadiens. But he is proven wrong, as Watson makes it back into a Rangers uniform on a medical deferral. Montreal retrieves three properties it sent to the Rangers for him: Fern Gauthier, John Mahaffy and Dutch Hiller.

Durnan was spectacular in his rookie debut in 1943/44, but Canadiens-watchers suspect that uncertainty over his military status is causing Montreal to hesitate in making a deal with Toronto for Bibeault. Hedging against the possibility that they won't be able to secure Bibeault, the Leafs bring to training camp in Owen Sound twenty-six-year-old Calgarian Frank McCool, who spent 1942/43 and 1943/44 playing Senior hockey for the Currie Barracks team in his home town. Ulcers undoubtedly led to his discharge from the army, and McCool, who has never played a minute of NHL hockey, brings his butterfly stomach and medicinal regimen into the Leaf camp as Toronto acquires his rights from New York.

If the Leafs or any other team expected the Canadiens lineup to be gutted by the new league constitution, they are profoundly disappointed. Whatever problems there might have been with Durnan's eligibility, they have evaporated by the end of training camp. He is injured during camp, and there is a hint of suspicion that Durnan is able to secure a medical deferral as a result. Conn Smythe, for one, is convinced that the Canadiens' depth of talent is due to the complacency of Montreal military district, which has issued almost twice as many medical deferrals as Toronto military district.

With Durnan's services assured for 1944/45, Montreal sends Paul

Bibeault to Boston—the Bruins' All-Star goaltender, Frank Brimsek, an American, is serving in the U.S. Coast Guard. Montreal's losses from the 1943/44 lineup have been minimal: Gerry Heffernan, a twenty-eight-year-old right-winger; Mike McMahon, a twenty-nine-year-old defenceman (who will resurface for fifteen games with Montreal and Boston in 1945/46); and Watson, who has gone back to the Rangers. At the same time, they have picked up Frank Eddolls, the outstanding defensive prospect whose rights Toronto traded away in 1943 to get Ted Kennedy from Montreal. After two years in the air force, during which he played for the Montreal RCAF team, Eddolls has been discharged in the manpower cutbacks and can begin his rookie season. The Canadiens have also picked up two army discharges: centre Ken Mosdell and defenceman Wilf Field. Both went into the army after the Brooklyn Americans folded in 1942; both had their rights secured by Montreal. The twenty-two-year-old Mosdell is a native Montrealer who played his Junior hockey in the city. The Canadiens insert Mosdell into their lineup and loan Field to a desperate Chicago team, with whom he plays his last NHL season.

The Rangers have been trying to secure the services of their veteran star Bryan Hextall, who has played seven outstanding seasons for them, but a Canadian judge won't let him back in a hockey uniform. Hextall has flown through his army medical with A-1 status, making him eligible for call-up. While he has not yet received his draft notice, a judge has ruled that Hextall cannot leave the country in the meantime to work in the United States as a hockey player. Hextall ends up sitting out the new season.[2]

With the bloody losses of the Scheldt offensive filling the obituary pages, sentiment even among sportswriters is swinging against the game and its players. "What strikes the observer looking in from the outside," notes the *Telegram* on October 18, "is why there has to be a border to be crossed before attention is called to the fact that army class A men are roaming around without being in uniform." It is, to be sure, a confusing autumn for sports fans and citizens in general. The Canadian army is in the fight of its life in Holland, and is still thrashing through Italy. Conn Smythe of the Leafs is telling the country that the volunteer army is under dire stress. Yet the armed forces still have hockey teams at home and overseas. And the National Hockey League is beginning another season with players who are not in the armed forces, who are being released by the armed forces or who are being rejected by the armed forces on medical grounds.

Telegram sports editor J.P. Fitzgerald is compelled to examine the mess on October 17. "Nobody can have any objection to men in fighting uniform playing hockey or any other game for recreational or conditioning purposes; just about everybody that takes this war seriously is hostile to young and fit men living on the fat of the land first as hockey players and secondarily, if at all, as military trainees.

"The NHL and other professional leagues have not got beyond their training camps as yet, but it behoves all and sundry clubs to weed out any and all candidates who are eligible and fit for the fighting forces.

"The war comes first or should and it is up to the several clubs to see to it that it does. Failing that the public has ways and means of making its feelings on the matter quite clear.

"As far as this column is concerned, hockey is no excuse for dodging military service."

Mr. Ralston, I would like an explanation concerning my husband's death in France. Mr. Ralston, Major Smythe is absolutely correct. Mr. Ralston, my son means more to me than those cowards back here can ever mean to their people. Mr. Ralston, Major Smythe should be punished by being awarded a DSO for his service. Mr. Ralston, we beg of you to leave our sons in Canada until they are properly trained. Mr. Ralston, I think there is something rotten about this government.

Mr. Ralston—

James Layton Ralston has lunch with Air Minister Chubby Power from 1:30 to 2:30 on Thursday, October 19, before entering the war cabinet meeting at 3:00, accompanied by General Stuart. Before the meeting, King briefly meets and shakes hands with Stuart in the antechamber. Stuart tells the prime minister he is glad to be back, but is sorry to have to bring the report he has. You have done everything that a man could to support the army, he tells King. You have given them everything they have asked for.

Ralston presents his report, repeating the arguments in favour of sending in the conscripts that he made to King yesterday. To head off any suggestion from King that the pace of the war be slowed, he tells his colleagues that Montgomery said the war could not be won by digging in: they had to press ahead through the winter.

There is a *great silence* after Ralston speaks. King lets the silence hang a while longer, then begins his reply, quietly. One of two persons begins speaking: it is either King the parliamentarian, concerned that a matter of such gravity receive its due process, or it is King the politician, stalling so as to make the issue go away of its own accord. The question raised, he tells his ministers, is the most serious one to come before the cabinet since Confederation. Adopting Ralston's recommendation will mean calling together Parliament, enduring bitter debate, then taking the issue from Parliament to the people in an election, which requires at least sixty days under the Elections Act. It would be well into the new year before they would have a result. And in the meantime, there would be the most bitter kind of election campaign waged from one end of the country to the other. Quebec and Ontario would be set against each other.

Conscription, he observes for all, clearly is not being asked for to win the war. This is not like 1917, when winning or losing was the issue. The war will be won. The momentum of the conflict has changed since D-Day. King recounts the gains made since the Normandy invasion and asks: In the light of all this progress, how could the Canadian people understand a sudden change in policy? Our Commonwealth allies, Australia, New Zealand and South Africa, have reduced their troop numbers. Canada is well on her way to demobilization; our air and naval strength is being reduced because of a surplus. Moreover, we are not being asked for total conscription—only conscription to provide reinforcements for an army that was made the size it is on assurances that conscription would not be required to reinforce it. King reveals he has discussed conscription with General McNaughton, who told him conscription was not necessary, and who also knew, says King, what it would do to Canadian unity and how unfair it would be to Quebec. He then makes essentially the same arguments against conscription from the domestic political perspective that he has already made privately to Ralston.

General Stuart makes his appearance, presenting his own report in support of conscription. King queries Stuart about his assurance, given two months ago, that there were plenty of reinforcements, as well as the assurances that the additional brigade in Italy granted in August would not drain manpower further. On the issue of having assured the government of there being plenty of reinforcements, Stuart tells the war cabinet he made a mistake. King is icily pleasant in response: *having given us the wrong information and having made a mistake, I hoped he would, as I know he would, do all to help the govt. out of the present situation.*

In discussing possible ways of reducing the size of the army in response to the reinforcement shortage, Stuart discourages the idea, saying he thinks the Allies are building up to a big decisive round, which might end the war at any time. He blunders by arguing that Canadian troops would want to play a major role in the final push, *and said something about ending up in glory.* King seethes. *I said pretty strongly that I did not think glory ought to be entered into where it was a question of saving of human lives.*

Stuart proceeds to describe for the war cabinet an end to the war in Europe that entails, as Ralston has already suggested, the armies fighting right through the winter; it is an image King finds frightening. Has Canada ever been consulted on this strategy? King asks. This is the first time he, the prime minister, has heard of such a strategy. Where Canadian lives are concerned, he tells Stuart, the government is entitled to know what is involved in the strategy. King presses his personal choice for finishing off the Nazis: taking longer and saving lives in the process, the way Churchill held off invading Europe. *This point had never been apparently thought of either by Stuart or any members of the Cabinet or Ralston.* But it is a moot point, as Canada has no real control over the Allied operational strategy. If Eisenhower is planning to fight straight through the winter, then the Allies will be fighting straight through the winter, regardless of the Canadian domestic implications.

St. Laurent then speaks, noting the bitter feeling between the men at the front and those at home who are not fighting. That bitterness is likely to continue whether anything is done about the NRMA men now or not until the war is over. The men fighting overseas, he predicts, are the young men who will govern Canada hereafter; the NRMA conscripts will be marked men through their lives. He calls unfair the assumption that wherever NRMA men are concerned, the issue is automatically equated with Quebec, as he understands, correctly, that only about one-third of the conscripts are from Quebec. No one, he posits, has said anything about the conscientious objectors, none of whom have fought, all of whom are Protestants. Because the Catholic Church admits the right to kill in war, there can be no conscientious objectors in their number. As a result, in St. Laurent's reasoning any reluctance by Quebec men to fight must be set against the number of conscientious objectors there are in English Protestant Canada. He concludes with a stern warning about the certainty of division in Canada for a long time to come if the conscripts are sent overseas.

The war cabinet meeting produces no resolution either way. Ralston has presented his argument in favour of conscription and Stuart has supported it. King is left groping for some painless solution—a solution that would not involve calling Parliament or an election. But the intransigence of Ralston blocks all expedient avenues.

On Friday, October 20, the Allied cause marks two important milestones: American troops take Aachen, the first German city to fall, and more than 100,000 American troops swarm ashore on Leyte Island in the Philippines. The pro-conscription campaign in Canada also takes two more steps forward. The *Globe* reports that the Canadian Corps Association has asked Ralston "to either make a statement reassuring the Canadian people concerning the reinforcement situation, or to implement his promise to make the 'Zombie' army available for overseas service." And Progressive Conservative leader John Bracken officially secures the nomination of the local riding association in Neepawa. His acceptance speech repeats the "criminal folly" charge over the government's not sending in the conscripts—a charge already laid by Drew and inspired by the accusation of "criminal negligence" made in the *Globe* by Major Spotton in support of Smythe's charges on October 12.

Another war cabinet meeting passes on the afternoon of the twentieth with nothing resolved. The ministers agree to leave the issue alone until they next gather, on Tuesday the twenty-fourth. After the meeting, King speaks with Norman Robertson of external affairs. The thought of bringing McNaughton into cabinet is circulating among King loyalists, and Robertson advises King that he will lose two other ministers in addition to Ralston if McNaughton joins the government. King is defiant: he tells Robertson it would not stop him.

A frenzy of lobbying ensues on Saturday the twenty-first as King's loyalists attempt to isolate Ralston and make his proposal as politically unpalatable as possible to the majority of cabinet. King's military secretary, Lieutenant-General Maurice Pope, takes the extraordinary step of going to Ralston and from 11:20 to 12:20 strives to convince the defence minister of the folly of his ways.

Pope was rattled by the war cabinet meeting on October 19, at which Ralston and Stuart advocated sending conscripts into combat.

"As I listened to the unfolding drama my heart was heavy," he will write, "and I think that I was really frightened officially for the first and only time in my life." What galls him is that at a time Ralston is asking for another 16,000 men from the NRMA ranks, the army "had already discharged, almost entirely for other than battle reasons, no less than 150,000 men. A paltry ten per cent of the strength we had thus rejected, much of it because we had set our physical standards somewhat high, was being allowed to threaten national unity." Pope tells Ralston that if it were October 21, 1943, no one could do anything but support his recommendation. But it is October 21, 1944. The enemy is beaten, he tells Ralston. Not only are we in the drive down the home stretch—we are in very sight of the tape.

He tries to convince Ralston to reduce the size of the infantry battalions instead of demanding conscription. The Canadian battalion is configured with four rifle companies. The British have dropped to three; the Germans have been using three in their battalions for fifty years. Surely the Canadians can as well.

He has no effect on Ralston's conviction. "I felt I might as well have addressed my exhortation to the rocky shores of Chebucto Head," he will write.[3]

Stuart's defiant address to the war cabinet has ruffled the feathers of those who were elected to lead and the civilian mandarins who serve them. Norman Robertson wants to get tough on the military: he tells King it is his position that the cabinet decides what the situation demands, and it is the army's business to fall in line. King is coming around to McNaughton's opinion of Ralston: *that there is something inhumanly determined about his getting his own way, regardless of what the effects may be on all others. In this I believe there is a desire to justify in his own mind his earlier convictions for conscription.*

King is convinced that the crisis in his cabinet goes beyond the electoral fortunes of his party. As the Liberals go, so goes the country. This is, after all, the political party that campaigned in 1935 under the slogan "King or Chaos." *One just cannot imagine how serious a break in the ranks of the government at this time would be to the whole future of Canada.* Ralston is becoming to King a danger not just to his ability to govern, but to the very survival of the nation.

The war was going just fine for King until Conn Smythe defied the discipline of his uniform and set Ralston back on his heels.

With one press release, its message so poorly countered by Ralston and his defence department, a right-wing hockey impresario appears to be on the verge (in King's mind) of driving the entire country into flaming ruin.

On Saturday afternoon King calls on his friend Malcolm MacDonald, the British high commissioner. He unburdens himself to MacDonald. *Malcolm at once said something to the effect that this is the most absurd thing he had ever heard of, to talk of conscription at the eleventh hour.* Practically the twelfth hour, and at a time when it is known that the war is being won, King grouses. The consequences of Smythe's campaign continue to ricochet as MacDonald suggests King communicate with Churchill, an idea that has already occurred to King. Now the British prime minister has to be dragged into the fracas. Churchill is away, meeting with Stalin, but he will be notified of an important private message arriving. King will bring one around the next day.

King has decided he should meet with McNaughton—the man Smythe wanted to oversee the entire Canadian war effort four years ago, when Smythe was last lobbing into the press his ideas on how Parliament Hill should be doing things. King tries to reach McNaughton, in part to let him know that there is nothing to a newspaper story mentioning someone else as a prime candidate for Governor General. But McNaughton is away, delivering a speech at Queen's University in Kingston.

That night, as it happens, the new minister of veterans affairs, Ian Mackenzie, tells King to look at the late edition of the *Ottawa Journal*, which contains excerpts from McNaughton's Queen's address. King is astonished and delighted. The inspiring words from the general are: "When you come, as you will, to places of authority and influence, and you face the acute issues which may divide our country part from part, may I commend this principle of action to your best thought and interest—compulsion is ruled out; we proceed by agreement, or for a time we rest content not to proceed at all."

This is out of the blue and without a word having been said to him, King marvels. *It makes pretty clear where he would stand if we got into an issue of conscription at this stage. I am beginning to think that McNaughton is right about what he said about the kind of tyranny that Ralston exercises over men and seeking to have his own way regardless.* Ralston's Conservative enemies have been accusing him of criminal folly in not sending in the Zombies; now

King is on the verge of tarring him with the brush of criminality. *It is nothing short of a crime*, he decides, *that, as Prime Minister, who has saved him from some pretty bad situations, to say nothing of giving him the chances he has had as minister, that he should allow me to be worried, as I have been, and the whole party to be brought to the verge of destruction just at the moment we are getting ready for a general election.*

That day, as Mackenzie King balances a colonel against a general, the Canadiens come to Ottawa to play an All-Star team of Quebec and Canadian Senior league players in a game sponsored by the Patriotic Association in aid of the Chinese Relief Fund. Over 6,300 fans watch Maurice Richard score the only goal of the opening period at 1:16, assisted by Butch Bouchard and Elmer Lach; he also assists on one of linemate Toe Blake's two goals as the Canadiens prevail, 5–4.

They are the masters of the new, high-speed head-manning game created by the two-line offside of 1943/44. "It's a new game that's a lot tougher on older players than anything," the Leafs' Schriner notes. "You have to do a lot more skating, and you have to readjust yourself to an entirely new style of checking."

The war cabinet meeting at 11:45 a.m. on Tuesday the twenty-fourth is the last opportunity for King and his key circle of ministers to thrash out the reinforcement issue before the full cabinet convenes that afternoon. It brings no resolution either way. *The truth of the matter*, King notes, *is that the Defence people want the NRMA men forced to go overseas without further consideration.*

The war cabinet wraps up at 2:00, with the full cabinet meeting set for 3:30. Outside the war cabinet meeting room, Chubby Power takes King aside to speak with him alone. The air minister voices his fear of some segments of the army taking matters into their own hands and having a "Curragh" incident. Curragh was a British garrison in Ireland at which officers with Conservative sympathies effectively mutinied in 1914 when the Liberal government of Herbert Asquith moved to enforce the Home Rule Act for Ireland. The officers, the conservative elite of His Majesty's armed forces, submitted resignations rather than move against Irish Protestant provisionals, who were seen by British Imperialists as patriots. Asquith was forced to pledge that British soldiers would not have to take action against their Protestant brethren. An army devoted to the idea of empire forced the elected government to change policy.

One cannot imagine a Canadian officer with more of the spirit of Curragh in his blood at this moment than Major Smythe, who is fiercely proud of his family heritage of English and Irish Protestantism. Moreover, he is a card-carrying Tory making life hell for a Liberal prime minister. King dismisses Power's concerns about a Curragh reprise, telling him he has no *concern on that score.* King is more worried about McNaughton and Ralston being drawn into a public confrontation on conscription, with McNaughton taking the position that the issue never would have arisen if the army had not been divided by Ralston and Stuart so that we could fight in Italy. But the Curragh question will not go away. There is no doubt that enthusiasm within the defence department for sending in the conscripts is widespread. The question remains of how much of this army is Tory, and is sufficiently impertinent to emulate Major Smythe by calling their government onto the carpet. Most dangerous to King is not an army in full and open rebellion, but an army that simply will confound the orders it is given. To revive the spirit of Curragh, rebellious officers only have to find some way not to do what their government expects of them. In the drive to raise voluntary reinforcements, particularly within the ranks of the NRMA, this will become a serious issue. If they agree with Smythe that it is up to the government to order the conscripts into combat, they will feel little motivation to save the government from legislating combat service by persuading the NRMA men to go voluntarily. Without firing a single shot, officers who are of Smythe's mind can bring off a powerful, even unseen, mutiny.

For an hour after the war cabinet meeting on the twenty-fourth, Ralston has lunch at his desk with Stuart. The closest allies in the pro-conscription camp are about to drop a bomb on the unsuspecting cabinet.

Ralston's subsequent address to the full cabinet advocating conscription is greeted by the intense silence King invariably encounters when conscription is the issue before his ministers. *Power and Macdonald were sleeping most of the time, or had their eyes shut and hands over their faces. The men who had not heard anything before looked intensely surprised, amazed and concerned.*

It is King's turn to speak. He begins by emphasizing that he does not want the discussion to be regarded as a debate between himself and Ralston. It is Ralston's duty, he explains, to give the military point of view. It is King's duty to raise points of national significance. King repeats his familiar point: that the issue of conscription cannot be separated into military and political aspects. The two realms are inseparable in this case.

He goes on the offensive against General Stuart's report, drawing attention to the fact that he is asking for the men necessary for the war against Germany. Stuart *did not say to win the war or to keep the army at full strength—just necessary for the war with Germany.* The important difference between him and Ralston, he underlines, is that Ralston claims that an undertaking had been given to keep the army up to strength, whereas King asserts that what he, the prime minister, said in Parliament, is that the issue was winning the war.

King picks apart the military's failure to communicate to the government any concerns about reinforcement shortages over the last few months. *I rather stressed the point that this was a fairly serious matter.* He stubbornly refuses to accept Ralston's opinion that the war will run into 1945. He notes for cabinet an intercepted cable from the Japanese ambassador to Sweden back to Japan from Berlin on September 15, which indicated no hope for Germany.

He reviews for the ministers the steps involved in extending the NRMA so that conscripts can be sent overseas. The cabinet will have to agree it is necessary. They will have to pass an order-in-council, recall Parliament and ask for a vote of confidence. The conscription issue, he says, would occupy Parliament until mid-January, and would not secure the men needed—now, then or thereafter.

I want for the men all the reinforcements needed, King says, short of choosing a course that would fail to achieve that and have serious consequences. There would be bitter controversy in Parliament and a divided Canada. He reaches back to the life of his grandfather, William Lyon Mackenzie, to the report of Lord Durham that followed the rebellion his grandfather led. Durham, King tells them, spoke of two nations warring in the bosom of a single state. We would have the same condition on a much larger and more dangerous scale. We would have the provinces warring with each other and I fear civil strife could not be avoided. Any attempt to enforce conscription now would be certain to lead to bloodshed in many parts of the country.

He plays the giving-comfort-to-the-enemy card: envisioning Germany taking heart from Britain's supposedly enforcing conscription on the Dominions, and from a divided Canada. The Nazis will think that if they can hold on longer, they could get a negotiated peace.

King adds a new wrinkle to the evils of conscription. It will have serious repercussions on the international peace initiative, he warns. On August 21, the foreign ministers of the Allies had gathered in suburban Washington, D.C., to map out the structure of the United Nations Organization, which would, it is hoped, maintain global peace in the postwar era. That initiative, King tells his ministers, will require peace to be maintained through force; participating nations will have to contribute to the application of this force. In King's scenario, a country that falls into civil strife over the application of conscription can hardly expect to be invited to participate in future peacekeeping efforts. If Canada cannot be relied upon to raise and maintain an army in this war, how will the international community rely upon it to raise and maintain an army for peacekeeping?

King cannot leave the issue without touching on the obligations the assembled ministers have to their party; that they must consider its political implications. He predicts the complete destruction of the party for an indefinite period. The CCF will gain control of the government, and not even the Tories, he suggests, would welcome that result.

More silence as King concludes his address. Jim Gardiner and Angus Macdonald then fall upon each other. Gardiner, approaching sixty-one, gave up the premiership of Saskatchewan in November 1935 after King returned to power to serve as his agriculture minister, a post he continues to hold. King also appointed him minister of national war services in July 1940 after the NRMA was passed, thereby making him responsible for the national registration program of men eligible for home defence duties. But Gardiner resigned from the position in June 1941, and remains adamantly opposed to sending conscripts into the fighting line. As a member of the Saskatchewan legislature during the Great War, he watched the Conservatives renege on their election promise to Gardiner's constituents to exempt young farmhands from overseas service. Gardiner contends that worse than civil war would result from trying to force active duty upon the conscripts. Canada has done more than her share of fighting, and should be furnishing food and supplies and other materiel, rather than taking on yet more combat duties. Macdonald laughs at the idea that Canada should not be expected to do more fighting. King interjects, saying Gardiner meant more fighting in terms of fighting in three or four places on land. King is tempted to add that, having lost a son in combat in the air force, Gardiner is entitled to say that Canadians have fought enough.

King is exasperated by the performance of his mines and resources minister, Manitoban Thomas Crerar, finding him *anything but helpful*. Indeed, Crerar (no relation to General Crerar) embarked on a tour of western Canada on October 2, speaking with citizens about the reinforcement issue. He had just returned to Winnipeg from Vancouver on October 19 when he received a message from King's secretary, telling him there would be a full cabinet meeting on the twenty-fourth and that he should be back for it.[4] He tells his fellow ministers about his trip, the talk he has heard against the Zombies. *He thought the people of Canada would not stand for our men overseas not being kept up to strength as long as there was a Zombie army in Canada to draw from. This was ignoring all the other national considerations and limiting the whole thing to what is really in the minds of some of them. A sort of vengeance at the NRMA men. Crerar said he had opposed increase in the army at every stage, but now felt that the Zombies ought to be sent overseas.*

After the full cabinet meeting, Crerar calculates that support for King among the ministers is running three-to-one in his favour. The only supporters of Ralston on hand were himself, Ilsley, Macdonald and Colin Gibson, the national revenue minister from Hamilton West.* Despite the fact that he still has the upper hand, King is angry that the Ralston issue should be commanding his attention while the other parties are gearing up for the election that must eventually come. He takes solace in the steadying words spoken at Queen's by McNaughton. *If McNaughton had been looking into the Council Chamber and hearing all that is taking place there, he could not have given wiser counsel. My job has been to try and proceed on that principle and try to have that principle prevail.*

---

*The son of Major-General Gibson, he was a captain in the Royal Fusiliers of the British Expeditionary Force for the entire Great War, during which he was wounded twice and was awarded the Military Cross, the Belgian *Croix de Guerre* and the Order of Leopold. From 1929 to 1934, he was the lieutenant-colonel in command of the Royal Hamilton Light Infantry militia, and was in command of the Hamilton garrison in 1939 when war broke out. In the spring of 1940, Gibson was elected to Parliament for the first time and given the national revenue post when Ilsley moved into the finance portfolio as Ralston replaced the late Norman Rogers.

The next day, Wednesday, King meets with Stuart. It is King's ambition to make the general understand the political implications of a military undertaking. *It was a side of the situation of which the General had taken no account whatsoever and with which he said, as a military man, he of course was not concerned.* King makes his basic point, that the purely military aspect of the problem cannot be divorced from the national and international political aspects. Among King's proposals is the novel idea that French soldiers should be brought into French-Canadian units to make up the reinforcement shortage. The idea, like the rest, falls on deaf ears. *What annoys me about the Defence Dept.*, King observes, *is that any proposal made, short of conscription of NRMA men, meets with instant rejection. There is not an attitude of trying to work out the situation. Stuart, I know, is genuinely worried, as he may well be, for if the government falls it will be due to the Army and the way they have overdone things and also misled the government.*

The cabinet gathers, and King's loyalists lambaste the idea of conscription. Dr. James H. King, the Senate leader, pronounces it political and national suicide. Gardiner notes comments made by Tommy Douglas, the new CCF premier of Saskatchewan, in the morning press. The CCF has devised a position in which it will not support any conscription of men without conscription of wealth as well. In other words, they will not support any measure of conscription, it appears, and Douglas has indicated his party would sweep Saskatchewan on the issue. Thus, the anti-conscription sentiment is not limited to Quebec. Parliamentary secretary Brooke Claxton (a future minister of defence) scores a direct hit on the conscriptionists when he elicits from Ralston the statement that there are 120,000 general service men already enlisted in Canada. *Ralston's statement caused Power to say: My God, if that is the case, what are you talking about getting more men under conscription? Ralston made out some sort of reply on figures which it was difficult to understand.*

After more bickering back and forth, Ralston rises to his own defence, and he does so quietly, from the perspective of his personal responsibility. He had said that he would see that the army was maintained at strength, Ralston reminds the cabinet. In visiting hospitals overseas, he has seen men being returned to the front too quickly. If we do not secure the necessary reinforcements, his integrity will be attacked. What he dislikes most of all, he confesses, is the fact that the *Globe and Mail*'s president and publisher, George

McCullagh, and his allies George Drew and Connie Smythe, would have the satisfaction in the end of saying, "I told you so," if they run short of reinforcements. He cannot see how he could remain in the government unless they can be sure of the reinforcements.

King is back at him at once, interrupting his address to say: Let me ask you a question, Ralston. Would your resignation from the government help to get the men that you say are so greatly needed? Unless it would, you should not even think of talking of resignation.

But Ralston has placed it on the table: conscription, or resignation. He has been waiting to make his position clear since returning from overseas. Power lets King know that Ralston told him the day he arrived back in Ottawa he would resign if he didn't get his way. C.D. Howe has already told King of Ralston's resignation plans. *It is clear that unless Ralston gets his way, he will resign*, King decides.

After the meeting, King and Chubby Power mull over the practicalities of a Ralston resignation. Power tells him: you will have to consider who you can get as minister. I suppose you would ask me, but I would not take the position. It is a moment that verges on comedy. *Little does he know that he would be the last person I would ask today in this crisis*, King notes. This is, after all, the Chubby Power who drank his way out of the picture when Ralston was in Italy and Conn Smythe was wreaking havoc on the government, when Canada, in King's mind, was facing its greatest peril since Confederation. In any event, King wants to avoid having to replace Ralston, and is willing to go as far as offering his own resignation to bring Ralston to heel. King is still counting on the fact that in a game of brinkmanship, Ralston will be the first to blink. If King resigned, Ralston he is sure wouldn't take on the task of forming a ministry and presenting conscription to the House, nor would any other member of the government. *I think I can make clear to my colleagues that while I can contend with the forces opposed to the govt., I cannot contend with my own colleagues. If we cannot get unanimity in the Cabinet, my influence is gone. I have succeeded for nearly 18 years in that task. It is apparent I have got to the time of my life where belief in my political wisdom is not what it was some years ago in the minds of some of my colleagues.* Before the week is out, he decides, he may be forced to call Ralston's bluff, if that is in fact what it is.

OUR SOULS TORN OUT

October 25, 1944

IN the Wednesday morning edition of the *Globe and Mail*, Jim Coleman examines the National Hockey League's contribution to the war effort and finds it wanting. "A former professional hockey player writes to point out that, after five years of war, the National Hockey League still hasn't sponsored a single game for war charities. This has been a favourite lament of this department, and we've worn the nail off the right index finger three times while writing about it.

"Individual teams have contributed proceeds of games to various funds, but, as a whole, the National Hockey League has shamefully ignored an important work. Apparently the league governors don't give a damn about possible postwar public opinion as long as the customers continue to jostle each other to get into the arenas.

"The Leafs, for one, haven't done anything about a war charity game as yet—we'll forward the letter to Major Smythe."

On October 25, the Wartime Information Board releases its latest figures on casualties and recruitment, which tell the pro-conscription, anti-Zombie, pro-Smythe, anti-King contingent everything it needs to know. The army is taking a beating in casualties, and Quebec is not coming through with its share of volunteer reinforcements.

There were 9,338 army casualties between July 31 and August 31, compared to 144 in the navy and 775 in the air force. Prince Edward Island leads all provinces with 46.5 per cent of all military-age males having enlisted. Ontario is close behind, at 44.4 per cent. Quebec is a distant last, at 22.8 per cent, and the province's critics are eager to propose that many, if not most, of those volunteers are anglophones.

Thursday, October 26: Mackenzie King plucks at the thorn in his flesh. Ralston has been meeting with his navy minister, Angus Macdonald, for more than two hours when he responds to the summons of his prime minister.

I am surprised that you mentioned in yesterday's meeting that you might find it necessary to resign, King says to him. That shouldn't be thought of by any of us. We must seek to be as united as possible, to find ways together to prevent any need of resignations.

The pronouncements of Smythe, Drew and Bracken, amplified by McCullagh's *Globe* and other conservative newspapers, have burrowed deep into the defence minister's conscience. I have thought the whole matter through, he tells King, but I cannot see, after what I have said in Parliament about using conscripts to keep the army up to strength, that I can do anything else out of self-respect than resign if we do not send the NRMA men overseas. I might live in obscurity in retirement, but at least I could feel that I had carried out what I said I would do.

None of King's arsenal of consequences has any effect on Ralston's resolve. I have thought the matter out, he responds, and I owe my position to what I have talked over with myself. But as of now, King presses, we do not know that we cannot get the men! Time is short, Ralston replies; I am satisfied we cannot get them. I have tried recruiting; others have tried. We have not yet tried recruiting by the government, King proposes. We have not yet attempted to see what we can do by extra inducements to the men— and besides, is the whole question not dependent on how long the war may last and what the casualties are from this time on?

Yes, Ralston agrees.

Well, that being the case, King presses, am I not right in feeling I should let this whole situation be known to Mr. Churchill? I should leave at once to cross by plane and let our allies know what is likely to develop so that they may consider what steps should be taken first. There has been mention of having our men in Italy brought to reinforce the men in the north along the Channel. General Crerar has told me there is nothing he is more anxious for than to be altogether at the end of the war. I cannot see why this might not be arranged, rather than create the situation I have described. And other arrangements could be made for our troops in Italy at this time. It is pretty clear that when our men have completed the task at the Scheldt, King says, they will be taken out of the fight for a time, and that will make a big difference.

King agrees that his flying to England to confer with Churchill is not the ideal solution. I recognize the difficulty of going overseas, he says, with the publicity it would occasion. He suggests that instead someone from England come here to confer, or that he communicate with Churchill by telegram—he has, of course, already drafted and provided one to the British high commissioner. But for Ralston, the clock is ticking. He discusses the time consumed in a crossing by King, the effect of not deciding on the issue at once. These men, he tells King, are needed before the year is out.

The meeting solves nothing for King. The thorn festers. He goes to the Governor General to recount the events of the past few days, including Ralston's threats to resign. Both men are confused and bewildered by the army's reinforcement situation. The Earl of Athlone asks him: Will you tell me how many men there are available in Canada today? Your Excellency, King replies, I cannot tell you that because I cannot find out. I can get no definite statement from the minister. King tells him that there are about 130,000 general service men in the country, and that the number of reinforcements required is 15,000. As for NRMA men, he offers a breakdown he has received from his influential assistant, J.W. Pickersgill. Thirty thousand are in operational units, 14,000 thousand in non-operational, 11,000 in training and 8,000 on leave—far fewer than the 80,000 fully trained fighting men George Drew has alleged.[1]

The G.G. brightens. *He said something to the effect about that being the wretched part of the whole situation.* Yesterday I had Stuart here, he tells King. I tried to pin him down on numbers, but he could give me nothing that was definite. It was all very inconclusive. I can make nothing out of him in what he presents.

The truth of the matter, King complains, is that the men on whom we have had to rely have not given us the facts or told us what was to be considered. *Rather, they have given us assurances in the opposite direction and now they expect us to clear up the whole situation.*

Getting exact information on numbers is the most important thing, the Governor General tells King. He cannot understand why King's government cannot get clear ones. Nor can he understand the state of Canada's training system. I have visited a couple of camps where I found that every man was general service, the earl observes, and I have visited others where some were G.S. men and some were not.

When the war cabinet convenes at three o'clock, considerable time is consumed by Ralston reading the reports by his officers who have tried to recruit from the NRMA pool. *One could see that the officers had been very strongly biased in favour of conscription. For example, one used the phrase: that we had been planting lilies and trying to raise men. The men said they would be ready to go if the government would order them, but they wanted to be ordered.*

The gap is widening between the King and Ralston camps. *The discussion was on the whole very disheartening,* King concludes after the meeting. The prime minister is almost alone in arguing with the conscriptionists. The rest of the cabinet for the most part remains silent. Howe, who is back from an air conference in Chicago and is the minister most impatient to put the war behind them and convert the country to a peacetime economy, contributes nothing. *He has said nothing all along.* Only St. Laurent wades in, sharply rebuking Ralston by saying it is only too evident that getting satisfaction with the Zombies is the reason he is taking such a course.

When the war cabinet gathers again that night, a summary of operations from the Chiefs of Staff reports that on October 24 Canadian army casualties in North Western Europe were nil. *It is ludicrous that Ralston should be talking of resignation in the face of a figure like that.* The news of the casualty-free day comes atop the report of the U.S. Navy's decisive blow against the Japanese fleet at Leyte Gulf, an epic engagement in which thirty-six Japanese warships were destroyed by an American navy that lost only six vessels. The fall—the obliteration—of Aachen by the Americans has given hope to some in the Allied effort that Germany might now collapse. The Russians are driving into East Prussia and Hungary, and the Canadians and British are sweeping up the Low Countries. King is outraged *that we should be having our souls torn out as we are by Ralston's persistent determination to have conscription or to attempt it at all costs.*

The blame for the crisis ultimately lies with the defence department, King is certain; *it has made a terrible mess of our whole war effort. The army has been far too large; the planning has been anything but sound. The judgment, far from good.*

On Friday, King is notified that a reply has been received from Churchill. He heads to Earnscliffe and takes a seat in the sun room, waiting for it to be handed to him. *A most lovely view across the river. A beautiful spot.* The British High Commissioner, Malcolm MacDonald, arrives shortly and gives it to him, cautioning him that it *in some ways was not too good.*

King is crestfallen. He thinks the close relationship he has forged with Churchill would have promised him something more forthcoming. *I saw that it did not answer the questions which I had asked. At least in an authoritative way. It evaded the question of the part that our troops would be taking between now and the end of the year by stating that the plans were not yet prepared but indicated that the Canadians would have an intense part in the fighting at the finish though not participating in the next operation. It also stated that Churchill had talked very confidentially with the Chiefs of Staff who indicated that the war might well run on—there again not doing more than indicating what might happen. The message made it clear it had no reference to numbers where it referred to the extent of future operations. It does not give the particulars that I wanted.*

The reply is a tremendous blow to King's efforts to push the consequences of conscription onto the international stage. Most illuminating, and depressing, is the attitude clearly expressed that this has been a British war, another war in which the colonies or Dominions have rushed to the aid of the mother country. It has not been about global security or any other high-minded goal. King reflects that the message indicates they *looked upon the war as theirs and that we were giving them help, not that it was a war which was of concern to freedom everywhere.* King has been fighting a war for old England and he has not even known it.

MacDonald offers him some solace, telling King he is sure Canada can still meet its reinforcement demands by methods other than conscription. The Royal Canadian Legion, however, will accept nothing less than the commitment of conscripts. Speaking at the twenty-fifth anniversary dinner of its Verdun branch, legion president Alex Walker says tonight: "At this moment youngsters of eighteen, nineteen and twenty are dying on the battlefields of Europe, while a fully trained army remains at home. I tell you that if this is the price of unity, then the price is too high."

King returns to confer with his war cabinet again at four o'clock, to lie to his ministers. It would be better not to reach a decision today, he tells them. He is waiting for more information from Officers Commanding in Europe. Once I have heard from our own men overseas, he promises, I will telegraph Churchill—concealing the fact that he already has Churchill's crushing response.

After misleading his war cabinet, King stays behind to have a word with Dr. King. The Senate leader is livid. He tells King that he would like to tell Ralston and Stuart, in King's presence, that he suspects a *determined plot on the part of the Defence Dept. to destroy [the Prime Minister] for not having agreed to conscription. That he felt sure of that.* Ralston's position is terrible, he rails. There are only a very small number from the army as a whole in the fighting line, and to think that out of 130,000 general service men in Canada alone, we cannot find 15,000 reinforcements. He accuses Ralston of mismanaging the navy and air force, failing to control Macdonald and Power, and allowing them to take men that Ralston should have been free to take into the infantry. When the facts come out, Dr. King predicts, Ralston will be the first victim and in a terrible position.

Next, Jim Gardiner approaches. I want to speak with you, he says. Something very bad has happened.

I could see that he was about to break down. I pulled a chair beside his and asked him what it was. Violet, my wife—I don't know what has become of her. She was at breakfast with our daughter Beth. He goes through his pockets, produces a scrap of paper. On it is a note to Beth from her mother, saying if she was not back when her father came in, to tell him she was not going. This means she is not going to drive up with me to my mother's, Gardiner explains, which we were planning to do this afternoon, although I had already decided not to make the trip when she thought it too far. There is another letter, he tells King. He cannot find it just now, but he shows it to King later. It addresses each of the children in turn, telling them they have been such good children. And that Jim has been the best, the kindest, of husbands. She reproaches herself a little for not having been more careful in the training of Beth, their youngest, and expresses a wish to be with their boy Edwin, who was killed in the air force. The letter also explains where the silver is stored, where her fur coat can be found.

Her mind has been failing, Gardiner explains. Everything is causing her concern. On one or two occasions she has said she wishes she had been taken instead of their boy. I don't know where she could be, or what has become of her.

Perhaps she has just wandered away, to sit down somewhere, King suggests.

Do you think I should have the police search for her? Gardiner wonders.

By all means, says King. I will get Commissioner Wood at once.

King telephones the commissioner. He comes to the council

chamber and is shown the letters. The commissioner takes down a description of Mrs. Gardiner and leaves immediately.

The self of spirit and the self of matter can never meet. Ultimately, one must eradicate the other. You must merge the two into the One and sacrifice the personal to SELF impersonal. You must pass the threshold into the realm in which love of pleasure is destroyed forever, and the roots of one's will to live are torn out.

And then your soul shall be delivered.

Word is not long coming from the commissioner. A body matching Violet Gardiner's description was found in Patterson Creek this morning, he tells King. It is in the hospital, not yet identified. Soon after, Gardiner telephones King with the same news. I am going out to the hospital, to see if it is the body of my wife and to identify it. King asks him to send word, to let him know when he can see him later. King has Premier Ernest Manning of Alberta waiting to meet him in the next room. But in the midst of his talk with Manning, King decides he should get to the hospital as soon as possible.

Commissioner Wood is waiting for King when he arrives. He guides him to the room where Gardiner has been left to wait while the autopsy proceeds. *The poor fellow could say nothing. He broke down. I just sat beside him quietly.*

Gardiner takes himself to task for not having been home sooner with his troubled wife, instead of being out west tending to politics, for not having taken more care with her. King tries to make him dismiss such things from his mind. *It was a matter of good machinery breaking down when something was thrust into it too great to bear.* She might have been spared a long breakdown and suffering by this, he tells Gardiner. *Now she was free and happy.* Gardiner has not yet told his older children, his daughter Florence in Montreal, his son Wilfrid in Kingston. Little Beth knows.

They sit together, alone, for the longest time as the autopsy proceeds. Gardiner turns to King and says: I hope you will stand firm against conscription. I will not stay in any government that favours it. I will join the CCF first.

If the majority in cabinet opts for conscription, King asks him, do you think I should go to the Governor General and ask him to call on Ralston to form a government to put it through?

You might have to consider that, Gardiner replies, but I hope you will remain the leader of the Liberal government. If Ralston becomes the leader, I will have to cross the floor.

I would have to do the same myself, King notes.

It is shameful, Gardiner pronounces, the way in which we had been deceived by being told nothing of the need for reinforcements until the last day or two.

King stays with Gardiner until the hospital is ready to have him leave. Come stay with me at Laurier House, King says, or have the children brought there. Gardiner thinks it better that he stay with Beth tonight, who is with her aunt. Can you arrange to keep things out of the papers? he asks King. The evening papers carry a notice of finding the body of a woman who has drowned, but who was not identified. *Nothing would go in. I shall be surprised, however, if something does not soon appear.*[2]

One of those evening papers carries the headline: "War at last lap—Churchill." The British prime minister made the statement in the House of Commons, and King decides that this statement, and not the one he has received by telegram, is the one on which he will base his argument for not supporting conscription at this time. But it will not be of much use to him. Churchill will repeatedly visit the last lap theme, emphasizing that, as in a race, there can be no letting up now.

❦

It is a seasonable autumn day, a weekday, in Winnipeg. When Bob Carse was shipped overseas, Betty Carse moved herself and her daughters—Nancy, seven, and Sharon, five—here from Calgary to live with her parents. In Calgary, while Bob was in training, the family lived in a house atop a hill next to the Currie Barracks training grounds, and the Carse girls would sit in the grass at the top of that hill, watching Daddy go through his drills.

It is lunchtime, and Nancy is home from school for the meal. A next-door neighbour runs to the house, crying, carrying a Canadian National Telegraph's message that has been left with her. It's for Betty.

MINISTER OF NATIONAL DEFENCE DEEPLY REGRETS TO INFORM YOU THAT M44432 RIFLEMAN ROBERT ALISON CARSE HAS BEEN OFFICIALLY REPORTED MISSING IN ACTION TWELFTH OCTOBER 1944 STOP IF ANY FURTHER INFORMATION BECOMES AVAILABLE IT WILL BE FORWARDED AS SOON AS RECEIVED

Nancy is told what is in the telegram. She is too young to understand what "missing in action" means. She shrugs off the news and nonchalantly heads back to school. Her grandfather runs out of the house after her, to bring her home again and make sure she truly understands what those words imply.

Betty Carse stands in the living room, shattered. She looks out the picture window and sees people walking by on the street, people living their lives, people carrying on as if nothing is out of the ordinary. She sees that the world has not collapsed in a heap because of the piece of paper in her hands. Its message has not caused the sky to darken or buildings to crumble. Everything that was happening the moment before the neighbour came in crying went right on happening the moment Betty read the telegram and understood that she might never see Bob alive again. Watching the world go by, Betty Carse in an instant knows she will be able to carry on, come what may.

Around three o'clock on the afternoon of October 12, the day Bob Carse's entire platoon disappears after crossing the Braakman, the Queen's Own Rifles follow in the path of Carse's Winnipeg Rifles as the Royal Engineers of the British 79th Armoured regiment ferry the QOR to the other side of the Braakman inlet. They are to relieve Joe King and the rest of the Highland Light Infantry at Biervliet, a few miles south and west, so that the HLI can press on for Schoondijke. The crossing unfolds without incident, but no sooner are the QOR ashore than shells begin falling from the German batteries across the West Scheldt on Walcheren. The regiment's history will record: "Major Cottrill was the only casualty," but such histories don't always keep track of the lesser ranks. Red Tilson, who has rejoined the Queen's Own today, is wounded and sent back behind the lines for treatment.

In his absence, the Queen's Own endure several days of miserable fighting in the Scheldt, fighting marked by cold, wind-driven drizzle, mud and water, and flooded fields surrounded by dykes that must be cleared one at a time of Germans. After taking Ijzendyke and Steenhoven, the Queen's Own approach a critical objective: the German stronghold of Oostburg, about five miles inland from the mouth of the West Scheldt.

After his wounding, Tilson drops back in rank to rifleman. He rejoins the 8th's headquarters on October 18, and remains attached to it through the twenty-fifth. On that day, the Queen's Own begin their attack on Oostburg, and the entrance to the town is secured. The next day, October 26, resistance collapses, and the Queen's Own round up about two hundred prisoners. Tilson now rejoins the regiment.

No sooner has Oostburg been secured and Tilson is back among the Queen's Own than 88-millimetre German guns on Walcheren begin shelling the town. The barrage lasts for several days; on the second day, October 27, it claims the life of Rifleman Tilson.

The former Junior hockey star and future Maple Leaf lasted sixteen months in uniform, including 180 minutes as a Kingston Frontenac Army forward. Many young men have served for far less time and lost their lives, but there are also many who have served far longer than he who have never made it anywhere near the front, and never will, and are still playing the game that promised him fame. He is buried in grave nine of a temporary cemetery in the corner of a pear orchard.

He is in a railway station, waiting to meet Sir Wilfrid and Lady Laurier. King is in the midst of a crowd when the train pulls in. He moves to where he expects the Lauriers to detrain, but they are not there. When he returns inside the station, he learns that there was another train, which had immediately followed, a short special one that the Lauriers were aboard, and that they have left before he can greet them. Moreover, King has lost his hat. He tries to find the Lauriers, and he wanders into *some mysterious place where there were a lot of gangsters and all sorts of evil-minded and evil disposed people. Men and women of fashionable sets who had gone to extremes.* He makes it through them, and is trying to get out of the place by its only entrance. *Was told there would be a terrible crowd out there. Better go the other way which was the more fashionable way.* King presses through, *but at the outset was held up with people who wanted to get money and who were attempting to use force to get their way.*

King wakes up. It is Saturday morning, the twenty-eighth. What can this vision mean? Not to lose his head. Not to go too far in any direction. Sir Wilfrid is synonymous with his own stance against conscription. He will have to be careful not to miss the course for which Sir Wilfrid and Lady Laurier stood. If I do, I will fall into evil company. The station is his position; Laurier his guide.

He pays a visit to poor Gardiner, who is staying at a neighbour's house. He seats himself on the sofa with Beth, and does his best to have her feel that her mother is still beside her and will be happy with her brother. You will find little messages coming from her in things you read, he tells her. *The little child simply smiled. Did not say a word all the time that I talked to her. I put my arms around her little back.*

King then meets with Malcolm MacDonald. They share a long walk and return to Kingsmere, where they enjoy a pleasant talk that begins over dinner and continues in front of the fire.

The high commissioner tells King his stand on conscription is fully right. It might be ten or twenty years before the country sees this clearly, but it will be recognized that you took a statesmanlike position. Had you taken any other, you would have been wrong and the country would have suffered increasingly.

The disappointing telegram from Churchill is on their minds. He loves to wage war, MacDonald explains. He has thought in terms of war all his life and really enjoys the waging of war. The prime minister considers how Senate leader Dr. King used the expression that Churchill was *very cruel.* King's assessment is that Churchill is *tremendously courageous but equally ruthless which perhaps is necessary once war has begun.* Remember, he tells MacDonald, what the elder Pitt said to the younger: Never try to use war as an instrument for gaining fame. *I think that will be found to be true of some men at least of today. No one will be able to accuse me of seeking by war or through or as a result of war to gain any fame. It will be rather the contrary.*

At 9:45 they turn on the radio to listen to the news. Instead they find a hockey game. Toronto and Montreal are both playing their home openers, the Leafs against the Rangers, carried nationally on "Hockey Night in Canada," the Canadiens against the Bruins, broadcast in French in Quebec.

In Toronto, Conn Smythe is sequestered in the comfort of his home. His wounds from the night of July 24–25 have left him in constant pain. He will not even see an NHL game for another four months, and relies on Foster Hewitt's broadcasts to keep in touch with the battles waged by his Maple Leafs. He would not miss listening to the Leafs' home opener, and it can only please him that they rally to defeat the Rangers 2–1 as Sweeney Schriner scores twice in the third period; in Montreal the Canadiens are downing the Bruins 3–2.

For a brief moment the two men locked in conflict over the country's war effort are joined by the sound of the Leafs at play. But a passion for hockey is no more shared by Smythe and King than is a passion for conscription. When he hears Hewitt's play-by-play, King promptly turns off the radio. The high commissioner leaves.

The prime minister goes to bed.

The crisis ignited by Conn Smythe is bearing down upon King. His health is suffering. His ears have been ringing. *The situation which I am now facing is the hardest that any leader could possibly face. If I do not lend myself to conscription, it will be represented to those who have sons or relatives overseas, that I am responsible for not supplying them with the necessary help and for their lives. If I were to do so, that I am responsible for the lives that would be conscripted and that in addition, it would be said that I had betrayed the people at home with reference to there not being conscription for overseas. However, one only has to realize that there are millions of men suffering today more than what one may be called upon to suffer oneself. One might even ask if the way of the Cross in a situation like the present is comparable to the pain that poor Gardiner is called upon to endure at this time.*

It is Sunday, the twenty-ninth. The day of Mrs. Gardiner's funeral. At the funeral parlour King finds Gardiner at the casket. He asks King if, for the private service and the one to follow at the church, he can stand between his girls, so that they are arranged with Beth between King and her father, then his older daughter Florence on King's other side, then his son Wilfrid. Gardiner wants all of them to travel together in one car. *I felt very touched at this expression of his affection and feeling that I could be of comfort and strength to them.*

King stares into the face of the late Violet Gardiner. He is impressed. *It looked like a woman that was facing her God and as if she had done something in His sight, and was prepared to stand and face God for all that it meant. There was no line of weakness in it. No expression of sadness. A certain firmness and impassiveness. Not so much an expression of sleeping as an expression of life itself.*

When I identified the body, Gardiner tells King, her face had a look of great gladness. As if she had found someone she had been looking for, some great joy. I am sure she had seen Edwin and is with him.

King notes, *I firmly believe it.*

The funeral is well attended. The King cabinet is out in strength. King reflects on the sight of all the ministers standing together. Perhaps Violet's passing might help them be a little less headstrong, more positive. He says this to his agriculture minister as their car is passing the Gardiner house, on the way to a private gathering.

Yes, Gardiner agrees, but what a frightful price.

THE SAINT COMES
MARCHING IN

Loyal toward his faithful subjects of Quebec, Laurier's successor
will resist his adversaries.
—Le Soleil, *October 30*

Late October, 1944

AMONG the Canadians embroiled in the opening hours of Operation
Switchback on October 6 was Sergeant Ken Bergin of the Regina
Rifles, who were part of 7th Brigade assigned to establishing a
bridgehead across the Leopold Canal. The Regina's casualties were
appalling; after his platoon was virtually wiped out, Bergin took
cover in a trench, into which the Germans lobbed several potato-
masher grenades. Bergin and a rifleman attempted to lob them back,
but they exploded in their hands, wounding five of the six men in
the trench. The Germans were quickly upon them; rather than
shooting them all, the Nazis took the Canadians prisoner.

The men have been taken to a hospital, a converted schoolhouse
in Breskens crammed with wounded from both sides. Here, Bergin
has an operation on a messhall table to repair his hands. When he
wakes up from the ether anaesthetic the next day, he discovers new
Canadian faces around him. One of them is a fellow from the
Winnipeg Rifles, wounded during the second phase of 7th
Brigade's operations when they crossed the Braakman and attacked
from the right flank. The wounded rifleman tells Bergin that before
he went into the army he played for the Chicago Blackhawks, and
that he'd like to go back to the Blackhawks when the fighting is
over. Rifleman Bob Carse and Sergeant Ken Bergin will be together for the next four months.

Carse's dawn patrol was detected by the Germans while they were
walking along one of the high embankments dividing the fields.
Carse was hit by a rifle bullet that entered his right arm above the
elbow and exited out his shoulder, knocking the insignia off his col-
lar and narrowly missing his chin. Through much of the unfolding
day, Carse and the rest of the patrol of nine men struggled through
the muck, the noise of their advance alerting more Germans. Taking

refuge in a farmhouse near the crossroads they were to help secure, they suffered shelling and small-arms fire from the Germans closing in. They held out for twelve hours, with two dead Canadians in the house, three of the surviving platoon members wounded, and two Bren guns no longer working, before being captured.

Bergin finds the wounded left-winger a thoroughly decent man. After being treated in Breskens, they are moved across the West Scheldt to another hospital at Middleburg on Walcheren Island. Carse is walking down a hall one day when he notices a door is ajar. He opens it and finds himself looking out on a street. A woman across the street, sweeping some steps, motions him over. Carse walks out into Middleburg to meet the woman. She gives him a glass of milk and tells him she is with the Dutch resistance, and that she can get him out. He refuses to go unless the other Canadians in the hospital can come with him. It's the team spirit, all-for-one, one-for-all mentality—and he walks back into the hospital, his absence never noticed. The Canadians are then contacted in the hospital by the resistance, who tell them that, while they cannot get them out of the country, they can at least send by shortwave radio personal information that will let their families know they are alive. The information eventually is successfully relayed by a ham radio operator in Boston.

One day while in hospital in Holland, Bergin and Carse go together to have their bandages changed. Carse's wound is healing on the outside, but festering on the inside. When he tells the German doctor about his problem, Carse is told to sit on the makeshift examination table. Without administering any anaesthetic, the German doctor plunges a lance into Carse's wound, completely reopening it. It heals a little better.

German military records indicate treatment of Carse's wound from October 24 to 26, just as his wife is learning he is missing in action. Assessments indicate a nasty injury, diagnosed as a shrapnel wound, that has turned septic, but on November 6, when Carse is in a hospital in Zug, Holland, the prognosis is much improved. While movement in the arm is limited, the wound is healing, and there are no bone or nerve lacerations. No further treatment is considered necessary. Rifleman Carse—whose trade on his German medical documents is specified as "Sportsmann (Hockey)"—is judged fit enough to be transferred to a prisoner-of-war camp.

Carse and his fellow wounded captives are kept on the move as the Third Canadian Army presses through the Scheldt. The end of the line in Holland is Gouda, where they are put in boxcars and shipped east. Strafing by Allied aircraft causes them to abandon the train several times. When their journey finally ends, they are outside Hanover in Fallingbostel, at an enormous prison camp for Allied prisoners of every imaginable nationality, known as Stalag 11B.

They are fed once a day, some dark bread like sawdust and a thin soup. Carse takes off his wristwatch, a Christmas gift from his wife, and goes looking for a deal. He finds a French prisoner who is willing to give up his personal stash: a loaf of bread, a pound of prunes and 300 cigarettes. The cigarettes give Carse an inventory of trade goods for currying favour with his guards. He also now has a smoking habit. If you smoke, a fellow prisoner tells him, you won't feel the hunger as much.

On Monday, October 30, King arrives at the East Block to discover his air minister, Chubby Power, *is again the worst of liquor.* With Gardiner burying his wife back home in Lemberg, Saskatchewan, this makes two ministers who will not appear for the war cabinet meeting today.

Having met with the Governor General on Saturday to explain his position, Ralston must again meet with his prime minister, who is accompanied by St. Laurent, to defend himself. After conferring with General Stuart and then Brigadier Delalanne in the morning, Ralston proceeds to his appointment with King and St. Laurent for a crash course in the consequences of conviction.

We must make an effort to avoid going to Parliament, King says. It would only open up discussion there and across the country on the pros and cons of conscription. Whether they go to Parliament to get approval for conscription or ask for a vote of confidence, the effect will be the same—the government's war effort will be impaired. The only solution is to keep cabinet united.

There should also be no election in wartime, King says. If the Liberals do have to call Parliament and ask for a vote of confidence, and if they are defeated, King will have to resign and ask the Governor General to call for someone else to form a government. If the largest majority against him comes from the Liberal benches, he explains, Ralston will have to accept the responsibility of applying and enforcing conscription and all the other policies of the government. He tells Ralston: I think you or anyone else would find that a very difficult task.

King is not well, and he says so. I have the fight in me to take on political opponents, he notes, but I cannot keep on with division in my own ranks. If I find in Parliament that the strain is too great, I would have to give up the leadership of the party and leave it to others to form what government they could.

He cannot make it clearer that Ralston is the source of his ills. *Ralston kept saying he was anxious not to impose, heaven knows he did not want to impose any additional burdens on me but he said this and he said that and he did not see how he could possibly stay unless his words could be implemented. He kept coming back to feeling sure the House would carry on conscription and told me that he relied on me to see that this was done as I had promised it would in short order.*

On the contrary, King tells his defence minister that the House would not consent to closure on debate at this time, regardless of what he might have said in the past. And unless the House is overwhelmingly in favour, the policy cannot be applied. A vote like 106–97 wouldn't be enough. And conscription will need overwhelming public backing to make it enforceable.

St. Laurent tells Ralston the public will probably accept King's view that conscription is only to be applied if winning the war is the issue. I myself and many others, the justice minister explains, could not possibly support introduction of conscription at this time. At one time I would have been prepared to support it, as you, Ralston, know, but not now.

Your resignation, King tells Ralston at the conclusion of the meeting, would not only mean defeat of the government, but possibly the end of my leadership and the end of the party. And no other groups exist that would be able to form a government and carry on the war effort.

From there they proceed to the war cabinet meeting, where King reiterates his desire to avoid summoning Parliament or having to call an election. To that end he produces a draft statement he could read to appeal to the NRMA men to go general. He reads the draft, which is favourably received.

If he cannot keep the cabinet united, King explains, if Ralston resigns, Parliament will have to be summoned. He will ask for a vote of confidence and allow full discussion of the conscription issue. If he cannot get the vote, then he will resign. He makes the same point he did with Ralston: he would not have the strength to carry on if the party were divided.

The threat of his own resignation has the desired effect. He is a master at forecasting calamity. King senses a waning in the conscriptionists' impatience for action, *as things were not pressed to an immediate decision before the meeting was over. Ralston seemed to ease up a little, but very little.*

King contributes still another repercussion of conscription: it might help put a Republican in the White House. The presidential election, only a week away, is a dead heat between Roosevelt and Dewey. *Were we to get out and seek to urge men to cross the seas, we would be helping Roosevelt who was stating the need and seriousness of the the war to his own people.* With conscription, King warns, *we would be playing into the hands of all the isolationist elements in the U.S. who would support Dewey. They would point out the way men in this manner were being coerced to fight in European wars. I think this made some impression.*

It is a long meeting; they remain together until seven o'clock. Afterwards, King takes stock of his cabinet's loyalties. In the pro-conscriptionist camp he places Ralston, Crerar, Macdonald, Gibson and Ilsley. Howe he must also add, noting that if he was not in favour of it he would have stayed in Chicago and missed this meeting. Most of the cabinet, though, is still with him. Power, in the grip of liquor and who knows where, has resisted conscription, but King predicts he will find *some way of not opposing Ralston and Macdonald.*

That night, King telephones his veterans affairs minister, Ian Mackenzie, to gather his impression of the meeting and where it is all leading. *He told me he found it all he could do to control himself in the Cabinet. He felt perfectly sure there was a conspiracy from the Defence Depts. to get me out. I said to him it was rather noticeable however that the men who wanted conscription were those opposed to our social legislation. He said that was quite clear. There was no doubt that that part might lie back of the raising of the conscription issue.*

The conscription lobby, King has concluded, goes much deeper than patriotism and dislike for the Zombies. *The same men who are for conscription are the same identically as those who opposed most strongly the family allowance and other social reforms in the budget: Ilsley, Ralston, Howe, Macdonald, Crerar and Gibson.* King is struck by the parallel his life is taking to that of Sir Wilfrid Laurier. He is back in the autumn of 1917, with the Liberal party crumbling as Laurier's *supposedly strongest colleagues left him, one by one, and joined their political enemies and became a party for conscription.* The defectors march across the floor to form another Unionist government and steal an election. There will be a true Tory party, stocked with conscriptionists from all parties who are also out to preserve their wealth by turning their backs on his social programs. The remnants of the Liberals in turn would combine with Progressives and Labour members to create a true Liberal party. It will be nothing less than a seismic realignment in national politics and the power bases of the competing parties as class allegiances force the fracturing of superficial bonds. *For my part I shall certainly become a member of the latter, rather than the former and do what I can to save Liberalism and the lives of the many whether in war or peace.*

He suspects that it was on the military's initiative that efforts were going to be made to force a decision on implementing conscription today, *but by taking the initiative myself I think I staved that off at least for another day.* But then what? How much longer can King delay the inevitable? As they speak, Ralston is holding a three-hour meeting with Macdonald and his deputy minister, Colonel Currie. Mackenzie tells King he should bring McNaughton into the government and tell Churchill Canada wants her men out of Italy and reunited as one army.

King is beginning to like the idea of McNaughton as defence minister more than the idea of McNaughton as Governor General. *McNaughton has none of the enmity towards French Canadians which so many conscriptionists entertain.*

If it comes to opposing Ralston and his conscriptionist friends, King resolves, *McNaughton will soon find himself at my side strongly fighting for the peoples' rights in this country.*

❦

The 30th Battery's sergeant-major, Nick Hatten, is in hospital in England, being treated for his pelvic wound from the night of July 24–25, when Turk Broda shows up at his bedside.[1] He has a broken bone in his foot, from playing army softball. Broda tells Hatten that the injury has prevented him from joining 30th Battery as he'd hoped.

Conn Smythe will give another reason for Broda's failure to clear England in the months after the Normandy invasion. In 1967, in the course of preparing Broda's nomination for the Hockey Hall of Fame, Smythe will write to Frank Selke, who is assisting him in assembling the nomination. In the letter, Smythe will aver that Broda "applied to come to my Battery so he could go to France, and through the usual army skullduggery his O/C kept him at the Base in England and would not release him to us."

Broda has become a sporting ringer within the Canadian camps in England. He wins an army softball title—Broda is a very good catcher. And as a goaltender minding the nets for the 32nd self-propelled artillery team, he records eight straight shutouts.

Broda is chatting with Hatten in the company of another soldier, who like Broda hasn't gotten past England in this war. Hatten hears a shrill sound from outside the hospital that sounds just like an incoming bomb. Hatten and another patient with front-line experience instinctively throw themselves to the hospital floor, leaving Broda and his friend dumbfounded and bewildered. The incident underlines precisely for Hatten the different sorts of war he and Broda have experienced. The noise, it turns out, has come from a British Meteor jet fighter at a nearby airbase.

As cabinet meets on Tuesday, October 31, another *Globe* editorial maintains pressure on Ralston, who it notes has still not responded to Conn Smythe's charges, even though he has been home from overseas for two weeks. "Citizens whose sons were killed after being transferred from one branch of the army to another and sent into action without sufficient training know the facts," the *Globe* intones.

King enters the cabinet meeting while it is under way. Have they been making any headway? They have not.

It is difficult to imagine how King can avoid taking the conscription issue before Parliament if his criterion for avoiding it is a united cabinet. His ministers remain deeply divided, and the advocates on both sides of the issue take turns venting their incompatible opinions.

Secretary of State Norman McLarty tables the agenda for securing enlistments that is the heart of the conscriptionist strategy: accommodate King for a spell, but get him to commit to a timetable. No more wriggling free. There should be an appeal for enlistments, McLarty proposes. If it isn't successful, conscription should be resorted to at the end of November. *They could begin putting men on ships now,* McLarty points out. His position uncertain to King only yesterday, McLarty has evidently joined the conscriptionist ranks. Ralston's recommendation is that the NRMA men be sent overseas to ensure that reasonable reinforcements are in place for the army. Having stated his position, Ralston returns to McLarty's proposal. Will the cabinet say that, if an appeal is not successful, conscription will be applied? It is a position backed by Macdonald.

King hedges. Let us take a month to find the volunteers. *By then,*

*the need not to conscript might be perfectly obvious but I did not
think it was wise to say that conscription would necessar[ily] follow at that time. That I thought we should hold to what our policy
had always been. Get the men by voluntary means and, if necessary
to win the war, then have conscription.* It is a policy that has carried
us through five years of war, he says, and we should say we believe
it can be carried through.

He cannot say if conscription would be necessary in one month
because, as he points out, he does not know the Allied war plans, and
he argues that he has as much right as Roosevelt and Churchill to be
informed. The defence officers certainly cannot tell him what will
come. King bitingly notes that Ralston had asked him to wire
Churchill to support sending men to Italy in 1943, but now is unwilling to let King telegraph Churchill about the present reinforcement
situation. (King of course has done it anyway and not told anyone.)

It has, however, become impossible for King to cling any longer
to the notion that the war will be over shortly. Today in the British
House of Commons, Churchill states: "I certainly could not predict,
still less guarantee, the end of the German war before the end of
spring or even before we reach early summer."

In the interests of the men overseas and their families, King
avows, I want to avoid a wartime election—above all, an election
based on conscription. I would not be party to bringing on such an
election if it could be avoided. If Ralston and any of his colleagues
find it necessary to resign, King will have to call Parliament together and ask for a vote of confidence. If it is carried, the government
will continue until the war is over, provided it doesn't outlast its
parliamentary term. If the government loses the confidence vote,
King will resign, but he expresses his hope that a new government
could be formed without having to have an election and that it
could continue until war is over. But King cannot help suspect that
his adversaries intend to tear a page out of the strategy book of
Borden and the Unionists. An election while the war is on is exactly what they will want. That way, they can benefit from the votes of
the soldiers and their relatives, which helped Borden win in 1917.

If Ralston resigns, Macdonald reveals, he will have to *consider
his situation very carefully.* Later in the meeting, the navy minister
says he could not face his people, in his riding in Kingston or back
home in Nova Scotia, after what he had said in the House on the
plebiscite of 1942 if conscription is not adopted. King notes: *It was
quite apparent that he had intended to do this from the start.*

It is plain to King that Ralston, Ilsley and Macdonald, all Nova Scotians, are closest on the conscription issue, and have been from the beginning. (Borden, for that matter, was a Nova Scotian.) He attributes Crerar's stance to personal dislike—King had suggested he would not be in the next cabinet and would instead be appointed to the Senate. Gibson has said little, but King correctly assumes he (an old school chum of Stuart's) is with them as well. William Mulock, the postmaster general, who was strongly against conscription only yesterday, has abruptly switched camps. A lawyer and apple-orchard owner, Mulock served with the Canadian Expeditionary Force's ammunition column in Siberia in 1919 and has represented North York since 1934. My constituency, Mulock explains, would expect reinforcements. *I am a little surprised at Mulock. I do not forget that Sir Wilfrid had somewhat the same experience. As I sat in Council, I thought of what was happening to me, was exactly the same as what had happened to Sir Wilfrid. I can see this whole thing has been worked out as a plot. Some of the men who were incensed at the proposal at the start are now coming around, being fearful.*

King retallies the two camps. He puts seven for conscription, eleven against, then calculates further. Power, still lost to alcohol, he decides is not in favour, nor is the grieving Gardiner. Howe he is sure will take the conscriptionist side. The count, he concludes, is thirteen to eight in his favour, but that split is not comforting. On the conscriptionist side are aligned two of his three war ministers, his minister of reconstruction and his finance minister.

Noting the division in cabinet, King asks Ralston if he should go to the Governor General and ask him to send for Ralston. Would you take the responsibility of forming a government and carrying on? King ventures. No, he would not, objecting to King's brinkmanship: you can hardly resign when you have the support of the majority of cabinet. King then turns to Macdonald: would you form a government? No. And you, Ilsley? The finance minister says he needs time to decide. It isn't something that can be decided in a minute. *It is pretty clear he has it in mind he may be the one to be asked to form a govt. If he does, heaven help him and help the govt. for he will go all to pieces before no time.*

I hope as many of you as possible will continue to help me carry on if these other gentlemen resign, King tells his cabinet. We must remember the King's government has to be carried on. It important to remember that a war is on, that further decisions must be made. I thank you for all the support you have shown in the years we have had together.

It was King's hope that some decision could be made on the conscription issue before the meeting ended. But it is now eight-thirty. A decision will definitely have to be made tomorrow.

King feels that the conscriptionists are overly optimistic of their chances in Parliament and in an election. Their agenda might carry in the House, but not by a large majority. And he continues to wonder if anyone could properly enforce conscription or govern satisfactorily for very long. But that might not be for him to decide. *The question I have had to ask myself tonight would be whether it would be wise to tender my resignation tomorrow on the score that practically all the Ministers of the War Committee and some of the others were deciding against me, and that I did not feel in these circumstances I could carry on the govt. and ask that one of the conscriptionist Ministers be called upon.*

He decides he should carry on, refusing resignations of ministers if they are offered, until Parliament assembles. If he cannot avoid accepting resignations, then he should fill up the positions with new ministers, if necessary before Parliament meets.

Should conscription carry in the House, the onus will be on its supporters to make it carry in the country. *That is a responsibility I should not like.* Holding power, he concludes, *is a small thing compared to standing firmly on what one believes to be the right. I was never more sure that I am in the right in not yielding to conscription at this stage of the war than I am tonight.*

All Hallows Eve. The children of Ottawa are running riot in the streets, bartering good behaviour for confections. A night for the underworld to rule, a last gasp of evil before the saints come marching in the morn. It is also the final day of Maple Leaf Gardens Ltd's fiscal year. Conn Smythe's garrison has posted another exemplary performance. Net profit is almost $90,000, and on January 15, 1944, the company was able to retire its first mortgage two years ahead of schedule. The next year will prove to be even more profitable for Smythe and his fellow principle shareholders; the company will buy back 9,565 preferred shares.[2]

King opens his mail. The first letter contains a small medallion from the Czech foreign minister. On it, a weeping mother and child cling to the body of their father. His hands have been nailed to posts. Serpents coil around the posts, and Nazi helmets are perched atop them. Czechoslovakia, crucified by the Nazis. The crucifixion image draws his mind back toward Laurier yet again: such a fitting symbol of what Sir Wilfrid had to endure with his own party and his own cabinet members. King feels himself experiencing the same martyrdom. *It will be a great relief to be free of it all for a time if that be God's will.*

King gets very little sleep. Writing in his diary keeps him up late, and he is awake at four, plagued by his own demons. He takes to walking, hoping it will quiet him.

It is November 1. All Saints' Day. Hope and goodness renewed. King's resolution has shifted dramatically. He will not simply wait for any resignation to come to him, to attempt to hold it off until Parliament is again seated. He has had enough. He wishes the thorn plucked once and for all.

Noon. King is already well into a breakneck day. He telephones Government House to arrange an appointment with the Governor General, and leaves for it immediately.

Going into the Governor General's office, he meets the earl's wife, Princess Alice, in the corridor.

These are busy days for you, she says.

Yes, Your Royal Highness. I fear I am wearing out the carpets at Government House going backwards and forwards.

The way is becoming clearer?

I see more light on the horizon beyond the troubled waters.

For a politician oft charged with making an art of evasion and delay, Mackenzie King can move with lightning speed when he feels the need. His episodes of foot-dragging should never be mistaken for weakness. It requires a particular kind of resolve not to act, as King often has. That resolve can also express itself in a ruthlessness no political opponent should underestimate. King is about to catch Conn Smythe and his Conservative allies, not to mention Ralston and his conscriptionist allies in the government and in the army, completely flatfooted.

King and the Governor General begin with small talk. Did you get out to Kingsmere this weekend? the G.G. inquires, then mentions Violet Gardiner. King tells him what happened, tactfully leaving the exact nature of her death in the dark, mentioning only a letter Mrs. Gardiner had written to her brother that didn't indicate anything was wrong.

Well, well, well, the G.G. remarks. Then waits. What could it be that King has for him on this occasion?

We're having a pretty trying time, King tells him. We've had steady meetings of the cabinet, carrying on till late in the evenings. King outlines for the G.G. the policy of launching an appeal to the NRMA men for enlistments, noting the split between Ralston and himself over committing to a timeline for conscription to be imposed. Ralston, he explains, probably will not accept anything less than such a commitment, which means King would have to come to His Excellency this afternoon and ask him to accept Ralston's resignation.

If Macdonald and Ilsley also tender resignations, I will ask you not to accept them, at least not until Parliament is called and the matter can be discussed there. I want to avoid an election in wartime, above all an election on conscription, and I must take every possible means to do that.

When I ask you to accept Ralston's resignation, I will also recommend for appointment General McNaughton as minister of defence.

King has held two successive meetings with the general, the first yesterday, the second shortly before calling Government House today for this appointment. King and McNaughton have proved to harbour synchronous states of desperation and revenge. King wants to be rid of Ralston; McNaughton is only too willing to have his final revenge on the defence minister who had him ousted from command of the army. The general is optimistic that reinforcement needs can be met without conscription. The conscription issue in Canada would work irreparable harm, he has agreed. He has also concurred that it might affect the presidential elections in a real way, and has observed that the Germans would, of course, construe a conscription-based election as evidence of the breaking up of the Empire and use it with their people to encourage prolonged resistance. When shown secret communiqués by King on the war's progress, McNaughton agreed that it could well be over shortly. *He stressed the fact that between now and a month hence when we would be committing ourselves to introduce conscription, the whole thing might greatly change, and the need be met in other ways or entirely removed. That he felt was the strongest of reasons for not committing oneself to any course in the intervening time.* It is ridiculous that there should be so many general service men not in action, McNaughton told him. Headquarters here is *full of people doing nothing*, and this was true of general service ranks throughout Canada. He admitted the Zombie situation is a problem. It will have to be dealt with, he said, but the thing to do is get them at work somewhere.

McNaughton is contemptuous of Stuart, and of Ralston too. The experience of having the army split and elements sent to Italy against his will still outrages him and leaves him with little if any respect for the architects of the policy that brought him down. Only this morning, he pronounced Ralston's insistence on having a date set for sending in the conscripts while attempting a recruitment campaign as *psychologically unsound*. One should not cross that bridge until one comes to it, he counselled King. Try to get the men first voluntarily, and only worry about when to use conscripts if the volunteer appeal should fail. He spelled out for King a war strategy entirely compatible with limiting the need for reinforcements. As an artillery man, he wants to see the guns pound the enemy positions, doing the dirty work, and then have the infantry fall in after to mop up. It is a strategy straight from the machine-age view of warfare, completely at odds with the iron-age scenario McNaughton's promoter, Conn Smythe, was expounding back in 1941, a reinforcement-intensive scenario that called for a round-the-clock rotation of men in pressing the attack. *McNaughton emphasized the importance of saving unnecessary destruction of life. I said it was amazing how indifferent men become to that in war.* McNaughton is also inclined to agree with King that Canadians have already done more than their fair share of fighting. They have cleared the areas around Caen and Falaise, and the Scheldt will soon be secured. Once that was accomplished, there might be an opportunity to rest some of the troops.

King is through with Ralston, and it has become evident that if he does not act, he will lose McNaughton as well. The general has allowed that the Conservatives have been lobbying him to join their ranks. They have any kind of money to use and are prepared to make all kinds of financial inducements to me, McNaughton revealed, but I would not think of accepting anything of the kind. A man could not be independent, and dependent at the same time on corporations and others, he remarked.

George Drew, McNaughton declared, is the most dangerous man in Canada. He must be gotten rid of. McNaughton had begun to feel an obligation to take on Drew when Mitchell Hepburn suddenly decided to re-enter political life. Providence, he mused, chooses strange tools to effect its ends. Hepburn has saved me from that job.

There is only one complication facing McNaughton in taking over the defence portfolio from Ralston: he has already told John Bracken that he has decided to take on work outside of politics.

Should he accept the cabinet position, the general would feel obliged to go back to Bracken and his people and *tell them quite frankly*
that an emergency had arisen and explain to them that if he came
in, he was coming in only to help meet the emergency. That it was
not a matter of party with him but of service to the country at the
time of great need. I told him, of course, that would be the right
thing to do.

As they went downstairs together at Laurier House after their
meeting today, King drew McNaughton's attention to a statement
by Bracken in the morning press in which he declared there to be
no difference between himself and Drew, that the Progressive
Conservatives are a united party. When Bracken took over the
national Conservative leadership in December 1942, after twenty
years as Manitoba's Progressive and then Liberal–Progressive premier, he did so on the condition that its policies move to the centre
of the spectrum, even beyond it, and that the word "Progressive" be
added to its name. When he made his leadership debut, he was
probably positioned more to the left than Mackenzie King. Now he
was expressing solidarity with the likes of Drew. King noted how
this amazed McNaughton.

General, King pronounced today, the time has come, I think, for
me to ask you to become minister of national defence, having the
supervision over all the defence departments as well as the army
side. I think this should be done immediately. Every hour is important. Ralston will probably tender his resignation this afternoon. I
will take it to the Governor General and ask him to accept it, and at
the same time I will recommend to him your appointment. I will
then return to the cabinet and let them know of the action taken.
Then I shall pass the order-in-council appointing you, and ask you
to come with me to be sworn in by the Governor General.

McNaughton's parting words to King were: I will be waiting at
the house for your call.

And now King is with the Governor General, watching his face
redden as he absorbs the news that King wants McNaughton not as
Governor General in the spring, but as defence minister before sun-
down. You have said something that filled me for a moment with
consternation, the earl explains, then lapses into silence. Finally the
G.G. asks: *What do you think of McNaughton?*

I had not talked with him about military matters when we discussed the Governor General's post, King says, but he seemed to
me to be the one person who possesses the knowledge required to

meet the situation successfully.

Does he have a following in Quebec?

I think McNaughton has always been a friend of Quebec, King offers. He reviews some of his talk with McNaughton and reports that the general *was quite positive he would be able to meet the situation short of conscription by methods he would propose....*

Whatever reluctance the Governor General might feel about McNaughton gaining political power, it is shelved. He agrees to approve McNaughton as defence minister. I expect to be down around four, King says, bearing Ralston's resignation.

When King arrives for the decisive cabinet meeting, Ralston, Macdonald and Ilsley, his three thorny Nova Scotians, are not yet there. King returns to his office and sends for St. Laurent. I have at last found a way out, he announces. McNaughton has consented to come into the government and believes that he will be able to secure the necessary reinforcements without any resort to conscription.

St. Laurent's piercing eyes looked straight ahead and he wondered what Macdonald and Ilsley might do.

Have you spoken with Ilsley? St. Laurent asks.

No, I have not. I thought it best not to say anything to anyone until in council.

Word arrives that all ministers are now present. St. Laurent and King rejoin the rest of the cabinet. It is now three o'clock.

Have they been discussing any matter? King asks as he takes his seat. Ralston speaks. He has something requiring cabinet approval. He reads a message from Canadian Defence Headquarters, a minor thing regarding paying tradesmen's rates to some petty officers who are reverting to the rank of privates. Cabinet gives its assent without discussion.

Now. King asks if there is anything further with regard to where they left off last night. *I was going to sum up the position at once, expecting the matter would be brought quickly to a head. Ralston said he did not know why he should begin, but he did begin, in an extremely moderate and mild way.*

Ralston explains how he, Macdonald and Stuart have been going over figures again to see what further men might be secured. He hands off to Macdonald, who addresses the matter of an appeal to the NRMA men. Macdonald reports that he telephoned General George Pearkes, senior officer in Pacific Command, at noon to discuss the appeal. Pearkes's opinion is that it would not be wise for King to address the camps—if the desired numbers are not secured, it would reflect badly on him. Perhaps a broadcast by King from Ottawa rather than a personal appearance would be best. Pearkes feels that the minister of defence and some other might speak. The men had not yet been addressed by civilians, although chaplains have done so. They might attract 2,500 men this way, though it might take two to three weeks to get them. Pearkes says they are not likely to enlist in a large body, but rather in groups. Their strongest source of recruits would be the 2,500 men who went to Kiska in Alaska on manoeuvres and performed well.

Men are not seen as likely to respond to an appeal, according to Pearkes, because some think the war is nearly over and they aren't needed. Others feel they've been badly treated and snubbed. And some have said they would be ready to go if ordered. And Pearkes doesn't think it advisable to say conscription will follow if they do not respond voluntarily.

King is surprised by all this. He is compelled to comment, without pressing the matter unduly, on the fact that this information was apparently not sought until today, and *we were led to believe days ago that the situation had been combed over and that we had the last word*. King cannot understand how cabinet could have been given earlier figures as the last figures, and that apparently it was not until noon that the commander responsible for the largest NRMA camp in the country was asked what he thought could be done.

Not everyone is taken with Pearkes's helpfulness. Edmonton's James MacKinnon, minister of trade and commerce, *came out quite strongly that he thought Pearkes was no good; that he really had not his heart in trying to get men; he really wanted conscription*. King contributes the observation that the press had commented on the offensiveness of some of Pearkes's speeches with regard to the NRMA men.

Ralston leaves the room momentarily. Macdonald, conciliatory, acting to broker the schism between Ralston and King, advises on what he thinks Ralston is prepared to consider in the way of a policy. King asks several times what Ralston is expecting. He repeats his own basic stance—no conscription for overseas service, with the government continuing to carry out the mandate given by the people in the last election. Their differences still hinge on the definition of what would make conscription necessary—necessary to keep the army up to strength, as Ralston argues, or necessary to win the war, as King posits. Ilsley attempts to manoeuvre King into conciliation by reading from a speech in which King used the word "maintain" in reference to supporting the army. *It is the one that Ralston has had his finger on right along.*

I agree that necessary reinforcements should be found, King replies, but I still believe they can be found voluntarily to the extent of "maintaining" the army. By that I meant doing what is necessary in the way of supplying reinforcements, having relation to all phases of the situation. I am prepared to agree to that. But, King emphasizes, I have never thought of anything else, as references to other parts of my speech will show.

Ralston has returned. As the discussion continues, King notices that Ralston is *particularly careful not to finally say that we would have to undertake to resort to conscription.* Instead, the conscriptionists continue to try to pin down King's own position on bringing in conscription. He will consider it, but *I did not think we should cross that bridge until we reached it.*

The meeting drags on. King has secretary Arnold Heeney phone Government House to say King would be by later than four o'clock. Later, he excuses himself to telephone McNaughton and tell him a decision probably will not be reached until late in the evening. He looks at the clock. The hands are aligned precisely at five minutes to five.

Six o'clock comes; the hands are aligned again. The Governor General waits. General McNaughton waits. Discussion has narrowed to the point of deciding when conscription can be implemented. This still leaves open what we mean by the necessity for conscription and I think we should clear that up, King proposes.

Ralston responds. There is a fundamental difference between us. But I think the decision on that has already been made, he concedes: most of council are apparently against conscription at any time. Ralston notes that King has been quite frank in the position he has taken. But there is still much that needs clarifying, in particular the question of the course of the appeal to NRMA men, which he is prepared to consider further. Perhaps we should take tonight to think it over.

King is astonished, and immediately suspicious. *This was so different from his previous attitude as to the necessity of not losing a day that I said to myself at once: here is a scheme to make the situation still more difficult for me. We will be met tomorrow by some condition of things which will mean going over the same ground again to no effect.*

King becomes convinced that if the discussions are held over until the next morning, all of its elements—his plan for an appeal to the NRMA men to volunteer, Ralston's readiness to speak as part of it—will somehow be turned against him. Everything will be *limited down to the smallest point, which would go to show that I was not willing even secretly among ourselves to give an undertaking. That if there was a failure to secure the necessary reinforcements I would not then allow a reference to Parliament.*

He keeps waiting, waiting for Ralston to repeat his basic position: that he will have to resign unless he gets his way, unless the government will commit to sending in the NRMA men if the voluntary appeal does not work. But Ralston will not. Is he wearying, or is he scheming? King suspects the latter.

I felt that the situation would be worse tomorrow if I did not speak.

We ought, if possible, to reach a conclusion without further delay, he begins.

I have been told each day that an hour's delay would prejudice the securing of men. I do not see how we will get any further by not reaching an understanding at once.

After what was said last night, I realized that some way would have to be found, if it could be found, to save the government and to save a terrible division at this time, and at the same time make sure of getting reinforcements, if that was possible at all. I had been asking myself: Is there anyone who can do this, who believes that our policy, which has worked so successfully for five years, and will work for the remaining weeks or months of the war? If there is, I owe it to the country that such a person's services are secured.

I believe I have the man who can undertake that task and carry it out. General McNaughton.

There is no man by whom the troops overseas would feel their interests are being more taken care of than McNaughton. There is no man toward whom the mothers and fathers throughout this country would have the same feeling more strongly. There is no man in whom the citizens of Canada as a whole would have greater confidence for a task of the kind. He has taken no part in politics. He is not a Liberal, a Conservative, a CCF, though he is very liberal-minded and very liberal in his policies.

There is a difference between a campaign being started by a man who has little faith in what can be accomplished and by one who believes that if he puts his heart into it he can secure results. Ralston has said that while he is prepared to speak, he does not think it would be to much effect. I know McNaughton feels otherwise. He believes that tackled in the right way he himself can find the men necessary for reinforcements by the voluntary method. I know this because I felt I must, as soon as possible, find someone who would undertake this task; I should find out as soon as possible whether McNaughton would be willing to undertake it. I spoke with him this morning, and I had an assurance from him that he thought we could get the reinforcements without resorting to conscription. He thought conscription would be disastrous for Canada, that he knew the French Canadians. General Crerar has referred to the whole conscription campaign centring on hatred of French Canadians, because of the so-called Zombie army, and spoke about the whole situation being a flame across the country. McNaughton knows the French Canadians, he knows the prejudices being worked up. It would be a terrible thing for Canada if this were permitted and if we had one province against the other. He is a strong believer in Canadian unity and believes it should be maintained, but not with conscription as an issue. He believes that an attempt to do anything of the kind would have an appalling effect through years to come.

I believe he can get the necessary reinforcements. He believes our men are being given an undue share of the fighting, being pressed too hard. Indeed, their lives are being unnecessarily sacrificed because of the extent of infantry fighting, resulting from the inadequate munitions and shells for guns, and guns themselves. I spoke of this yesterday, and Ralston made some statement to the effect that the infantry has never been without plenty of ammunition. McNaughton thinks that Drew is the greatest menace to Canada of any man in the country, that linking up with him on conscription would be a terrible thing. This whole business had come up since Drew began his agitation.

The people of Canada will say that McNaughton is the right man for the task, and since Ralston has clearly said that he himself does not believe that we could get the men without conscription, while McNaughton believes we can, and that he, Ralston, would have to tender his resignation, as he has said at different times he would if we pressed eliminating the conscription part of reinforcements, then I think that if Ralston feels that way he should make it possible for us to bring General McNaughton into the cabinet at once, the man who is prepared to see this situation through.

Ralston tendered his resignation to me some two years ago and has never withdrawn it. It has been a very trying thing for me to go on, day in day out, for this period with his resignation not with-drawn, but simply held. No one can say that McNaughton is not the best person who can be secured.

With that, King draws from his pocket the September exchange of letters between McNaughton and Ralston—the exchange that con-firmed McNaughton's promotion to general as he resigned from the military. King now turns that correspondence coldly against Ralston. He refers to a statement by Ralston holding that, while they have not seen eye to eye on some matters, he and McNaughton share a belief in the sincerity of each other's conviction. King also reads a passage in which Ralston praises McNaughton's perfor-mance in training the volunteer army, his great skill, the certainty of his desire to serve Canada.

There can be no misunderstanding McNaughton's qualifications, King says, having ruthlessly placed the words of recommendation for McNaughton in the mouth of the man he is replacing.

The hardest thing for any man to do is part with a colleague, King continues, especially one who has been as close as Ralston has been, and one for whom one has such high respect and, indeed, affection. But these are times of war, the worst war the world has ever known. The situation is particularly dangerous in that when it comes to a government going under at this time, with all the conse-quences that would produce in Canada and in other parts of the world, I feel no man can allow satisfying his own conscience to out-weigh what his conscience must tell him would be the consequence for all, to outweigh what he owes to the army, to the country and to the war effort. Ralston had taken up the words "Canada's war effort" as used by Crerar. Instead of furthering it, it would destroy the total effort, destroy it in reference to finance and other matters. I don't think we ought to allow this situation to drag on at all. The strongest of reasons has been given repeatedly why it should not, and I think we should decide at once what is to be done.

There was intense silence.

Thomas Crerar will record how he is "completely surprised" by the turn of events, as he thinks are "practically all other members of council." He has seen much confusion in King's mind in the course of the meeting. He has heard him declaring conscription would be enforced if necessary and advisable, then that it might be necessary but not advisable, and then that both conditions had to be met. He has heard him declaring he would not be the prime minister of a gov-ernment that introduced conscription, and at other times declaring the men overseas must be supported. On two occasions he has heard King tell cabinet he should talk to Churchill and get his advice, and once that he might consult Roosevelt.[3]

Ralston replies in the quietest voice. Of course I will give you my resignation at once. I wish to thank you for the opportunity given me to serve. I know I am limited in some things, but I have done the best I possibly could. Ralston speaks of the companionship they have all enjoyed, what it meant to him to share in the work with his colleagues. I sincerely hope the new move will be successful. I am not sure that it will be, but I certainly hope it will.

Ralston concludes by announcing he will retire to private life. His political career is over.

No words, King says, can express what we feel of his integrity, his service. It would be mere heroics to use any words regarding what we all know so well. This is not a personal matter. It is what the situation at the moment seems to demand. King thanks him for all he has done, *and again expressed how hard it was for me to say what I felt I had to say in the interests of Canada's war effort.*

Ralston gathers up his papers, turns to King and shakes his hand. He says something to the prime minister, but the exact words in the hair-trigger dignity of the moment elude him. They are something to the effect of, "Thank you for the opportunity I have had." Cabinet rises as one, forming a complete circle around the table. Ralston shakes hands with every member.

As Ralston moves to leave the chamber, King detains him at the door. The resignation: would it be possible to have it tonight? *He looked very anxious and strained and said could he have until morning? I said by all means, but please say nothing to anyone, to keep the matter wholly secret and confidential, until the other appointment was made. This he agreed to do....*

It is six-thirty. Ralston goes home for dinner, then returns to his office at eight forty-five, remaining there until two in the morning, spending a substantial part of that time reviewing the development with Macdonald, his closest cabinet ally. King heads to Government House to inform the Governor General of the afternoon's proceedings, and to explain what had taken so long. *It was apparent from H.E.'s face and manner that while he was saying nothing he was greatly concerned. I think his mind related all the time to the trouble there had been with McNaughton in Britain and the effects this might have on the High Command there.... Whatever H.E. said of McNaughton was very nice but it was not enthusiastic.*

He asked me if he might send word to the King; said he would like to get the word over as soon as possible. I said certainly....

Mackenzie King has blood on his hands. It is his own, or it is Ralston's, or it might be a commingling of both. In speaking with Mackenzie on this day, he tells his minister of veterans affairs: You will recall how in our caucuses, when I was speaking about waiting for the last term of Parliament, there would be endless demands that would be very hard to meet. That in regard to conscription I felt that I must be prepared to face what Sir Wilfrid had to face over conscription. After what was said by certain of my colleagues last night of what would follow, I realized that I had to face being crucified by some of my own party because I would not yield to conscription.

The passion of William Lyon Mackenzie King. The Czech medal dangles. Sir Wilfrid and Lady Laurier are somewhere in the station.

Malevolent forces are at work, aiming to destroy him and the government. Ralston was not deliberately attempting such a thing, but he has been their tool. *There is plenty of circumstantial evidence to make that as clear as day. They are the same forces that do not want social legislation.*

King confidently notes that McNaughton has many friends in military circles, a far greater following than Ralston. Only overseas will there be *consternation,* because of McNaughton's particular views about how the war should be run in the field.

Of course it is a terrific blow to Ralston. He has been more afraid of McNaughton than anyone. This will give McNaughton the chance to get the Canadian army together as one. It will give him a chance for much else. He will be a fine Minister of Defence to welcome back the men and will get [a] tremendous ovation from them wherever he appears. While I am deeply sorry to offend Ralston in any way, I cannot forget that he was prepared to have me and the government destroyed politically.

Conn Smythe has been blindsided by McNaughton's appointment. How can he possibly register dissent? This was the man he championed so vociferously in 1940 as deserving control of Canada's entire war effort. He wrote newspaper articles in support of his promotion; he even wrote Mackenzie King personally, and C.D. Howe as well. He cannot say that the McNaughton of the fall of 1944 is a different McNaughton from the one who charmed him in the summer of 1940. McNaughton would not have stood for conscription then, and there should be no surprise that he does not support it now. Conn Smythe went out on a limb for McNaughton in 1940, and he now must sense—and rue—how far above the ground and from the trunk that limb extends. But Smythe can only blame himself for his present perch. He was the one who made such a racket about having McNaughton promoted four years ago, and he has been the central figure in the campaign to send in the conscripts that has led King to dump Ralston in favour of McNaughton.

The prime minister is acutely, even gleefully, aware of the bind in which McNaughton's appointment places Conservative cheerleaders like Smythe. Let them try to attack him—*they have been lauding him to the sky.*

The press naturally must gather Smythe's reaction to the defence portfolio drama. On November 2, he is compelled to issue a statement, which presses the conscriptionist cause without evincing any criticism of McNaughton himself:

> In answer to the questions the newspapers have asked me, as far as I am concerned, the issue is not the merits or demerits of McNaughton or Ralston. The issue is still the sending of trained reinforcements to the fighting Canadian forces in Italy and on the continent. The appointment of General McNaughton has not added one man to the fighting forces.
>
> Prime Minister Churchill in Parliament last week stated that no mention of bringing back the five-year men should be allowed, as it was only raising false hopes, and that we were now facing the grimmest part of the war. General Alexander under Rome Nov. 2 date-line stated that the Allied forces in Italy have been numerically inferior to the Germans throughout most of the campaign. Our troops are fighting for you and me under these conditions, and they are short of trained reinforcements. It is up to you and me to see that every available trained fit Canadian be sent overseas at once. We voted the Government the necessary authority in the Plebiscite to send the draftees overseas. If they aren't sent, the onus is on McNaughton.

The statement is cleverly put. The issue cannot be the merits or demerits of McNaughton, because if it is, by corollary the issue would also be the merits or demerits of Smythe, who so relentlessly championed McNaughton as the man who deserved to direct Canada's entire war effort. The press either has a short memory or chooses to forget recent history: Smythe is not challenged on his lack of enthusiasm for the appointment of a man he described (in his letter to C.D. Howe of July 3, 1940) as being "known throughout Canada from coast to coast to be the best posted and most up-to-date Canadian on modern warfare."

In a story carried by the Canadian Press on November 3, an unscathed Smythe turns up the heat on the new defence minister, asserting that McNaughton will be able to provide reinforcements for the Canadian army overseas only if he enforces conscription immediately.

"That's the only way General McNaughton would inspire me with confidence," he says. "What worries me is that while we are trying to get reinforcements over, the men are short-handed and many are dying every hour of the day because of lack of reinforcements. The point is not an argument on McNaughton or Ralston, but it is the question of enforcing total conscription and in that way getting trained reinforcements over to help our men."

The conservative press sees no good news in the fall of Ralston and the rise of McNaughton. "A government which is not prepared to place the war and the reinforcement of soldiers ahead of its own political ambitions deserves to be driven from office and replaced by an administration that will do its duty without fear or favour," expounds the *Telegram* on November 2, and advises the Conservatives to demand an election if the Liberals don't bring in conscription.

A November 3 *Globe* editorial proposes that McNaughton's acceptance of the defence portfolio "will come as a terrific shock to the men overseas and the people of Canada. Under the known circumstances it has to be assumed that in taking this office he has agreed with the Government's cowardly and shameful policy of keeping the zombie army in futile idleness in Canada, and refusing to provide adequate reinforcements to the army he once commanded.... The general has taken on heavy army responsibilities, and the heavier responsibilities of a discredited government policy."

George Drew produces the least diplomatic response to the news of McNaughton's decision to join King's cabinet. Stung by McNaughton's decision to go back on his word to Bracken and enter politics—as a Liberal defence minister opposed to conscription—the premier of Ontario puts pen to paper. I would not insult a yellow dog, he informs the general, by calling you one.[4]

THE PLOT THICKENS

An Ottawa message brought the news of the resignation of Col. Ralston as Minister of National Defence, to be succeeded by Gen. McNaughton, former commander Cdn Army Overseas.
—FLAK, *November 3, 1944*

November 1, 1944

THE Canadians fighting for Walcheren have been exhausted, physically and mentally and in fighting numbers, by the offensives culminating in the debacle of the causeway assault. The narrow, 1,200-yard mound of cobblestones and mud linking South Beveland with Walcheren has been tested by the Black Watch, which sustained yet another bout of terrible losses. The Calgary Highlanders have also had a go, but the Germans used flame throwers to drive them back. The French Canadians of Les Maisonneuves picked up where the Highlanders left off, and some managed to reach Walcheren. But the losses were horrific, and the men were called back. There must be another way to take the island.

The Canadian infantry are pulled out of the fighting line. In their stead their commander, Lieutenant-General Guy Simonds, turns to the Royal Marines commando brigade attached to the Canadian army. Simonds employs them in a fresh strategy codenamed Infatuate: using artillery and aerial bombardments to breach the dykes and flood out the Germans, he creates beaches on which the Marines can carry out amphibious assaults. In the portion of their assault around Westkapelle at Walcheren's most seaward point, the Marines suffer three hundred casualties as twenty of twenty-seven landing craft are sunk or damaged. The attack, while bloody, is ultimately successful. On November 8, Walcheren is in Allied hands. But in five weeks of fighting, there have been 6,367 Canadian casualties. It will take virtually every volunteer, officer and enlisted man, in the reinforcement pool, to bring the army back up to strength.[1]

On November 2, the Toronto *Telegram* publishes an anonymous letter objecting to a photo recently run of some of the star players with the RCAF Bombers hockey team in Winnipeg: "The picture on your sports page of hockey players is a little more than I can stand. Two of my boys went overseas four years ago—one has been killed, the other is in Italy. All these hockey players in the picture have been in for nearly three years and are still in Canada. And are playing hockey. Please don't tell us that they are ever going to fight."

Sports editor J.P Fitzgerald does his best to defend the men in the photograph, some of whom were NHL stars before enlisting and will play when the war is over, others who will begin their NHL careers at the end of hostilities. Fitzgerald wonders why it is necessary to "heap obloguy [*sic*] on these men. They are in uniform and it is no fault of theirs they still are in Canada. Presumably they are in training for active participation in the war and there is no reason why they should not be playing hockey or baseball or soccer or any other game in their spare time or for conditioning purposes.

"It's quite possible that the odd athlete throughout the length and breadth of the land is pulling strings to keep from getting into active fighting, but by and large the vast majority are ready and willing to get going.

"Anybody in this or any other war can testify that hanging around camps is the most trying part of preparation.

"Unfortunately no soldier, sailor or flyer is in a position to demand that he be given this or that job, much less that he be sent overseas forthwith.

"That is the function of higher officers and in view of recent charges that untrained men have been sent into the fighting line it is unlikely that they will make that mistake again.

"The hockey players in this particular case are in uniform, are on the active list and no man can do more. They are not zombies nor made for Canadian service only and it would seem that the time has passed when even the military authorities will dare to build up hockey teams for home consumption."

Fitzgerald has tabled a remarkable rationale for the lengthy military hockey careers of some volunteers: the military is only taking heed of Conn Smythe's charge that volunteers have been poorly trained, and is making sure that these boys are fully trained before sending them into combat.

Tonight, in Montreal, the Maple Leafs of Hap Day and the Canadiens of Dick Irvin meet in their first encounter of the season, their first game since Montreal eliminated Toronto in the semifinals the previous spring, their first game at the Forum since March 30, when Montreal won 11–0. The summer has not caused the bitterness of the 1944 playoffs to fade. If anything, the wartime antagonism between French and English Canada that has blossomed in recent months in the heat of the debate over the NRMA has given this rivalry fresh and angry overtones—at least to the fans.

The game degenerates into a brawl. After Toe Blake ties the game at one apiece midway through the second period, the penalty parade begins, most of them meted out to Montreal. Murph Chamberlain, Elmer Lach and Ray Getliffe all do time. Nick Metz of Toronto joins them.

The fisticuffs start in the third period. Getliffe earns a minor and a ten-minute misconduct; teammate Leo Lamoureux is awarded a major and a ten-minute misconduct. From the Leafs, twenty-year-old Bill Ezinicki, a new recruit who won a Memorial Cup with the Oshawa Generals last spring (and had played with Red Tilson on the 1942/43 Generals), picks up a major. Minor penalties also go to Lach, Butch Bouchard and Maurice Richard of Montreal, and Toronto captain Bob Davidson. Rarely during the period are the teams at even strength.

Referee King Clancy, a star of the Leafs before the war, hands out eleven penalties to Montreal, five to Toronto over the course of the game. The Forum fans pelt the ice with papers and bottles; a chair is launched from a private box. Somewhere in the midst of the penalties, Toronto scores three unanswered third-period goals—Schriner from Lorne Carr, Gus Bodnar from Schriner and Pete Backor, and Carr from Schriner. The Leafs have won 4–1 on the strength of three power-play goals. As Clancy leaves the ice, a fan slugs him in the face.

"There's nothing wrong with hockey when teams go out and play like that," league interim president Red Dutton crows. "What a game! It reminded me of some of those battles between the Maroons and the Canadiens! Those are the games that fill the rinks." Those games between the Maroons and the Canadiens were as good as a war on ice between French-speaking Catholics and English-speaking Protestants. With the Maroons gone since 1938, the Canadiens have been icing a lineup that is a blend of both cultures, but the idea of two of the country's founding cultures scrapping so heatedly when the Leafs and the Canadiens now meet is what is most important at the turnstiles.

On the ice, culture is no more an issue than it is in the rivalry that persists between Toronto and Detroit. This rivalry, at the level of the trenches, is the time-honoured one of athletes concerned about bragging rights. But up in the seats of the Forum, what did the Montreal fans see and sense when Clancy handed out twice as many penalties to les Canadiens as to the Leafs? What motherlode of resentment and anger moved them to the brink of rioting? Over a hockey game?

Today's paper also carries a notice that Bob Carse, the former Chicago Blackhawk, is missing in action.

❧

"Every year, about this time," Jim Coleman writes in his *Globe and Mail* column of November 3, "this department is deluged by mail from indignant correspondents who enclose clipped pictures of professional hockey players, with bitter comment pencilled in the margins. Judge Macdonell, in a city court early this week, epitomized these pencilled comments when he observed that it was 'perfectly disgusting that husky hockey players were able to obtain military deferments.' These critics are wrong, we think, when they insist upon pointing the finger of scorn at individual hockey players. If anyone should be blamed, it should be the club owners who have countenanced and counselled this 'war job' hanky panky in the past few years.

"Two and a half years ago this bureau was ingenious enough to predict that the manpower shortage and draft requirements would knock the National Hockey League out of business, and once went so far as to advocate that, if necessary, professional sports should be abandoned for the duration.

"That prediction certainly stood up well, didn't it? Since then the National Hockey League has enjoyed two of the most successful seasons, financially.

"Again we say there is no point in tossing harpoons at individual hockey players. If deferments have been obtained they couldn't be obtained any more readily by a professional hockey player than they could be obtained by a bank clerk, a bellboy or a newspaperman.

"However, to question as to whether hockey clubs have exerted influence to have players deferred for medical reasons is a matter which we will leave to the conscience of the club owners. We're damn sure that a lot of mutton-headed players have listened to some shockingly poor advice in the matter of military service....

"For two and a half years we have been ingenious enough to believe that professional hockey has been about to be shattered by a fine old scandal. Here it is the winter of 1944-45, and the bomb hasn't burst."

❦

"I should like to climb on the post-war bandwagon and predict a great boom in professional and amateur hockey," writes Lance-Bombardier Doug Gillespie of 30th battery in the November 3 edition of *FLAK*; the battery is now on the south bank of the Scheldt, where it scans the skies for enemy aircraft during Infatuate. "Though the calibre of hockey in the National League runs well below peacetime standards, Canadian and American citizens have been packing the arenas in ever-increasing numbers. Toronto Maple Leafs in each of the past two seasons have drawn more customers through the turnstiles than in any other season since the Garden [*sic*] was built. This is the same throughout the League.

"At the conclusion of the war, the armed forces will release such stars as Apps, Schmidt, Taylor, Brimsek, Bentley, Colville, Stanowski, Reardon, Patrick, Drillon, Roy Conacher and others. These players back in the line-up along with the young blood now performing in the big league will ensure the fans of a much better quality of hockey, and interest will grow accordingly...."

❦

On or about November 6, Bob Carse of the Chicago Blackhawks and the Royal Winnipeg Rifles is marched out of Stalag 11B and into a train boxcar as part of a group of prisoners being transferred to a new POW camp. The boxcar offers only standing room, and the men devise a stand-up, sit-down routine to offer rest. They cross what used to be the German border with Poland and end their trip at Stalag 8C outside Sagan in Upper Silesia. The camp is about seventy-five miles northwest of Swidnica, where Conn Smythe was interred in 1917.

The camp is segregated along racial and ethnic lines, with sectors delineated by fences topped with barbed wire. Prisoners from India have their own area; so do black South Africans. The Canadians are tossed in with the white South Africans, who do their best to make them comfortable. They are next door to Stalag Luft 3, a prison camp for Allied airmen. On the night of March 24–25, 1944, seventy-six prisoners tunnelled their way to liberty in the breakout immortalized as the Great Escape. Only three prisoners made it successfully out of occupied Europe. Fifty who were recaptured were executed. As winter descends, Carse can hear from Luft 3 the sound of shooting. And scoring.

Members of the RCAF are interred next door. Military hockey has come to Upper Silesia.

Replying to your letter of the 4th, Air Force Routine Order 1795 dated August 19, 1944, instructed that personnel who have served two years or more in Canada only, provided their services have not been terminated on grounds of misconduct or inefficiency, would not be subject to recall for military service. The Navy works on the same basis.

I trust this is the information you desire.

—letter written November 7 to Toronto Maple Leaf coach Hap Day by S.H. McLaren, Associate Director, National Selective Service, Department of Labour

A war within a war; a day within a day; a picture within a picture. William Lyon Mackenzie King is standing at the Cenotaph in Ottawa, marking the eleventh hour of the eleventh day of the eleventh month, twenty-six years to the minute since the guns marshalled by Andrew McNaughton fell silent and the Great War was over. General McNaughton, paying tribute to comrades who fell in this and the last war, honouring the memory of his own son, lost in the air force in 1942, is by King's side; and so, in his own way, is Sir Wilfrid Laurier. A package was sitting on the hall bench at Laurier House last night, and King put off opening it until this morning. As he moved to unwrap it, he looked at the clock. The hands were perfectly aligned at twenty-two minutes past ten. *I said this is significant.* The paper torn away, he found a colour print reproduction depicting Laurier attending the coronation of George V. Laurier is at the centre of the composition, which shows the coronation parade in London. As King stands at the Cenotaph, the parallels between this moment and the Laurier image strike him. Both have a prime minister, members of cabinet, a central statue, police escorts, a nation's capital. Here he has the Governor General with him, the King's representative—the King being George VI. Adding significance are documents presented to him at the ceremony requiring his signature. They pertain to Canada's treaty with China. King contemplates Laurier's responsibility for Canada coming to sign her own international treaties. *If Sir Wilfrid had wished to make his presence to me known at this most significant hour, I do not see how that could have been brought about more effectively even beginning with the editorial in the* Citizen.

The miserable conscriptionist press. The nerve the *Citizen* had, printing that editorial that very morning. "Laurier's Better Way."

How could they even argue that if Laurier were alive today he would approve of conscription, based on the fact that he had suggested a plebiscite on the issue in 1917? *This lying article on the part of the conscriptionist press is appalling.*

McNaughton is striving mightily to meet the reinforcement shortage without conscription, but it is a struggle. The surprises come quickly. In his meetings with King leading to his appointment as defence minister, McNaughton asserted that a shortage of artillery ammunition was a factor in the number of infantry needed to do the fighting. He must now concede that the ammunition shortage is, on close examination, a thing of the past, only temporary. He has concluded that the reinforcement situation cannot be met exclusively by volunteers from the general population. They are going to have to convince some of the Zombies to go general. But this could be difficult, as McNaughton discovered, almost immediately, that they are being too well paid as conscripts to want to volunteer.

What a moment that was, when McNaughton informed the war cabinet on November 3 that some of the Zombies were being allowed to hold jobs that paid them as much as six or seven dollars a day, at a time when general service men were making $1.25. King saw universal *surprise* in the faces of his ministers when McNaughton revealed this, noting that it naturally had to stop. Any reader of the Toronto *Telegram* of November 2 knew all the facts about ongoing work assignments for conscripts. With wretchedly bad timing for the anti-conscriptionist cause, the first of 530 French-Canadian NRMA men had just begun arriving in the Toronto area. They were mainly members of the Régiment de Joliette augmented by conscripts from Valcartier, Borden, Petawawa and Farnham. About two hundred Joliette men had already been sent to the Simcoe Basic Training Centre several months ago to help bring in the Norfolk County tobacco crop, and then pitched in with harvesting fruit. The Toronto-area arrivals have been assigned to work on track maintenance for the CNR and CPR and in other construction duties. One of those jobs is helping complete the Sunnybrook Military Hospital in Scarborough—ironically a duty J.L. Ralston insisted they be assigned to while he was still defence minister. Labour Minister Humphrey Mitchell was embarrassed in cabinet by this development. The *Telegram* revealed that any monies earned in excess of the basic soldiers' pay and the cost of board and lodging would be given to the soldier. "It would appear that if the weather is reasonably good," the *Telegram* reports, "the men will receive from $10 to $15 a week more than they would get as soldiers." *No-one in cabinet seemed to acknowledge they knew men were receiving extra money. They understood employers were to pay for labour at price other labour would receive, but surplus pay was to go to the state, for war purposes. Mitchell said there had been no such agreement. Ilsley and others thought there had been.* Two days into his new post, General McNaughton was able to shame his fellow ministers with their own ignorance. And he now understood what a difficult time he will have trying to convince NRMA men to go active when they are making such handsome wages as conscripts.

McNaughton wanted to organize an appeal to the NRMA immediately, but King dithered. They could not begin one until the U.S. presidential election was over, on the seventh. And then there was the Victory Loan drive, which ended on Armistice Day, the eleventh. Then they could go ahead.

In this way the appeal lost precious days. McNaughton did address a Canadian Legion gathering in Ottawa on November 6 with King, but their reception was frosty. As McNaughton and King stand together at the Cenotaph, they know every imaginable veterans' group is aligned with Ralston.

Ralston is gone from cabinet, but is still there in spirit. He has his supporters in and out of the government, not the least of whom is General Stuart, whom McNaughton has fired. Not a firing, but a leave pending retirement, just the way McNaughton's firing was a medical leave; and Ralston's departure was a resignation, but King is having a hard time convincing some of his own cabinet ministers of the fact. When he read to cabinet on November 7 a draft of a speech he was to give the next day over the CBC, there were objections to its comments on Ralston. There is nothing there about Ralston having been prepared to stay on with the administration, Angus Macdonald said. And he did not resign.

But he did resign. That is King's position. The fact that Ralston did not walk into the fateful meeting on November 1 with a letter of resignation in his hand, lay it on the table before King and say, "I resign," is not important to King. Nor is the fact that King had to request the letter, and wait until the next day for it. *I then had to go over the ground again about his saying repeatedly that he would have to resign and would resign if his recommendation was not accepted; that he had put it always on the ground that he would have to resign in virtue of what he had said in parliament.*

Macdonald warned King that Ralston might take exception to King's account. Well, I will try to be sure that nothing could possibly be misinterpreted, King said. I will seek to make reference to Ralston's sincerity, words like that.

In his radio speech, King reviewed for the nation the circumstances surrounding Ralston's departure. He told the country how Ralston had come back from his overseas tour to ask for conscription, how King realized he would resign unless his recommendation was followed. How King then sought the advice of General McNaughton, who believed the volunteer system had not been exhausted. How a volunteer army is more effective and the country more united as a result. How only about 8,000 of 60,000 Zombies were sufficiently trained as infantry reinforcements to be ready for combat at an early date. How Ralston had resigned and McNaughton had replaced him.

He reviewed for the country the history of conscripts. How, to date, about 68,000 men have been called up, of which nine thousand are on extended leave, on compassionate or other grounds. He told the country that not all the NRMA men are Quebecers. Only 23,000 are from that province, only 25,000 in all are French-speaking. He told the country that of another 82,000 draftees, 33,000 were "wastage," which included men discharged for medical or other reasons. That another 6,000 of those 82,000 enlisted as volunteers in the navy or airforce, and the remaining 43,000 for general service in the army. Finally, King appealed directly to the NRMA men in the listening audience to consider volunteering.

The speech does not go over well, at least not with Ralston, who has kept his silence publicly over his disappearance from the cabinet, indicating only that he has left it to King to do any explaining. He is infuriated by King's speech, and on November 12 he strikes back with his own account of what transpired.

"I had understood Government policy to be that if there was need for reinforcements overseas and volunteers were not available, NRMA personnel would be sent," he tells the press. "This was what I had taken from the Prime Minister's speeches in 1942. It was in effect what I, as Minister, had repeatedly said in the House since."

Ralston offers to the press the text of King's speech at the end of debate over Bill 80 on July 7, 1942, in which he minimized the number of legislative steps that would be required to send in the conscripts—just the order-in-council and a motion of confidence. The reinforcement crisis is immediate and not postponable, Ralston asserts. There will be outright shortages in fighting lines in December because of a lack of men in reinforcement pools; these shortages would increase in the new year.

Ralston's retort is not quite as bad as King expected; neither is it entirely true, he assures himself. *Repeated the error that I had asked him to resign, etc. I could see at once that it was part of a plot to keep up this controversy and to get me out on the conscription issue.* Furthermore, King believes that Ralston has breached the confidentiality of cabinet and exposed state secrets.

Ralston's departure has not solved King's basic problem of cabinet unity. At the war cabinet meeting on November 3, Thomas Crerar handed him a letter. It followed the arguments Ilsley had made that very day, pressing for what the government intended to do if the appeal for volunteers is not successful. After receiving the letter, King braced himself for the resignations that he expected would follow: first Crerar, then Macdonald, perhaps Howe too. Howe, who is a friend of McNaughton's, *might at least wait until we've had appeal.*

Of his three defence ministers, that would leave him only with Power—missing again, apparently owing to drink, on November 1, then suddenly in the hospital on November 2 with appendicitis.* The issue, for King, is no longer being argued on the basis of merit or logic. Lies and deception and misrepresentation—that is what his world is steeped in now. He faces plots and vengeance. How could Crerar, who opposed Ralston more than anyone on increasing the size of the army over the years, now favour conscription? He has also received a letter from Macdonald, pressing for a date to be set for the end of the appeal to the NRMA men. He is suggesting, as Ralston did before he departed cabinet, that it be November 30. While Macdonald has made it clear he won't be running again in Kingston, his veiled intention, King is certain, is to lead the Liberal party in Nova Scotia and regain the premiership. *He will use his power in that position to help to get conscription in that province and defeat the administration of which he has been a member right along.*

Ralston and Macdonald are still working together, he can see. McNaughton is sure there is a plot: the army was built up to avoid

---

*In his memoirs, Power wrote that he returned to his Quebec City riding on October 27, and was admitted to hospital there on November 2 for an emergency appendectomy.

conscription, but some are nonetheless determined to have it. The general wants the government to go before Parliament and reiterate its commitment to voluntary enlistment for overseas service. He and King agree that there will be *immediate trouble involving bloodshed* if conscription is imposed on the Zombies.

King decides to recall Parliament and ask for a vote of confidence: *I could not go on this way. That was the only alternative to public controversy.* King has the press notified that he has instructed the Speaker of the House, James Glen, to request the members of the House to return to their seats on November 22. He then speaks with the Governor General, who expresses his consternation with Ralston. The earl likes Ralston, but cannot understand him. It is wrong for the controversy in the newspapers to be kept up, he tells King. I hope it will not continue. The G.G. cannot help but return to the issue of McNaughton's religion. One of drawbacks of McNaughton's appointment, he tells King, is that he's a Catholic, and as such will not be able to visit any Protestant churches. *I said I did not know what his religion was.* In cabinet the next day, Macdonald will observe that someone said he, McNaughton and Power were all Catholics, helping to save the Catholics—meaning the French Canadians—from enlisting. McNaughton will note that some of the papers have spoken of him as a Presbyterian. For the record, he will tell his colleagues that he is Anglican and his wife is Catholic.

King's resolution swings wildly. He voices his confidence that he can carry the House. He tells Power that they are going through the conscription crisis of the fall of 1917 all over again, and that he would not think of *handing over anything unless I found myself without a party.* Over dinner St. Laurent urges King not to allow the Conservatives to carry out their plans without his first appealing to the people, presumably with an election, should he be defeated in the confidence vote. The people should get to have their say. But King does not have the determination he expressed to Power earlier. It would be best to go to the Governor General and ask others to be called upon, he tells St. Laurent. They will have difficulty forming a government and carrying out conscription, and while they might extend the term of Parliament, they would have to have an election. Then they would be defeated. King's sentiment seems to be to cut his losses and reap the political benefits down the road.

On the evening of the thirteenth, the *Globe and Mail* goes to work calculating how the House of Commons will align behind the

King and Ralston. At least 40 of 161 Liberals will support Ralston (presuming he even asks for support), along with the Conservatives and Social Credit. The position of the CCF remains unclear to the conservative paper. With eleven seats vacant, if every non-Liberal vote were to back Ralston along with the 40 Liberal renegades, the Ralston camp would number 113, leaving the loyal King ranks at 121. Based on these numbers, King could win a confidence vote, but it would be a paper-thin victory. It might not be strong enough for him to carry on governing.

While the *Globe* calculates, Karl Homuth, Conservative MP for South Waterloo, addresses a memorial banquet of the Kitchener branch of the Canadian Legion. "You people have read the statements from Major Connie Smythe," he says. "Some of you have, perhaps, received personal letters bearing out these facts. I not only have letters from officers overseas, but I have families in my riding whose sons, almost children insofar as warfare is concerned, are now lying in hospital or are buried in Europe."

His wounds confining him to his home, Conn Smythe's existence is limited to words, public utterances on the subject of reinforcements. He has become a patron saint of the uncompromising war effort, his notoriety ennobled by his own suffering. Like his nemesis Mackenzie King, his world in the fall of 1944 is defined by lies and deception. The government is not being honest about the reinforcement situation because it wants to hold on to political power by not offending voters in Quebec. And like King, he fears insurrection, a palace revolution. The offer of the NHL presidency—that was just director Ed Bickle's and acting general manger Frank Selke's way of manoeuvring him right out of Maple Leaf Gardens. He has also not forgiven Selke for the deal that sent Frank Eddolls to Montreal in exchange for Ted Kennedy, no matter how well Kennedy has done.[2] In Smythe's mind Selke and Bickle have been acting as if Smythe is never coming back, as if Selke is more than an interim general manager.

Conn Smythe built this club and the building in which they have achieved their glories, in the same way that Mackenzie King built the Liberal party machine that has managed to hold on to power since 1935. Both men see themselves as irreplaceable focal points of their respective institutions, fonts of strength and greatness for those around them. They are leaders accustomed to winning, to having their opinions heeded and their orders obeyed. The captain who made the mistake of beginning an inspection of 30th Battery ranks at Petawawa without waiting for Smythe was never allowed to make that mistake again. *You're not trying to take my battery away from me, are you, captain?* So long as Smythe can reassert his grip on the Gardens, Selke has no more of a future within the Maple Leaf organization than J.L. Ralston did in the Liberal cabinet.

But Smythe's ambition at the moment exceeds the confines of the Gardens. He also wants to tell King how to prosecute the war and who belongs in his cabinet. His assessment of the reinforcement situation has been consistent, if one-dimensional. It can be summed up as: we have 60,000 Zombies who are trained to fight; make them fight. And the public by and large appears to agree. With the exception of a few bitter letters to the editor and the awkward shifting of some sports columnists, the idea that not just Zombies, but hockey players too, should be in the fight does not catch hold in the public imagination.

The newspapers project a mad cacophony of contradictions. There are pages full of notices of men missing in action, men killed, men wounded, men captured. There are politicians like Bracken, supported by men like Smythe, charging that the army desperately needs more reinforcements, that every NRMA man in the country must go overseas at once. And then, like missives from a parallel universe, there are sports stories relating the latest exploits of armed services hockey teams—teams like Newmarket Army, which features in its lineup Leaf star Billy Taylor, who enlisted shortly after Red Tilson in June 1943, who continues to shoot pucks while volunteers who have been in the army for far less than a year are dying in Europe—while Tilson lies in a temporary grave in a Dutch pear orchard.

During this new season, the press items are jarring in their incongruity. On one page: a notice about a young Toronto amateur athlete who has died in combat overseas with the RCAF, the span between his enlistment and his loss six months. On another page: professional hockey players on RCAF teams in Canada who have been in the service for two, three years, some of them Maple Leafs. In the sporting press there is a surreal matter-of-factness in reporting that players who have received medical discharges from the armed forces are back on the rosters of NHL teams, judged by the army too unwell to aim a rifle but found healthy enough by desperate coaches to withstand the rigours of professional hockey. And this when men overseas are sent back into the fighting line after being wounded two, three or more times.

On November 14, the Toronto *Telegram*'s sports department turns verbal somersaults in extending congratulations to a soldier who has been discharged on medical grounds just in time to resume a hockey career. Like Taylor a star with the Memorial Cup–winning Oshawa Generals of 1939, he volunteered at the start of the war, went through officers' training and received the rank of captain, the *Telegram* salutes. "Our young man went to war.... Did his various duties over a four year period," the paper vaguely sums up. "Then it happened.... An old injury spoiled everything.... Came sickness...hospitalization...convalescence...and...finally...honorable discharge.... Came the next step...the road back to civilian life.... The chance again to play hockey." Last night, he marched into Conn Smythe's Maple Leaf Gardens and signed an agreement to play for the new Gardens attraction, the Senior team to be known as the Toronto Staffords and run by Harold Ballard.

In fairness to the discharges, there are injuries that cannot be tolerated in the fighting line that can nonetheless be made tolerable for sixty-minute bursts by team trainers and doctors. A bad knee or shoulder that won't see a player through basic training can be nursed through a hockey season with drugs and therapy. Even so, there is no public warming to an underlying contradiction in Conn Smythe's stance: that he should be calling for the most dramatic measures to support the boys overseas while the professional hockey system of which he is a part embarks on another profitable season. On November 8, his own coach, Hap Day, upon hearing that new Leaf recruits Bill Ezinicki and Pete Backor have been summoned for their second army medicals to assess their suitability for service, unabashedly expresses his own priorities at this time of national crisis: "Certainly hope we don't lose either right now." (He loses Ezinicki.)

It is as if the Zombie army has anaesthetised the citizenry against feeling any broad resentments toward the continued existence of professional sports, or toward the fact that many athletes who are in the armed forces appear to be carrying on as athletes. In the NRMA men, the country has found a focal point for its contempt and impatience. The public wants hockey—to watch, to cheer. It does not want the NRMA men in Canada any more. Canadian citizens—at least the ones who buy tickets to professional hockey games—by packing arenas with sellout crowds have tacitly given their approval to the fact that young men are playing hockey instead of fighting overseas or contributing to war work, the latter now being impossible on even a part-time basis, thanks to the change in the league constitution. And overseas, men in uniform have been delighted to receive the specially arranged game broadcasts by Foster Hewitt on the BBC. One Canadian soldier will recall being moved to tears by the sound of Hewitt's play-by-play crackling from an English radio. Hockey, in a strange but not altogether absurd way, is part of what they have been fighting for. It is an essential element of the nation's character. When the war is over, the fans will readily forget about who did and did not fight, and why. Many of the fans faced the very same decisions about whether or not to go, and arrived, like the players themselves, at their own decisions. To suggest to many fans that there should not be hockey while there is a war on would be to suggest that there should not be books, magazines, newspapers, radio programs, movies and plays. No one writing the screenplay for a romantic comedy to distract the citizenry and those in the services from the daily carnage is accused of forsaking personal duty to the state and humanity. Why must the athletes be singled out for excoriation above all other entertainers?

Professional sport—not just hockey, but other commercial pursuits like baseball and football—is trapped in a mass of contradictions. It matters because it is entertainment, a harmless distraction that a beleaguered public is entitled to enjoy, yet it is also supposed to matter because it is part and parcel of society's backbone. It matters because the men who play the games are symbols of courage and sacrifice, but these men must not be expected to be sacrificed courageously on some battlefield just because they are a symbol of it. The games must go on because they are part of the nation's heart and soul; the games must go on because, even if they have nothing to do with the nation's heart and soul, the war effort will not benefit in any material way if they stop. Just as Lieutenant-General Pope can argue that Canada's presence or absence in the Allied forces will make no difference to the outcome of the war in the Pacific, hockey fans can make the same argument about the practical contribution NHL players can make to the war overall. With only about ninety men needed to form the lineups of the six-team National league in 1944/45, ten NHLs would have to shut down to produce enough men for just one regiment. About six hundred National Hockey Leagues would be required to match the total size of the NRMA force. In professional baseball, about four hundred men are required at spring training—barely a drop in the manpower pool the U.S. armed forces are drawing upon.

But there is, of course, a larger principle involved. A call to arms is a call to arms. Once certain classes and categories are unofficially exempted, beyond those judged to be in industries and endeavours essential to the war effort, beyond the conscientious objectors, the farmers, the infirm, then society is playing a wink-and-nod game over worthiness, which devolves into a question not of valour and honour, but of expendability. Some must die for a freedom that others have the reserved right to enjoy. A Red Tilson is considered expendable, and is expended. A Billy Taylor must be harboured.

Here's mud in your eye and more power to your arm. I would have written you before congratulating you on the now famous interview but I've been holding off hoping for results which now seem to be rolling in. My hope now is that the late Minister won't allow his loyalty to Willie prevent him from speaking his piece like a little man and telling the country what we all know, to wit, that the bottom of the voluntary reinforcement barrel has long been reached.

It's an interesting situation, and fraught with great opportunity for a man like yourself, with the money and, one hopes, the ambition to get into public service....

My interest in the matter is very personal now that I have an 18 year old boy in the Army who as sure as Hell will be on the western front before his 19th birthday, after six or seven months of training, unless the policy is changed. Not that John won't have to take his chance, but, by God, 18 year olds have neither the physique, stamina, endurance, or training to do the man's job required. Naturally, I don't want to be quoted, as while I'm quite ready for civil life again, I want to go back in my own time and not be kicked out by Canada's lemons of political high command soldiers.

Just a line more. Do your best to contradict the theory that these Zombies are no-good cowards. Eighty percent of them will go, & go willingly, when the Gov't tells them to, so don't let people get diverted into contempt for the Zombies, from the real issue, which is that the Gov't is the no-good collection of cowards in asking men to lay their lives on the line when it is not even prepared to lay its political future there.

—*undated letter to Conn Smythe from Major Harry Robinson, commander of an anti-aircraft battery in Prince Rupert, B.C.*

On November 14, General McNaughton releases figures disclosing the number of men in the home defence army and their provinces of origin. While Quebecers form the single largest group, they are not in the majority. Of 58,000 NRMA men, just under 36 per cent—20,800—are Quebecers. Fifteen thousand are from Ontario, 13,800 from the Prairies, 4,300 from the Atlantic provinces and 4,100 from British Columbia.

The CCF is no longer concerned about offending its western power base by supporting the idea of sending in the conscripts. "My personal opinion is that we have to see to it that our men are fully supported and reinforced, whatever that means, and this can only be ascertained when we have access to the information in the possession of the government which includes relevant reports and documents," says M.J. Coldwell on November 15. "If it is shown that the need is there, we must use all means in our power to reinforce our men overseas.

"That would mean sending the home defence forces overseas if the situation is serious enough to demand it. It must all be predicated on the information given to the House."

November 16—it has been nine days since the U.S. presidential election. Roosevelt pulls up at Laurier House in his large car, alone, with space beside him for King. He looks well and happy, smiling cheerfully. You left a burden around the corner, he tells King, who climbs into the car. King puts an arm around Roosevelt and tells him how deeply he loves him for himself, and how much all their associations have meant to him.

Suddenly they are seated together in the House of Commons. There is so much excitement that King has to call out "Order!" Roosevelt is about to take the oath of office. I am being sworn to protect the Constitution and to uphold the Atlantic Charter, the president declares, then leaves his chair and seats himself on the floor in an open space beside King's desk.

Eight o'clock. King receives his wake-up call. He ponders the comforting vision. It must symbolize the help he could be receiving through Roosevelt in his hour of need, both before and during the upcoming House session. *My burden will be eased through some action of his, and both the political, the Constitution, and the social, the Atlantic Charter, will be met and upheld.*

Fortified by the vision of Roosevelt, King then receives reassuring news from McNaughton, which the general repeats for the cabinet that afternoon. He does not hold out much hope of finding more volunteers from the "hard core" conscripts now in the camps, but he reports a gain of upwards of three thousand trained men available in Britain. He makes clear all ships up to the end of December are booked full, and that the acute reinforcement shortfall might not come until late January.

King has his plan for the new session of the House. On the first day, he will table his exchange of correspondence with Ralston regarding the defence minister's resignation. Then he will adjourn until the next day, when the House will meet in secret session so that members will know the pertinent reinforcement facts that cannot be publicly disclosed. He has had the idea of making McNaughton a senator so that he can get him into the House for all this, but McNaughton won't accept the appointment.

The president of the Progressive Conservative party, Charles P. McTague, has offered in the press his impression of King's forthcoming strategy. King will be goaded into asking for a vote of confidence. When he finds he cannot win it, he will accept the House's verdict of conscription, dissolve the house, and go to the country in a general election. King is completely baffled. *How a man's mind could conceive of such a thing, I don't know but it does indicate what Tories would like me to do. They do not want to be the ones to be responsible for conscription in a general election.*

❧

It all seems to be going well, until Sunday the nineteenth. King hears from McNaughton, who informs him he has encountered *a rather formidable difficulty*. The commanding officers of the NRMA camps are revolting.

Come by at four, King tells him. McNaughton arrives very early, at three-fifteen, a bad sign. King sees the clock hands aligned, pointing to the right.

They settle into the library of Laurier House. McNaughton produces telegrams from the commanding officers in Winnipeg, Calgary, Vancouver and Toronto, all to Lieutenant-General J.C. Murchie, Chief General Staff in Ottawa, all saying that McNaughton has misrepresented their position in a statement he has made to the press. In it, McNaughton expressed his confidence, after speaking with them, that the volunteer system would succeed. On the contrary, the commanders say they told McNaughton they didn't think the volunteer system would.

It is a potentially fatal error for the reinforcement drive. McNaughton has alienated the NRMA base camp commanders, just when he needs their help in getting their men to go general. *The General explained that his confidence lay in the fact that while they had spoken frankly of their doubt, they had nevertheless given the assurance they would make another try and that he, himself, felt with that attitude and all the forces that were at work and would be now coming to work, for example the individual efforts from men's families; the Parliament meeting, public opinion shaping up, etc., etc. That everything would come through all right.*

I have to handle these commanders carefully, he tells King. If they begin to oppose me, I might have a revolt on my hands, a situation that would be very difficult to manage. It is important to avoid a quarrel, *to explain quite clearly what he meant and express the hope that they would, with that understanding, do their best to further the new policy.* He shows King the reply to them he has drafted and a statement he intends to give to the press, *all of which I thought was exceedingly good.*

McNaughton blames Pearkes for the rebellion. He was a friend of Stuart, McNaughton explains, and while McNaughton was in charge of the First Canadian Army he sent Pearkes, commander of the 1st Infantry Division, home in 1942 to look after Zombies. Montgomery had been determined to get rid of Pearkes, declaring he "has no brains."[3] McNaughton is sure Pearkes, a Victoria Cross recipient in the Great War, blames him for being sent home.

King reminds McNaughton how he had said to him after a recent war cabinet meeting that *our men were suspicious of Pearkes. They felt he had never tried to make the voluntary system go.* McNaughton replied at the time that he was sure Pearkes would be loyal and helpful, King adds. He also reminds McNaughton how he avowed that Pearkes had been very close to him in England, had grown up under him, how he felt he knew Pearkes thoroughly and trusted him absolutely. Well, King has had his fill of trust. *One soon finds out how little one can trust men when a popular tide is running in an opposite direction*, he counsels McNaughton.

The general then tells King that Macdonald has been pressing him for information about total men overseas, the number of available reinforcements. He is reluctant to relinquish these figures, feeling they should be reserved for cabinet. Remember, King says, that whatever Macdonald asks for, it is for the use of Ralston and his friends.

I have come to see that, McNaughton admits.

We'll get through all right, McNaughton predicts. If I can get this business settled, I would be perfectly happy. I would feel I had accomplished my real work, even if I never do anything else in my life.

It has been a challenge for McNaughton to cope with the campaign against him. *Telegrams calling him everything from Judas Iscariot down.* He reflects on how much the conscription lobby has set back their effort to recruit voluntarily. King could not agree more. However, McNaughton says, the situation is there. We shall have to do the best we possibly can to meet it.

When King rises the next day, Monday the twentieth, he inspects his list of inspirational morning readings for the coming week. All are from the Crucifixion.

It is all coming together now. A convergence of images of suffering, loss and betrayal. The cross he thought poor Gardiner had to bear. The Czech medallion. Laurier crucified by his own party. McNaughton branded as Judas. The image touches even Conn Smythe, who will reflect that he half expected to be crucified by the government when he made his September 19 statement. King has been sure his turn would come.

It looks as if this were to be my week in the Garden of Gethsemani and that I shall come to know something of the Station of the Cross. I shall have to go through something of the nature of Christ's passion.

THE CROSS HE BEARS

I allowed my wits to wander at times, and to imagine as I looked at
Mr. King presiding at the head of the [cabinet] table that behind
him I could see the wraith-like figure of Sir Wilfrid, and behind
Laurier that of old John A....
—*Lieutenant-General Maurice Pope*, Soldiers and Politicians

WHAT does English Canada know of Quebec in the autumn of
1944? It is a strange land that speaks a foreign tongue, populated
by citizens who worship in the Church of Rome, whose political
life is populated by the most extraordinary characters. In just the
past few months they have elected provincially a premier, Maurice
Duplessis, who practises an autocratic nationalism; those who cast
ballots for him turned their backs on Liberal premier Adelard
Godbout, who had brought in compulsory elementary education
and given women the vote. Godbout himself blamed those women
for turfing him out. His government had supported King's conscription policy, though opposing compulsory overseas service
after Bill 80 was passed, and as he complained to King after the
election loss, these newly enfranchised women did not want their
sons and brothers to have to fight. Duplessis would never make
them fight. And what to make of Montreal? After spending four
years in a military prison for inciting defiance of the NRMA draft
registration, Camillien Houde has been reinstated as mayor by the
city's adoring electorate. No wonder NRMA medical deferrals are
about twice as common in Montreal as they are in Toronto.
Quebec's most ardent nationalist politicians are still calling the war
an exercise in support of British imperialism.

Out of this strange, contrary world skates the Montreal Canadiens,
Stanley Cup champions, led by the Punch Line, whose members,
Elmer Lach, Toe Blake and Maurice Richard, respectively, speak
not a word of French, French and English fluently, and only the
most basic shards of English. The puck does their talking. And this
season, Richard has begun to speak volumes with it.

At first, the 1944/45 season promises little in the way of the
extraordinary from Maurice Richard. The Canadiens do begin the

season on a tear, winning four of their first five games, but Richard doesn't get his first goal until the third game, when he contributes one in a 3–2 win over Detroit at home on November 4. In a rematch the next day in Detroit, Montreal again wins 3–2, but Richard is blanked. The team as a whole has averaged only 2.25 goals per game in its first four contests. Then, in its fifth game, in Chicago on November 9, Montreal demolishes the woeful Blackhawks 9–2, with Richard recording a hat-trick.

On November 11, Armistice Day, Montreal plays a subdued game against the Leafs in Toronto and loses 3–1 as Richard cannot score. Back in Chicago on November 12, Richard scores once as the Blackhawks are defeated 4–2. It is his first of five goals in five straight games as Montreal defeats Boston twice, the Rangers once, and ties Detroit. Then it is back in Toronto again on November 24, where Montreal is shut out 2–0. Toronto has won all three of its first encounters with Montreal this season and Richard has never scored. But in a rematch back at the Forum on November 26, Richard produces his second hat-trick of the season as the Leafs go down 4–1. In their final game of the month, a home match against the Rangers on November 30, Richard scores again as the Canadiens falter and lose 7–5 to the league underdogs. In its first fourteen games, Montreal has nine wins, one tie and four losses. Maurice Richard has scored thirteen times.

Adored and worshipped in Quebec, Richard will always be feared and admired, and never entirely fathomed, in English Canada. He becomes notorious as much for his ferocity as his goal-scoring. Through practice and sheer effort, he will learn English, but it will not make him any more accessible as a sporting star. He is no wise-cracking, easily quotable Babe Pratt. His fiery glare, his hatred of losing, his pride in winning, make him a kind of demon of the rink. If he represents Quebec for English Canadians, it is because they equate Quebec with what Richard is when he is in the game—something primal and untamed, even incomprehensible. He will not be the most beloved Canadien of his time for anglophones. That distinction will be held by Jean Béliveau, who will come to the Canadiens in 1953 exhibiting ferocity and determination, but also a gentlemanly charm rare to the game. In anglophone perception, Richard has Duplessis's rough-hewn power and charisma. Béliveau will be a shooting and scoring St. Laurent, refined and statesmanlike. English Canadians will one day think of Jean Béliveau as a perfect governor general. They will never think of

Maurice Richard that way.

❧

The resurrection and the light. The unifying light of Liberal thought, sweeping across the country, radiating from Quebec. A passion play of betrayal and crucifixion ending with resurrection. Renewal and rebirth. The eternal reconfirmed. Divine guidance proffered.

At the war cabinet meeting on November 20, General McNaughton reviews figures on men available for overseas service. His report indicates *a somewhat better showing, but still leaves the lack of reinforcement for January an acute serious problem. There was a considerable discussion on the poor showing of French regiments, and the considerable need for additional reinforcements.*

How long can they wait for conscripted men to go into battle of their own free will before the government is forced to order them to do so? It has been almost three weeks since Ralston left cabinet, and McNaughton feels that it will be another fortnight before they can be sure of how the appeal to the NRMA is going. That is a week later than the Ralston camp has proposed for making overseas service compulsory. And what will the government do once McNaughton's fortnight is over?

It is apparent the government is still going to put the decision off and off, Macdonald grumbles. Every day's delay, he charges, is making things more difficult. Ilsley is also impatient to put an end to the appeal. We are gambling with human lives, he declares, and lays down his position: they should pass an order-in-council without calling together Parliament to send the NRMA men overseas. Thomas Crerar makes an ultimatum. If the government tries to go on with volunteer enlistments beyond November 30, he will resign. Mulock indicates that nothing would satisfy the people short of sending in the Zombies if they do not go voluntarily. King concludes that Gibson is of the same mind. And then there is Howe—a Howe exasperated with the drifting state of the government, with the government's almost solitary preoccupation with conscription at a time when he is supposed to be engineering a peacetime economy. Whether the government sticks to its volunteer program or opts for conscription is secondary to the priority of having a firm policy. In other words, pick one and follow it, and be done with it.

McNaughton attempts to inject a dose of consequence into the debate. Here is what enforcing conscription will mean, he tells his fellow ministers. The men who will have to maintain law and order in Canada should any opposition arise to conscription, the men who will be responsible for seeing that trained NRMA men go overseas, will for the most part be NRMA men themselves. I fear there will be bloodshed, which could spread like a prairie fire throughout the country.

I am for passing an order-in-council, Ilsley retorts, bloodshed or not.

McNaughton has joined the ranks of cabinet ministers who suspect a Curragh incident is unfolding under their noses. There is a real conspiracy right in the defence departments not to have the voluntary system work, he says in conversation with King after the war cabinet meeting. If given a fair chance, I believe it could succeed, but instead of helping, everything is being done from different sources to enforce conscription. The veterans, King observes, are opposing the voluntary system. Indeed, the Royal Canadian Legion won't have anything to do with the appeal.

We should stand by what I have said and what I believe in, and what I came into the government to help try to carry out, McNaughton declares. We should not yield on conviction. There is no use discussing little details—it is a matter of principle and we should stand on principle.

Yes, King agrees. Principle it will be, then.

Which brings him back to martyrdom. If most of the war cabinet resigns over the reinforcement issue, he announces, *I did not see I would be of any further use.* I am against a wartime election. I don't believe I have the strength to go through one, and if I bring one on through dissolution, I will be accused of making it impossible for reinforcements to be supplied. I will be blamed for lives lost in the war, whether due to that cause or not.

When Gardiner, who is also at the post-cabinet meeting, speculates on how the election might pan out in the West, King replies: We are far beyond discussing any questions of election. We are faced with an appalling situation in the country, which involves the possibility of civil war. I will not take any course that might bring that on, or that might lead to any accusation that I have not done everything in my power to get men overseas.

That night, King listens on the radio to statements on the reinforcement issue made by commanding officers in the West. The spirit of Curragh is palpable. *It is quite apparent that there is a conspiracy there. One after the other has been coming out and saying that the NRMA men were just waiting for the government to do its duty and send them overseas. That looks like the Army defying the civil power. These men in uniform have no right to speak in ways which will turn the people against the civil power.*

He goes to bed depressed. *Appalling* is the word that comes to mind time and again as he contemplates his situation. He has been forced to admit, at least to himself, that he could not carry on if Ilsley resigns. *Macdonald and Crerar do not mean much. We would be better off without Crerar. Macdonald has ability and knows his own department, but is contentious and difficult. He has been very trying over the last two months.*

By the time the cabinet convenes late on Tuesday afternoon, King has settled on his course of action. He realizes there are irreconcilable differences, he says. There is a volunteer wing and a conscriptionist wing. Both sides are equally sincere. This difference, he tells them, will disappear when the war is over. In the meantime, I want to keep the party united, in service to Canada and to the world. We must try not to let bitterness make the cleavage too wide so that we will be able to reunite.

He lays out his plan. Everyone is agreed that the appeal should run for a certain length of time. This means a definite time must be set for the end of the appeal. If there are not enough men to solve the reinforcement shortage when the appeal is over, I will make it possible for conscription to be enforced without having to go to Parliament for a vote of confidence. I am determined not to have a dissolution and an election in wartime. I will resign and ask the Governor General to call on some member of cabinet to form a government to carry through with conscription.

The cabinet plunges into one of its silences at King's mention of resignation. It is one thing for a prime minister to lose the services of a navy or a finance minister. Can a navy or a finance minister stand to lose the services of a prime minister? Which is the more likely to have the strength to carry on?

King has proven himself, again, a master of brinkmanship. For the sake of your principles, he might as well have said, I am prepared to sacrifice my political life, for I am not prepared to make your principles mine. Now comes the test: how firm are their own principles, and indeed, what are they? Is their courage of conviction greater than their instinct for political survival? Can they kill him with a clear conscience?

He saw dismay and regret on the faces of some of the ministers when he spoke of resigning as their leader. *What strikes me as so*

cruel on the part of some of the Ministers is that they are quite pre-
pared to gain all the strength that comes to them through my lead-
ership but they are not prepared to help me maintain that position;
rather are doing everything in their power to undermine me.

Ilsley's resolve falters. If you resign, it will make carrying out
conscription more difficult, he complains. I cannot see why, King
blithely, triumphantly replies. *He at once realized what the job*
would be. Even Crerar was nonplussed. Angus Macdonald was
quiet for a time; Ilsley not saying too much.

Mr. King has a perfect right to expect those who are opposing
voluntary enlistment to assume the obligation of carrying out conscription, Power says. The conscriptionists, he lectures, are not
being fair to him.

It is clear that King can carry cabinet as a whole. I will want to
tell caucus and then the House what my attitude will be, King
informs his ministers. It is Angus Macdonald's turn to gamble a
trump card. It is apparent the government is not for conscription, he
observes, and that there will be no conscription under it. Perhaps I
should resign at once. Macdonald explains that he had intended to
resign along with Ralston, but had yielded to persuasion to stay on
to help the government through a crisis. Now he is inclined to go
home and write King a short letter of resignation. Ilsley is of the
same mind: I will not be able to stay in a government with no policy
for conscription.

At least wait until the issue has been discussed in caucus tomorrow before deciding, King asks Macdonald. The conscriptionists
object to having the issue put before caucus, feeling it will put
them in an unfair position. You will have the support of caucus,
Macdonald warns King, but you will be defeated in the House as
many of our people join with the Conservatives and Social Credit.
King is disgusted. *In other words, Macdonald is really prepared to*
go in with the Conservatives and Social Credit to help defeat the
Liberal administration of which he is a member.

Macdonald is no great loss to King, who fully expects to have his
resignation the next morning. But for Ilsley he launches a special
appeal. I must be honest with cabinet, King says. My strength will
not last if my war cabinet and half the rest of cabinet leaves. You,
Ilsley, have charge of the nation's finances. You are the only one in
cabinet who knows the whole financial situation. What will become
of the country's war effort if you resign? I hope you will stay at
least until we see how the next few weeks of the appeal go.

Ilsley comes around to a conciliatory stance. He is willing to give the public appeal two weeks, but he will also have to tell Parliament his feelings on what he would have to do if the appeal is not successful. You will be quite free to do that, King replies; members will discuss the question fully. I do not want to control anyone.

It has been a precarious victory. King has lived to fight another day. If he can stop the conscriptionist members of his own caucus from casting their lot against him with the Conservatives and Social Credit, his confidence motion will carry.

Speaking with St. Laurent after the meeting, the most solemn one this government has ever had, King expresses his fear of attempting to carry on governing without ministers of the calibre of Ilsley and Howe, and without practically every minister from Ontario. Howe, still weighing his position, would be the greatest loss if he gets off the fence on the wrong side of the issue. And King is concerned about how weary the undecided, irreplaceable minister of reconstruction appears.

🍁

Dear Major:

Many thanks for your recent letter.

I thought I would write a few lines and give you up to the minute news with regards to the changes that are expected within the next few weeks.

Well Sir, to start with, a meeting was held last Monday [November 13] for all N.C.O.'s. The purpose of this meeting was to try & convince NRMA (Zombies) to turn Active. A reward of one extra days leave was promised an N.C.O. if he induced a man to join Active and five extra days leave for the Zombie. If they hold the rank of Bdr. it will be immediately confirmed on turning "GS". Yesterday, Major General Lafleche* from Montreal was in camp & made a final plea. He spoke to all French Canadian men in the drill hall & I understand his speech was met with cheers & jeers.

Well Sir, I really don't think this will help the reinforcement situation an awful lot because a large number of these men

---

*Major-General Léo LaFlèche served as deputy minister of defence from 1932 to 1939 and entered cabinet in October 1942 as minister of national war services, making him the highest ranking and most influential French-Canadian commander of the war. He was stained by controversies surrounding the awarding of the Bren gun contract in 1938, which left him distrusted by some, including General McNaughton.

have been around the camp since 1941 are being paid for their rank, which I think was one of the biggest mistakes ever made, they also receive trades pay & are well satisfied with present conditions. For instance Sir, an NRMA man can apply for a certain course & when this is completed they are allocated to a battery office. Up until a few days ago, we had eight batteries in this centre & the Draftees were all 2 I/C of these battery orderly rooms. Active men (low category) have to work under them & I am in that position at the present time.

Well Sir from what I hear & see, this centre will be closing up within the next few months....
—*November 22 letter to Conn Smythe; name removed*

Wednesday, November 22. This morning, Thomas Crerar writes his letter of resignation and formulates his plan of action. There will be the sitting of the House at which King will table the exchange of letters with Ralston. Afterwards, caucus will meet, and King will ask for continued support of his voluntary overseas policy. When the meeting is over, Crerar will hand his resignation to King.

He goes to lunch at the Rideau Club. Howe takes him aside, and gives him the most extraordinary news: I am going to break with the prime minister at caucus. I have thought the matter over and I have decided that the only course of action is to use NRMA men as reinforcements. A few minutes later, Crerar sees Gibson, who has always supported sending in the Zombies, and Gibson tells him that Mulock would also stand with the conscriptionists.

King's triumph of Tuesday is rapidly disintegrating. Howe's decision has changed the chemistry of the cabinet split entirely. But as it turns out, the most crippling damage to King's strategy has come from within, from the most unexpected source. That morning, just as King has begun to prepare for the day ahead, and as Crerar is drafting his resignation, King's telephone rings.

It is McNaughton.

I have quite serious news, the defence minister says. I have been advised by the staff at military headquarters in Ottawa that the voluntary system will not get the men we need. It is like a blow to the stomach. I told them that this was the most serious advice that could be tendered, and that I wanted it in writing. As soon as I have it, I will come to see you. I also have the resignation of the Winnipeg base commander. If the other base commanders resign, the whole military machine will begin to disintegrate. There will be no controlling the situation.

Poor Andy. Only yesterday he was insisting that the volunteer system has not failed, that he has found three thousand to four thousand men, although recruiting in French Canada remains a serious problem. It is all for naught. His army has failed him, again. First it was split against his wishes, and no sooner has he regained control of it than it threatens to disintegrate entirely. He is confronting anarchy, and he has said as much to his prime minister, the prime minister who gave him another chance, who counted on him to save him.

It is over. Five years of resistance and evasion by King are over. Twenty-seven years after Robert Borden introduced conscription, it is happening again. Quebec was right to view the NRMA in 1940 as the thin edge of the wedge.

King looks at the clock. Five minutes to eleven. Hands aligned. He finds himself strangely relieved by McNaughton's message. He accepts it as an absolution, a release from the promises he has made and the sin others will say he is about to commit. Is McNaughton a traitor, a Judas? Not at all. He has saved William Lyon Mackenzie King from his own convictions. If this is the advice tendered by McNaughton, who came into cabinet to rescue the government, then it is King's duty to agree to pass the order-in-council that will send the NRMA men overseas and go to Parliament to ask for a vote of confidence, rather than put before the House the motion he had drafted and was intending to hand to the clerk today.

This really lifts an enormous burden from my mind as after yesterday's Council it was apparent to me that it was only a matter of days before there would be no government in Canada and this in the middle of war with our men giving their lives at the front. His mind executes a breathtaking bit of gymnastics. If he continues his volunteer policy and the government collapses, there will be more chaos on the home front than if he introduces conscription. Thus, introducing conscription is the wiser course. King is ready to make an about-face, and in so doing he shall save the nation.

❧

The House session is perfunctory, its only item of business King's tabling of the correspondence between himself and Ralston. He says nothing of the news from McNaughton. King speaks of Ralston with affection, telling the House how he misses having him at his side. He is dismayed by the *pretty rowdy* behaviour of the

Conservatives. *Tories rather overplayed their part in emphasising the haste with which things should be done.... Most absurd part of Tory performance was a motion without notice; also members standing to over rule the Speaker when there was no question of Order.*

The meeting of the Liberal caucus that follows the House sitting is just as businesslike. King asks the members to read the correspondence tabled. He doesn't want to discuss its contents now. King says cabinet will review it tonight, and they can all discuss it at caucus tomorrow morning.

At the end of caucus, King sends for St. Laurent, and breaks to his Quebec lieutenant alone the news of his talk with McNaughton. This raises serious questions of the relations between the army and the government, St. Laurent remarks, and speculates about the possibility of *a Palace revolution*. They are back in the territory of Curragh again. King evidently pitches him on his philosophy of the lesser of the two evils—that maintaining his position of volunteers only, and having the government collapse, would cause more strife than imposing conscription. *I spoke of how impossible the whole matter of Government, law and order might become.*

He was very much perturbed. What you are suggesting might mean the loss of all of our seats in Quebec, St. Laurent says. The justice minister, with only three years in the federal government (and a son serving overseas, "a fine officer" as Conn Smythe will recollect), notes that he would have to give up public life. But he does promise to King *to follow my judgment and lead.*

After caucus, Macdonald approaches Crerar. Those of us who feel alike should meet to discuss our course, Macdonald proposes. We can meet in my office, Crerar offers. Crerar invites Gibson and Howe, and Gibson goes to Mulock. Only a few minutes after caucus has dispersed, the like-minded ministers are gathered in Crerar's office.[1]

It is happening again. In 1917 Crerar was in his tenth year as president of the United Grain Growers when as a Liberal by sentiment he made his dramatic political debut: he accepted an invitation to serve as the minister of agriculture in Borden's Unionist government. In the election on December 17—an election that marked Mackenzie King's forty-third birthday—Crerar was elected with a huge majority in the Manitoba riding of Marquette. When the war was over and Crerar found himself unhappily rubbing shoulders with Conservatives, he led a party of nine western

Liberals back across the House floor. Along came the National
Progressive party, which took the reform instincts of several farmers' movements onto the national stage. The National Progressives
needed leadership, and Crerar agreed to provide it, breaking ranks
with the Liberals for the first time in fact, for the second time in
spirit. In the 1921 election, the National Progressives took sixty-
four seats, fourteen more than the Conservatives. By limiting the
Liberals and their new leader, Mackenzie King, to twenty-one seats
in Ontario and three seats in the Prairie provinces, Crerar's
National Progressives were able to deny them a majority government. But the National Progressives were so internally fractious, so
collectively indecisive about their role in Parliament, that it fell to
Arthur Meighen's Conservatives to serve as the official opposition.
On November 12, 1922, the day after the fourth anniversary of the
Armistice was marked, Crerar resigned the party's leadership. He
had viewed the National Progressives as a protest movement that
would lose its raison d'être once King's Liberals produced some
sensible policies, foremost among them support of free trade.
Crerar made his way back yet again to the Liberal ranks, although
he did not stand for election in 1925 as he concentrated on his
UGG presidency. In 1929 he left the grain growers post and was
sworn in as King's minister of railways and canals, but he failed to
secure a seat in the 1930 general election that brought the
Conservatives to power. Elected again in 1935, Crerar was given a
seemingly unwieldy portfolio: minister of the interior, of mines, of
immigration and colonization, and superintendent of Indian affairs.
All were amalgamated into the ministry of mines and resources in
1936, and Crerar has held the portfolio ever since. Twenty-seven
years after answering the Unionist call, the time has come for
another revolt by Thomas Crerar.

We are in a serious situation, Crerar tells his fellow ministers.
The action we are contemplating might bring about the downfall of
the government. We should not be influenced by any false modesty,
but should face the responsibility involved with a possible fall of
the government as men capable of seeing our duty and doing it.
Whatever action we take should be taken together. It's not necessary that we send King a joint resignation, but our resignations
should go in at the same time. Mulock then reads to the group the
letter he proposes to send to King; Crerar reads the one he wrote
that morning. They have just finished reading the letters when
Ilsley arrives, and agrees to their plan of action.

After dinner at Laurier House, King returns to his office to meet with Chubby Power, the only defence department minister he had who opposed conscription when Ralston was in cabinet. Power agrees that the step King proposes is the right one, that it is *the only one that could be taken to save the existence of the govt.* But Power also feels that he will have to resign. I am not running away, he tells King. I have done my job. *He looks pretty pale and frail. I spoke to him about friendship for him; what a friend I would be through the years. He said no man could have been more so; promised he would not speak out in Council, but would have to take a stand or quietly drop out.*

The full meeting of cabinet follows. Twenty-one ministers are assembled, some having to settle for a seat on the sofa. Six are about to resign because King will not implement conscription. An unknown number are about to resign because he will.

King recounts his conversation with McNaughton earlier today. McNaughton now has the full data, King reports, and while he feels the voluntary system might have succeeded, it now looks as if it cannot be counted on to succeed. General McNaughton feels we need a way of securing a margin of safety against the possible failure of volunteer recruitment to meet reinforcement needs. He proposes we take a limited number of NRMA men and train them to meet the situation, and reluctantly I have to agree with him.

King is surprised his proposal of limited conscription for NRMA men is received so quietly. In the case of Crerar and his conscriptionist associates, they are dumbfounded. "This, of course, was a complete right-about-face," is how Crerar will recollect the moment. Power, despite his avowal to King after dinner that he will remain silent in cabinet, is vocally opposed. Gardiner, King's other stalwart anti-conscriptionist, suggests that King has reversed his position in the face of threatened resignations. King denies this, which is true—he knows nothing specific of the plan forged by Crerar, Macdonald, Howe, Mulock, Gibson and Ilsley, but, as Crerar will reflect, "I think he realized quite clearly what was about to take place." Debate follows on how the call-up should be shaped—how many men, how long. If we are agreed on general principles, Macdonald proposes, can we not just leave the details to be worked out? *Ilsley completely silent through night, just a question or two. Seemed relieved.*

King's francophone Quebec ministers say nothing beyond Major-General LaFlèche's report that he has been able to secure more volunteers at Petawawa. Gardiner and Power move to submit their resignations. King begs them to stay on. It will be impossible for me to lead the party any longer unless I have the support of long-standing members. I can fight enemies from without, but not from within our own household. He tries to make them understand how this course of action was necessary to save the country from the disaster of the government's collapsing in wartime. I do not intend to have on my conscience the thought that I had not done everything possible to ensure the lives of the men overseas, he tells them. I wish to do everything possible for these men while they are fighting to save our lives and to make it possible for us to sit in council and discuss the situation.

His only difficulty comes when he proposes ignoring caucus altogether tomorrow and simply presenting the new conscription policy to the House in the afternoon. St. Laurent is aghast. It would mean the government's policy reversal would strike the Quebec backbenchers like *a blast from the blue;* they would have no more warning of it than the Conservatives or the CCF. King quickly concedes the point. He will tell caucus in the morning, and then the House.

King is as satisfied with the results of the cabinet meeting as he could hope to be. He is still prime minister. There is still a Liberal party. Afterwards, Dr. King, his Senate leader, comes to him, *his voice trembling, almost breaking down.* You have done the right thing, he tells his prime minister. You have literally saved Canada.

Today has gone well. Tomorrow will be very difficult and the following day possibly most difficult of all. But I believe the right decision has been reached. The only decision that could save our country from chaos while our men are sacrificing their lives for freedom overseas. We must above all keep them first in our thoughts. I have left nothing to be done up to the present which could lessen their security. What has been done today will bring fresh courage to them and strengthen the hearts of their loved ones at home.

Arriving back at Laurier House, he is struck by a heavy nosebleed. Blood gushes down his face as he enters his bedroom. *I could not help thinking how symbolical blood was of crucifixion.*

DELIVERANCE

Late November 1944

THE great goaltenders, almost all of them, are gone. Johnny Mowers of Detroit, who won the Stanley Cup in 1942/43—in the RCAF. Turk Broda of the Leafs, who won the Stanley Cup in 1941/42—in the army. Frank Brimsek of the Bruins, who won the Stanley Cup in 1938/39 and 1940/41—in the U.S. Coast Guard. Davey Kerr of the Rangers, who won the Stanley Cup in 1939/40—retired after the 1940/41 season. Sugar Jim Henry, who replaced Kerr in the Rangers goal—in the army. Chuck Rayner of the defunct Americans and now the property of the Rangers—in the navy.

Frank McCool, who couldn't crack the Blackhawks or the Rangers lineup, and who spent two years knocking around in Senior hockey with Currie Barracks, is doing a serviceable job with the Leafs. The Rangers—God knows how the Rangers even ice a team. At least they haven't been pushed to the extreme of 1943/44 when coach Frank Boucher, forty-two years old, retired from the ice since 1938, put on a uniform and played fifteen games at centre, and it wasn't saying much for the strength of the league when old Raffles collected fourteen points in the process. Boucher has had Tubby McAuley, a complete newcomer to the league, in the nets for the last two seasons. Bless Tubby, his effort has been beyond heroic, but last year the Rangers allowed 310 goals in fifty games, when Montreal was allowing 109. After losing Mowers to the RCAF in 1943, Detroit began using a twenty-six-year-old Québécois named Connie Dion, a five-foot-three graduate of the Cornwall Army team. But after twelve games in the net in 1944/45, Dion is sent down to the American league and the Red Wings pin their hopes on an eighteen-year-old from Owen Sound named Harry Lumley, a kid labelled Apple Cheeks because his face is scarcely ready for a razor. The Bruins are coping with Paul

Bibeault, and the Blackhawks have been using Mike Karakas, a capable veteran called up from the American league who starred with Chicago before the war. Of course, in Montreal they have Bill Durnan, a big ambidextrous shooter's nightmare who was lurking in the Senior system with the Montreal Royals when the Canadiens finally convinced him to move up to the big league in 1943, whereupon he won the Vezina and made the first All-Star team as Montreal won the Stanley Cup.

But wherefore the offensive stars? There is no Apps, no Taylor, no Hextall; no Schmidt to Bauer to Dumart; no Bentley or Patrick or Colville of either given name. The marquee players are few and far between. And yet, given the new rules, and the inconsistent quality of the goaltending, the complete deterioration of professional hockey is not unfolding as predicted. Scoring overall in the league is not soaring out of control any more. It is actually dropping. After the half-goal-a-game surge of 1943/44 when the two-line offside was introduced and average team scoring exceeded four goals a game, production in the new season will end up being down by almost fourth-tenths of a goal, marking the beginning of a nine-season freefall that will see it drop below 2.4 goals per game.

The game is changing. Defences have adjusted to the new speed and there isn't the epidemic of breakaways that plagued goaltenders in 1943/44. Less scoring has not, and will not, mean less offensive action. The game has a fresh pace, the pace defined and exploited by teams like the Canadiens and their Punch Line of Richard, Blake and Lach. When Sweeney Schriner returned from his one-year stint in navy hockey for this season, he noted that they had used the two-line offside rule in the games he played with the Calgary navy team, but they didn't play the way the NHL is playing. This is a whole different game.

New stars are emerging with the new rule and the new game it has inspired. Maurice Richard completed his first full season in 1943/44. The Leafs have a pair of nineteen-year-olds at centre: Ted Kennedy, who will go through the fifty-point barrier in his second season, and Gus Bodnar, who produced sixty-two points in 1943/44, his rookie effort, and beat out Durnan for the Calder. Detroit has a ferocious nineteen-year-old left-winger from the St. Mike's Junior program named Ted Lindsay, and their new goaltender, the eighteen-year-old Lumley, will have the season's second-best goals-against record (tied with McCool) at 3.22. They are all stars of the present and the future, and after the war the league's

general managers will go on a youth craze, eager to sign the kids
who have formed their skills playing the new high-speed head-
manning game at the Junior level.

For professional baseball, the Second World War has been a period to endure; when the war is over, the priority will be restoring
the game to its greatness. For hockey, at least from the perspective
of the NHL, the war has not been a debilitating experience; rather,
the war years have proven to be a period of renewal and rebirth.
The death of the Brooklyn Americans franchise in 1942 left the
league at six teams, but the American Hockey League lost more
teams; from a business viewpoint, the war has proved fruitful for
the NHL, hobbling the AHL just as it was becoming a serious chal-
lenger to the NHL. Those AHL franchises in smaller markets that
do not have developed transportation infrastructures—aka decent
streetcar systems—suffer disproportionately at the box office when
fans cannot spare gas rations to get to a game. And with its box
office dependent on star players often on loan from NHL clubs,
AHL revenues suffer when those NHL clubs call up better players
to fill gaps in their lineups created by starters departing for the military. The AHL's reaction—to limit member clubs to three NHL
loaner players, which would allow the league to develop its own
quality talent pool—serves only to anger NHL figures like Conn
Smythe, who smell an attempt to establish the AHL as a full rival.
It is a war the AHL will not be able to win.[1]

In the lexicon of nostalgia to come, the NHL clubs that survive
the war will become known as the "Original Six," as if the teams
that went before them—the Maroons, the Tigers, the Bulldogs, the
Pirates, the Wanderers, the Eagles, the Americans, the Senators, the
Quakers and their kind—as if all of those teams and all of the players who starred on them belonged to some other pursuit; as if the
history of the game did not begin until a war was on and the players who had made the game marvellous were out of the game,
many never to return. They will be gone because, a few years older
with a war behind them, they will have to confront a game that has
changed utterly, that has been rebuilt for youth and speed. The very
youths who have usurped their positions will be defining the new
game's qualities. The tables will be turned. It will be the veterans
who will have to live up to the standards of the rookies.

No battlefield casualties have been required to usher in a new
generation of stars. The game itself has demanded fresh reinforcements and new strategies from its commanders.

They crucified him.

So reads the first line in the devotional diary entry of William Lyon Mackenzie King on the morning of November 23, the morning on which he must go before his caucus and explain why he has reversed the government's policy on conscription and will now pass an order-in-council committing 16,000 NRMA men to combat duty.

He does his best. He is there to speak foremost to his Quebec wing, and to them he apologizes on behalf of the Protestants in Ontario for the way in which the people of Quebec have been insulted by the Orangemen and their ilk. The men of Quebec are in a minority in Canada, in both race and religion, and he understands that. He pays tribute to how Quebec has done so much in the past to preserve the Empire, her people standing by the English in 1776 and again in 1812. *Tried to let them see I really understood their position.*

He is remarkably successful. Before the day is out, he will have lost only two Quebec backbenchers who cross the floor of the House.

He returns to his office to settle on the wording of the order-in-council; McNaughton was up until five in the morning, working out the details of the call-up he will present to the House. Power comes in to see King and hands him his resignation. *He shook hands with me and thanked me in a warm and friendly way. He was sorry that he had to take the step but did not see how he could possibly do otherwise.* He also faces the loss of Gardiner, who has lost more than enough himself in the course of this war: first his son, then his wife, and now the struggle to fend off conscription. He cannot carry on, and tearily insists he must resign. King, however, is able to convince him to stay on.

A brutal session of the House awaits King, and McNaughton, for whom special permission has been granted to address the members. Only three weeks after replacing Ralston, having avowed that volunteer recruitment could carry the day, McNaughton must now go before his Conservative enemies and put forward a policy that Ralston himself would have waited until the end of the month to introduce. And he will have to face questioning from Ralston himself, who still has his seat in the House.

The day after being removed from his cabinet post, Ralston wasn't sure he wanted to set foot in the House again. He and King spoke on November 2 in the minister's office in the defence building, after Ralston and McNaughton met and power was formally transferred to the general. *I said to him I felt so sorry that we were not to be together. That I hoped it was only temporary. He replied that he had 'phoned to his law firm in Montreal and was going back to practice. He had also 'phoned his constituency to say he would go down to explain to them the position. That his wife had said she did not want him to be back in Parliament. I said: Oh no. He must stay in Parliament.... I assumed he could, if he wished, resign at once though I would prefer to have him stay on through the foregoing nomination for the next Parlt.* As they spoke, King envied Ralston the freedom he now had. *In fact I think I said that to him.*

Ralston is free, in a way—free to have his revenge on King and McNaughton, for ending his political career and then passing an order-in-council he would have been happy to promote.

The sitting is a confusing one for the Conservatives. The about-face on conscription has caught them off guard, but it is not total conscription, and they smell blood in McNaughton's failure, Ralston's presence and King's reversal before his Quebec wing.

Just being back in the House energizes King. The press gallery is packed, the thrust and parry of Parliament under way. He is pleased by the applause he receives from the Liberal side of the House when he reads the order, though a few members sit on their hands. *The Tories looked greatly disconcerted; no applause from them.* He hears Richard Hanson, the Conservative House leader from 1940 to 1943, call out "Surrender!" *I thought the Order seemed favourably received in the other groups but not markedly so. There was an element of real surprise on the other side of the House.*

Then comes McNaughton, accompanied by Major-General Gibson and Brigadier Delalanne, complete with tables to support their volumes of records, to assist him with the information he must present. McNaughton's arrival is like a red flag before a Conservative bull. *From that moment on, after McN. came in, the Tory Party were in a very nasty mood. Graydon called on Ralston as though he were to be the prosecuting attorney and McN, in the witness box. Lawyer after lawyer of the official Opposition monopolized the time questioning and really browbeating McN.*

King can see the general is tired. He is fifty-five years old, he has been up all night, and he has never before appeared in the House of Commons, much less before the badgering tactics of a hostile Opposition. *I saw he got flushed around the temples at times but he maintained a sweet calm. Once or twice he gave a retort which was well deserved.*

McNaughton explains to the House that the draftees will go overseas in batches of five thousand in December and January, with the remainder getting there by May. Ralston wrings one important concession out of his successor from the total-conscriptionist perspective: that not all of these reinforcements need necessarily be NRMA men. King feels that McNaughton makes a very good impression, and that the sympathy of the House is with him. But he is also grateful that the exchange between Ralston and McNaughton never turns bitter. They have *maintained a quiet dignity and avoided anything like an open conflict.*

Veteran parliamentarians remark that the day has taken them back to 1925, when King was nursing along his precarious minority government and at times his ability to maintain control hung on the vote of a single member. That is a far more dire reading of the day's proceeding than King himself would subscribe to. The next morning, Friday, he awakens full of joy that he is past his *day of crucifixion...the process of resurrection has already begun.*

❧

Conn Smythe has won the battle, if not the war. While Mackenzie King remains in charge of the country, toppling the Liberals from power was not a stated priority of Smythe's. It may well still happen—King must survive a vote of confidence, and the Conservatives are gearing up to promote defections in the Liberal benches. In the meantime, Smythe's campaign to send in the Zombies has achieved sterling successes. Foremost is King's reversal of policy, producing an order-in-council that will do just that. Smythe's hounding of Ralston helped firm the defence minister's own enthusiasm for conscription, and when he lost his cabinet post, the conscriptionists gained a political martyr. Smythe has even gotten his way with McNaughton. Having promoted him relentlessly more than four years ago as the man to head up the entire Canadian war effort, Smythe now sees McNaughton doing just that as defence minister, and most importantly as a defence minister who has successfully turned into government policy the alleged necessity of committing conscripts to combat.

In a little more than eight weeks, Conn Smythe's simple press release has grown into a juggernaut of public opinion that has rocked the King government and threatens still to bring it down. It is entirely appropriate that, when the order-in-council is tabled,

Smythe should immediately be sought out by the press for comment.

He pronounces himself cautiously satisfied. "If they [the government] are going to send the draftees over," he tells Canadian Press that evening, "then the victory is a great one for the boys over there. But if the home defence draftees are not sent now, then it will be a body blow to the boys overseas who believe in democracy and expect that it will work at home and give them the help they need."

King visits the Governor General, who must be bewildered by the comings and goings of the prime minister, his appointments and his policies. To sum up his position, King has lost confidence in the ability of his government to control the army. Curragh has come to roost in Ottawa. Conscription, which he has said all along would tear the country apart, is now the only way to keep the country from tearing itself apart.

King explains how McNaughton *had been left at the mercy of his military advisers. That if I did not accept that advice he would be able to get nowhere with the army and might be confronted with a sort of palace revolution.* The situation, he advises His Excellency, was desperate. *The only way it could be saved was by myself being prepared to be crucified between those on one side who would be resigning for one reason and those on the other who would resign for an opposite reason.*

And so, King took it upon himself to be crucified. And lo, he has risen.

The alleged quasi-coup is the only item on which King and Lieutenant-General Pope are in serious disagreement. Pope hears the whispers of an army revolt and a "palace revolution," and simply will not believe it, and never will. He saw nothing untoward in the senior staff at National Defence Headquarters advising McNaughton that the required reinforcements could not be found voluntarily. "I am confident that there was not a single principal staff officer at NDHQ who did not know from his intimate knowledge of the situation that in this the Government was setting out to flog a very dead horse," he will observe. "But dutifully they gave it a try." He will not be so confident of the behaviour and motive of the base commanders, however. "I have not here in mind the attitude and conduct of army officers in the districts and it is no part of my purpose to try to condone anything they have said and done."[2]

Pope was not privy to King's decision to replace Ralston with McNaughton, but he will conclude that the prime minister likely made an issue of the Curragh factor, "that he must have played it up so as to win over his hesitant colleagues." He will also reach into Conn Smythe's world to fathom King's strategy in November. "In many an evenly contested game of baseball or hockey, there comes a time when the players feel that their only course is to play their hardest, and safely, to wait with what patience they can muster what in sporting language is called 'the breaks' of the game. I wonder if the game of politics differs greatly in this respect." To Pope, King's strategy was to buy time, replacing Ralston with McNaughton and launching the appeal to the NRMA men, in hope that the breaks would come his way and turn the game in his favour. For a moment, in effect, Mackenzie King was Conn Smythe in 1940, replacing Dick Irvin with Hap Day. It worked for Smythe. But for King the breaks went the other way.

The first sign of genuine trouble emerges on the evening of November 23, when nearly one thousand soldiers from the NRMA camp at Vernon, B.C., on Okanagan Lake stage a protest parade through the town, shouting a CCF slogan: "Conscript wealth and industry as well as manpower."

The Conservatives want to see as many as possible of the Zombies in action as soon as possible—ironically at a time when the participation of Canadian troops in front-line duties has eased dramatically. After the bloody and costly struggle to secure the Scheldt ended on November 8, the Canadians having been relieved on November 1 by British troops under the First Canadian Army's command, Montgomery rewarded the Canadians with a well-earned respite, just as Chubby Power predicted he would. Though Canadians continue to fight in Italy, it will be three months before they see serious action again in northern Europe, and plans are being made to pull the Canadians out of Italy in January and send them north as well. While the daily carnage in Europe for Canadian troops has receded, the losses in France and Holland continue to reverberate in the public conscience. English Canada wants the conscripts sent in. It wants the fighting men relieved. Even the editors of the Liberal *Toronto Daily Star* made up their mind to advocate that the Zombies be shipped out, just before King reversed his policy. The CCF can no longer pretend to be a pacifist movement. Firmly anti-war under J.S. Woodsworth at the beginning of the conflict, five years later M.J.

Coldwell is leading a party that is resigning itself to the fact that its own constituents want the Zombies out of the camps and into the thick of it.

King's capitulation and support for limited conscription does not go nearly far enough for the *Globe and Mail.* King must fall, and its editors know just the person to do it: James Layton Ralston. On Saturday, November 25, the *Globe* editors publish an open appeal to Ralston to lead the effort to bring down the Liberals. The *Globe* argues that Ralston has a moral obligation to bring King down. "His duty is to fight the thing through to the end.... It is his responsibility to see that all the facts are exposed in the free air of Parliamentary debate and to give leadership to the members in forcing a decision on the basis of those facts without concern as to where the chips may fall. He cannot have fulfilled his trust to the men in Holland and Italy until he has done so."

The corvette HMCS *Shawinigan* leaves Sydney, Nova Scotia, on November 24 to escort a merchant ship, the SS *Burgeo*, across the Cabot Strait to Port aux Basques, Newfoundland. On this route on October 13, 1942, a U-boat sank the passenger ferry SS *Caribou*, with a loss of 137 lives. The two vessels arrive in Port aux Basques that night, as the Maple Leafs are defeating the Canadiens 2–0 at the Gardens. The *Shawinigan* leaves the merchant ship in port for the night to patrol the local waters. In the morning, the corvette is to rendezvous with the *Burgeo* and escort it back to Sydney.

On the night of November 25, the merchant ship arrives back in Sydney, without the *Shawinigan*; the corvette never appeared for the rendezvous. A search is launched, which turns up no trace of her. The navy resolves that the *Shawinigan* was torpedoed during the night by a U-boat and lost with all hands. Subsequent searches will recover several bodies, carried far from the probable sinking area by tidal currents. One of them is positively identified as twenty-year-old Able Seaman Dudley "Red" Garrett, former Leaf property and a New York Ranger for half of the 1942/43 season.[3]

King is sitting in the House on Tuesday, November 28, when he is told McNaughton has received word from Pacific Command that the Zombies are revolting in B.C. According to the report, about 1,600 men in the Fusiliers de St. Laurent, Prince Edward Islanders and Prince Albert Volunteers at Terrace Bay in the northern interior, paraded as a demonstration without disorder on Monday. About one-quarter of the garrison have been able to control the remainder by intimidation, occupying well-organized positions with six-pounders mounted. The attorney general has been asked to close local liquor stores and prevent the movement of liquor into the base. Brigadier Roy and Lieutenant-Colonel L'Heureux are attempting to regain control of French-Canadian units.

With this knowledge fresh in hand, King rises to deliver a three-hour oration to the House in which he warns of anarchy. But mainly he takes the House on a personal tour of the conscription crisis, along the way noting how "some persons"—declining to name Conn Smythe, George Drew and John Bracken—made representations to the effect that volunteers were not being properly trained, that these men were obliged to go into battle unprepared, and how these representations were distressing to the mothers, fathers and relatives of men overseas, as well as the men themselves. He tells the House he always regretted that an immediate reply was not made to these representations. He believed it was because Ralston wanted to be doubly sure of his facts before making any reply. King remarks that Ralston sent back word from overseas indicating he didn't think there was any justification for allegations of insufficient training. Then came his October 13 telegram expressing his concern about the reinforcement situation.

In recounting how cabinet debated the conscription issue in the weeks that followed Ralston's return from overseas, King charges that "new situations were being created within Canada which were very unsettling. A measure of unrest was being organized the like of which has not been seen in the history of Canada before, not even in a political campaign. One may condemn this movement. The day will come when it will be exposed and fully condemned."

This movement then set upon his appeal for volunteer enlistments. "How was the public appeal supported?" King asks. "The moment that we started on the public appeal, that moment the opposition to anything of the kind on the part of the interests that lie behind this organized effort to force conscription began to make themselves felt in every direction—in the press, by meetings and the like, sending representations to members, and so forth, with the result that instead of the appeal reaching the ears of the people the ears of the people were dinned by the efforts that were being put forth by those who were determined they were going to have conscription no matter what the cost might be." It was then, he declares, that he decided Parliament must meet.

After reading his 1942 speech in which he declared his policy of "not necessarily conscription, but conscription if necessary," King asks for a vote of confidence on the following motion: "That this House will aid the government in its policy of maintaining a vigorous war effort."

He could have called an election over Ralston's resignation, he says. "Yes, I could have swept the whole province of Quebec, carried every seat in it. I could have carried seats from one end of this country to the other and I have not the least doubt that I could have come back to this Parliament as prime minister as the result of an appeal in circumstances such as these." But that would have meant two months of political warfare in the country during an international war.

So now they have conscription. Why? The military had advised the necessity of conscription. The government had obliged. Now the House must express its views on whether it is ready to support the present ministry in carrying it out.

He turns to address his own cabinet members, declaring he is prepared for any one of them to take over his responsibilities if the House has greater confidence in them than in him. "No man in the world would be more relieved to be free of responsibility at a time like this than I would, after carrying on for the years that I have, at the age I have reached," he assures the House. He looks to the leaders of the Conservatives, the CCF and Social Credit: Would they accept his responsibilities? I am nearing my seventieth year, he explains, and I find the load growing heavier day by day. I will need the support of men of like mind to carry on.

He turns again, to address the Quebec members of his caucus, imploring them to pledge themselves to service "not only for the salvation of France and Belgium but to the salvation of this world from the domination of an enemy that would destroy human freedom and Christian civilization wherever they are to be found."

King then invokes Laurier, reading from a speech the late great prime minister made thirty-three years ago—making Laurier's words his words, and his words Laurier's: "If there is anything to which I have devoted my political life it is to try to promote unity, harmony and amity between the diverse elements of this country. My friends can desert me, they can remove their confidence from me, they can withdraw the trust they have placed in my hands, but never shall I deviate from that line of policy. Whatever may be the consequences, whether loss of prestige, loss of popularity, or loss of power, I feel that I am in the right, and I know that a time will come when every man will render me full justice on that score."

King explains that he wishes to repeat "those words as my own, having in mind at this moment all that Sir Wilfrid Laurier meant to me as a leader, all that he meant to me as a friend, all that he meant to me as a great Canadian and a great statesman.... I wish to use those words to this House of Commons today and I want them to be words that will be remembered by my fellow citizens when I am gone."

In 1973, twenty-three years after Mackenzie King is gone, Conn Smythe will offer these words to the *Toronto Star*: "The French people have given us our best prime ministers, starting when I was a little boy with Laurier."

When the House sitting is over, King confers with McNaughton on the uprising in Terrace Bay, and asks St. Laurent to join them. *I have seldom seen the look of greater concern on anyone's face than that which came over St. Laurent's face as he thought of the situation as it might develop. The gravity of the situation was apparent the moment McNaughton told us what he had said in Council might happen.*

If the troops begin to resist, McNaughton explains, I do not have the soldiers to enforce law and order. He could call out the militia, but most of its men are employed in materiel industries such as munitions; bringing them in would harm ammunition production. The defence department has no plans for meeting a situation like this. *They had evidently taken it for granted that all that had to be done was to say the men would be conscripted and they would be.*

Here, King recognizes grimly, is exactly what McNaughton told the cabinet would happen if we had to resort to conscription. *The officers had lied by saying that the men were ready to go and were anxious to go but wanted to be ordered by the government. Ministers who repeated the statements were completely in error.* Radio reports also indicated that the men were resisting the call-up because they did not like a "phony" conscription. More lies. *This again was Tory inspiration and entirely wrong.*

They are virtually helpless in the face of open revolt. King imagines what might happen when armed men are permitted embarkation leave in Quebec before being shipped out. He sees them in their homes, weapons primed, refusing to go. What can be done? McNaughton tells him: nothing. We can only trust the people themselves.

We do not have the forces necessary, whether army or police, King realizes, to maintain law and order if it comes to that. *Here indeed would be a state of anarchy, not merely in the philosophical sense of no government existing, but as well in the actual sense of civil strife. One can only pray to God that we may be spared anything of the kind.*

He greets the news of the rebellion as an affirmation of his leadership. King sees himself as the last bastion between the country and total anarchy. If they are to be spared outright insurrection, it will be because of the belief the people of Quebec still have in him and now in McNaughton. *It makes very clear that had I not taken the course I did, and the government passed into the hands of conscriptionists, that a measure of civil war would have been inevitable.* King has now convinced himself that conscription, as enacted by him and not anyone else, is saving the country from the very catastrophe that would seem to be brewing.

McNaughton is not so confident of the effectiveness of his personal charisma in averting civil war. He calls in representatives of the press, and asks them to be careful not to sensationalize the uprising.

Early Wednesday afternoon, the twenty-ninth, the revolt at Terrace Bay is discussed by the war cabinet. King resolves that steps must be taken immediately to censor the newspapers and to make sure radio reports are prevented from sensationalizing the situation. McNaughton is informed that an officer out west tried to have the press play down the story, but that Gillis Purcell, head of Canadian Press, is of the opinion that the defence department has no right to interfere; his resistance is such that a story on the government's efforts to hush up the Terrace Bay rebellion could go out today.

Get Eggleston and Frigon at once, King declares. Both are having lunch. The deadline for evening editions of the newspapers is two o'clock; at 1:45 Wilfrid Eggleston, the director of censorship, and Augustin Frigon, general manager of the CBC, are brought in to meet with the King.

The prime minister is particularly exercised by the fact that the word "mutiny" has made it into the press. The press, King counsels, must use the same methods and judgments with regard to Terrace Bay that it does when handling news affecting troop movements and incidents in general that can have an impact on the war effort overseas. It is not a matter of politics, King says, but of patriotism.

If once shots were fired and blood began to flow, no one could say where the whole condition of things would end, and we as a government were helpless in avoiding a situation without co-operation of the press and radio.

King suggests bringing all press service heads to Ottawa immediately and having the situation explained to them. Eggleston advises that if the defence department would provide censorship with directions on what should not be published, they could be followed. Until now, he notes all such censorship has been carried out voluntarily, and McNaughton agrees with Eggleston that things should continue that way. A defence department officer is to be assigned to provide guidance; in the meantime, King asks that direction come from McNaughton in instances of conflict between the press and the government.

King then joins the afternoon session of the House, in time to hear Victor Quelch of Social Credit indicate his party's support for King's motion. So much for the possibility of dissident Liberals banding with the Social Credit to bring down King. This gives King ten non-Liberal votes (all from Alberta) in his favour, a step toward addressing the haemorrhaging of votes in his French-speaking Quebec caucus. While his francophone members are not leaving the party on masse, the vast majority of them cannot be counted upon to support him.

King has scarcely joined the proceedings when Angus Macdonald shows him a letter from Air Marshal Leckie, chief of staff of the air force, which indicates that General Pearkes of Pacific Command has ordered the air force to make a demonstration flight over the rebellious camp.

King is *terribly alarmed*. See McNaughton at once about it, he tells Macdonald. King bolts from the House as well, and reaches McNaughton ahead of Macdonald. McNaughton is mortified. That is terrible, he frets; *these men must be crazy*. I must stop this at once. He had forbade using the air force in a demonstration role against strikes and civil unrest back when he was Chief of Staff. *It was one of the worst things that could possibly have happened. For a moment it made him almost despair. We did not wait to discuss matters further.*

McNaughton proceeds directly to his office, hoping to have the flights stopped, although they have gathered from Macdonald that it is too late to keep the planes on the ground. King is left to wait and wonder if conscripts are busy shooting down pilots from their own air force. They are, after all, armed.

McNaughton returns to tell King all is quiet. A flight, which was ordered yesterday, had indeed been made, but McNaughton was able to get word out to the camp just before the flyover occurred that it was a routine manoeuvre, that the planes were not armed. McNaughton instructs Pacific Command that *on no account was this kind of thing ever to happen again.*

A close call. McNaughton shows King another one, a news story that has been spiked. Men from Terrace Bay are declaring that under no condition will they be moved. Others are saying the government doesn't have enough jails or life sentences for all of them. There are promises to resist with firearms. None of it will reach the public now.

If you had not taken the action you did in council, McNaughton tells King, in immediately sending for the chief censor and the general manager of the CBC, all of this would be in the press this afternoon, and the situation would be completely out of hand. McNaughton has also learned that half of the men had paraded, with the rest remaining quiet. One train of conscripts has left today from Terrace Bay. The situation appears to be easing.

King does not blame the rebellious men; he blames the officers. *It is a crime that French Canadian regiments have been kept out in British Columbia under command of a man like Pearkes, and the group he is heading there. Ralston has been wrong, terribly wrong, on all this.*

Wrong or not on this or any other matter, Ralston is about to address the House. It is the moment the Conservatives have been waiting for. He can bring down the government. There are some three dozen Quebec Liberals who will oppose King just to oppose conscription. There are the Conservatives and possibly the CCF who will oppose King because he is not bringing in the kind of conscription they want. If Ralston adds his voice to the discord, he could draw away enough moderate Liberal conscriptionists, cabinet ministers among them, to bring King down, or at least to make his victory so narrow that it will effectively serve as a defeat. King will have to resign. The Unionists will be reborn, with Ralston as their leader.

As a private member of the House he has a fifty-minute limit on his speaking time, but King magnanimously waives it. Ralston will have all the time he needs to say what he must. And it is as grim an attack as King has ever sustained in his political career. It lasts for two hours as Ralston dismisses, item by item, King's account of the crisis and Ralston's role in it.

He vigorously disputes King's charges that he was late in bringing to cabinet news of reinforcement shortages. Further, there was an actual shortage when I came back from overseas, he stresses. The reinforcement pools were heavily depleted. And as for King's observation that nothing had been said about reinforcement shortages during the Quebec Conference with Churchill and Roosevelt, Ralston contemptuously offers that the conference "had not the faintest thing to do with the battles going on in Europe."

He had been concerned about King's statements regarding the NRMA at that time, he reveals, telling the House that he did not like the idea of releasing NRMA men in September, as they might be needed. I would have liked to have had the voluntary system work, Ralston says, but it had not.

"I have not any ambition but to be a good Canadian and I know that my place is not on the towering heights of leadership but in the humble valleys working with my fellow men.... I confess I should have liked to have finished the job but that has not been possible." He dismisses completely the sincerity of King's proposal, made in cabinet on October 31, that Ralston consider forming a government himself. Ralston calls it "the strangest doctrine I have ever heard enunciated in this House. If I were not respectful for the Prime Minister I would call it just plain nonsense. I will call it rhetoric instead.... The Prime Minister in his speech gave the impression that he was in genuine search for a successor. I want to say nothing of the kind occurred.... He asked a purely hypothetical question, going something like this: 'If I went down to the Governor General tonight and offered my resignation and recommended you take on, would you accept?' And as a matter of fact I said 'no' and neither of the others accepted." King interjects, but Ralston rolls on. "When the Prime Minister stands up and takes me to task for having indicated that I would have to resign if the policy was not carried out, I submit he is taking a position which is absolutely untenable. It simply means that if a man does not propose to carry out the policy of the government he must stay in the government or else be prepared to accept the premiership of Canada."

Rarely has any parliamentary democracy seen anything like it—a government member so determinedly eviscerating the character of his leader. The press, the opposition, the government benches are in varying measures fascinated, energized and repulsed by Ralston's performance. All that remains for the former defence minister to do is perform the coup de grâce: twist the knife and put King out of his misery.

But he does not. He leaves him bleeding, yet breathing. Ralston tells the House he will not vote for a Conservative amendment calling for immediate conscription of all 60,000 NRMA men. It would amount to a vote of non-confidence, something Ralston says he is unwilling to cast. He cannot help note that he would have stayed in government as defence minister if King had adopted the plan McNaughton eventually put forward for limited conscription. "When I resigned, I didn't want a change of Government; I wanted reinforcements. That's what I want today."

Ralston gives his support to King's confidence motion, on the understanding that if yet more troops are needed, the government will pass the necessary order-in-council and commit the fresh conscripts without again putting the issue before Parliament. "That is correct," King promptly tells Ralston and the rest of the House.

Ralston has, in the final analysis, kept the foremost trust George McCullagh's *Globe and Mail* set upon his shoulders; that invested in him by the fighting men overseas. "To put it bluntly," he says, "I think that, unsatisfactory though the method is, action is more important than method, and I believe these men will be despatched more quickly and more certainly if this House completes the action which the Government has at last taken, by approving the motion, than by any other course which the House can take at the present time."

Though he has declined the call to side with the Conservatives, Ralston emerges as a hero of the conservative press. The *Globe* salutes Ralston's performance and calls King "completely discredited." The Montreal *Gazette* says much the same thing: "Layton Ralston has probably saved the government, but he has damned it forever. In two hours in the House of Commons Wednesday he built up his case with deadly precision; he spoke coldly and quietly with calculated self-possession; he glanced sternly about him and he stared accusingly at the Prime Minister as he made it plain that he has never forgotten the treatment he received at his hands; and all who witnessed the performance left the chamber convinced that it will take a rash man to trifle with the feelings or the word of Layton Ralston in future."

For King, the Ralston speech has been distasteful and anticlimactic. He knew before Ralston had said a word that he would not break with the government; he had learned as much from St. Laurent earlier in the day. King's public statements of affection for Ralston are far from his mind as he mulls over the impact of the speech. *It was plain from the way he spoke that Ralston carried a good deal of resentment, intensified I think by the attitudes of both Macdonald and Ilsley.*

King assures himself that, on balance, he has emerged from Ralston's diatribe with more dignity than Ralston himself. *Ralston's statements gave me a chance in one or two corrections to get out more clearly than would otherwise have been possible to our men the point to which I had come in the Cabinet, namely that of being ready to tender my resignation if anyone would agree to take over,* he records. *All this will help our French Quebec supporters to see that there has been no duplicity on my part. That I had gone to the limit on everything.*

And it was just not a very good speech. *I thought Ralston spoke much too long. He went far too much into detail. He had his material written out in a meticulous way and made it apparent to the House the kind of a colleague he was, namely one who would bend in nothing and rather boasted of this attitude himself.*

And far from having rallied discontented Liberals to his side, Ralston, King concludes, has isolated himself further. *Altogether, as he was speaking I could see that our men were getting more resentful of his attitude. When he was through it really was a sad and humiliating spectacle to see him still at his desk shaking hands with Tories who came across to congratulate him. Not a man from our own side that I could see anywhere around joined in the congratulations. Before adjournment in the lobbies the men were indignant. They felt he had gone too far.*

The conservative press can say what it likes about the triumph of James Layton Ralston and the demise of William Lyon Mackenzie King. By any measure known to the prime minister, the day has belonged to him.

❧

On November 30, the day after Ralston's speech, McNaughton reports at King's request to cabinet on the events at Terrace Bay. King deigns to omit any mention of Pearkes's calling in the air force as a weapon of intimidation. *I did not bring up the fool action...not wishing to antagonize.* McNaughton reports on his efforts to defuse the hostility in the NRMA camps. Among other things, McNaughton is making sure that the camps they are being

moved to before shipping out are bright and cheerful, that they are
not run-down, with broken windows and the like, that officers and
friends meet them on their arrival so they can head off in the right
spirit. It is easy to see why the rank and file of the army have so
long admired the general. But the problems are not entirely behind
them. Yesterday, McNaughton revealed to King that there had been
trouble on a train transporting conscripts to New York, where they
were to board their ship. *Several of the men tried to break away but
were overpowered by their own men. A lot of them got away without incident. How little the public knows what powerful forces have
to be contended with.*

After cabinet, King enjoys a half-hour conversation with Hugues
Lapointe, Liberal MP, major with the Chaudières, and son of
King's late justice minister Ernest Lapointe. Hugues was elected at
the age of twenty-nine in the riding of Lotbinière in the 1940 election, eighteen months before his revered father's death, and he says
to King he realizes his constituents chose him only because of his
name. He would be going to see them this weekend, before
addressing the House in the new week. He promises King that he
will do his utmost *to try and have them understand the situation in
a way that would leave him free to help us. I told him that no matter what he did, I would understand his position.*

If your father had been with me, King tells him, I might have
been able to prevent the army reaching the size it has. It also would
have helped if Power had not allowed the expansion of the number
of men in uniform. He tells the younger Lapointe that his father's
successor, Louis St. Laurent, had to be modest at the start, being
new, but has emerged as a tower of strength.

In Hugues Lapointe he confronts a remarkable fusion of charac-
teristics: a member of his caucus from a riding that will not countenance conscription of any sort, the son of a valued and departed
ally, and a fighting man who experienced the beaches of Normandy
and knows, as King never can, the scale of sacrifice made by the
country's volunteer army, and yet who does not believe in conscripted reinforcements. King does his best to make Lapointe
believe that his father *would have done anything possible to have
prevented the govt. getting into Tory hands and certainly to prevent
anarchy which is what we were really facing at the time I took the
steps I did. I told him that he would realize where we would be as a
party if we failed to give reinforcements where we were told they
were absolutely necessary.*

In the course of their conversation, Lapointe reflects on his war. His company, he tells King, was the first to go forward after landing on D-Day. He lost half his company in the process, and they then had to fight continuously, without sufficient rest, for thirty-five days. The men, he says, were magnificent fighters, but they simply would collapse from the strain at the end of several days of patrolling. In taking Calais and Dieppe in September, Lapointe remarks, the Canadians fought with a few brigades—in similar tasks, he asserts, the British employed entire divisions. Our men, he advises King, were unfairly pressed forward and were given more than their share of the fighting. But he cannot say anything publicly about it. He also feels the army is too large and it should be made smaller, but he tells King he recognizes that, as prime minister, he cannot make any suggestion of interference in military planning. *I am glad he is going to be in Canada for some little time before going overseas,* King concludes. *He will be a helpful influence with the men there.*

The next day is December 1, a Friday. King speaks with MP Robert Mayhew on the phone, extending his congratulations on the speech he made to the House in support of the government's new war policy. Mayhew, a cardboard-box magnate from Victoria, B.C., *suggested that the French [Canadian] troops should be taken out of B.C. I told him that this is what was being done. He said the trouble out there is that the whole army is Tory. They have a force that will not help anybody.*

❧

On Saturday, December 2, Conn Smythe makes his first return to Maple Leaf Gardens, though it is not to watch a hockey game—his condition is still too poor for him to sit through a Leaf match. He comes to the Gardens because he has had a note published in the newspaper, inviting the relatives of his 30th Battery men to meet him today so they can share news. About one hundred people show up, ranging from wives and girlfriends to parents. He makes sure he speaks personally with every one of them. He is especially touched to meet Shirley Rule, whose husband Eric pulled Smythe clear of the burning ammunition truck when he was wounded. Eric Rule's gallantry has earned him the British Empire Medal.[4]

❧

The November 26 hat-trick against Toronto is the beginning of a scoring run by the Rocket. In seven games, Maurice Richard scores ten times. He registers one goal in a 7–5 loss to New York on

November 30, another in a 2–1 road victory over Chicago on December 3, another in a 4–1 defeat of the Bruins in Boston on December 5, and after a nine-day layoff (during which the fate of Mackenzie King's Liberal government is being decided in the confidence motion debate and vote), he picks up another as Toronto and Montreal tie at two apiece at the Forum. The layoff means the Canadiens have ground to regain in the schedule, and must play three games in four days. Two nights after tying Toronto on the fourteenth, they are host to Boston, and the Bruins go down 8–5 as Richard scores twice. Then it's onto a train and down to New York for a game the next night at Madison Square Garden, in which Richard contributes a goal as Montreal wins 4–1.

There is another easing in their schedule as Christmas approaches. After a five-day layoff, Montreal hosts Chicago at home on December 23, and Richard fails to score for the first time in seven games as Montreal edges the pesky Blackhawks 2–1. A Christmas break follows, and Montreal earns another five-day layoff. Richard takes advantage of the respite to move to another house. On December 27, the day before he must face the Red Wings at home, he is busy lugging a piano with the help of his brother. He gets only two hours' sleep, and doesn't think he's in shape to play. Try, Dick Irvin tells him. The Forum fans witness a signature performance in the history of the building and the franchise as Richard contributes five goals and three assists to a 9–1 demolition of the Red Wings.

Two nights later the Rangers are in town and Montreal has an easy go of it, winning 4–1, although Richard is held scoreless. Over the month of December, Richard scores eleven times in eight games, giving him twenty-four goals in twenty-two games.

May the present unfortunate crisis in Canada be considered a frame-up by the French population? Buttressed, perchance, by the Roman Catholic Irish-American population, to the south of our fair land? There may be some intermingling— and that intermingling may be far more, and other, than you are pleased to believe. Has not the always-politically-dangerous Roman church just organized arch-dioceses in both Ohio and Indiana? And is not the surge forward of that group—the best ORGANIZED in the world—something to reckon with in the Dominion? One cannot lose time now in recalling the folly of England in permitting for a moment the French retention of their language, since they were, and are,

merely conquered folk permitted to remain on British terrain
because of British generosity!
*—anonymous letter sent to both J.L. Ralston and General
McNaughton, December 3, 1944*

The week in the House beginning Monday, December 4, which
brings the final days of debate that conclude with a vote on the
government's confidence motion on Thursday, is saturated with
acrimony. The rhetoric poured upon King by his Conservative
opponents defies the bounds of House civility. About nine hundred
lines must be struck from Hansard on Tuesday. Some of those
offending words are contributed by Dr. Herbert Bruce, Progressive
Conservative from Toronto Parkdale, who scandalized the
Commons the previous summer with his corrosive comments
regarding Quebec during the family allowance debate. Bruce's
assertion that King prefers "to break his pledged word and sacrifice
the lives of our Canadian boys on the battlefields of France and
Italy rather than lose votes in the province of Quebec" must be
struck from the official record.

Such attacks do not bother King. He has become accustomed to
them during his political life. The words that truly wound him
come from people he respects. On December 5, Hugues Lapointe
offers the House a moving and dignified oration on why he cannot
support his own government's motion. He is angered and dismayed
by the efforts of politicians to divide English from French
Canadians. He saw no such division in the field among the fighting
men. As a soldier of equal rank to Conn Smythe, Lapointe witnessed first-hand the terrible losses incurred by the infantry in
Europe, and his own regiment was among those cited by Smythe as
a source of dissatisfaction with the quality of reinforcements. If his
reinforcements were improperly trained, if his volunteer ranks
deserved to be relieved by conscripts, he is in an ideal position to
say so. His own government wants to send them in. But as a man
who has led French-Canadian volunteers into battle, he will not
countenance draftees, anglophone or francophone, being forced to
relieve them. He stands as he believes his father would have stood,
had he lived: foursquare with the original Liberal policy opposing
the use of conscripts overseas. Lapointe's father had reassured the
Quebec population with the words "Jamais, jamais," on the conscription issue. Never will always mean never to his son.

King concedes to himself that parts of the speech Lapointe made to the House that night *were exceedingly fine. He spoke as a soldier who had served gallantly in battle. It was doubly effective and very telling in that he himself explained he had heard nothing about the need for reinforcements until he came back to Canada a few months ago. He also took a stand against even a limited measure of conscription as not being necessary and not likely to do any good. It was an entirely sincere speech and a very brave and courageous one.*

King professes himself to be amazed that Lapointe could not bring himself to support the government on the confidence motion. How could he not? He has said that the people want no one but King for prime minister. But Lapointe has turned away from King because he cannot forgive a broken pledge; he has told the House that to do so would mean a loss of faith in public men.

King cannot understand how Lapointe, and the French-Canadian Quebec members who share his sentiments, can abide by the potential consequence of their stance: turning over the government to *a conscriptionist gang for the rest of the war, including the war against Japan, simply because I had not held to the statements made at the time of the elections in 1940, when in 1942 the same country released me wholly from these obligations in the light of the changing situation of the war throughout the world. I confess that what Lapointe has said has hurt me more than anything in the Debate. It will do more to unsettle our own members in the House than anything that has been said and will do more harm to the Liberal party in the province of Quebec than anything else.*

🍁

Approaching mid-season, Montreal is leading the league because it can both score goals and prevent goals. It has the Punch Line up front and Bill Durnan in the net. Detroit, Toronto and Boston also have scoring ability, but of those three only Detroit and Toronto can keep their opponent under wraps with any consistency. Boston, Chicago and New York have the misfortune to allow more goals than they score, and it is being left to them to scrap over the fourth and final playoff spot. New York is in the worst position—its goals-against is by far the worst of the league, as it is allowing twice as many goals as Montreal. Averaged out, the typical New York Ranger game of 1944/45 ends 5–3 in the opposition's favour. But New York stays in the hunt for the final playoff spot by scrapping for more ties than any other team. It is winning fewer games than Boston and Chicago, but it is also losing fewer. Montreal is sure to finish first overall, with Detroit and Toronto to decide who finishes second and third.

The Canadiens are without dispute the dominant team. In All-Star voting this season, five of six first-team selections go to Montreal players: Durnan in goal, Butch Bouchard on defence, and the Punch Line of Blake, Lach and Richard up front; only Detroit defenceman Flash Hollett prevents a Canadian sweep. In addition, Dick Irvin is named the first team coach for the second straight season, and defenceman Glen Harmon makes the second team. In 1943/44 only Durnan made the first team, although Bouchard, Lach and Richard made the second team. Before then, there hadn't been a Canadien player on an All-Star team since 1939/40, when Blake made the first team. And before that, there had been Blake, and Blake only, from the Canadiens back to 1937/38, when defenceman Babe Siebert made the first team. Lach, Richard and Blake will also sweep the top three places in the 1944/45 scoring race. The last team to sweep the top three positions in the scoring race was the Bruins with their Kraut Line of Schmidt, Dumart and Bauer in 1939/40. But of those three, only Schmidt made the first All-Star team that year. The Punch Line is the first to sweep the first-team selection since the All-Star team was introduced by the NHL in 1930/31. Before Blake, no Canadien forward had been named an All Star since Aurel Joliat in 1934/35. Now, every great forward is deemed to be a Montreal Canadien; every great forward is deemed to be playing together on the same line.

Bill Durnan is well on his way to winning his second Vezina and making the first All-Star team for the second straight year. Before Durnan, no Montreal goaltender has won the Vezina since George Hainsworth in 1928/29; no Montreal goaltender before him has ever been a first-team All Star. Until 1943/44, when Durnan made his debut and the Punch Line played its first full season together, Montreal had not won at least half of its games or scored more goals than it allowed since 1936/37. The Montreal Canadiens of 1944/45 are exhausting all available superlatives.

On December 7, the third anniversary of Pearl Harbor, Mackenzie King faces Judgment Day. The time has come for the House to vote on his confidence motion, as well as on two proposed amendments: that of the Conservatives, who are asking for full and immediate conscription of all NRMA men, and that proposed by King's former public works minister, Montreal's P.J.A. Cardin, who resigned over Bill 80 in 1942, which opposes conscription of any kind.

The Conservative politicking has never let up, and House leader Gordon Graydon delivers a speech full of venom. King is astounded—not so much by its specific content as by what he views as its ineptitude. Graydon has behaved *like a school-boy and with the worst judgment possible* in making a speech *all on the line of petty politics—one might say peanut politics in which he talked of the CCF and Liberals combining against the Tories by using the old simile of Liberals and CCF becoming curious bed-fellows in an effort to divide the Tories. Not a word on the significance of the resolution in reference to the war and the maintaining of forces overseas.*

Graydon's amendment for all-out conscription is voted down emphatically, 170–44. Cardin's amendment opposing any conscription suffers an almost identical fate, obliterated 168–43. King instantly recognizes his own wisdom in the votes. The extremes of the issue have met with almost exactly the same degree of opposition. The middle of the road can seize the day.

A golden moment emerges before King when CCF leader M.J. Coldwell presents a motion of his own, calling upon King to drop the words "its policy of" from the confidence motion, which as tabled reads: "That this House will aid the government in its policy of maintaining a vigorous war effort." King reads an elaborate rationale into Coldwell's action. The CCF will be embarrassed in front of the nation if it fails to support the government in pursuing limited conscription. Therefore it has asked for an amendment it does not think we will accept. When we do not, it will have its excuse not to support the government. But King has no problem amending the motion. He can't even recall how the words "its policy of" came to be included in the simple statement. Their presence or absence changes nothing. King spots Ralston studying the motion with great gravity, sniffing out some subterfuge.

I saw in an instant that if we accepted the amendment, the CCF would have to vote with us on the motion as amended.... I at once said that I would accept the amendment.

King is correct in assuming that, by accepting Coldwell's motion in good faith, the CCF members will have no choice but to support him with their eight votes, and the sight of the left wing of the House joining the Social Credit component of the right wing in standing by his government will help shore up support among his own ranks. That leaves the Conservatives. Their day has been a tactical disaster. Left and right alike are falling into line with King.

Having passed an order-in-council providing for limited conscription, and with King having assured Ralston in this House that if more conscripts prove necessary he will respond with a simple order-in-council, there is no good reason beyond stubborn partisan politicking for the Conservatives to deny King his confidence vote.

Yet the Conservatives cannot bring themselves to voice any measure of confidence for King's government. And so they stumble into an alliance with the dissident Quebec Liberals led by Cardin when the vote is held. *Tory Ontario and the anti-war Quebec groups tied with each other,* King marvels. *I don't think men were ever more discomfited or political opponents, both foes and friends, more completely confounded, than were the official opposition and those of our own party who did not support the main motion.*

When the vote is counted, King is amazed. His government is alive by a count of 143 to 70. One hundred twenty-five Liberals have joined with eight CCF and ten Social Credit members in support of King. Opposing him are thirty-three Progressive Conservatives and thirty-seven dissenting Liberals, of whom thirty-four are from francophone ridings.

King is like Henry V at Agincourt. The scale of his victory staggers him. A seventy-three-vote margin. *It took me some time to realize that I had 2/3 of the House with me. I had been expecting 30 of a majority—some said we might have 40. Gordon Ross at one stage had said to me he would not be surprised if we went as high as 50. I never believed that. I never thought beyond 30 or in the 30s.*

Divine intervention is the only explanation. God's will, working in concert with a manifestation of spiritual power. King is certain of it. An answer to prayer, God's law enacted, the power of faith in action.

The result was really a miracle.

After the day in the House is over, King notes in the press that it was four minutes past one when the vote was counted and announced. The clock hands aligned.

When I rose to thank the House for the confidence it expressed in the govt.'s undertaking to maintain a vigorous war policy, I was given a tremendous ovation. Never before have I received such a place from the H. of C. nor do I believe any other leader has received anything greater.

Thank you, King simply says, and immediately moves to adjourn.

The conservatives will not concede victory, miraculous or fortuitous, to King. "Surely no Canadian Government has presented a spectacle of a more nerveless fumbling in the face of necessity, nor won a more dismal victory," the Montreal *Gazette* fumes the day after the motion has been carried and the Orange Conservatives of Ontario have been left holding hands with francophone anti-conscriptionist allies. "Had the government only done promptly what it has had to do finally, great would have been the gains for this nation. There would have been no suspicion that we were hedging our war commitments at the most furious moment of the war, just because we believed that the war was near its end. There would not have been the spectacle of our neighbor to the south sending its drafted 18-year-olds to the front because of 'urgent military necessity' while we refused to use our drafted Home Defence Army. We would not have presented to the enemy this suggestion that we might be deciding to limit our commitments, with the further encouraging hint that what Canada had seen fit to do, others might do also. We would not have presented to our fighting men this debate as to the degree to which we should back them up, nor would they have heard the Prime Minister suggest that, because they were fighting so well under the voluntary system, no compulsion should be used in sending them reinforcements. Nor would we have presented to ourselves this spectacle of tension and bitterness and strife."

For the *Ottawa Citizen*, however, the performance of Graydon and the Conservatives is one of the most striking aspects of the debate and vote. In their performance as the official opposition, the *Citizen* avows that "political ineptitude reached a new low level."

And from the *Winnipeg Free Press* editorial page on December 14 comes a voice of understanding for Quebec's position on compulsory service:

"Quebec's opposition to overseas conscription does not spring from any fear of, or desire to escape from, the pains and sacrifices of the field. To believe so is basically to misunderstand the case of Quebec. In the debates of 1917, the Quebec members in denouncing conscription frequently told the House that their own sons were in the trenches. Likewise in the recent debate, some of the Quebec members who spoke against the Government were but recently back from the battlefront. It was the same Hugues Lapointe who led the assault on the channel ports, who denounced the King Government. And many other Quebec members—older men—are represented overseas by their own flesh and blood.

"In fact, conscription in Quebec long ago ceased to be a matter of military policy and became a symbol of racial domination. Quebec has always felt that Canada became involved in wars not because of Canadian interests but because of the emotional pull of the English-speaking majority."[5]

❧

On the afternoon of December 8, the third anniversary of Japan's invasion of Hong Kong, Mackenzie King drops by Government House to confer with the Governor General. The crisis is behind them. They have a policy of conscription neither of them really wanted, they have seen cabinet ministers threaten to or actually resign, they have seen draftees mutiny, and they have seen relations between English and French Canada sink to perilous depths of enmity. But they have not seen King's government fall, and they have not seen the country collapse into civil war and anarchy.

But there is still a war to be won. I am more than convinced that only Providence will save the situation, King tells His Excellency. The real fight continues to be between good and evil in the beyond.

There were forces at work that led Coldwell to move the amendment he did, he assures the Governor General. It enabled me to get a majority of at least twenty more than I would otherwise have secured, and helped to make the vote the telling one it was before the country.

I believe absolutely in the survival of human personality, and in those who have gone being able to continue under Divine guidance to influence situations, he adds. King does not say which human personalities came to his assistance, but who else could have been leaning on the course of destiny but Sir Wilfrid himself? What more could King have done to call his spirit down into that august chamber than to read his own words back into Hansard on November 28—veritably channelling him into his old prime minister's desk at the front of the Liberal ranks, which King now occupied? Death had delivered the party's leadership from Laurier to him. Periodicity had inflicted upon him the same ordeals that had beset Laurier. Together, in spirit and in flesh, they had triumphed at last.

God bless Mackenzie King. Resurrected, revitalized, reconfirmed. *Rex.*

COUNTERATTACK

December 7, 1944

ON the third anniversary of Pearl Harbor, General Douglas MacArthur begins the American reconquest of the Philippines with an invasion of the island of Leyte; over the next few weeks 80,000 tenacious Japanese troops will die trying to defend it. Two days after American infantry come ashore at Leyte, James F. Byrnes, director of war mobilization and reconversion in Washington, orders the selective service department to resume induction of men in the twenty-six to thirty-seven age group. Since April 1944, the American draft has been concentrating on men in the under-twenty-six age category; Byrnes wants to use the men in the higher age bracket to replace those released by the armed forces to work in war plants, which are facing a serious manpower shortage.

With American troops pressing toward the Rhine in Europe and the land war in the Pacific escalating, the United States is entering a critical phase in its ability to continue mustering men and materiel. On December 15, Americans begin a new offensive in the Philippines, making the first of several landings over the next five weeks on Mindaro to secure airfields to aid in the forthcoming main assault on Luzon and the ultimate objective of Manila. The next day, Hitler delivers a terrible surprise through the Ardennes forest by launching a last-gasp blitzkrieg aimed at recapturing Antwerp. The engagement known as the Battle of the Bulge—so called because the Germans drive a wedge deep into the First U.S. Army's line in Belgium— results in American troops being completely overrun by ruthless Panzer assaults in the greatest defeat of U.S. arms since the Revolutionary War. At Malmédy on December 17, SS soldiers massacre eighty-six American prisoners, one of only several such atrocities during the offensive. By December 22, the Germans have the town of Bastogne completely surrounded, trapping the 101st Airborne and elements of the 10th Armoured; on December 24, the Second Panzer Division has reached Foy-Notre Dame and is only three miles from the river Meuse, some sixty miles from the front as it stood on the night of December 15.

The same day that Foy-Notre Dame falls, the *New York Times* runs a large, admiring feature on how well professional sports have thrived during the war. With Allied forces, largely American, on their way to suffering almost 100,000 casualties in the Ardennes, there could not be a worse time for America's leading newspaper to proclaim the remarkable ability of sporting leagues, franchise owners and professional athletes to prosper at a time of national crisis. The next day, Christmas, James Byrnes directs the national selective service to review the military qualifications of professional athletes. The NSS quickly complies, issuing a memorandum to local draft boards on December 26, just as the German thrust is being halted at Foy-Notre Dame, ordering a review of professional athletes previously deferred on medical grounds. As the Associated Press relates, "Byrnes said it was difficult for him and the public to understand how men can be physically unfit for military service and yet be able to compete with the greatest athletes of the nation in games demanding physical fitness. A substantial number of these athletes hold 4-F classifications due, principally, to injuries sustained in sports competition." Many of these 4-F ratings are thought to be borderline cases.

Just how prevalent 4-Fers are in professional athletic ranks is soon revealed. Of twenty-eight members of the Washington Redskins football club, thirteen are playing because 4-F ratings have kept them clear of the armed forces. Another ten hold 1-C ratings—discharged from the military because of medical disabilities. These disabilities are overwhelmingly sporting injuries—as the *New York Times* reports, they run the gamut from twisted knees to stomach ailments to perforated eardrums and bum shoulders. Professional baseball has kept the game alive overwhelmingly on the strength of officially disabled men. On December 30, it is reported that 223 of 530 men in major-league baseball owe their continuing careers to a 4-F rating.

Sportswriters do their best to defend the practice, and the players. "These lads appear physically fit mainly because their dressing rooms are equipped with whirlpool baths, baking machines, massage tables and adhesive tape," writes Arthur Daley in the *Times* on December 29. "Some of them have to wear special braces and the majority of them are the most artificially 'physically fit' athletes imaginable. It is only with the aid of these mechanical gadgets plus constant massage and the liberal use of adhesive tape, that they are able to cavort on the gridiron, the diamond or anywhere else. They require persistent personal attention in order to continue for the brief spurts in which they operate. In the Army or Navy* they would get none of that, and it was Army and Navy doctors, it should be remembered, who assigned each of them 4-F status in the first place."

The point is made, but the damage to the reputation of athletics has been done. With sports, particularly basketball, already in the midst of gambling and corruption scandals, the war turns against professional sports, the customary wellspring of heroes. To conserve oil and rubber being consumed by bettors and their automobiles, Byrnes puts an end to thoroughbred racing. The imperative to conserve strategic materials leads to speculation that baseball will not be permitted to begin spring training—a moot decision if enough of its players have their 4-F ratings revoked. The able-bodied male is now just as strategic a material as oil and rubber. With thousands of Americans falling in the snow of the Ardennes and on the beaches of the Pacific, and with the draft being stepped up to help address the shortage of war workers, ensuring the continuation of professional sports is the lowest priority among war planners in Washington.

On December 28, Betty Carse receives another telegram.

MINISTER OF NATIONAL DEFENCE NOW WISHES TO INFORM YOU THAT INFORMATION HAS BEEN RECEIVED THROUGH INDIRECT CHANNELS THAT M4432 RIFLEMAN ROBERT ALLISON CARSE PREVIOUSLY REPORTED MISSING IN ACTION HAS NOW BEEN REPORTED PRISONER OF WAR STALAG 11B GERMANY PRISONER OF WAR NUMBER UNKNOWN STOP THIS INFORMATION SUBJECT TO OFFICIAL CONFIRMATION STOP WHEN FURTHER INFORMATION BECOMES AVAILABLE IT WILL BE FORWARDED AS SOON AS RECEIVED

---

*The air force is not mentioned because the United States at the time didn't have one. Air operations were conducted under the aegis of the army or navy.

On January 8, the Canadian military lists Rifleman Carse as an unofficial POW, held at Stalag 11B.

On January 2, Montreal is in Boston and Maurice Richard scores once in a 6–3 win. Montreal has eight wins and one tie in its last nine games. But then the Canadiens must face the Leafs at Maple Leaf Gardens on January 4, and they continue to meet frustration with Hap Day's tight-checking charges. Richard fails to score for the fourth time in six meetings with Toronto as the Leafs win 4–2.

Two nights later, back at the Forum, the Canadiens launch a fusillade of scoring that produces twenty-five goals in three games. Richard scores once as they bury Chicago 10–1 on the sixth; on the eleventh Toronto receives its comeuppance at the Forum as Richard scores twice in a 7–4 win; and in Detroit on the thirteenth Richard gets another as Montreal wins 8–3.

These are the first victories in a nine-game winning streak, the first victories in a greater run in which Montreal goes eighteen games without a loss, producing sixteen wins and two ties as they outscore the opposition ninety-seven to thirty-nine. The streak includes two more romps, both at home—an 11–3 defeat of Boston, in which Richard scores once, and a 9–4 defeat of New York, in which Richard scores twice. He also picks up his fourth hat-trick (counting his five-goal night against Detroit on December 28) of the season in a 6–3 road defeat of the Red Wings on January 21. In a nine-game span from January 20 to February 10, during which Montreal wins eight and ties one, Richard sets a record by scoring fourteen times. For the month of January, Richard produces twelve goals in eleven games, and has thirty-six goals in thirty-three games on the season.

On December 8, the day after his government secured its vote of confidence in the House of Commons, Mackenzie King set himself to the task of lining up a riding for his defence minister, General McNaughton. He quickly found one: Grey North on the shore of Ontario's Georgian Bay, some twenty-three thousand souls, an even mix of urban and rural voters with its main population centres at Owen Sound and Meaford. It is a longstanding Liberal seat. Backbencher W.P. Telford, who has agreed to resign to make way for McNaughton, won the seat in 1926, lost it in 1930 when the Conservatives came to power, regained it in 1935 and held it in 1940. Though he did not carry the riding with a majority in 1940, his victory margin over the Conservative candidate was more than 1,800 votes.

McNaughton *will doubtless be elected there,* King noted on December 8—perhaps even by acclamation. In King's mind, the opposition parties should have the grace to permit McNaughton unopposed admission to the House ranks—as defence minister he should be in the House, answering questions and reporting on the progress of the war and the government's policies. But within days King was perturbed to learn that the Conservatives, at least, have no intention of allowing McNaughton to reach the House unchallenged. They will have a candidate on hand to give him a run for his money. The CCF also decide to enter the race.[1]

For the February 5 by-election, the Tories choose as their man the forty-six-year-old mayor of Owen Sound, in the Toronto *Telegram*'s words "a short, stocky, pugnacious looking" Garfield Case. In the Great War he was rejected three times as medically unfit, but finally made it into the ranks of the Royal Flying Corps in 1917. He served in Canada for two years before being discharged in 1919 with a 50 per cent disability. Raised on a farm near Aurora, Ontario, Case had attended Ontario Agricultural College in Guelph. Upon his discharge, he ran the Saskatoon Grain Growers Association Co-operative in the town of Imperial. He came to Owen Sound in 1932 and went into the insurance business; his first foray into politics was in 1940, when he was elected to the city council. He secured the mayor's chair by acclamation in 1942, 1943 and 1944.

The CCF produce an enigmatic candidate: Air Vice-Marshal A.E. Godfrey. As an ace with the Royal Flying Corps in France in the Great War, Godfrey shot down nineteen Germans and was awarded the Military Cross. At the beginning of this war, he was made head of Western Air Command; subsequent postings led to his being named deputy inspector general of the RCAF for eastern Canada in 1942. He retired from the military in 1943; now fifty-four, he was serving as executive assistant to the president of the industrial firm Parmenter and Bullock in Gananoque, Ontario, when the CCF made him their Grey North candidate.

The Liberals turn out in force to help clear McNaughton's path to a House seat. William Mulock, the postmaster general, becomes his campaign chairman. Fellow cabinet members Ian Mackenzie and Colin Gibson appeared on the hustings in support. The retired air vice-marshal does not seem to pose a serious threat to McNaughton.

The Conservative effort is also lagging; by the end of January, Case's campaign has peaked.

❧

On January 25, U.S. navy secretary James Forrestal orders a crackdown on 1-C medical discharges being enjoyed by professional athletes. A ruling similar to the navy edict was issued by the U.S. Army one month earlier, according to United Press. All ships and stations have been ordered by Forrestal not to discharge from the navy, marines or coast guard apparently able-bodied athletes on medical grounds unless those cases are reviewed by superior officers in Washington. A re-examination of all professional athletes granted a 4-F rating has revealed that all but two are in fact now judged fit for service.

The argument that professional sport is an indispensable thread in the American cultural fabric is not heeded by Forrestal, who declares it "unessential to the national health, safety and interest." At the time Forrestal issues his order, Americans are embarking on some of the bloodiest fighting of the war. Their assault on the main Philippine island of Luzon began on January 9 with 68,000 men of the American Sixth Army going ashore at Lingayen Gulf. Americans will still be fighting for Luzon in July. The fact that major-league baseball will need about four hundred men for spring training is of little concern to men like Forrestal.

Two days before UP announces the Forrestal order, it is matter-of-factly reported that the Boston Bruins will sign a defenceman who has been playing for the RCAF Hurricanes. He has been discharged from the service on medical grounds, but he is obviously fit enough to become a Bruin two weeks later and play the last five games of the season and seven more seasons in the NHL.

❧

Supposedly stung by internal criticism that the party has not done enough for their Grey North candidate, and with less than one week to go before the February 5 by-election, the Conservatives launch a massive frontal assault on General McNaughton. Party leader John Bracken, just back from an overseas tour of the troops, heads promptly for Grey North on his return.

On January 29, King is confident that the Liberals will be able to hold off the Conservative challenge. Chubby Power, though persona non grata after resigning his cabinet position over conscription, has observed to King that Garfield Case *appears to have gotten in wrong by a letter he had written a few months ago saying he was*

*not in favour of conscription though in favour of the
Conservative...platform. It will be interesting to see where Bracken
gets off at when he goes to Grey North. I rather imagine he will
come out with some story which he will say he obtained while overseas, making things as unpleasant as he can for McNaughton. McN.
expects this kind of an attack but said he himself is quite prepared to
continue in the quiet way he has and ignore whatever is said.*

On Tuesday the thirtieth, King notes to himself: *I believe
McNaughton will win and win handsomely. A good candidate is 2/3
of the battle. He is an excellent candidate. Already the tide in North
Grey has begun to swing strongly in our favour.*

John Bracken sweeps into the riding on Wednesday the thirty-
first to campaign right through the remainder of the week in preparation for election day the following Monday. The Conservative
strategy is to make conscription the election issue. With Bracken's
arrival, candidate Garfield Case steps into the background to let the
big boys wrestle over the big issues. Embarrassed by their performance in the confidence vote, which left them allied against the
government with dissident Quebec Liberals, and unable to forgive
McNaughton for entering the King cabinet, the Conservatives have
resolved to give no quarter to the general who was once their dar-
ling. They pronounce themselves dissatisfied with the King–
McNaughton scheme to send only 16,000 NRMA men overseas.
Nothing less than all 60,000 of them will do. Performing with a
vigour never before seen, Bracken rolls into Grey North with a fury
and a vengeance.

Speaking at the Legion hall in Owen Sound on his first day in
town, Bracken declares that the people of Grey North are deciding
the future of Canada, that they are bearing "the greatest duty and
the greatest challenge ever imposed on any Canadian electoral constituency since Confederation. The obligation is to say emphatically to our men overseas that reinforcement needs will hereafter be
dealt with as the military problem it is and not as a political expedient, which the government has made it."

Reflecting on his recent overseas visit to Canadian troops,
Bracken intones: "Shocking though the story may be to you, those
men have the definite conviction that Canadians at home are letting
them down.... They feel they are unnecessarily handicapped when
they cannot be sure of a full team in battle." The soldiers, he
reports, "told me Ralston was not wrong. They told me this was an
understatement rather than an overstatement." Plainly it is their

duty to reject McNaughton. "The election of General McNaughton will do no more than confirm in office a man whose policy has failed lamentably to give your men the support they have so desperately needed."

❦

At Stalag 8C in Sagan, the prisoners have managed to build themselves a radio, and they use it as often as is safe to keep abreast of the war's progress through Allied news broadcasts. On January 12, the Soviet Union launches the single largest offensive of the war—larger than Germany's blitzkrieg through France and the Low Countries in the spring of 1940, which involved 120 divisions; larger by far than the forty-five divisions assembled for the Allied Normandy invasion in June 1944, which involved about 155,000 troops and paratroopers in the initial action of June 6. The Soviet offensive throws 180 divisions, about 3.8 million men, against Germany's eastern front. Stalin's strategic plan calls for an end to the war in only forty-five days. The Soviets enjoy a numerical advantage of ten to one over the German defenders.

Moving across western Poland and Hungary, the Soviet offensive drives before it a ghastly parade of refugees, concentration camp internees and prisoners of war, whom the Germans force-march through a harsh winter, back into Germany. The infirm are abandoned; stragglers are shot.

Bob Carse and the rest of the men in Stalag 8C know the Russians are coming—they just don't know when. On February 1, the Soviets are across the Oder at Steinau, about seventy-five miles east of the camp.

That day, Carse's Chicago Blackhawks are in Montreal, and so is the NHL's board of governors, to decide on the playoff format to be used in the spring. The day also marks the return to public life of Conn Smythe. No longer to be heard simply through missives dispatched to the press, Smythe is now out in the world in flesh and blood, and voice. He comes to Montreal for the league meetings, and so takes in his first NHL game since returning home from overseas in September.

Maurice Richard scores in the first period, the only goal Montreal can manage as the struggling Blackhawks hold them to a 1–1 tie. It is Smythe's first look at the new two-line offside game as played by the NHL, and his first real look at Richard, the player everybody is talking about. He now has thirty-seven goals in thirty-four games.

He appears assured of breaking the league scoring record set by Joe Malone of the Canadiens in the NHL's first season, 1917/18, the last time French and English Canada were at each other's throats over conscription, when Malone produced forty-four goals in only twenty games. No player has scored forty goals in an NHL season since 1929/30, when forty-three were notched by Boston's Cooney Weiland, forty-one by linemate Dit Clapper and forty by Montreal's Howie Morenz. And when the war came along, no one had even scored thirty goals since Toronto's Charlie Conacher produced thirty-six in 1934/35—this despite the fact that the NHL season was steadily getting longer.

The average number of goals per game climbed rapidly during the war. Teams averaged about 2.5 goals per game each in the late 1930s. In 1941/42, when average team scoring reached 3.1, the Ranger's Lynn Patrick broke through the thirty-goal ceiling with thirty-two in forty-seven games. In 1942/43, when the team scoring average jumped again to 3.6, Doug Bentley of Chicago produced thirty-three goals in fifty games.

The great leap forward came in 1943/44, when the two-line offside was introduced and the game was broken wide open. Average team scoring shot up to 4.08, and a record six players made it into the thirty-goal club: Doug Bentley with thirty-eight; Herb Cain of Boston, Carl Liscombe of Detroit and Lorne Carr of Toronto with thirty-six; Bill Mosienko of Chicago with thirty-two; and Bill Cowley of Boston with thirty.

Cowley's was the most impressive performance of 1943/44, as he produced his thirty in only thirty-six games, at which point his season was cut short by a separated shoulder. Producing an average of one goal per game over a season has proved an elusive accomplishment in recent years. Up until 1925, the league's top scorers routinely produced more than one goal per game. In 1925/26 Ted Kennedy's mentor Nels Stewart became the first scoring-race winner not to manage a goal-a-game pace, producing thirty-four in thirty-six games for the Montreal Maroons. Team scoring overall was in steady descent, suppressed by restrictive passing rules, and it wasn't until the modern blueline offside rule opened up the game and doubled scoring in the league in 1929/30 that a player again came close to the one-for-one target, when Weiland missed it by one goal over forty-four games. Ever since, the feat has remained well beyond the reach of even the best players. Richard is on pace to surpass Weiland's "modern" scoring record and the rate at which he amassed them, and the fans in rinks around the league know it.

"It still seems strange to me," Smythe confesses after seeing the new brand of NHL hockey as demonstrated by Montreal and Chicago. "I guess I'm going to take a while to get used to it all again. I guess one rule still applies, though. The good hockey players are still the best, and the team with the good players wins." And how good does he think Richard is? "When he went in for that goal I could see why it was they have been comparing him with Howie Morenz. He's terribly fast and looked like Morenz for a moment there, but the comparison ends there."

Despite his grudging praise, Smythe is mesmerized by Richard. Everything he has heard about him is true. Seeing him in action on the Forum ice, he knows two things. First, that with a player of his extraordinary talent on hand, the game will do fine in the postwar years. Second, that he must have him as a Maple Leaf.

He offers the Canadiens $25,000 for this son of francophone Quebec. All the loathing that this war has built up between Toronto and Montreal, in the political and sporting arenas, means nothing to Smythe in the face of a powerful talent, a talent that can make the fans forget about the makeshift matches of the war years, a talent that can fill a rink to standing room with paying customers.

Richard was a Maple Leaf once—a Verdun Maple Leaf, in his Junior days. But Richard as a Toronto Maple Leaf? It is almost impossible to imagine. Richard is a purely offensive player; Hap Day's two-way close-checking regimen would drive him mad. But more important is how this son of working-class Montreal, a Catholic who is still learning English, would fit into a Leaf regiment back under the command of Conn Smythe, who will soon have the Gardens board allied with him and have Frank Selke off his payroll.

Smythe has been party to one of the most vituperative attacks on the character of French Canadians in the nation's history. Quebecers have been cast by Conservatives as duty-dodging traitors, cowardly Zombies. Their Catholicism has been cast by the most avid members of the Orange Lodge as an evil to be resisted. Conn Smythe's relationship with his son Stafford came perilously close to termination in his rage over Stafford's marriage to a Catholic in a Catholic ceremony. Smythe is not so xenophobic that he will not employ Catholics, even Irish Catholics like King Clancy, or underwrite the hockey program of a Catholic school like St. Michael's College. But his suspicion of Catholicism is deep-

seated. When scout and old crony Squib Walker wrote to him overseas in March 1943 to complain about his salary negotiation problems with Frank Selke, Smythe replied that Selke "is not the
strongest friend in the world when the chips get down as is probably due to the RC in him." In Conn Smythe's world, religion is a
final litmus test of character.

Smythe's business priorities have always been strong enough to
make him see the profitability in any relationship, no matter how
unholy. But Maurice Richard would be a disaster as a Maple Leaf.
He is too spectacular, too *Montreal*, ever to be assimilated. Even as
a Canadien he stands apart as a talent. In Toronto this distinctive-
ness would work against him, not because Richard plays the game
the right way and the Leafs play the wrong way, but because
Richard plays his way, and no other way, and he carries too much
cultural baggage for his idiosyncrasies not to carry additional shad-
ings when the time comes to criticize his effort and attitude.

"I played for myself, the team and the fans," Richard will reflect
in retirement. "I don't think I would have done half as well anywhere else—in fact I would have refused to play anywhere else—
because of the rapport I had with the fans here." His wife Lucille
attends every home game in which he appears. His father only
misses two in his entire career.

Maurice Richard as a Maple Leaf would be a one- or two-season
phenomenon. And then the fans, mystified and tortured by an endless series of incidents—Hap Day complaining about Richard's
backchecking, Richard benched, Richard sullen, Richard refusing
to speak to the press in his halting English, Richard cut off from the
community that adores him—would be greeted by a newspaper
story along the lines that Smythe has cut a five-player deal and
Richard is on his way to Chicago. He might do all right there, he
might not. He might end up frustrated, alienated, spent and discard-
ed, the answer to the trivia question: who was that guy who scored
all those goals for the Canadiens at the end of the war, and then
faded away just as Germany surrendered?

Montreal, as it happens, declines Smythe's offer. Richard will
become, as a Toronto sportswriter will salute him fifteen years
later, a symbol of the French-Canadian race; he will become, as a
Quebec sportswriter will one day salute him, a mythic figure for
the people of the province on a par with Parti Québécois leader
René Lévesque and folk singer Felix LeClerc.

Since he's just a one-way player, Smythe will quip, I would have paid $100,000 for him. If he could have backchecked, I would have paid $200,000.

❧

The league board of governors are meeting in Montreal on Friday, February 2, when Conn Smythe turns his attentions to Grey North. If the people there are told the facts about McNaughton, he assures the press, "they will have the sense to throw him out." The general cannot be "trusted with the Canadian Army." Conn Smythe's opinion of McNaughton has come a long way since June 1940, when he was imploring the prime minister himself to make him his minister of war.

John Bracken has turned the Zombies ruthlessly against McNaughton. Today it is reported that, while 8,300 conscripts did arrive overseas on January 20, 7,800 who were given leave for Christmas and New Year's prior to their embarkment failed to report back on time. Of those, 6,300 are still AWOL. Bracken challenges McNaughton with an allegation that NRMA men showed up overseas without their rifles and ammunition because they threw them overboard.

Mulock's report back to King on Saturday is *decidedly hopeful. The poll of newspapermen in the constituency indicates McNaughton at the top. McNaughton, the most favoured, C.C.F. next, and Conservative last. I believe this will be the order. I also believe that McNaughton will have a substantial lead. I shall be greatly surprised if that is not so. His speeches have been, I think, excellent, particularly what he said in this last broadcast about certain newspapers and control by a reactionary, very wealthy small group, who have a stranglehold on the Conservative leadership, differentiating from the old party led by Sir John and the present piratical gang was well done. He has immensely strengthened his stature in the Dominion. The fight will help us I am sure in the general campaign.*

On the political battlefield of rural Ontario on this day, King's confidence is not so readily supported. McNaughton loses his temper, unaccustomed to close quarters, no-holds-barred politicking. In his allegations about the NRMA men in transit, Bracken, he charges, has "slandered not only me but the Canadian Army. I resent that." He insists there is no truth to the weapons-jettisoning story. The closest he can get is a rumour, and only a rumour, that one man threw away his rifle. And he rejects the Conservative arguments that supporting the boys overseas means sending in all 60,000 Zombies.

Reinforcements, McNaughton insists, are adequate.

It is brilliant, below-the-belt campaigning. The Conservatives are hitting hard and fast at the last minute, forcing McNaughton to take the defensive on unsubstantiated rumours, forcing him in the process to defend the Zombies. The Conservatives are making a final, dramatic push.

Bracken takes to the podium today and plays a trump card, the Quebec card. The Conservative leader has settled upon an ingenious stump position on the Zombies. He levels all the criticism against Quebec that the most right-wing supporter would relish, then absolves himself of Quebec-bashing by blaming Mackenzie King for brainwashing the poor duty-dodgers. "For twenty-seven years, Mackenzie King taught in one section of Canada in case of war they would not have to bear their share of the burden," he thunders. "Is it any wonder only twenty-two per cent of their available manpower is in the armed forces as compared to forty-four per cent of your boys? If you had been taught the same thing, maybe your boys would not have gone to be shot at.... It isn't the fault of the habitant of Quebec. It is the fault of those who taught that section of Canada it need not carry its fair share in war, and so you are carrying an extra burden and the French-Canadians are being accused of not carrying their fair share."

The Conservatives also unveil their eleventh-hour secret weapon: wounded war veterans.

Major George Hees and Captain Howard Sale arrive in the riding to address a crowd on Saturday night. Hees was wounded in action in the Scheldt pocket on November 2; Sale, in Italy in March 1944.* They have come to Grey North to tell the electorate that General McNaughton is dead wrong and that the fighting men are depending on them to reject him and his policies.

Hees makes emphatic assertions about the reinforcement situation. "We never had enough infantry reinforcements and after the Scheldt battle our reinforcements were so low we had to get men from other arms. They had to be trained and their training period was one month. One month, and they went out incapable of taking their place in the units to which they were sent. Not only did they hamper themselves, through their lack of training they became casualties and they jeopardized the lives of fully trained men." If

---

*A Toronto *Telegram* account of Captain Sale's address reported that he had been wounded in Italy in March 1943. This would have been impossible, as no Allied troops were even in Italy at the time.

the government does not bring in full conscription of all NRMA men, Hees assures the audience, the morale of the fighting men will be affected.

"The Canadians went into D-Day without visible reinforcements," declares Sale. "If anyone, be he general or not, says this is just a political issue, he was never more wrong. It is not a political issue. It is a pressing need. If General McNaughton says we do not need reinforcements, he is wrong, wrong, wrong."

In criticizing the practice of remustering men from other service arms to meet reinforcement needs, Sale asks the crowd to consider this: If the Maple Leafs needed a player, would they turn to a baseball team for one? Would the Leafs take Joe DiMaggio? In his emotional knockout punch, Sale invokes the memory of his brother Julian, who was killed in the air force a few months earlier. "I can't let that boy down," he says. And nor, he might as well say, should they.

The only slip in the final weekend blitz by the Conservatives comes in the address by Major Hees, who presents himself as practically the last man taken out of the Scheldt when wounded on November 2. It is news to most people when he reveals that the First Canadian Army has not been in active combat since then. For three months, General Crerar's troops have been recuperating with Montgomery's blessing after the casualty-ridden Scheldt offensive. One might imagine that people would wonder how there could be such a drastic shortage of men when the army in northern Europe has been idle for three months, but the question does not seem to surface.

More important to the reinforcement issue, the Canadian forces are to be pulled out of Italy and will join up with Crerar's men in March, thereby creating the unified force McNaughton had argued for, at the expense of his command, in 1943. If this were public knowledge, McNaughton would be able to offer a compelling rebuttal to the relentless Conservative charges that there are not enough reinforcements, that all the available NRMA men must be committed. But it is an operational secret. Perhaps the officers campaigning for Case would not have been so adamant about the need for reinforcements if they knew the Canadian divisions tied up in Italy were shortly going to be available in northern Europe. Perhaps the Conservatives themselves would not be able to campaign so vociferously about the need for every available NRMA man to be shipped out if they knew this.

It is not so secure a Liberal riding, Grey North. Of twenty-one elections since Confederation, eighteen have been decided by fewer than five hundred votes. And the period of Conservative dominance, from 1908 to 1926, included a decisive victory in 1917, when conscription was the issue.

King's tone remains upbeat on Sunday, though anxiety seems to be creeping into his self-assurance. *Have naturally been thinking much of tomorrow's by-election. Feel confident McNaughton will win. Will be greatly surprised if he does not. Bracken I think has hurt himself in the charges he made about N.R.M.A. men throwing their kits and guns into the sea—wholly unsubstantiated. His language too has been unworthy of public men. I doubt if Coldwell has made much impression either way. I still look to see the Tories at the bottom of the poll.*

On Monday, February 5, election day, King can admit to himself his misgivings. *A little concerned over the possibilities of the election in Grey North. All day I have been much less certain than I was a few days ago. My main concern has been with the C.C.F., feeling that the young people may take the bit in their teeth. That has been perhaps my greatest concern. So far as the Tories go, I have been fearful of the Orange complexion of the constituency and the use that may be made of the Orange crusade against the French and the Catholics. The fact that Mrs. McN. is a Catholic would be used for all it was worth among Orangemen and what I equally fear is the power of money in the constituency—the buying up of votes. The Tories will spend no end of money for that purpose. I have not, however, had any fear that Case would win. My thought has been that he will come 3rd. I was a little concerned last night when I saw the snow coming down fairly heavily, some wind, and heard of drifting of snow in other parts of the province....*

There was indeed a heavy snow on Sunday, which has raised fears among Liberals that it might affect the turnout among rural voters, where the party's strength lies, but as many voters cast ballots on Monday as did in 1940—about 16,500. After the polls close at six, McNaughton convenes with his team at the home of Roly Patterson, who won the local seat for the Liberals in the 1943 provincial election. Gerry Rau, who was McNaughton's aide-de-camp when he was in charge of the First Canadian Army, comes in with the first poll. Thirty-two votes for McNaughton, fifteen for Case, seven for Godfrey. At the Progressive Conservative headquarters, Case's campaign manager, Karl Homuth, MP for South

Waterloo, reveals the first poll to come out of Owen Sound: 106 for Godfrey, 102 for Case, 97 for McNaughton.

King receives the news of the first returns about 6:45 p.m. With five of 127 polls reporting, he is told Case is ahead with 120 votes, McNaughton has 109 and Godfrey 54. *This relieved my mind immensely as it drove away all fears of C.C.F. winning the election. Case's strength is pretty certain to lie in Owen Sound of which city he has been Mayor and all the wards of which he will know pretty well and control. He may also roll up quite a vote in the other towns but the country I think is pretty certain to come our way.*

King is soon given the results of eight polls and Case has surged ahead with 273 votes; McNaughton has 171 and Godfrey 59, *which relieves my mind even more in regard to the C.C.F. It gives me concern, however, as to what in all probability has been going on behind the scenes in the Tory tactics. I cannot see how with the kind of thing Case has stood for as a candidate he could count for anything. However this lead is significant. It is now apparent that everything will depend on the country vote and how well it has been gotten out. It begins to look as though the Orange Order felt that its chance had come and under the guise of patriotism at a time of war had been riding the white horse for all that it is worth, by a whispering campaign directed against the province of Quebec. All a part of the Tory conscriptionist campaign related to the Zombies.*

At 7:05, 40 of 127 polls have reported and Case is out front with 1,899 votes. McNaughton has 1,687, and Godfrey is fading at 804. King receives the count at 7:10. *A neck and neck race between Case and McNaughton, rather too favourable to Case. Again I fear the effect of money and the Orange vote.... When we had reached this point I felt pretty sure that the Tories had won and the C.C.F. would be at the bottom of the poll.*

There is soon a call for King from Owen Sound. McNaughton wants to speak with him. *He said there were reasons that he could not speak of which accounted for the defeat, that he was by no means downhearted, though disappointed after the way in which all of them had worked. He read to me what he thought of saying over the radio....*

Mulock then gets on the line. The postmaster general makes it clear that he believes bribery and corruption are behind the unfolding Case victory. *He said they have evidence of extensive use of money. I said they had better collect the evidence and be prepared to expose the whole business. Perhaps the C.C.F. would help in having that done....*

Shortly before eight, seventy-eight polls are in: Case has accumulated 4,798 votes, and McNaughton has slipped behind him by 624.

When it is over, Garfield Case is on his way to the House of Commons with the support of 7,338 voters. McNaughton has only been able to rally 6,099 to his side, while Godfrey's performance, at 3,136, is so poor that he must forfeit his deposit. It is a conspicuous setback for the CCF, who had seemed to be on a roll with the Canadian electorate in late 1944, and it does not reflect well on the ability of M.J. Coldwell, who came out to campaign for Godfrey, to sway voters beyond the CCF hard core.

But above all it has been a tremendous blow to McNaughton. He is enraged by the Conservative campaigning, and publicly declares the election a victory for "the forces of Tory reaction," offering no congratulations to Case. For his part, Case unabashedly attributes his win to Bracken's last-minute campaign blitz.

After making his statement in the offices of the Owen Sound *Sun–Times,* McNaughton brusquely leaves. Turning back to reporters as the entourage heads down the stairs, Gerry Rau says, "See you in Moosomin."

Moosomin is, of course, McNaughton's home town. It will be announced shortly that McNaughton will continue as defence minister and vie for the seat of Qu'Appelle, the Saskatchewan riding encompassing Moosomin, in the next election. Judging by the timing of Rau's gibe, McNaughton went into election night prepared for defeat, with a contingency plan already in place.

John Bracken suggests that McNaughton should resign as defence minister in light of his defeat in Grey North. The riding, the *Telegram* opines the day after the election, "indicated that Gen. McNaughton should be demobilized."

Flush with the victory over McNaughton, Conn Smythe now takes on the government on the issue of hockey players being tied up by military duties. He is vexed by the cases of players placed in the reserve rolls after being discharged, making them unavailable to the NHL because they are not allowed to cross the border to work. The most famous case is that of New York Rangers star Neil Colville, who enlisted in the army in 1942 to play for the all-star Commando team organized by Rangers coach Frank Boucher. After the

Commandos won the Allan Cup in 1943, Colville transferred to the RCAF. He qualified as a navigator, and then had his services declared almost, but not quite, superfluous as the air force began demobilizing some of its ranks. Since January 16, Colville has been on the RCAF reserves list, subject to call-up. In the meantime, he can't leave the country to work, which means he can't play full-time with any NHL team. Even a Canadian team has to cross the border to play the four American teams in the league.

As one of the stars of their 1940 Stanley Cup victory, he is eagerly sought by the Rangers. By Conn Smythe too, for that matter, who offers New York $30,000 for him—more than he thinks Maurice Richard is worth. The Rangers turn Smythe down (on Colville's orders), and in the meantime Colville stays in shape by playing with the Commandos in the Quebec Senior league. As an amateur now, Colville can be called up to play in a maximum of three NHL games, and Frank Boucher does just that for New York's dates in Toronto and Montreal. But if Colville is to play in Montreal on March 10, which would be his fourth league appearance, his status with the RCAF will have to be resolved so that he can return to the professional ranks.

Having always been a powerful figure within the league, Smythe now has formal clout. Red Dutton has been persistent in his refusal to carry on serving in the president's position. A Great War veteran, Dutton has lost two sons in combat in this war, and he has a thriving contracting business out west he is determined to return to. The Montreal league meetings have resulted in a decision on February 2 to address Dutton's intransigence by appointing a three-man executive committee: Dutton, Smythe and Red Wings owner James Norris, Sr., who will run the league until a permanent replacement can be found for Dutton.

Coincidentally, major-league baseball is approaching a new season with no commissioner in place, and is under the gun from Washington over the 4-F status of many active players. On February 1, the day Chicago is playing Montreal at the Forum, Congress takes a legislative step that is potentially fatal for sports relying on American athletes by passing the May–Bailey Bill. Dubbed a "work or be prosecuted program," the bill prescribes that any draft registrant aged eighteen to forty-five who is not a member of a force on active duty and is not excepted or deferred from training and service is liable to work in war production or in some endeavour in support of national health, safety or interest. Baseball, as the navy's James

Forrestal has made clear, is none of those things.

The game receives a shot in the arm from FBI chief J. Edgar Hoover, who feels the athletes have been dumped on unfairly. On February 4, he tells the press there is a "wide misconception in the public mind" about the attitude of players toward the armed services. "All the publicity about this situation has left the impression that some of the athletes themselves may be at fault. From our part in the war prosecution, we know this is not true. If any ball players—or other athletes—were attempting to dodge service, it would be our job to look into such cases. But our records show there are few if any such cases among the thousands of ball players, and they are entitled to a clean bill of health." Hoover counsels the league to be more aggressive in putting its case forward for the continuation of the game.

Perhaps Smythe takes heart from this statement, because on February 6 he is attacking the government over the uncertain status of players like Colville. "Nobody points out that we have 165 of our men in the services," Smythe complains to the press. "Three of our Maple Leaf players, Fox, Garrett and Tilson, were killed overseas. It is time we quit pussyfooting, time we laid our cards on the table. The Government is unaware of our contribution because nobody has had the gumption to tell the plain facts. Why should we cringe and cower? Why should we be booted around as though we were doing something dishonourable and against the war effort?"

As with the crisis in reinforcements and with the suitability of McNaughton to represent Grey North or lead an army, Smythe is eager for the plain facts to be known. But the plain facts are not plain. True, many NHL players have been lost to the armed services during the war, but they have not in general been going into front-line combat. Smythe's attempt to project deep sacrifices by his club verges on the ridiculous. The three dead men he has offered up were not Maple Leafs proper. On December 5, 1942, the Leafs traded eighteen-year-old prospect Red Garrett and Hank Goldup to New York to get Babe Pratt. Garrett had never made a regular-season appearance as a Maple Leaf; he played twenty-three games for the Rangers in 1942/43, then joined the navy and was killed in action— not, technically, overseas, as Smythe has said, but aboard a torpedoed corvette off Port aux Basques. Red Tilson was a Junior amateur prospect when killed in Holland. Jack Fox was another Leaf prospect who never actually played for the team. No bona fide Maple Leaf has been, or will be, killed in action in the Second

World War. (Hec Kilrea, a former Leaf and Red Wing star who retired in 1938, is wounded in action in Italy.) When the war is over, the NHL will be hard-pressed to identify one established player who left a starting position to serve in the armed services and lost his life in the process.[2] Smythe is free to argue that players have made contributions to the war effort on or off the battlefield, even argue that in playing military hockey they have served to boost morale among regular enlisted men and the crowds they have entertained, but it is sheer bravura to assert that the league has made great sacrifices in the Allied cause. If facts are to be laid bare, then it should be known that the war has been profitable for these teams. Maple Leaf Gardens has hosted sellout crowds paying full ticket prices to watch teams stocked with fill-in players who, because of their inexperience and/or mediocrity, are cheaper to pay. As a product hockey has scrambled, but as an enterprise it has not suffered. In 1916/17 the NHA resolved to donate 5 per cent of its gate to the Red Cross. No such munificence has been demonstrated by the NHL in this war.

Smythe's outburst on the NHL's deserving to get its players out of the clutches of the armed forces is very nearly his version of Montgomery's gamble at Arnhem—a polemic too far. Neither the league nor the public rallies to his cause, the way so many responded to his charges that the lives of reinforcements were being thrown away and that it was time to send in the Zombies. He has blundered into an irreconcilable contradiction. How can he possibly argue that the army is desperately short of reinforcements to the point that all NRMA men must go overseas (and the defence minister be sacked for not having already agreed to do so) and at the same time complain that the military is tying up hockey players? True, those coming out of the navy or air force are part of the general demobilization, and one can understand a certain frustration when some are placed in reserve and not allowed to work outside Canada rather than being released outright. But NHL teams have benefited this season from the services of young men who have been released by an army that by Smythe's own definition is desperate for reinforcements.

On February 6, while Conn Smythe is complaining about NHL talent tied up by the armed forces, Mackenzie King receives word that the Canadian army in Italy will be moved to Europe in about one month's time. He is hopeful that the war in Europe will end in April at the latest.

McNaughton returns to Ottawa from Owen Sound, and visits

King at eleven in the morning on the seventh. *He was looking very cheerful. Not a bit tired and was in good form generally. I congratulated [him] on the splendid showing he had made against the kind of conditions I knew he had to contend with.*

Though he might appear cheerful, the general is full of rage. The destruction of discipline in the army must be stopped, he tells King. The crackdown should start with Bracken, who has made completely untrue and reckless statements about the NRMA men throwing weapons overboard. Proceedings should be started against him by either the defence department or the justice department. Connie Smythe should be court-martialled, and so should the officers who came to speak at the meeting.

McNaughton sees the hand of George Drew behind the vicious campaign inflicted on him. He shows King the copy of a speech Bracken made that he understood Drew had actually written. *Altogether it was plain the document had just been put in Bracken's hands.* He then tells King of the trench warfare waged by the Conservatives. Some of them came into the riding on Friday night, distributing liquor that night and on Saturday, *and money had been spent freely in the purchase of votes.* McNaughton is sure that they can prove thousands of dollars were spent in such bribes. *He described how the meetings had been interrupted by people that were paid; soldiers telling untruths, etc.* And paranoia about the Liberals being in the pocket of anti-Imperial Quebec was whipped up. An article attributed to *L'Action Catholique*, purporting to describe King's new program, which called for separation from Britain, was reprinted in the *Globe* and broadcast to voters at eight in the morning on election day. The Orange Lodges and the Tory scrutineers were told *to listen in to get their cue to influence the people as they went to the polls. McN. said the Lodges were simply bought out brazenly, and ordered by others to change [their votes] against McNaughton. One of our own Liberals had been asked what price he would be prepared to accept to pull out of the campaign. McN. seems convinced it was money and liquor and the appeal to prejudice, saying his wife was a Roman Catholic, and that sort of thing, which had influenced the vote at the time.*

The *Globe*, he claims, played an active role against him in the campaign. The newspaper sent up people to circulate stories about the reasons he resigned his command in 1943 and the like. McNaughton has been girding himself for an all-out counter-offensive against these Tories, which he tells King might reflect badly on Ralston. I have actual documents, one of them from Eisenhower protesting against taking part of the Canadian army to Italy, and Ralston's misgiving before the army officers that if they were not taken, the whole fighting might be over without our having any casualties. It is McNaughton's contention that Ralston and Stuart all along pursued a course that would get Canadians right into combat, *even against the will at the time of the British authorities as well as Eisenhower, the head of the American command. He spoke of the documents being very serious. They would involve Montgomery's determination to get control of the army in Europe. He gave me other information which he had cabled to Canada at the time of taking away the Canadian forces [to Italy] which I know never came before the War Committee.*

King recalls how Ralston said repeatedly that Canada would have no real voice in peace if we did not do more fighting. *I kept telling him the Chiefs of Staff knew what they were about to do; were holding the Canadian army intact for the best of reasons. Now we have received word the Canadians are being brought from Italy to join other forces; that will save, so McN. said, many thousands of men in meeting any reinforcement situation. The whole situation has been created by the necessity of keeping up the lines of supply and communication that were never anticipated. I have no doubt that McN. has been completely vindicated on the stand he took.*

Even so, King cannot see any good political reason for an explosive public retort by McNaughton. *I counselled him against making a martyr of Bracken. That there would be difficulty in getting convictions against him but to seek some way of having him put in the position where it would become clear before the public that he made the statement he did without any authority. Also I told him to hold back anything about Ralston, Montgomery and others while the men were fighting at the front. He would be all the stronger in the end. As for other things, I was for following them up as rapidly and completely as possible....*

There will be no court-martial of Conn Smythe, however. He has already been discharged from the army. He is free to fire at will.

OVER THE TOP

> The strength of that Canadian army was as close-in fighters. They went at it like hockey players.[1]
> —*Corporal Dick Raymond, 3rd Canadian Division*

February 8, 1945

As the Montreal Canadiens dismantle the New York Rangers 9–4 and Maurice Richard scores goals forty and forty-one, the First Canadian Army goes back into action after a three-month respite following the costly Scheldt offensive. General Harry Crerar, back in command after his hospitalization with dysentery, is in charge of a Canadian army in which Canadians are in a minority. The First has ballooned to thirteen divisions with the addition of non-Canadian divisions—nine of them are British, and they join the American, Dutch, Belgian and Polish forces Crerar's command has already accumulated.

On February 1, before the Yalta Conference began, approval was given to General Eisenhower's battle plan for the final phase of the European war. The First Canadian Army is to work in concert with the Ninth U.S. and Second British armies under the umbrella of Montgomery's 21st Army Group in a final drive across the Rhine, north of the Ruhr. The Canadians will concentrate on bridging the Rhine and then clearing the Netherlands of the final pockets of German resistance.

Crerar launches Veritable on the eighth, and in two days the 9th Infantry Brigade—the brigade of Joe King's Highland Light Infantry—smashes through the Siegfried Line. The Canadians are now angling southeast toward the 16th U.S. Corps; both forces are converging on the city of Wesel, where the river Lippe flows into the Rhine. The fighting through the wooded strongholds of the Reichswald and Moyland Wood is costly, but the objectives are met, in part because of the sacrifices made by Bob Carse's former comrades in the Winnipeg Rifles in subduing Moyland Wood on February 21.

The outcome of the election in Grey North has changed the whole picture, Mackenzie King concludes on February 8. *It has made wholly clear the inadvisability of holding an election while the war is on.... We have now very strong evidence that the war may be over by the middle of April. My own feeling is that the end will come before that....*

Though never one with a mind for military strategy, King at once is struck by a warrior's epiphany. He looks at the election in Grey North and recalls the Battle of the Bulge. *I see very clearly a parallel related to the situation on the western front as it developed by General Rundstedt's attack over an area that was slightly defended. He got his armies well into the field of his opponents. It looked, for the moment, as if Germany had renewed her strength and might be in a position to carry on, if not successfully, at least pretty well along the line of a stalemate. The effect, however, was to realign the forces for the allies, drive Rundstedt back beyond the line from which he had advanced and made possible in the end a speedier and more certain victory for the allies....*

We went into Grey North with the highest and best of intentions— to permit another session of parliament before an election, so as to avoid an election in war time, especially in the interests of the men overseas and in accordance with the wishes of their families and friends at home. Instead of co-operation, in carrying on until the war is over, we have reached the climax of obstruction from Tories and C.C.F. alike. From looking upon Grey North as a defeat, we can make it the corner stone of victory. That, I believe, we can do.

He visits the Governor General tonight, who touches on the Grey North by-election. *I mentioned the corruption.... He was quite emphatic about my being right about not having another session and also in not announcing the date of an election until the war was over if that was at all possible. He volunteered this of his own accord. I mentioned that it might be June before we would have the election in the way I was thinking at present. Of course the unexpected defeat in [Grey North] had made it necessary to reconsider old plans. He spoke of being quite incensed at Bracken's remarks as to soldiers having thrown rifles and ammunition overboard. Says that that was unpardonable.*

They discuss a possible successor for the earl as Governor General, Lord Airlie. It cannot be McNaughton now. He has sunk as deep as anyone can into the mire of domestic partisan politics.

On February 10, in a home game against Detroit, Maurice Richard scores twice as Montreal wins 5–2. He now has forty-three goals in thirty-eight games, equalling Cooney Weiland's output and surpassing his pace. The next night, February 11, the Canadiens are in New York and beat the Rangers 4–3, but Richard does not score. His next opportunity to surpass Weiland and match Joe Malone's ancient record of forty-four goals will come at Maple Leaf Gardens on February 17.

Also on February 11, Cadet Sylvanus Apps of the Officers' Training Corps in Brockville, Ontario, appears in a hockey game at Kingston, Ontario, playing for the Ottawa Army All-Stars. Apps scores six times, but the All-Stars still lose to the Barriefield Vimyites 11–9.

On February 12, all speculation on the arrival of the Soviet army ends at Stalag 8C when the entire camp is assembled and given a medical inspection to determine who is and is not fit to march. Bob Carse is determined fit; Ken Bergin is not. Those considered strong enough are put on the road toward Germany. The rest are simply left behind. Two days later, the Russians overrun the camp.

Carse and his companions are force-marched in freezing weather with only the clothes on their backs, with guards jabbing rifle butts into those backs when a satisfactory pace is not maintained. The POWs pray that the Soviets will catch up with them and liberate them. They probably would, had Stalin not decided during the Yalta Conference of February 4–9 that a quick end to the war was not in his best interest and ordered the Soviet advance to engage in mopping-up exercises rather than a sustained offensive press. At Stalin's behest, the Allies set a target date of July 1 for the end to the war in Europe. The closest the Soviets ever come to catching up with Carse's column is about forty miles.

They sleep outside every night, in the depths of winter. Carse is almost dead when he is allowed to spend a night in a barn while his German escorts take shelter in a farmhouse. That night, Carse and his fellow prisoners catch, kill and eat a chicken. When they take to the road again the next day, a woman who lives in the farmhouse distributes raw potatoes to sustain them.

Bob Carse, starving, freezing and tormented, marches nearly four hundred miles in thirty-one days, all the way across Germany, all the way from one front to the other, all the way to Stalag 9B at Frankfurt-am-Main. His presence at the new camp is confirmed by

the Canadian military on March 12. Already malnourished, he contracts dysentery on March 15; his weight plummets to 110 pounds.
Carse's life is in the hands of General Patton's Third U.S. Army,
driving east across the Rhine.

❧

On the night of February 13, RAF Bomber Command sends forth
796 Lancasters and nine Mosquitoes in two waves in a raid on the
mediaeval German city of Dresden. Six planes are lost. The resulting firestorm, as well as the bombing of the railway yards the next
day by 311 B-17s of the USAAF, kills an estimated fifty thousand
people.

❧

McNaughton's anger about discipline in the army has not entirely
extinguished. He relieves General Pearkes of Pacific Command.
Pearkes is rumoured to be planning to run as a Progressive
Conservative in the next federal election in Nanaimo, a rumour that
will prove correct. Agriculture Minister Jim Gardiner is not surprised by the rumour. Pearkes, he says on February 17, has been
"acting for the Tories ever since he came back from overseas and
there's no reason why he shouldn't run for them.... I'd say further
that statements by General Pearkes and some of his officers have
done more than anything else I know of to cause the high incidence
of absenteeism in the army. The story has been continuously coming out of British Columbia that the [NRMA] troops in the camps
had been advised not to volunteer; that the act of volunteering
would only be playing into the hands of the government and they
ought to make the government compel them to go overseas." King
regrets Gardiner's outburst, and Pearkes threatens to slap Gardiner
with a libel suit.

It is the anniversary of Sir Wilfrid Laurier's death. That night, the
Canadiens and the Leafs meet in a Saturday-night match at Maple
Leaf Gardens. No team has given the Canadiens more trouble this
season than the Maple Leafs. In their seven games to date, Toronto
has won four and tied one, although since the Leafs won their first
three matches Montreal has had the edge in performance, winning
two and tying one and outscoring Toronto fifteen to eleven. This
proves to be another hard-fought meeting. The game is tied at three
when, with less than five minutes to play, Maurice Richard gathers
up a rebound in a goal-mouth scramble and rolls the puck past
Frank McCool. There are 14,922 fans on hand, Maple Leaf fans,
more than two thousand holding standing-room tickets, and as they

watch their team lose they applaud Richard for tying Malone's record. Richard has become a marquee player whose reputation rises above his particular uniform. He represents the league's ongoing prosperity because, as he has demonstrated in Toronto, he can pack an arena in any NHL town. He is making Conn Smythe money, and he isn't even a Maple Leaf. He is the enemy everyone needs.

"You know," Leaf coach Hap Day reflects, "I think a lot of us are underestimating the class of hockey now being played in the NHL. I notice some of the stars of other years coming back into the play. But I don't notice any of them setting the league on fire. There is nothing wrong with hockey when it's played like the Leafs and Canadiens played it Saturday night."

Now that Conn Smythe is back on his feet, albeit walking with the limp he will have for the rest of his life, the unenviable war record Maple Leaf Gardens has assembled—of having gone through the entire conflict without the Leafs holding one war charity game—is addressed. Over the last few years, many events related to the war effort have been held at the Gardens, events generally in support of Victory Loans and war savings stamp drives. But apart from an intramural Leaf game back in 1942 held in conjunction with a Victory Loan drive, Maple Leaf Gardens hasn't produced any event of an explicitly charitable nature in conjunction with its main attraction, the Maple Leafs.* For sports journalists like Jim Coleman and Clary Settell, all the Victory Loan and war stamps events don't add up to much when the Leafs themselves haven't been employed in any charitable manner.[2] The Gardens is practically in a race against the Allied armies to put on an event before Berlin falls. Had Stalin stuck to his original six-week timetable for the eastern offensive, the

---

*On October 29, 1942, a pre-season intramural game between the "Blues" and "Whites," featuring Maple Leaf players who had joined the armed forces, was held at the Gardens. Press coverage before the game indicated that the Kiwanis Club would be selling tickets, and that all proceeds would go to unspecified war charities. Former Maple Leaf Gardens publicity director Stan Obodiac, writing in *Maple Leaf Gardens: Fifty Years of History* (1981), stated that the game was co-sponsored by the Kiwanis Club and the Victory Loan drive, and asserted that this event raised $10,000 for (again unspecified) charities. A pitch is known to have been made to spectators during the game to buy Victory Bonds. As noted, contemporary sports journalists like Coleman and Settell were under the definite impression in late 1944 that the Leafs had yet to participate in any game that produced dollars for a war charity.

Gardens would be losers. But with the Red Army occupied with delaying actions, the Gardens is able to host a hockey extravaganza on February 21 while the Nazis still have armies in the field, a game between the "Leafs" and the "Maroons" featuring some of the greatest names in NHL history playing with stars of the Junior game. Smythe has called in every marker he has. The Leafs have culled from their celebrated past Red Horner, Charlie Conacher, Busher Jackson, George Hainsworth, King Clancy and Hap Day; they have New York Americans goaltender Roy Worters, the first netminder to win the Hart Trophy as the league MVP, and his old teammate Eddie Convey; they also have those two superb Rangers of yore, Bill Cook and Frank Boucher; and they have two present-day Leaf stars tied up by the military, Billy Taylor and Alex Levinsky, and the Rangers' Bryan Hextall. Among the stars on hand to make up a Maroons squad are goaltender Davey Kerr, who won the Vezina when the Rangers won the Stanley Cup in 1939/40; Eddie Shore, the Bruins' dangerously tenacious rushing defenceman of the 1930s; and Lionel Conacher—"The Big Train" himself, the Maroons star of the 1930s, named the greatest Canadian athlete of the first half of the century.

The Maroons win 6–3, but the biggest winner is the Navy League of Canada. With 13,844 in attendance and the use of the Gardens donated, the event nets $11,994 for the volunteer organization, which runs the Sea Cadets program and provides a variety of support services for men in the Royal Canadian Navy. It is reported, rather mutedly, in the press that the proceeds will go toward the production of ditty bags for Canadian sailors. There is no question that the Navy League has done much good in this war in support of Canadian sailors. But with the RCN's role in the war winding down, the Navy League is a curious choice as the beneficiary of charitable dollars. (It may or may not be significant that the Navy League chose the Gardens as the site of a major meeting last November 18.) The country is full of wounded and permanently disabled sailors, flyers and soldiers, and widows and orphans of fighting men. The world is brimming with refugees—last October, when the Canadiens played a charity game in Ottawa, the beneficiary was the Chinese relief effort. On September 8, 1943, the Canadian Jewish Congress held a rally in this very building, at which two Russian Jews who escaped Nazi atrocities spoke to a crowd of 12,000. During the rally author Solomon Asch lashed out at Canada's policy of restricting Jewish immigration despite the unfolding holocaust. In the face of all this need, Maple Leaf Gardens has decided to put its charitable effort into ditty bags. It is a disappointing outcome for an event that has drawn upon so much goodwill from the paying customers and the oldtimers who came out for the cause.

While Maple Leaf Gardens is holding its ditty-bag extravaganza, Conn Smythe's 30th Battery and the rest of the 6th LAA regiment are on German soil as the First Canadian Army moves out of the Netherlands toward the Rhine. The Luftwaffe threat had dimmed to such a degree that the 30th were retrained on rockets in the lull after the Scheldt offensive, but the renewed offensive in February has put them back on their Bofors. On the day of the fundraiser game the regiment has one of its most productive performances of the war, downing three ME 262 jet fighters.

In Ottawa, McNaughton tells the war cabinet that he might ask for another order-in-council in late March, allowing him to send more NRMA men overseas. King sees a frustrated McNaughton trying to extricate himself from the Zombie mess by shipping them to Europe, out of his hair. *I pointed out to him privately that unless they were actually needed overseas he would only be helping his opponents by having it appear they were right in feeling reinforcements were so greatly needed. He is giving this matter further consideration.*

On Sunday, February 25, the Provost Corps and the RCMP sweep into Drummondville, a town of about ten thousand some sixty miles northeast of Montreal in the eastern townships. They have come to town to find draft dodgers, and the reception is vigorously hostile. An estimated two thousand people riot, with four RCMP cars overturned and dozens of army trucks damaged. Sixty people are taken into custody; all but eight are released. The remaining eight are taken to Montreal, where Maurice Richard is attempting to break Joe Malone's NHL scoring record of forty-four goals in a game at the Forum against the Maple Leafs. After tying Malone's record in Toronto on February 17, Richard had the opportunity to break it in a game against the Blackhawks in Chicago the following day, but the brawl-filled match ended in a scoreless draw. The Canadiens then enjoyed a one-week layoff before playing their next game, this one at home against Toronto.

The Leafs follow a now-standard game plan, assigning Bob Davidson and Nick Metz to checking duties on Richard. But in a goalmouth scramble, Richard collects the puck, moves out to the penalty shot line thirty feet from the goal and banks the puck into the net off Frank McCool's skate. Joe Malone, who will turn fifty-five in three days and who like Chubby Power was born in Sillery, not a stone's throw from the Plains of Abraham where the two solitudes of Canada were born, is on hand to present Richard with the puck. And it was in Quebec City in the spring of 1918 that an aggressive pursuit of draft-dodgers produced the riots that spurred Borden to eliminate all exemptions from conscripted service.

Montreal wins 5–2. It has taken Richard forty-two games to score forty-five goals. Montreal, which has lost only five games all season, is assured of winning the season championship with eight games to go. Detroit and Toronto are well back in second and third place, and Boston is struggling to claw its way into the fourth and final playoff spot ahead of New York and Chicago.

Of the eight Drummondville men brought into Montreal by the Provost Corps and the RCMP today, three are released. Of the remaining five, three are identified as deserters, one is charged with failing to report for military service, and one with failing to possess a national draft registration card. It is a meagre haul for an action that resulted in so much damage and angered so many Quebecers.

On February 26, the First Canadian Army launches Blockbuster, its objective the heavily defended wooded ridge of Hochwald, about ten miles southeast of Moyland Wood. It will take until March 4 to subdue Hochwald, until March 10 to clear their area of operations west of the Rhine of Germans. More than 5,300 Canadian casualties result, but at least I Canadian Corps, pulled out of Italy, has now joined the First Canadian Army for the final two months of operations.

On Wednesday, March 7, Mackenzie King meets with Gordon Graydon, House leader of the Progressive Conservatives. A conference on the United Nations initiative will begin in San Francisco in late April, and King has resolved to include opposition party leaders in the Canadian delegation. He won't have anything to do with John Bracken, however, and has decided he can exclude him by specifying that in the best parliamentary tradition a party leader must actually hold a seat in the House of Commons.

Graydon ends up staying to chat with King for forty-five minutes. They were the most determined adversaries in the last sitting of Parliament, when King was striving to avoid defeat at the hands of the Conservatives on a confidence motion. Face to face and in the privacy of King's office, Graydon is conciliatory, telling King *he had been put into a very difficult position. I told him a little of the inside. He agreed it would have been a terrible thing if I had let go. There might have been a state of anarchy. He thought Ralston had been let down by some of his officers.*

Ralston should have dealt with Connie Smythe at once, King tells Graydon. We could have gotten along in the crisis if there had not been determination on the part of some to force conscription.[3] Graydon admits he feels sorry for McNaughton. I thought he did extremely well in Grey North, he offers. *I told him I thought the whole business was very unfair, unparliamentary, etc. He said he himself was as I knew not his own master; very difficult position. Could not control his own people in Parliament.* He promises to lend what help he can to the government in the forthcoming session of the House, but concedes he may not *be able to keep his own men at bay.* King tells him that the new session is only to seek approval for the appropriations of supply for the war effort and a resolution in regard to the San Francisco conference.

In the war cabinet meeting today, McNaughton impresses King with his accounting of the number of men now available for reinforcements. The army has come up with ten thousand more men from within its own ranks—ten thousand more than the government was told were available when McNaughton took over as defence minister in November. Six thousand of them are in England, men who are trained and should be fighting, but have been holding down *easy jobs.* The other four thousand have been found in the general service ranks in Canada. McNaughton now feels an order-in-council permitting him to send more conscripts will not be necessary until well into April, and probably not at all. In fact, only about 13,000 of the 16,000 NRMA men slated for overseas service are ever committed, and of those, only 2,463 reach field units.

After Maurice Richard breaks Joe Malone's scoring record, the Canadiens steamroller runs out of steam. On March 3, Richard doesn't score and the Leafs beat the Canadiens 3–2 at Maple Leaf Gardens. He now has forty-five goals in forty-three games. The next night in Chicago, Montreal is stunned by the sad-sack Blackhawks; Richard scores once as the Canadiens lose 6–4. For the first time in the season, the Canadiens have suffered back-to-back losses. Richard now has forty-six goals in forty-four games.

When Boston comes to town on March 8, the Canadiens manage a 3–2 win, but Richard is kept off the scoreboard, and a sprained ankle knocks Frank Eddolls out of the lineup. Richard has forty-six goals in forty-five games. On March 10, Montreal drubs the Rangers 7–3 at home, but Richard again cannot find the net: forty-six goals in forty-six games.

Montreal is at Madison Square Garden the next night and the team goes on another scoring spree, winning 11–5. Richard contributes two of them: forty-eight goals in forty-seven games. Four days later, on March 15, the Canadiens swing into Detroit for what promises to be a dress-rehearsal for the Stanley Cup finals. Detroit shuts down the freewheeling Montreal offence, winning 2–1 as Richard scores the lone Canadiens goal. He now has forty-nine goals in forty-eight games.

On March 17, Syl Apps graduates at the top of his class at Officers' Training Corps in Brockville with the rank of second lieutenant. The army's adjutant general, Major-General A.E. Walford, comes to Brockville to present Apps with the Sam Browne Belt in recognition of his performance. Apps returns to OTC in Brockville to serve as an instructor, but then volunteers for active duty with the 6th Canadian Division, a 24,000-strong force being formed for the invasion of Japan, and moves to Victoria, B.C., to await the call to action.

That night, Montreal is at home to host the troublesome Blackhawks. The Canadiens have won all nine of their games so far against Boston; won nine and lost one against New York; won eight, lost one and tied one against Detroit; and won four, tied one and lost five against Toronto. After outscoring Chicago thirty-one to nine and winning every one of their first six matches, Montreal has been unable to make any headway against a club struggling to avoid last place. Their seventh and eighth games ended in 1–1 and 0–0 draws. Then came the 6–4 shocker. The Blackhawks, who have won all of twelve times this season, give Montreal another close game; while the Canadiens win 4–3, the Blackhawks keep Richard scoreless. Though they cannot make the playoffs, by defeating the second-place Red Wings 5–3 the next night in Detroit the Blackhawks relegate the Rangers by one point to last place.

Having lost only five games all season before March, Montreal has lost three of its last seven games. And Maurice Richard now has forty-nine goals in forty-nine games.

The next night at Boston Garden, in its final regular-season performance, Montreal is on the way to losing four of its last eight games. With the Canadiens trailing 2–1 in the third period, Richard bears down on nineteen-year-old Harvey Bennett, the latest net-minding fill-in for Frank Brimsek. Bennett came out of Regina with Red Tilson to play for the Oshawa Generals. Now Tilson is dead, and Bennett is all that stands between Maurice Richard and the record book. Richard flicks NHL goal 101 past Bennett. Goals 102 and 103 follow within minutes as Richard's teammates put Montreal ahead 4–2 to close out the season on a winning note. Bennett has just played his twenty-fourth and last NHL game; Maurice Richard has become the first NHL player to score fifty goals in one season, and he has done it in fifty games. No player, not even he himself, will match the feat of fifty in fifty for thirty-six seasons. No player will score fifty goals again until Bernie Geoffrion reaches the plateau in sixty-four games in 1960/61, the season after Richard retires.

How has he been able to do it? Maurice Richard's feat of fifty in fifty will be debated endlessly over the ensuing years. His scoring pace will be dismissed by some as an anomaly of the war years, abetted by the presence of hapless opponents like Bennett. Even if overall team scoring is down from the heights of 1943/44, the 1944/45 season surely has been a shooter's dream, with teams still averaging an inflated 3.7 goals per game. But there is one facet of his accomplishment that cannot be overlooked: if this has been a shooter's dream, why has no one else in the league come anywhere close to matching his pace? It has not been like 1943/44, when half a dozen players scored thirty or more goals. This season, not only is Richard the sole player to score forty or more goals—he is also the sole player to score thirty or more. His linemate Toe Blake and the Leafs' Ted Kennedy manage twenty-nine, and the rest of the league trails them. Richard is in a class of his own.

A key to his success is assuredly the depth of talent of the Canadiens, and the skill of his Punch Line. He and linemates Blake and Elmer Lach tie up the top three spots in the scoring race, and Lach becomes the first player in the league to record more than fifty assists—he gets fifty-four—in one season as he wins the Hart Trophy as the player most valuable to his team. The Canadiens score more goals than any other team, and allow fewer goals than any other team. As the heart of the Montreal offence, Richard's line produces almost half of the team's goals—105 of 228. The Canadiens also win more games than any other team. Of their fifty games, the Canadiens win thirty-eight, tie four and lose only eight—and of those eight losses, only two come at home. The Canadiens have won so many that second-place Detroit, with thirty-one victories, is the only other team in the league to win more than half its games.

Over the course of the season, Montreal inflicts a few devastating losses on opponents. But the idea that Richard's scoring prowess is somehow due to Montreal's running up the score on teams weakened by wartime player shortages does not hold up to scrutiny. He is a consistent threat, registering goals in thirty-four of fifty games over the season; only in four games does he score three or more goals, and his longest scoreless streak is two games. By comparison, the next player to produce fifty-in-fifty, Mike Bossy in 1980/81, will be far streakier, scoring in just twenty-seven of the games and producing more than half of his goals—twenty-six—in just eight games, while going scoreless three times for three games.

Richard's individual performance has nothing to do with how many goals are being scored by the Canadiens as a whole. He scores just as many goals against third-place Toronto (eight) as he does against last-place New York, even though Montreal only manages a total of twenty-eight goals against the Leafs, its worst team performance, and sixty-one against New York, its best. While the Canadians do produce 27 per cent of their season's scoring against New York (when 20 per cent would be average against one team in a six-team league), Richard produces only 16 per cent of his individual scoring against the lowly Rangers, who like the fifth-place Blackhawks hold him scoreless in four of ten games and limit him to eight goals. Against Boston, he scores ten times, a statistically perfect performance for a fifty-in-fifty season in a six-team league.

If a culprit for Richard's performance is required, then it rests in Detroit, for it is, surprisingly, against the second-place Red Wings that Richard has most success. In ten games he scores sixteen times and is only held scoreless once. The secret to his success seems to be his way with rookie netminder Harry Lumley. Only eighteen, Lumley is a great new goaltending star who will win the Vezina and the Stanley Cup and twice be named to the first All-Star team, but in 1944/45 Maurice Richard has his number. Of the sixteen goals he scores against Detroit, two come against Connie Dion and one against Normie Smith, who starred for Detroit in the 1930s. Against Lumley, who plays the final thirty-seven games of the season for the Red Wings, Richard scores thirteen times. In ten games against Frank McCool, Richard has scored eight times, a total he manages in just two games against Lumley; against Mike Karakas in Chicago, who is named to the second All-Star team behind Durnan, Richard scores just seven times.

Perhaps Richard has set a record because he has found one goaltender whose inexperience has allowed him to push his production well beyond the forty-goal mark. He certainly has an edge over Detroit that his own team does not share. Montreal scores 20 per cent of its goals against the Red Wings in 1944/45; Richard gets 32 per cent of his goals against them. But then, everyone else in the league who is not a Red Wing has been shooting at Lumley too, and no one else has come close to matching the Rocket's pace. Perhaps Lumley sticks out in Richard's streak because he is the goaltender to have the misfortune to be in the net on December 28, 1944, when the Rocket has finished moving a piano and has five goals in him to uncork.

In his second full season in the league, Maurice Richard has established himself as the game's pre-eminent scoring machine. He may never score fifty goals again in his career, but over the next five seasons he will be the only player to score forty or more goals. He will do it with forty-five (in sixty games) in 1946/47, when the next best effort is thirty by Boston's Bobby Bauer and Detroit's Roy Conacher; he will do it with forty-three (in seventy games) in 1949/50, when the next best effort is thirty-five by Detroit's Gordie Howe. Only in 1950/51, when Howe scores forty-three and Richard forty-two, does the NHL have another forty-goal man. And no one else will join their circle until Jean Béliveau scores forty-seven in 1955/56. If an asterisk belongs beside Maurice Richard's 1944/45 performance, it is not because there is a war on. It is because the modern game has found a modern hero.

CITIZEN SOLDIERS

Military sociologists take as their premise the proposition that any system of military organization expresses the social order from which it springs....
—*John Keegan*

March 20, 1945

THE best-of-seven* semifinal series between the Leafs and the Canadiens begins this Tuesday night, with the Leafs looking to three men in particular to carry the series for them. Of twenty-eight goals scored against Montreal by Toronto this season, fifteen came from the sticks of just three players—Mel Hill, Sweeney Schriner and Nick Metz, each of them contributing five. None was around for the drubbing suffered by the Leafs at the hands of the Canadiens in last spring's semifinal. Hill was out with a broken ankle, Schriner in the navy, Metz in the army. Montreal's offence against Toronto this season has been provided overwhelmingly by the Punch Line, which produced eighteen of Montreal's twenty-eight goals, with eight by Richard, six by Lach and four by Blake. Although Bill Durnan is considered far the better goaltender, the two teams have been dead even on goals-against over their ten encounters, and Frank McCool has proven himself capable of clutch performances for Toronto as he led the league in the regular season with four shutouts. And while the two teams finished in a dead heat in total goals against each other, Toronto had the better record in their ten encounters—five wins, one tie, four losses.

Toronto has been plagued by injuries this season, but is coming into the series relatively healthy. Coach Hap Day actually has a few reinforcements on hand this season, compared to last. Nick Metz's brother Don has been released from the air force, and is coming

---

*The series actually employed an unusual points system, as a limit was placed on overtime duration so that fans could catch the last streetcar at a time of gas rationing. Because it was possible a game could end in a tie, the points system was used, with two for a win and one for a tie. Since no ties occurred in the series, it played out as a standard best-of-seven, with the first team to win four games declared the winner.

along to Montreal, though he is not yet ready to play. He was training to be a pilot when the RCAF decided it already had enough of
them, and he switched to navigator instruction. Then the RCAF
began discharging airmen in general, and Metz was at last released.
He has done some skating over the winter, but has hardly played any
hockey and his skills are rusty. Day puts him through practice drills
while the rest of the Leafs brace themselves for the Canadiens.

Day has decided to take on Irvin's league-leading lineup with a
minimum of bodies. Just as the British have cut their regiment's
complement of rifle companies from four to three in the face of a
shortage of trained men, Day reduces the size of his own fighting
force. A hockey team at this time normally employs three forward
lines. Day devises a two-line system, with his teenage centres leading them. Ted Kennedy is, as usual, between Bob Davidson and
Mel Hill; Gus Bodnar is between Sweeney Schriner and Lorne
Carr. He has Nick Metz—who scored the last-second goal in the
1942 semifinal that put the Leafs into the finals against Detroit—on
hand to go on with fill-in John McCreedy (back from the air force)
and Art Jackson as a utility third line whenever his main six forwards need relief.

There is an almost eighteenth-century flavour to Day's essential
strategy. Military history is full of battles in which small forces subdued much larger ones, even ones with more man-for-man ability,
by sticking to a rote strategy: closed ranks; discipline in the line;
load, aim, fire, reload; hold your position; do not break and run. It
is Day's intention to play a tight-checking game with relentless line
changes, to keep the match from opening up and allowing the
Punch Line to roam and charge at will. Montreal is cavalry;
Toronto is musketeers.

Kennedy has spent the bulk of his season's games against
Montreal in such a checking mode. In ten games, he produced only
one assist, but his two-way play helped Toronto stay even with the
league powerhouse. Of the three Punch Liners he has unblemished
admiration for Toe Blake, a formidable all-round player. His own
linemate Davidson is much like Blake, Kennedy thinks, a complete
player, lacking only Blake's above-average scoring touch. Lach he
finds chippy, an opponent not averse to throwing you an elbow. As
for Richard, he is a scoring hazard who behaves like a bee-stung
bear. He differs from most players in that he seems to Kennedy to
make no distinction between a legal and an illegal check. A clean
check is as much a cause for retaliation as a dirty one. Richard may

be able to score, but he is also driven to even the score.

Kennedy's outstanding regular season has ended in disappointment. Going into the last two games on the past weekend, he had twenty-nine goals and was within a snap of the wrist of joining his idol Charlie Conacher and Lorne Carr in the select circle of Leafs who have scored thirty goals in a season. The Leafs lost their last two games, 4–3 to the Red Wings at Maple Leaf Gardens on Saturday night, 6–5 to the Rangers in New York on Sunday, and despite the fact that the Leafs produced eight goals during those losses, none was contributed by Kennedy. It was the closest he will ever come to breaking the thirty-goal barrier.

The Leafs have proceeded straight from New York to Montreal for the opening game of the semifinal, and 11,738 fans are in the Forum to see their Canadiens take the first step toward another Stanley Cup. The Canadiens greet the Leafs with a near-intact line-up from their 1943/44 triumph. The only significant change is the loss of Phil Watson to New York, but on defence they have added Frank Eddolls, who has come back from his end-of-season ankle injury to play in the series.

The game is a whirling dervish of confusion for Kennedy—sixty minutes of rapid-fire line changes as he, Hill and Davidson swap ice time with Schriner, Bodnar and Carr; checking, checking, checking, reining in Richard, Blake and Lach and any other Canadiens who try to come close to McCool, holding them to just twenty-two shots while the Leafs themselves manage only eighteen in return. Conn Smythe is on hand, watching his first playoff game since 1942, when the two teams head into the final minute scoreless. Kennedy wins a faceoff in the Montreal end and skates for the front of the net; a bouncing pass comes his way from Davidson and he takes a golf swing at it, hoping only to keep it in play. The red light behind Durnan flares, stunning the Forum crowd. Toronto is ahead 1–0 with twenty-two seconds to go, and that is how the game ends.

In the dressing room after the victory, an ashen Frank McCool declares, "I could die right now, I am so happy."

While the Leafs are defeating the Canadiens 1–0 at the Forum, erstwhile Leaf Billy Taylor and Newmarket Army are taking on the HMCS *York* Navy Bulldogs at Maple Leaf Gardens. The crackdown on military hockey in the winter of 1943/44 may have knocked military teams out of Allan Cup contention, but play goes on in district leagues and exhibition games. And because the Allan

Cup has been shelved this season, some military teams have been back in Senior competition. Tonight, 4,000 spectators are at the Gardens to watch Newmarket Army, paced by Taylor's four goals and two assists, defeat the Bulldogs 10–7.

❦

On Wednesday, March 22, professional baseball draws a reprieve from the U.S. war effort when war manpower commissioner Paul McNutt hands down a ruling that will allow the National and American leagues to begin spring training in all haste. Players who were exempted from the draft for medical reasons have been expected to pitch in with jobs in war industries rather than play ball, but McNutt has decided they no longer need do so. Any player under contract who played in the professional game last year "may be recalled to their principle [sic] employment." While the ruling does not exempt physically fit men from the draft, it has recognized that baseball is the principal business of the 4-F men, and that they have a right to earn a living at it. McNutt allows that he came to this decision in no small part because of the widespread demand he witnessed in fighting men at home and overseas that the game should continue.

The baseball ruling caps an entire wartime of soul-searching over the role athletes and athletics should play in a time of national crisis. The McNutt decision has more to do with the players' basic right to pursue a legitimate profession, but by his own admission he let the fighting men decide the fate of professional sports. The soldiers, airmen and sailors informally voted for the heroes of peacetime to play ball.

Canada has gone through much the same soul-searching over sport and war. The situation has been complicated by the NRMA, which has no counterpart in the U.S., where everyone drafted faces combat duty. But both countries have experienced the incongruity of outwardly able-bodied men playing games for money while their brothers and neighbours have gone off to fight and in some cases die. In Canada, however, there has been no Forrestal or Byrnes deriding from the vantage point of a senior government post the continuation of professional sports in wartime. The debate in Canada has been contained within newspaper columns and letters to the editor; it has been left, for the most part, to sportswriters and their readers to debate the pros and cons. In the end, sport has muddled through, because people want it to. And as Toronto *Telegram* sports editor J.P. Fitzgerald pronounces on March 22 in reflecting on the McNutt ruling, the idea "that because he's an athlete a player should be in the army always was silly and unjust." Opinions can change greatly when a war that a country is winning convincingly is coming to an end. Less than six months ago, on October 17, when Canadian troops were in the thick of the desperate Scheldt offensive, Fitzgerald argued in the very same column that "it behooves all and sundry clubs to weed out any and all candidates who are eligible and fit for the fighting forces. The war comes first or should and it is up to the several clubs to see to it that it does.... As far as this column is concerned, hockey is no excuse for dodging military service."

The fans have voted consistently all season on what sort of uniforms they want athletes to wear. When the Leafs lost to Detroit at Maple Leaf Gardens last Saturday night to close out the 1944/45 home schedule, regular-season attendance for Leaf home games reached 305,000. In the entire history of the Gardens, attendance for Leaf home games had never before exceeded 300,000.

The war has served to expose to the core the symbolic structures of professional sports. Inspired by a regimental model, the Maple Leaf franchise has made out its players to be warriors. But what kind? Military history gives the player several roles to choose from: the conscript, the regular, the militia man, the mercenary and the slave.[1]

The Leafs have turned out to be a combination of all of them. As a practical structure the team functions as a regiment in a regular army, its members trained, full-time professionals who serve their native land and crown. But they are expected to exhibit the sense of civic pride and obligation demonstrated by the conscript and the militia member. This is the conscript as citizen soldier, not the conscript saddled with the duty-shirking reputation of the Zombies. Yet the team's identity is still incomplete. While the team is set within a league in which every other club is an enemy, players as mercenaries are hired by and moved between warring parties. The mercenary model may be the most accurate one of the game from the perspective of the players, but from the perspective of the team it is a model that must be denied. The paradox of the game is that the team's managers and owners strive to operate the club on the regular-army model, while projecting to the public a militia/conscript purposefulness and treating the players to a large degree as mercenaries, professional hirelings whose services are a matter of price, not allegiance or pride. General managers may expect allegiance and pride, no one more than Conn Smythe when his Maple Leaf jersey is pulled on, but they also expect allegiance and pride to be portable sentiments. A Maple Leaf must be able to turn himself into a Canadien, and vice versa, otherwise the entire system of trading would collapse. And finally there is the more ancient model of the slave soldier, whose skills and body are the property of the army employing him. The practices of selling and trading players, of ownership of players, of a player becoming the property of a club at birth because he falls within its territorial boundaries, of a player becoming a property because his rights were secured as a boy (without his even knowing it), only make sense from the perspective of the warrior as property, not as patriot or professional.

Hockey is organized, formalized, institutionalized, ritualized war, and the players are soldiers of every stripe.

When he acquired the Toronto NHL franchise in 1927, Conn Smythe set out to make hockey something greater than it is. Not a rogue's game or a bloodsport, but a statement about pride and character. It has made him lots of money, but it has also made the professional game exceed its own possibilities. While the Second World War has tested the game's worth, it has also tested the fans' loyalties, and the war has proved that the fans want the game he helped make great. They want it almost unequivocally. They accommodated the contrariness of warriors on ice and warriors in fact; they made the game survive and prosper by their very determination to have it. No one force-marched civilians into the arenas, or made them—and fighting men overseas—tune in to games on the radio. A game that struggled through the 1930s and into the war will emerge from the war with a powerful momentum delivered by the public affirmation of its importance.

The time has passed when fans should think that being a Leaf had anything to do with being a warrior in the literal sense. The losses of the last few years on land, sea and air should have cured them of any such delusion. The Leafs are the Leafs, gallant and courageous to be sure, but a phenomenon enclosed entirely within their garrison. The battles they fight are altogether different from the ones the Queen's Own Rifles or 30th Battery are fighting in Europe. The remarkable lesson of this war is that the people pouring through the Gardens turnstiles are able to sustain two distinct groups of heroes: those overseas and those on the Gardens ice.

The Leafs are not a pale imitation of the heroes of the Great War that inspired the logo on their uniform. For the fans, the Leafs are heroes whose heroics cannot be measured by the yardstick of the sacrifices of another generation's war. Nor has the past, as a war reborn, been able to supplant the devotions of the present. The war has been an incongruity, an intrusion on their relationship with the team they have come to adore. The need to defeat Hitler has not supplanted the need they feel to defeat Montreal.

In the final analysis of the citizenry, the Leafs are, in effect, a Zombie army—an army of home defence, a militia unit charged with keeping Toronto safe from enemies like Montreal. But these are Zombies the public can embrace and adore. They have played this season with a sense of duty and commitment, even obligation. The fans know what the team's role is and what they expect of it. None of them want to send it off to fight foreigners in foreign lands. The Leafs are needed at home, now more than ever.

❦

All along the Rhine, on a front stretching two hundred miles from the First Canadian Army's position southeast of Arnhem to the First French Army's position north of Strasbourg, the Allied forces mount a co-ordinated assault on the last physical barrier standing between the Allies and the German heartland. The First U.S. Army was able to cross halfway down the front on March 7 when it encountered a bridge at Remagen the Germans were unable to sabotage, but the bulk of the Allied attack must wait until the final week of March, when all forces have closed up to the river.

General George Patton's Third U.S. Army makes a lightning strike on the Rhine on the night of March 22, establishing bridgeheads at Mainz, where the river Main meets the Rhine some seventy miles south of Remagen, and at Oppenheim about ten miles south of Mainz. The defending Panzergrenadier division is surprised by Patton's thrust. The next morning, he telephones General Bradley, commander of the 12th Army Group, and tells him, "Don't tell anyone, but I'm across. I sneaked a division over last night. But there are so few Krauts around there, they don't know it yet." Patton's army is just twenty miles from Frankfurt-am-Main and Stalag 9B.

On March 23, the First Canadian Army crosses the Rhine in Operation Plunder, a night crossing carried out under artificial moonlight created by searchlights mounted on tanks—a technique pioneered by Canada's Guy Simonds in Operation Spring, back on July 24, 1944, when Conn Smythe was wounded. At home today, George Drew's minority Conservative government is defeated in a confidence motion after presenting its throne speech. One of the throne speech's measures proposed giving Ontario control of the categories of immigration to be allowed. Drew's party has pledged to stand against any large-scale immigration policy until veterans and those in war industries are assured of peacetime jobs. Defeated 51–36, Drew has no choice but to dissolve the legislature and call an election. This summer, Ontarians will be voting for both federal and provincial candidates.

Tonight in Montreal, the Leafs and Canadiens convene for their second game of the semifinals. In the opening minutes Canadiens defenceman Murph Chamberlain drives Gus Bodnar headfirst into the boards, sending him temporarily from the game. While Chamberlain is off serving a penalty for the vicious hit, Ted Kennedy collects a pass from Bob Davidson and puts it behind Durnan at 4:02. The Leafs are up 1–0 and Kennedy, not having scored all season against the Canadiens, now has the first two Leaf goals of the series.

This is a more wide-open, free-wheeling game, far less disciplined than the first one. A brawl in the first period runs on for twelve minutes as different pairs of antagonists take their turn in the centre ring. When the fisticuffs are subdued, major penalties have been dispensed to Toe Blake and Wally Stanowski, with minors to Butch Bouchard, Maurice Richard and Bob Davidson.

At 8:15 of the second period, Bouchard draws Montreal even with an unassisted effort. At 10:58, Lorne Carr converts a Sweeney Schriner pass to restore Toronto's lead. Nick Metz then drills a shot past Durnan from just inside the blueline while Lach is off serving a minor to give the Leafs an insurance goal.

The Leafs hold off Montreal all the way to 17:21 of the third, when Elwyn Morris is off for hauling down Chamberlain. Bouchard's second goal of the game, assisted by Richard, draws Montreal to within a goal, but McCool and the rest of the Leafs keep the Canadiens at bay to preserve their 3–2 lead and win their second straight game.

As promising as the series start is for Leafs players and fans alike, no one can seriously believe that Toronto will sweep Montreal. Waiting to board the train back to Toronto for game three the next night, Conn Smythe admits, "This strain is terrific. I don't know whether or not I can stand it."

Ted Reeve is travelling with Smythe, writing his sports column for the *Telegram*. Reeve's age finally caught up with him in the field and he was forced to leave 30th Battery and return to journalism. "They have sailed into the Flying Frenchmen as though they felt they could lick 'em every night and a couple of matinees, too,"

Reeve writes of the Leafs following the game. "They seem to feel that they may not be the world's champions of hockey but they are the world's champions of Les Canadiens, at least.... Canadiens are a good hockey team, but as of now they are up against something special in the way of team play and team spirit."

At the Rhine bridgehead of Rees, Scotland's famed Black Watch regiment of Britain's 51st Highland Division storms the town of Speldrop on the night of March 23, but is hammered by a German counterattack. When the Black Watch pulls back, one platoon remains trapped in the town. The 3rd Canadian Division, temporarily under the command of the Second British Army, is given the task of clearing the river bridgehead, and it falls to Joe King's Highland Light Infantry to recapture Speldrop and liberate the men of the Black Watch.

At 5:30 a.m. on Saturday, March 24, Major Joe King's B Company of the HLI leads the assault on Speldrop, which is defended tenaciously. In the battle to secure the town's outskirts, two of B Company's three platoon leaders are killed and the third is wounded. King personally takes over supervision of all three platoons' objectives, "moving freely through the company area, swept by machine gun and mortar fire and under direct fire from three tanks," as the regimental history will relate. Flame-throwing Wasp tanks are called in to burn the Germans out of their positions. So ferocious is the fighting that only fifty prisoners are taken. By eleven o'clock on Saturday night, Speldrop is in Allied hands and about twenty members of the Black Watch have been rescued, in no small part owing to Joe King's bravery and singleminded determination.

More than 15,000 fans are crammed into every nook and cranny of Maple Leaf Gardens on the night of March 24 to watch the Leaf miracle continue to unfold. Instead, the Leafs fold. At 11:42 of the first period, Murph Chamberlain steps out of the penalty box, collects the puck and sends it to Elmer Lach, who puts Montreal up 1–0. In the second period, Montreal notches three unanswered goals by Chamberlain, Bob Fillion and Dutch Hiller. In the third, McCool is cut in the head but stays in the game. Davidson scores at 9:02, but it is too little too late as Montreal wins 4–1. Canadiens centre Ray Getliffe rubs salt in the wound by offering that Davidson didn't even score the lone Leaf goal—*he* did, while trying to clear the puck.

Joe King's B Company spend Sunday night and Monday morning attacking a German stronghold in a large group of buildings in the north part of the town of Bienen, next door to Speldrop. Bienen must be neutralized for the offensive to move forward, as it rests on a bottleneck formed by a lake to one side and flooded land to the other. The stronghold is full of snipers, and it is dangerous work clearing the buildings, but Major King is again in the forefront of the action, supervising the work. One sniper, credited with killing six Canadians, is only fourteen. "By his initiative, courage and leadership, Major King contributed greatly to the success of the Battalion's assault and the rapid expansion of the bridgehead," the regimental history will observe. In recognition of his heroics at Speldrop and Bienen, Major Joe King receives the Distinguished Service Order.

At Mainz, Patton's forces swing north to form a pincer movement with the First U.S. Army and more of his own forces who have crossed on the night of March 24 farther north, encircling German troops a few miles upriver from Mainz around Wiesbaden, which falls on March 27. His forces at Oppenheim quickly press about thirty-five miles east, skirting south of Frankfurt-am-Main to capture Hanau and Aschaffenburg, both on the Main, on March 25.

What follows will dog Patton's reputation through history. He assembles Task Force Baum to liberate prisoners of war. But his target is not Stalag 9B, close at hand—it is Oflag 13B, an officers' camp near Scheinfurt, more than forty miles behind enemy lines. Patton may or may not be aware that his son-in-law, Lieutenant-Colonel John Waters, is held at Oflag 13B. On the night of March 26, the 294 men of the armoured task force roar forward. They liberate a camp full of Russian prisoners on the way, whose inmates, now armed and soon fuelled with liquor, go on a rampage through the countryside. At Oflag 13B, the task force tanks crash through the prison gate to find more than six thousand POWs, of whom 1,291 are American. They only have room to transport 250 back. In the meantime, the strike has attracted the interest of three German divisions, who surround and obliterate the task force. All but one of the 294 men are listed as missing in action. And Bob Carse, across the Main at Frankfurt in Stalag 9B, still awaits liberation.

On March 26, the last confirmed kill of an enemy aircraft by the 6th LAA in this war is credited to 30th Battery. On March 27, the last British civilian death of the war is recorded as a V2 rocket hits Kent.

❧

The Leafs and Canadiens reconvene on Tuesday, March 27, for game four. Rejuvenated by their 4–1 win on Saturday night, the Canadiens pick up where they left off. Lach scores just twenty-three seconds into the game, then sets up Richard at 2:13 for a 2–0 lead. Toronto survives the rest of the period and goes into intermission to regroup. After the period, Conn Smythe notes, "Five good men could win this league now." For Ted Reeve, those five men are among the following: Babe Pratt, teenage playoff fill-in Jackie Hamilton (back from the navy), Bob Davidson, Ted Kennedy, Sweeney Schriner and Elwyn Morris.

Nick Metz has been lost with an injured knee and his brother Don has been inserted in the lineup; Ted Kennedy is playing on a sore ankle. Two and a half minutes into the second period, Kennedy sets up Mel Hill and it's a one-goal game. The Leafs overwhelm the Canadiens with an offensive press that rains twenty-three shots on Bill Durnan in the period, while Frank McCool faces only three. Durnan is brilliant, but not impermeable, and at 16:15 Don Metz and Gus Bodnar set up Sweeney Schriner for the equalizer.

The Leafs stumble at the beginning of the third. Babe Pratt is off serving a minor when Bob Fillion restores the Canadiens' lead at 3:47. But Pratt redeems himself with a solo effort that ties the game up again at 9:16. Regulation time ends with the teams tied 3–3. The players have been exhausted by the constant hard checking of the contest; Butch Bouchard, the Canadiens' captain and emotional heart, is visibly exhausted. At 12:56 of overtime, Gus Bodnar beats Durnan to win the game 4–3 and put Toronto up 3–1 on the series. They have held Maurice Richard to one goal in four games. But to beat Montreal on this night they have had to outshoot them 56–25.

Ted Reeve is completely captivated by the teenager on Davidson's right. He proclaims Kennedy to be "that big, battling, good stickhandler, who is so solid on his skates and so cool in the clinches." Reeve writes that "it has been many a day since we have seen a finer prospect either for centre ice or, as he fills out, a place on the rearguard. A little more speed, which should come when he finishes growing, and he might be another Milt Schmidt."

❧

A deep strike takes Patton's Third Army another forty miles northeast of Hanau to Lauterbach by March 28. With the U.S. First driving east and southeast from the Remagen bridgehead, a dangerous salient is created in the German defensive line between the rivers

Main and Lahn. As March draws to a close, the remaining defenders around Frankfurt-am-Main are in danger of being cut off and destroyed or captured.

On Thursday, March 29, the sleeping giant awakens at the Forum. Leo Lamoureux scores on the very first Canadiens shot, forty seconds into the game. Within minutes, Butch Bouchard and Eddie Emberg, who has been called up from the Quebec Aces Senior team, have made it 3–0. Lorne Carr and Ted Kennedy get the Leafs back in the game before the period is over, but late in the second Richard scores and the Leaf checking game crumbles; they break ranks and scatter. The Rocket scores three more goals in the third to finish the game with four goals and one assist; Elmer Lach contributes one goal and three assists. When it is over, Toronto has been routed 10–3.

The teams board the train to head to Maple Leaf Gardens for game six the next night. The Leafs do not want to step inside the Canadiens' garrison again this spring. If they can't clinch the series on home ice, they doubt they can pull it off in a deciding seventh game back in Montreal.

Maple Leaf Gardens is packed again, with 14,400 customers. At 16:58 of the first period, defenceman Elwyn Morris gives them hope when he scores on a breakaway after Montreal's defence gets caught up ice pressing an attack. Two minutes later, though, Maurice Richard has the game back on an even footing, shaking off Bob Davidson's tenacious checking to score in an impressive effort in which he knocks his own rebound past McCool.

In the second period, Toronto goes ahead on a handsome goal on which Schriner takes a pass from Carr, splits the Montreal defence and beats Durnan. The Leafs hold the lead through to the intermission. Then, at 1:58 of the third, Gus Bodnar tips a long Babe Pratt shot out of the air and into the Montreal goal. Toronto is up by two, and Montreal is pressing hard.

At 15:26, Butch Bouchard lets go a low one from inside the blueline that beats McCool and brings Montreal to within a goal. The next four and a half minutes are electric terror for the Leafs and their fans. Reaching for the insurance goal, both Kennedy and Hill have breakaways thwarted that almost result in goals on the Montreal counter-rushes, but McCool holds the fort. In the last minute of play, Toe Blake splits the Leaf defence and closes in on McCool. Practically every man on the ice, save Durnan, ends up in a heap on McCool's doorstep as the Leafs desperately claw the

Canadiens to a standstill. The puck stays out of the Leaf goal. When the clock stops moving, Toronto has won the game 3–2 and the series 4–2. The Montreal Canadiens, the greatest Canadiens team Dick Irvin has seen in twenty years, have been toppled. The Toronto Maple Leafs are on their way to the Stanley Cup finals.

THE FINAL OFFENSIVE

March 30, 1945

BILLY the Kid Taylor marks another spring with another hockey championship. His Oshawa Generals defeated Bob Carse's Edmonton Athletic Club Roamers at Maple Leaf Gardens in 1939 to win the Memorial Cup. His Toronto Maple Leafs defeated the Detroit Red Wings in 1942 to win the Stanley Cup at Maple Leaf Gardens, with Taylor setting up the final goal by Sweeney Schriner. Tonight, his Newmarket Army team downs the HMCS *York* Bulldogs 10–5 at Maple Leaf Gardens before 5,400 fans to win the Toronto military district title. He is approaching the end of his second year in the army, and it is at least consistent with much of his life that the highlights of his career as a fighting man have come in Conn Smythe's ice palace. As a young amateur prospect, Billy the Kid would be put onto the Gardens ice during Leaf intermissions. Wearing a custom-made Maple Leaf uniform, the Kid would dazzle and amuse the fans with shooting, skating and stickhandling demonstrations. The war has brought more of the same for the Kid. A different uniform, perhaps, but it's the same act. Billy Taylor can still put on a show in the major's garrison.

While Taylor is helping win a hockey championship for Newmarket Army, the First U.S. Army, having fought almost seventy miles eastward from its Remagen bridgehead on the Rhine, reaches Marburg. Here it turns north and meets up with the Ninth U.S. Army at Lippstadt on April 1, entrapping Germany's Army Group B. Surrounded, the Germans hold out less than three weeks, and more than 300,000 troops are taken prisoner.

On April 2, about a hundred miles to the south, Bob Carse wakes up at Stalag 9B to discover that there are no Germans in the camp. Every one of them has fled in the night, leaving the prisoners to their own devices. Emaciated and starving, Carse is still strong enough and determined enough to walk out of the camp in the company of a few fellow prisoners, wading across a small river and heading in what they hope is the right direction.

They come upon some infantry. They are Patton's men, and they direct Carse and his companions farther back behind the lines to a medical aid station. A medical corpsman offers a welcome home of sorts when he tells Carse he's from Pittsburgh, and spent many nights sitting in Duquesne Gardens, home of the American league's Pittsburgh Hornets, watching Carse perform with the Providence Reds in 1939/40.

Carse is then transferred to a U.S. field hospital; in only four days his weight climbs from 110 to 125 pounds. A medical officer is stopped short when he is inspecting Carse's I.D. tags.

Bob Carse? The Bob Carse of the Blackhawks? I've seen you play in Chicago lots of times.

So it happens that Carse comes to learn, in conversation with this officer, that the 1944/45 Stanley Cup is over. Carse was captured before the season started. It has played out its entire course by the time he is again in touch with the game he left behind. We are left to imagine what he thinks when he learns that the league's rookie of the year, the goaltender who has recorded three shutouts in the seven-game final series, is the same one who tried out for the Blackhawks with him in 1939, without success, and who was playing Senior hockey at Currie Barracks in Calgary when Carse enlisted.

Conn Smythe has been with the team for playoff road games, in the dressing room for pep talks, but Ted Kennedy cannot say he has ever actually met him until this day, when the season is over and the Stanley Cup is stamped with the names of the 1944/45 Maple Leafs. He is in Conn Smythe's car, just he and Smythe and coach Hap Day, and they are going to the opening game of the Maple Leaf AAA ball club.

Nobody scored more goals than Ted Kennedy in these playoffs. He got nine over thirteen games. It was an especially noteworthy performance in that, in seven games against the Red Wings, the entire Leaf team only scored nine times. Five of the seven games ended in shutouts—three for Frank McCool, two for Harry Lumley. Toronto began the series by winning 2–0 and 1–0 in Detroit with Hap Day's two-line close-checking strategy, then won 1–0 back at Maple Leaf Gardens to go three games up. Whereupon memories turned back to the 1942 series, when Detroit was up three games to none on Toronto, and the Leafs of Hap Day roared back to win four straight. The Red Wings moved to avenge the humiliation, winning the next three games and forcing a deciding seventh match in Detroit. There, Mel Hill put Toronto ahead in the first period, enough offence for Day, who then had his charges wrap the Red Wings in his patented suffocating checking game. After two periods it was still 1–0, but eight minutes into the third period, Murray Armstrong, back from military service, tied the game. It was doubtful the Leafs could survive overtime. Frank McCool scarcely had enough resolve to come out for the third period, slugging back his ulcer medication between periods, calmly informing Day he could go on. Babe Pratt put him out of his misery, shoving the puck under Lumley to send Toronto ahead once and for all.

The playoffs reaffirmed Conn Smythe's love for this team. "I've been mixed up with hockey for a long time, but I don't think I ever wanted to win a championship as much as I did this last one," he will confess in a speech in October. "I remember as if it were yesterday when we played off for the Junior OHA Championship many more years than I care to confess, and how we wanted to win that one. Again when we and the Varsity team played for the Allan Cup in Vancouver after being defeated the two previous years, how much we desired that championship. Then again the first championship in the Gardens. What it all meant to us, having never been a championship team. And then again after ten years, winning in 41–42 to break that famous saying, 'Always a bridesmaid, but never a bride.' This last championship, however, seemed to be the one we wanted most of all."

"When I left this land," he tells his audience, "I had in my mind a clear-cut, fine picture of what professional hockey and the players meant. I didn't worry about the statements made by some people with respect to the patriotism of professional hockey players, because in 1940 I had signed up all the players and my questions included, 'would you immediately, should the country call on you, enlist and fight in the army, or whatever service you desired?' and each and every one signed with that understanding and with that in their hearts. That they weren't called by their country is not their fault. We must all of us be careful in statements we make..."[1]

For Smythe, with this championship, the dogged, determined Leafs have lived up to their inspiration: the men who fought at Vimy Ridge and Passchendaele, wearing the maple leaf insignia on their tunics. It is their spirit he has wanted to see come alive in the men who sport the uniform of his hockey team, and this spring, against Montreal and then against Detroit, he has seen it live and breathe. No player has embodied that spirit more than the teenager riding in the car with him, the kid he could not bear to have in exchange for Frank Eddolls.

And now the kid named Ted Kennedy—finally, truly face to face with Conn Smythe—turns and says, Mr. Smythe, my brother Joe is a major over in Europe in the Highland Light Infantry, and he wrote me and said that if I got the chance, I was to thank you for him and the men, for what you said about the reinforcements.

Conn Smythe replies: Why, thank you, Ted. You tell him that was very kind of him to say that.

He is in a swiftly moving train, trying to catch two white rabbits. He succeeds in capturing both by their ears, and when he looks into the next car, he sees his mother and father. He tells them all about chasing these animals and finally catching them.

Then he is awakened. It is seven o'clock in the morning, on Monday, May 7. William Lyon Mackenzie King is in San Francisco, attending the conference that is helping decide the shape of the United Nations.

Norman Robertson of external affairs intended to telephone him with the news at four in the morning but thought better of it, given the hour. So King is told instead precisely at seven. The war in Europe is over.

King has always thought of the number seven as significant. How appropriate that he should hear the news at the seventh hour of the seventh day of the month. *May the 7th is a beautiful day for a word of the kind.*

The first message brought to him reads: "May 7—London. Surrender of all German forces in Europe to Allied Expeditionary Force and Soviet High Command was signed at 01.41 hours this morning, Monday, May 7, by representatives of German High Command and General Eisenhower and General Susloparov, to take effect midnight Tuesday–Wednesday, May 8–9."

He thinks of the rabbits in his dream, and he understands. The first one in hand is Germany surrendering to the British. The second one is Germany surrendering to the Russians.

As soon as he is alone again, he kneels at his bedside to thank God for His guidance through the years, and prays for the strength to carry on. He then bathes and dresses immediately and returns to the room. Looking out his window onto the open square, he sees only a few people, and pigeons flying around the statue of St. Francis. He turns and looks at the clock and sees the hands aligned at seven-forty. King picks up the picture he has brought with him of his mother and father, to touch their faces with his lips. Later on, he looks to a little picture of his mother on the dresser, a picture taken at Kingsmere. *This is what we were made for*, he says without even thinking.

He dictates a telegram to Colin Gibson, who has taken over the air minister's portfolio from Chubby Power. The moment Churchill broadcasts the announcement of the surrender, Gibson is instructed, the Union Jack should be flown as usual from the top of the Peace Tower on Parliament Hill. It should continue to fly there until after King has made his own broadcast. When King's broadcast begins, the Canadian red ensign, which has been flown by the Royal Canadian Navy, should be hoisted to the top of the mast and remain there throughout the day as a tribute to the important part Canada's armed forces played in winning the war in Europe. It will stay flying until Thanksgiving Day.

In the afternoon, Robertson asks him about the flag. Shouldn't we just keep the red ensign flying for good once it is up? Robertson knows King's ambitions to give Canada its own flag. This is not the way, King counsels. A resolution from Parliament is the proper course to take to settle that question. This will be simply a tribute to the fighting men. During the election campaign, King will advocate that the country have a national flag of its own.

He sends another message, to the Prince Albert constituency, agreeing to accept the riding's nomination if offered for the coming federal election. *Tonight, I believe I shall win that constituency. This victory in Europe is going to help immensely in the campaign. I am entitled to some credit for the timing.*

At about ten o'clock that night, King receives word that his dissident MP P.J.A. Cardin is giving up the political movement he started, the Front Nationale, and might even drop out of the campaign altogether. He is angry about the way Chubby Power has been telling Quebecers he broke his promises to them in bringing in conscription, but if it is true that Cardin is stepping aside, which it is, *it means that as Liberals, we shall again sweep Quebec. This has been a good day—a happy day, in some respects of work, but one in which the burden has been greatly lightened from the knowledge that Nazi militarism has, at last, been destroyed.... That the multitudes of innocent people have had to suffer so terribly for the guilt and the folly, vain glorious ambition of a handful of gangsters. Nothing like it has been known in the whole of history. It is, however, the story of the Cross told this time on a world scale; instead of the Founder of Christendom being crucified, Christendom itself has been crucified by the same forces, but Right has triumphed over Might. God's mercy over man's folly and wrong. The law of peace, work and health begins now to triumph over the law of blood and death.*

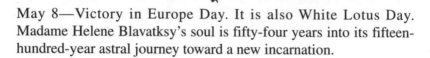

May 8—Victory in Europe Day. It is also White Lotus Day. Madame Helene Blavatksy's soul is fifty-four years into its fifteen-hundred-year astral journey toward a new incarnation.

EPILOGUE

ON June 4, 1945, George Drew is successfully returned to power as premier of Ontario with a majority government; Conn Smythe delivers his riding nomination speech. On June 11, 1945, William Lyon Mackenzie King is successfully returned to power as prime minister of Canada with a majority government. He has been proved right about conscription: it fomented a division within Liberal ranks that would disappear in peacetime. The Progressive Conservatives of John Bracken cannot capitalize on the discord a wartime election might have delivered. While there is still a war against Japan, it is essentially a distant one for Canadians. The fact that the war in Europe is over is what matters. Conscription has faded as a campaign issue. Despite the best efforts of the Conservatives in the weeks and months following the confidence vote in December 1944 to make reinforcements overseas a pressing issue, the issue fizzles, perhaps in part because the dire shortages of reinforcements Bracken and his fellow Conservatives were insisting were imminent did not materialize. There was no need to send in more than the 16,000 NRMA men Andy McNaughton agreed to commit to combat, when only 2,463 of those conscripts even made it into the fighting line.

King's caucus is reduced from 178 to 125, but given the calamitous discord facing the party only six months ago, he has done well. He has lost only seven seats in Quebec. The party has lost twenty-one seats in Ontario, which go the Conservatives' way as they increase their representation in the province by twenty-three. But the election has been a disappointment for the main opposition parties. The Progressive Conservative breakthrough under Bracken has not happened. Their only progress has come in Ontario; in the rest of the country they have no more than a handful of seats from any province. As for the CCF, their apparent strength in 1944 has vanished. They improve their number of seats from eight to twenty-eight, but almost entirely on the strength of their showing in Saskatchewan, where they win eighteen of twenty-one ridings. They pick up five ridings in Manitoba, four in British Columbia and one in Nova Scotia. In Ontario and Quebec, they have none.

General Pearkes, who was rumoured to be seeking election as a Progressive Conservative in the federal riding of Nanaimo when he resigned in February, does just that, and is successful. He embarks on a long and eventful political career. The controversy of his role in the conscription crisis will pale in comparison to the controversies of his role as defence minister in John Diefenbaker's shortlived Progressive Conservative government. In 1957 the defence department scraps the Canadian Avro Arrow fighter development program and, under the new NORAD defence agreement with the United States, replaces them in their tactical role with Bomarc missiles. The missiles, it turns out, are to be equipped with nuclear warheads. After bitter public debate, nuclear weapons are declared to be unacceptable on Canadian soil; in 1960 Pearkes leaves elected life to serve for eight years as lieutenant-governor of British Columbia.

General McNaughton proves unelectable. Defeated in his by-election bid in Grey North in February, his decision to seek the Saskatchewan seat of Qu'Appelle in the June 11 election bears no fruit. The fact that it encompasses his home town of Moosomin makes no difference to an electorate in a province that swings overwhelmingly in the CCF's favour. McNaughton is not prepared to try a third time to seek public office. Nor can McNaughton serve as Governor General now. His time in public office has tainted him with the bitter politics of conscription. Instead, he moves into the realm of international affairs and serves with distinction at the United Nations and in other high-profile diplomatic postings.

Mackenzie King does not live to see the day Canada has a native-born Governor General or a flag of her own. After retiring in 1948, he dies of influenza in 1950. The first Canadian G.G. is Vincent Massey, a candidate King considered and rejected in favour of McNaughton. Massey is appointed in 1952 and holds the position during the new Liberal government of Louis St. Laurent. The new flag does not arrive until 1965.

King is at least able to see the war through to the end. Roosevelt dies on April 12, 1945, his armies still in battle. Churchill witnesses victory in Europe as prime minister, but is then defeated in the first

British general election in a decade in July. When Japan surrenders on August 14, 1945, King is the only one of the three leaders of the democratic Allied powers who attended the Octagon conference in Quebec the previous September still in office. And King is at least able to see his successor as Liberal party leader, Louis St. Laurent, defeat John Bracken's successor as Progressive Conservative party leader, George Drew, in the 1949 election—not only defeat him, but reduce the number of Progressive Conservatives in the House from sixty-seven to forty-one. Drew retreats back into provincial politics, where he becomes a model of Tory moderation and the architect of Ontario's Progressive Conservative's Big Blue Machine.

When war in the Pacific ends after atomic bombs are dropped on Hiroshima and Nagasaki, Lieutenant Syl Apps is in Victoria, waiting to take part in the invasion of Japan that is now unnecessary. That fall, he is back in uniform as captain of the Toronto Maple Leafs.

The recovery of Bob Carse, near death when liberated by Patton's men on April 2, is a cause for medical wonder. After a few days in the care of an American field hospital, he is transferred to No. 11 Canadian General Hospital in England on April 8. Carse is treated for malnutrition and peripheral neuritis—a catch-all condition prompted by malnutrition that encompasses Carse's complaints of swollen ankles, areas of numbness, a spasmodically jerking knee, and a general absence of tendon reflexes. On May 1, Captain Stansfield, the medical officer in charge of Carse's case, is able to report, "The dysentary has stopped, and he is gaining weight rapidly. The tendon jerks have not come back." Stansfield has Carse discharged to the No. 1 Canadian Repatriation Depot, so he can be shipped home. He arrives back in Canada on June 3 and heads to Winnipeg to be reunited with his family.

After Carse's 30-day disembarkation leave, a Winnipeg military doctor's July 9 report notes: "This soldier has responded quite well to extra diet and has gained well. He states that he has not got back his former pep. Physical examination now reveals a well nourished soldier with no evidence of organic disease. His knee jerks are absent and there is no other evidence of peripheral nerve involvement. He is not yet fit for full duties." Carse is recommended for discharge.

He is interviewed on July 10 with regard to his future. "Carse has above average education and...above average army intelligence and ability," observes his interviewer, Captain Jones. "In civilian life he held a job as Service manager in a large service station at $40 per week and in the winter played professional hockey in the National Hockey League. He is co-operative and frank, willingly answering any questions asked of him. He converses intelligently and with interest.... Carse has as yet not fully recovered his former pep.... His experiences in the POW camps undermined his health, but he is well on the way to recovery. He hopes his wounded shoulder will recover sufficiently well to enable him to return to professional hockey after his discharge." Captain Jones considers Carse a fine candidate for becoming an army physical training instructor, as "Carse is very interested in remedial P.T., both to a view of his own recovery and to instructing in it. He is well motivated and...well suited to this type of work. He has the necessary education, [physical] ability and intelligence."

But Carse's future lies outside the army. On July 26, Captain Russell, army counsellor in Calgary, sends him on his way. "CARSE has a good education and is of above average intelligence and ability," the captain reports. "He is co-operative and frank, of athletic build and good appearance. His re-employment in his former capacity as service station attendant during the summer, and professional hockey player (NHL) in winter is already arranged. He was wounded once and suffered considerably from under nutrition as a POW for 6 months, but reports that he is now well on the road to recovery and that neither affliction will interfere with his future plans. It appears that his re-habilitation is well on the way." Captain Russell recommends that Rifleman Carse return to the gas station and the hockey arena. On July 28, Bob Carse is officially a civilian again after twenty-two months in the Canadian army. Those twenty-two months included about five days of actual combat.

He is overwhelmingly determined to pick up his life right where it left off, as a Chicago Blackhawk. Despite his assurances to Captain Russell that he has already arranged a spot for himself back in the NHL, his future as a professional hockey player is anything but certain. Six months after a skeletal Carse walked out of Stalag 9B, he shows up at the Blackhawks training camp. It is less than a hero's welcome. After two weeks, Bill Tobin offers him a spot with the farm club in Kansas City, take it or leave it. Carse decides to leave it, and goes home to Edmonton; the Blackhawks waive his rights.

He gets a job pumping gas at a local service station owned by a couple of local Senior players, and agrees to play with the

Edmonton Flyers Senior club. The goaltender is Tubby McAuley, who played so courageously, and hopelessly, for the New York Rangers in the last two wartime NHL seasons.

Carse plays like he was never away from the game. Sensing a major mistake, Tobin writes to Carse and asks him to name his terms for coming back to Chicago. But he is too late. The Montreal Canadiens have put him on their negotiating list.

On January 10, 1946, the Edmonton Arena hosts Bob Carse Night, a special salute to the city's home-grown war and hockey hero. He is somewhat taken back by the adulation. "I feel deeply honoured by this whole thing," he says before the celebration. "At the same time I am entirely aware that my contribution to the war effort was insignificant compared with that of many who will be in the arena tonight. There'll be ex–prisoners of war looking on who spent years—not months as I did—in those awful camps. Still more in the seats will bear the scars of wounds—scars to be carried along through life, in certain cases. My hat is off to all these. And I can't forget the fellows who aren't coming back. They gave it all...great former [Junior] teammates like Mel Lunde, Mike Patrick, Harold and 'Scotty' Sutton, 'Happy' Douglas and others. When you think of them...well...you can see why it's easy to be humble about it all."

At the arena that night, Carse is presented with a new wristwatch to replace the one his wife gave him that he bartered away to the French POW for bread, prunes and cigarettes.

Carse is elected to the Western Canada Hockey League All-Star team and named the Flyers' MVP. The team makes it to the WCHL finals, where it loses to the Calgary Stampeders. For Carse, that is just about enough hockey. He has started selling insurance with Great-West Life, and has plans for a new house and the land to build it on. Then Al Sutphin, owner of the Cleveland Barons of the American league, comes calling, having been tipped off to Carse's abilities by scout Gail Egan. Sutphin makes Carse the proverbial offer he can't refuse—$11,000 for two seasons. And that is more than many NHL players are making.

The Carses sell everything, up to but not including the girls' most essential toys, and head to Cleveland with only what will fit in their car. Carse forms a line with Pete Leswick and Johnny Holota, and they lead the Barons to first place in the western division. The team wins thirty-eight of sixty-four games, more than any other club, but falls to Hershey in the playoffs. Carse hauls in the accolades, official and unofficial. He finishes second in the scoring race, leading the league with sixty-one assists. The next-best effort is forty-four. His linemates Holota and Leswick finish third and eighth in scoring. Carse and Holota make the first All-Star team, Leswick the second. No player garners more All-Star votes than Carse.

The Montreal Canadiens call him up for 1947/48, but Carse by then has given his best years to the game, and to the war. He is twenty-eight now; it has been eight seasons since he made his professional debut with Providence and Chicago. He is a half-step behind the elite professional level; in twenty-two games with Montreal, he manages only three goals and three assists, and returns to Cleveland, where he continues to star. Accumulating fifty-four points in forty-three games, Carse is instrumental in Cleveland's again finishing first in the league's western division. In the playoffs, he contributes nine points in nine games as the Barons win the league championship, sweeping Buffalo in four in the final. He rounds out his playing career as a Barons mainstay, returning to the top-ten scorers list and making the second All-Star team in 1949/50. In four seasons with the club, he averages more than a point per game, and is eventually voted into the Barons hall of fame. Retiring after the 1949/50 season, he makes Cleveland his permanent home, continuing in the insurance business with Great-West Life. He and Betty expand their family with two more daughters—Mary Jane in 1949, Brenda in 1954. And without the efforts of Bob Carse, there would be no amateur children's hockey in the Cleveland area today.

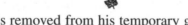

Albert Tilson is removed from his temporary grave in a Dutch pear orchard and reinterred in grave 12, row D, plot 2, in the Canadian military cemetery in Adegem, Belgium.

In the spring of 1945, the *Globe and Mail* presents to the Ontario Hockey Association a new trophy to honour the most outstanding Junior A player over the regular season. "The 'Albert "Red" Tilson' Trophy is so named," explains the OHA in the minutes of its 1945/46 annual general meeting, "in order to perpetuate the memory of one of our finest Junior players, who lost his life during the invasion of Europe." With that vague salute, Rifleman Tilson gains the most vaporous immortality. The 1995/96 official Ontario Hockey League guide will curtly explain that "The trophy was instituted by the *Globe and Mail* in memory of the late Albert 'Red' Tilson who was killed in action in Europe during World War II." Red Tilson, the Oshawa General from Regina who went all the way to Kingston to enlist and played three games for Kingston Frontenac Army in

the Ontario Senior league in the fall of 1943, who appeared in a
Toronto Marlies uniform when he shouldn't have at the behest of
Harold Ballard, who was wounded after crossing the Braakman
during the Scheldt offensive of October 1944, who died some two
weeks later in Oostburg during German shelling from Walcheren,
fades from memory almost as quickly as he is eulogized.

❧

In 1947, the American Hockey League names its rookie of the year
award in honour of Dudley "Red" Garrett.

❧

Major Joe King waives his right to career counselling on being
demobilized from the Canadian army on January 26, 1946. "The
purpose of this final counselling interview has been explained to
me," he submits, "but I feel it unnecessary because I will be taking
a position where I intend to remain for some time." Under "future
plans (if any)," King has noted, "I have a position arranged as
salesman with International Business Machines."

Married in the fall of 1942 before going overseas, Joe and his
bride Agnes have a daughter soon after he arrives home from
Europe, decorated and alive. He rises rapidly within the IBM
Canada hierarchy, becoming vice-president of marketing. He is
being groomed as the next company president when he boards a
Trans Canada Airways flight in Montreal on November 18, 1963,
to return to Toronto from a business trip. The plane crashes shortly
after takeoff in St. Thérèse, killing all 118 people on board.

❧

Turk Broda never does progress beyond his basic calling of truck
driver and sporting ringer while in the Canadian army. As the army
advances across Europe, the YMCA moves in behind it to refurbish
rinks and make recreational hockey possible for the fighting men.
In Holland he plays on the 4th Division team and records nine
shutouts in ten games. He makes it all the way into Czechoslovakia
as a star entertainer.

The war experience tries him, which is saying something for a
man as uncomplicatedly happy-go-lucky as Broda. While in
Amsterdam in January 1946, waiting to be shipped home, he loses
six teeth in a practice with the Canadian forces all-star team when a
player lets one go from three feet away. "Can you imagine getting
it from some joker after catching the best from the best of them?"
he exclaims. He announces that he's had enough of hockey and is
quitting the game.

Conn Smythe changes the Turk's mind. After winning the Stanley Cup in the spring of 1945, the Maple Leafs are going nowhere in 1945/46. Arriving home from overseas, Broda is granted disembarkation leave from January 29 to February 27, 1946, and plays fifteen games for the Leafs. Despite his presence, the team misses the playoffs.

"Broda has no definite arrangements made for his employment for the summer but has many good contacts to obtain work," states Captain W.R. Bentley, army counsellor in Toronto on March 25, 1946. "He is well known in professional hockey circles as goaltender for the Toronto Maple Leafs and should have no difficulty capitalizing on his name for obtaining suitable work for the summer. His object is to establish himself with a firm and obtain leave of absence to play hockey so that he will have a job to return to each summer and finally be fully employed in it when his hockey days are over. Work as a salesman seems to be his most logical choice as, in this kind of work, his name will certainly be of great assistance. As for his future in hockey he has already signed a 1946/47 contract with the Toronto team.

"Failing work as a salesman he will seek factory work which he has done before and is physically able to return to.

"Another proposition he is considering is to accept an offer of partnership in a recreation club in Brandon[. T]his business involves operation of a restaurant, dance hall and bowling alleys. Again his reputation as a hockey player will be useful in establishing himself in a business of this kind but, at the moment, he definitely considers this an alternative." Captain Bentley's official recommendation: "Return to former employment as Pro Hockey Player."

There will be no sales jobs or restaurant/bowling alley/dance hall in Turk Broda's future. Frank McCool's NHL career ends as soon as Broda is out of the army. Broda is to be a Maple Leaf again, and when not a Maple Leaf, he is driving a gravel truck at C. Smythe Ltd. (Smythe also gives jobs to some of his 30th Battery veterans. Shanty McKenzie goes into ticket sales at the Gardens; Buck Houle becomes the bookkeeper for C. Smythe Ltd.) With Broda back, the Leafs begin an unprecedented run of championships. Conn Smythe kicks out Frank Selke, his suspected schemer, who lands in Montreal, and takes over as managing director again. The Leafs win an unprecedented three straight Stanley Cups between 1947 and 1949, and add a fourth in 1951.

The league has a new president—Clarence Campbell, the lawyer who put together the Edmonton Athletic Club Roamers team of 1934. Fresh from his duties with the Canadian military at the Nuremburg war crimes trials, he accepts the presidency at the beginning of the 1946/47 season. In 1947/48 he is forced to come to terms with the gambling scourge that has tarnished other sports. Leaf Babe Pratt was suspended for nine games in 1945/46 for gambling on league games (a suspension that effectively ended his NHL career). This season, Billy Taylor, having bounced from Toronto to Detroit to Boston to New York, is suspended for life, along with Don Gallinger of Boston, for betting on his own team's games. Back in 1939 Taylor was the future of the Maple Leafs, leading the Oshawa Generals to a Memorial Cup over the EAC Roamers. During the war, he was the Leaf star who went into the army and spent two years helping Toronto military clubs win games. After the war, he led the league in assists as a Red Wing. Now he is disgraced and banished.

Syl Apps's last season is 1947/48. His captaincy is handed to Ted Kennedy, who now wears Charlie Conacher's old number nine. Like Apps, Kennedy neither smokes nor drinks, though profanity is another matter.

Kennedy's last season is 1954/55. He collects fifty-two points, one of his best outings, and wins the Hart Trophy, becoming only the second Leaf, after Babe Pratt in 1943/44, to be named the player most valuable to his team. No Leaf name will be added to the trophy's base over the next forty-some years. He makes a half-season comeback in 1956/57, but it does not work out.

By then Dick Irvin is dying of cancer. Ted Kennedy is sitting in Conn Smythe's office at Maple Leaf Gardens when Smythe dials Irvin to deliver parting words to the man who brought Smythe's Leafs their first Stanley Cup in 1931/32. He hands the phone to Kennedy and says, Now, Teeder, I want you to talk to Dick. Kennedy knows Irvin has never quite forgiven him for turning his back on the Canadiens organization in 1942, and it is important to Smythe that the chill be lifted before Irvin is gone.

Dick Irvin's funeral is held in Montreal, but he is buried in Toronto's Mount Pleasant Cemetery. Conn Smythe personally handles the burial arrangements, and makes sure six members of the 1931/32 Stanley Cup team are on hand as pallbearers. After his father is buried, the late great coach's son, Dick Jr., hears the major's distinctive bark to him: Don't ever forget that your father saved the Canadiens franchise.

❧

The war leaves two great legacies to the game: the new high-speed style of the two-line offside, and two powerful Canadian clubs with a fierce rivalry. By the time the season is extended to seventy games in 1949/50, the Montreal Canadiens and the Toronto Maple Leafs are playing each other fourteen times over the regular season. No game at Maple Leaf Gardens or the Forum is more alluring to the fan and the players than one of their encounters. The nation's ancient duality of French and English, the clashing city states of Montreal and Toronto, the bitterness of the war years both on and off the ice, underpin the conflict. The Zombie controversy, the country's divided war effort, is not explicit in the emotional investment of the fans, but it rests deep beneath it. If the rivalry had its big-bang beginning, then it was the playoffs of 1943/44, when the Leafs were obliterated by the Canadians and Hap Day complained about grown-ups playing kids. The relationship between the clubs was baptized in resentment, and for at least another twenty years the two organizations will squabble over which team is not just better, but superior. And as the Canadiens pursue greatness in peacetime through wars on ice, the team is legitimized as a symbol of Québécois pride.

The game that emerges from wartime is also far more violent. Though the game has always been rough around the edges, its scoring stars have traditionally accumulated a bare minimum of penalties. During the war, the top-ten scorers were particularly subdued, as if the game was collectively conscious of the unseemliness of brawling in a game while young men were fighting and dying in a war. Penalties among the top players began easing off in the mid-1930s, and, with a handful of exceptions, during the war years a typical scoring star accumulated less than twenty minutes in penalties over the season. In 1943/44 Herb Cain of Boston won the scoring title with only four minutes in forty-eight games.

This pattern quickly changes. In September 1946, Clarence Campbell, the incoming new league president, describes hockey as "a game of speed and fierce bodily contact. If these go out, hockey will vanish." That season, Maurice Richard becomes the first top-ten scorer to accumulate fifty penalty minutes since 1939/40, and his minutes climb steadily as the game lives up to Campbell's edict: 69 minutes in 1946/47, 89 minutes in 1947/48, 114 minutes in

1949/50. It is as if the game—not just Richard, but the entire game—has responded to the passing of war with a reinvigorated combativeness. Perhaps the speed of the game encourages penalties, but perhaps as well a public that has already been shocked and even numbed by the calamity of war is more receptive, even desirous, of a game that is rediscovering its innate violence. Perhaps the game must now live up to a standard of ruthlessness set by the greatest, most terrible war in the history of humankind. During the war, brawny young men duking it out in an arena—not just playing, but fighting as a matter of course—would have been an unpalatable entertainment to many spectators. After the war, when the battles against the Nazis have vanished from the headlines and the local pages are cleared of their scores of notices of young men killed, wounded, missing or captured, the quota of conflict and casualties is taken up by professional sport. Hockey comes to serve not as an embodiment of battlefield patriotism, as Conn Smythe had envisioned his Maple Leafs doing when he gained control of the franchise in 1927, but rather as an embodiment of the sensation of being at war.

On March 13, 1955, Maurice Richard's increasingly flamboyant temper erupts in a terrifying outburst in Boston, when he poleaxes Bruins defenceman Hal Laycoe with his stick and then punches linesman Cliff Thompson. Clarence Campbell suspends him for the last three games of the regular season and the playoffs as well. Because of the suspension, Richard misses what proves to be his last solid chance to win a scoring title; teammate Bernie Geoffrion edges him out by one point. When Canadiens fans riot on March 17, attacking Campbell in his Forum seat and going on a rampage down St. Catherine Street, social scientists will come to see more than a mob of angry sports fans. They will see the first flaring of what will become known as Quebec's Quiet Revolution, a renewed expression of Québécois nationalism. Campbell is the appointed hatchet man of the Anglo-Saxon oligarchy, Richard the incarnation of Québécois pride.

Montreal loses the Stanley Cup for the second straight season in a seven-game final against Detroit. It will not happen again. With Richard reinstated, with his old Punch linemate Toe Blake taking over as coach from Dick Irvin, the Canadiens surpass the Maple Leaf feat of the late 1940s by winning five straight Stanley Cups. Richard himself has hobbled through the decade, an extraordinary talent who by his own estimate misses more than 160 regular-season

games through injuries. Another fractured ankle in 1958/59 mini-
mizes his contribution to the fourth Cup win. When he retires after
the 1959/60 victory, a four-game sweep of a Maple Leaf team
emerging from its 1950s doldrums, Richard is elected to the
Hockey Hall of Fame with all possible speed.

Conn Smythe and the printed record

How much to trust Conn Smythe?

That is an essential dilemma in writing about the man whose actions in the fall of 1944 almost brought down the Mackenzie King government. Conn Smythe made a public complaint about operational military issues—the training of volunteer reinforcements and the need to send in the conscripts—that were charged with political consequences. Indeed, his initial statement to the *Globe and Mail*, printed on September 19, 1944, named a political figure, Defence Minister J.L. Ralston, and not a military one such as General Crerar or Stuart, as the presumed respondent, and so demonstrated that in his mind the issues ultimately were political ones. Which begged the question, then as now: Was Conn Smythe motivated by a sincere concern for the army in the field, or by partisan politics? Was he using his public notoriety to press for a badly needed policy change, or was Smythe merely the point man in an anti-Liberal, pro-conscription campaign whose ultimate goal was bringing down the King government?

Certainly Smythe was prominent in Conservative politics, fraternizing at the highest level with men like Ontario premier George Drew and *Globe and Mail* publisher and president George McCullagh. As this book has noted, Smythe delivered Drew's nomination speech before the 1945 federal election. On October 30, 1943, Drew, as the newly elected premier, was chosen to drop the puck at the opening faceoff of the Maple Leafs' first home game of the season. We know Smythe met with Drew while he was in hospital overseas; we also know McCullagh visited Smythe the day he arrived at Chorley Park Military Hospital in Toronto on September 18, and collected from him the statement the *Globe* published the very next morning. One can infer that the Smythe campaign against

the conscripts' remaining an army exclusively for home defence
was something cooked up between himself and Drew while Smythe
was being treated for his wounds in England, and then was
launched with all possible speed in concert with McCullagh once
Smythe was home. This is exactly what one of his few public critics, Edna Blois, charged.

What else would support this position? One can argue the campaign was purely political because Smythe did not, as his critics
and internal defence department documents accurately noted, make
any complaint to a superior officer about the reinforcement problem after he was wounded at Caen on the night of July 24–25. He
had almost two months in which to do something through formal
channels before he made his opinions known in the *Globe*, but he
did nothing. His silence was uncharacteristic, as there were other
times in his service when he showed no hesitation in registering his
convictions within the command structure. On January 18, 1944,
Major-General J.V. Young, Master General of the Ordnance, wrote
Smythe in response to one such outburst:

> Thanks for your letter of 20th December. You have opened
> up a keg of nails in your criticisms with respect to towing
> vehicles for various Artillery equipments. We quite realize
> the fact that better towing equipment could be made avail-
> able but before we can proceed to develop such a vehicle it
> is necessary for us to have some specifications from the
> Artillery with which to work; how much and what stowage
> is required is a case in point, and so on…. We have continu-
> ally pressed for specifications but until now have not got
> anything concrete. If you could get your ideas across to any-
> one and get it on the way to us, it would be splendid.

Clearly Smythe was waiting to make a noise until he was back
home, and he was going to do it on the public stage. And the fact
that Drew and national figures in the Progressive Conservative
party moved with such speed to support him, at a time when the
party was preparing itself for a federal election, suggests collusion.
It is also clear that Smythe was essentially recycling the argument
Drew had made after the fall of Hong Kong: poorly trained volunteers were being sacrificed, and it was time to commit the conscripts to combat roles.

Interestingly, Smythe's campaign was heavily foreshadowed by

Drew in a speech to the Young Men's section of the Toronto Board of Trade on October 27, 1942. Speaking on the subject of the fall of Hong Kong the previous December, Drew raised the very issue of concerned Canadian officers or citizens speaking out against government incompetence in prosecuting the war. "Under what he described as the 'loose provisions of the Defence of Canada Regulations,'" the *Toronto Telegram* reported, "Col. Drew stated that many Canadians have been restrained from uttering embarrassing criticism, many by prosecution and the resultant concentration camp. However, he said, a mere trial, whether successful or not, will discourage most from exercising his 'fundamental British birthright of free speech. After all, who is really helping the enemy, the man who places before the public weaknesses which should be cured, or a political leader who seeks to obscure a vital national issue?'" Two years before Smythe raised the issue of inadequate reinforcements and the need to send in the Zombies, Drew had stated the circumstances under which the Smythe campaign would begin. In Smythe, one might conclude, Drew found a man not afraid to face trial, and who may well have believed himself to be immune to prosecution, given his public popularity.

Smythe's campaign was short on hard evidence. He offered up a list of regiments from whom he said he had gathered complaints, but no officers from those regiments stepped forward (at least publicly) to back him up. In fact, one officer, Major Hugues Lapointe of the Chaudières, was publicly in complete disagreement on the reinforcement and conscription issue, albeit in his role as a Liberal MP.

In his autobiography, Smythe recounted spending his convalescence collecting names of officers and supportive testimony before going public with his charges on September 19. No such evidence of fact collecting survives in Smythe's private papers, a very large collection in the Ontario Public Archives. This doesn't mean Smythe didn't conduct this fact finding, only that his papers have left behind no evidence of who he spoke with or what they said. Some letters on the subject do survive (as this book records), as well as the original drafts of his various public statements in the fall of 1944. But in the final analysis, there is no raw material backing up his two months of preparatory research—only the drafts of the statements he made and the responses he received.

Smythe was always one for a good story, and at least one aspect of his account of his campaign is doubtful. His autobiography related how, after his wounding, he was transported with blood dripping on him from his wounded sergeant, an experience that he asserted inflamed his determination to right the wrongs in the field. If he meant his battery sergeant-major, Nick Hatten, then this scene was unlikely, as by Hatten's own recollection he and Smythe, though wounded side by side, took entirely different routes of treatment and convalescence.

Smythe's account in his autobiography of meeting a wounded major from Les Fusiliers at the casualty clearing station on the night he was wounded and listening to his bitter complaints about the state of reinforcements must be greeted with some scepticism, since he did not include Les Fusiliers in the list of regiments he released on October 3, 1944. One must also remember that Smythe's autobiography was published posthumously, which meant he never had to defend any of his statements.

In his memoirs, Smythe also told of officers from the French and Italian campaigns being brought to him with stories of their own while he was sailing home on the hospital ship *Lady Nelson*. This certainly could have happened, for it is important to remember that the issue of inadequately trained reinforcements was not something that Smythe cooked up by himself. It was a very real concern within the fighting ranks. Smythe had no personal experience with reinforcement problems in his anti-aircraft battery, which did not suffer serious casualties until the night Smythe himself was wounded, but he appears to have become a lightning rod for every story of inadequate reinforcements in the infantry ranks.

In all, Smythe's retelling of his public campaign in his memoirs is highly selective in its details. George Drew is never mentioned, nor are any other Conservative political figures. He makes it sound as though he was cruelly persecuted by the Liberal press, when in fact the Liberal press was feeble in its counterattacks and the Conservative press was relentless in pressing his case.

Even if Smythe was working in concert with Drew and others to promote the issue as a cause for sending in the conscripts, it does not mean that Smythe was merely a mouthpiece or a dupe. He was a man of opinions, and those opinions were always ones he legitimately held. If Conn Smythe said the reinforcements were a problem, then he most assuredly believed it. Even so, Smythe certainly would not have distinguished between solving a reinforcement issue and helping elect John Bracken as the next prime minister. Smythe's personal politics were well to the right, and closely held. As this book has pointed out, many Liberals believed that the conscription issue was a political Trojan Horse for the Conservatives. St. Laurent, according to Chubby Power's memoirs, was convinced of this. "The big interests were bound to destroy King because he had embarked on a program of social legislation and had not been favourable to the C.P.R. or the banks," Power summed up St. Laurent's "formula" after lunching with him on December 14, 1944. "Family allowances were considered by the interests to be a drain on financial resources, and the interests objected to paying them." The Conservatives could get the public to elect them on the strength of the conscription issue, and once in power move on their real agenda, which was dismantling the new social programs, such as the family allowance act, despised by the conservative business elite. Conn Smythe would not have been unhappy to see this happen. In Power's summary of St. Laurent's "formula," King "had no alternative but to accept conscription, or hand the reins of power over to people who would destroy all social legislation...."

There is no surviving correspondence between Smythe and George Drew in the Smythe papers that could shed light on whether or not they colluded in the conscription campaign. While there are letters to or from Smythe in the George Drew papers at the National Archives of Canada, they will not be released for public inspection until 1998. Some answers may become available then.

Smythe described himself later as having been naive about his campaign—he thought it was simply a matter of him making his point and the government looking into it to see if the problem was real or not. But this was Smythe at his most disingenuous. He most certainly understood what he was getting himself into, and what was at stake. And his own political ambitions were still alive in these crucial days. He had dabbled with the idea of running for office since returning home from the Great War and becoming enamoured of the Conservative party around 1920. His position with the Maple Leafs was unclear when he was shipped home in September 1944, and it was crystal clear to others where his anti-Zombie campaign might lead. As Major Harry Robinson noted to him in his letter that autumn, "It's an interesting situation, and fraught with great opportunity for a man like yourself, with the money and, one hopes, the ambition to get into public service...."

Materials and Methods: The King Diaries

One cannot read the diaries of William Lyon Mackenzie King and not be struck by their narrative power. It is more than the detail of his private and public lives that so impresses; it is the way events unfold over days, weeks, months and years, the way he harnesses characters, experiences and observations in story lines that keep the reader compulsively moving on to the next entry.

When I began working on this book, I realized that a fundamental challenge and opportunity was making use of the material in the diaries in a way that preserved, even enhanced, their narrative power. Fortunately for me, the relatively short time frame of the essential part of this book allowed me to use daily observations by King, in snippets or their entirety, to convey the unfolding drama.

The beauty of a diary is that there is no opportunity for the diarist to rewrite or obscure. The day is recounted as it was experienced, on first impression, and that is a valuable thing when delving into the mind of a politician, who might with hindsight prefer to portray events in an altogether different light, or pretend they never actually happened. Other diaries are used in this book—for example, the desk diary of Defence Minister Ralston for the period of the conscription crisis, and diaries kept by Colonel Dyde and Colonel Weeks as they accompanied Ralston on his tour of Canadian troops overseas that same autumn—but there is nothing in them that has the power to move and enlighten the way Mr. King's does. (Ralston's diary is simply a tally of appointments.)

I have used the King diaries with great respect for their content and for the man who painstakingly and faithfully wrote them, but also with a writer's desire to maximize their essential narrative power. At times I have felt more like the late prime minister's editor or co-author, and I have been impressed by his ability to create, at a stroke, memorable turns of phrase and anecdotes. The best I could do was not so much improve upon them as make them more accessible to the general reader. Making complete sense of them requires a shelf full of reference books and research material. They are full of people who do not receive proper introductions, as King was writing for himself, about persons he already knew. He also writes, as a diarist will, in recollective shorthand. An expression like "the situation" says all it needs to for King himself, but for the general reader some elaboration is required. As well, when King briefly remarks on something as monumental as the setback of Arnhem, the reader needs to understand what in fact happened at Arnhem, and how that military disaster might have impacted on King's circumstances and state of mind.

The diaries' narrative is also not always linear. His recounting of a critical meeting seldom unfolds as it did in life. The account loops back upon itself, covering an important exchange perhaps in several separate passages; sometimes one event can take successive days of entries to be drained by King of its detail and significance. A writer concerned with telling a coherent story needs to address these idiosyncracies; to cut, paste and elaborate.

I wanted the material from the diaries to remain as much within King's frame of mind as possible, because if they stayed that way, it would be possible for the reader to enter that frame of mind. Otherwise, one would be gaining the facts, but losing the man, and the man himself is one of the most important subjects within the story I set out to tell.

King's diaries provide the narrative backbone to the period of the book dealing with the conscription crisis, that is, between mid-September and mid-December 1944. King's observations are augmented by my own observations of him and his opinions and by various collaborative or complementary materials, such as the abovementioned Dyde, Weeks and Ralston diaries, documents found in the Ralston, Smythe and McNaughton papers (including an unsigned summary of the events of the conscription crisis from a pro-conscriptionist cabinet minister's perspective, prepared by T.A. Crerar on December 26, 1944), statements preserved in Hansard and the daily press, and observations made in the autobiographies of Chubby Power and King's military adviser, Lieutenant-General Maurice Pope. (For a more detailed account of materials employed, see the bibliography and endnotes.)

As to how King's diary entries have been distilled into a narrative backbone, I settled upon the following method. Much of the time, I simply paraphrase him while attributing observations to him. When he is in lengthy conversation with his cabinet ministers, or with the Governor General or General McNaughton, for example, all sides of the dialogue are drawn from King's own account. Because they appear in the diaries as personal and private recollections in the past tense, with all the narrative idiosyncracies outlined above, and because this book unfolds in the present tense and cannot take three days of activity, as the diaries sometimes do, to cover everything King can recall from a few particular hours, I have had to act the respectful editor in making reasonable reconstructions of meetings and the conversations that took place.

Exchanges made in these conversations are drawn directly from King's diaries. (Additional dialogue is also contributed by Weeks and Dyde, by the unsigned Crerar memo and by the Pope autobiography.) No opinions are offered that cannot be found in a primary source. Actual statements recorded by King have sometimes required smoothing and minor elaboration so that they make sense to the reader. These minor alterations do not change the basic message King set down. I have been extremely careful not to put words in people's mouths, to add opinions or exchanges one might reasonably argue to have been plausible, as one could if writing a full-blown historical novel or film script. If the source material is not set down by King (or one of the other sources cited), then the words have not made it into my narrative.

The diaries do provide narrative challenges. It is sometimes not clear from King's recollections whether an exchange with a particular person took place in a meeting, or before or after it, or in a different meeting the same day. I have done my best to assign events to their most likely place in the narrative time line. When I have been completely flummoxed, I have simply left them attached to no particular moment in the pertinent day.

Similarly, it is often impossible to recreate the order of events in a particular meeting based on a diary entry. Indeed, in his account of his meeting with General McNaughton on October 31, King begins with the words "Without following the sequence...." I have striven mightily to impose some order on such exchanges. This has sometimes meant moving material around from within King's non-linear account, or drawing from material set down by King on a subsequent day. For example, in King's meeting with McNaughton on October 14, it could be inferred from the day's diary entry that

King proposed making McNaughton the next Governor General. Only when King recounts his visit to the Governor General on October 16, in the course of which he recounts for His Excellency's benefit the meeting with McNaughton, is it revealed that McNaughton himself asked to be considered for the post. Consequently, I have blended material from two different accounts of the meeting set down by King himself on separate days to create one account that I feel is as close as one can get through King to what transpired.

As King scholars well know, King never meant for his diaries to be read by people like you or me, although some historians believe he wrote with an eye fixed on posterity. He intended them to be used as a reference for his official biographer, and then to be destroyed. Fortunately, trustees of King's estate recognized them for the extraordinary works they are, and made sure they were preserved for the benefit and elucidation of the Canadian people.

A typed transcript of the handwritten diaries prepared by the University of Toronto forms the basis of the microfiche record I worked from at the university and at the National Archives in Ottawa. Every now and then, it is plain that the typist slipped and not the prime minister, and I have corrected errors that one can reasonably assume were not made by King himself. He does make the occasional slip, and where I have used verbatim quotes I have set the corrections in parentheses. Other minor errors on his part, whether syntactical or factual, I have patched up where paraphrasing has been used. For example, King at one point in his diaries refers to a speech made by McNaughton at McGill that we know he made at Queen's. King, on second look, probably would have known that, too. McNaughton was making speeches at several universities at the time and King's error is too petty to preserve or to point out in my paraphrasing.

Where I have felt it important or illuminating that some verbatim part of his diary be highlighted, I have used italics for the passage or particular words. Paraphrasing outside the italics runs the gamut from the very broad, when I am simply trying to sum up his observations or the activities described, to the very narrow, in the case of dialogue. As a rule of thumb, most words presented as spoken in this book are substantially as King recorded them. There are some passages that run practically verbatim but have not been set in italics, as I have had to make minor repairs to syntax, content and tense. King's chilling address to his cabinet of November 1, in which he justifies his firing of Ralston as defence minister, runs for about 1,100 words in this book with only very slight changes from its appearance in the diary.

Except in the case of speeches quoted from Hansard, or statements made in the press or set down in documents, quotation marks are not used. Dialogue in this book as a result appears as part of the flow of the narrative. This is partly my own choice of narrative style, partly because I am conscious of the fact that the words I have presented as spoken cannot be literal representations of what was said. We have no sound recordings to verify who actually said what, and I did not want to cross the line into the realm of the historical novel. The narrative is a factually grounded account of what transpired. I do not want it to be misinterpreted as an incontrovertible record of what happened. Quotation marks, to me, would convey absolute veracity. The narrative I have written is intended as a conscientious, creative presentation of events as I have been able to determine them. Other writers can approach the same material and construct their own passages of dialogue. If you want to know exactly what King committed to paper, rather than what I can say with confidence probably happened, based on the material, then read the King diaries.

King emerged from his diaries as complex, compelling, flawed certainly, inspired unquestionably. He was one of the most successful politicians this country has ever produced, and its greatest diarist.

ENDNOTES

Prologue: A New Season

1. The response to the call for conscription by British colonies and dominions is explored in *The Rise and Fall of the British Empire* by Lawrence James.

Rites of Spring

1. Upon Squib Walker's death in 1951, Conn Smythe's letters to Walker were returned to Smythe by Walker's widow. These letters thus made their way into the Smythe papers.
2. The Blackhawks brochure is preserved in the private papers of the Carse family.

The Warrior

1. The relationship between sports and games and the defence of Empire is explored in Lawrence James's *The Rise and Fall of the British Empire*. Mr. James's work provides the quote by J.E.C. Weldon and the passage from *Through the Sikh War* by G.A. Henty.
2. The interview in which Conn Smythe related his devotion to theosophy was conducted by Jack Batten and published in the article "King Conn" (*Star Weekly*, October 8, 1977). This interview, and others Smythe gave in the final years of his life, are contained in clippings preserved in a file at the Metropolitan Toronto Reference Library.
3. The author is indebted to Bruce F. Campbell for his work *Ancient Wisdom Revived: A History of the Theosophical Movement*, in his discussion of Madame Blavatsky and the history of theosophy. Mr. Campbell's book provides the quotations from Madame Blavatsky's works that appear in this chapter. Albert Smythe's experiences with theosophy are drawn from materials in the Smythe papers.
4. John Keegan's *A History of Warfare* is the author's primary source for his discussion of the origins of the regiment. It also supplies the quotes by Keegan in the text and accompanying footnote.
5. Conn Smythe's observations on the Great War inspiration for the Maple Leafs name were made in a speech he delivered to the club organization in October 1945; a draft is preserved in his papers.

6. Smythe's concerns about how his warrior ethic would be perceived in the face of actual warfare were expressed in his memoirs. His precise observation was: "When the war came I had to face that. Had I been talking fiction or fact? Was I a fraud or did I live up to my own principles? I had made myself out to be a warrior and tried to make my players be warriors, too. I thought it was up to me to lead, set an example."

7. Smythe's memoirs placed his decision to form a sportsman's battery in early 1941, but his correspondence to Frank Ahearn preserved in his papers clearly demonstrates he had this in mind in December 1939. His memoirs' timeline of officer's training and the actual formation of the battery appears reliable.

Men at Arms

1. Irvin's reputation as a hard-driving coach is refuted by Bob Davidson, who played for him as a Maple Leaf in the 1930s. He told the author he found Irvin's coaching style to be based on letting the players do what they were good at. Davidson's teammate, Hap Day, was in Davidson's opinion much more of a disciplinarian when he took over from Irvin as coach in 1940, more committed to the concept of a playing system and a team regimen.

2. Biographical information on General McNaughton in this chapter is culled from several sources: Granatstein's *The Generals*; McNaughton's personal papers at the National Archives; *The Canadian Encyclopedia*; *Who's Who in Canada*; and a draft of a profile of McNaughton contained in the Smythe papers. *The Generals* makes note of the accuracy of McNaughton's artillery at Vimy Ridge and its role in the Canadian success in that battle.

     The profile of McNaughton in the Smythe papers was prepared as part of the draft-McNaughton campaign. Smythe was privy to detailed information about McNaughton's life, as indicated by a letter from W. Dowson of Willowdale, Ontario, to Smythe on June 10, 1940, which accompanied a draft of the article. "Enclosed herewith is the first draft of the build up on Gen. McNaughton from the details which you sent me on the 6th inst. I have seen the editor of the local paper and he will print it…. You will not receive anything for the article and we nothing for our work. We work for Canada." Smythe instructed Dowson to have his name removed from the article, explaining that he wrote his own articles and speeches. The article cites Conservative pork barrelling as one of the reasons for McNaughton's fall from grace in the Bennett government, and also outlines McNaughton's ambitions for a research centre at Valcartier. The Smythe papers also preserve some of the paraphernalia of the lobbying campaign, such as the poster and bumper sticker.

3. Conn Smythe's flight training regimen is spelled out in his private pilot's log book, which is preserved among his papers. It also notes that in June and August 1941, he took along a passenger named

McNaughton on flights. The author could not verify if this was in fact General McNaughton. If so, it is the only firm evidence the author could find of the two men knowing each other, though they must have met at some point in their lives. McNaughton had a son in the RCAF, who was killed in 1942, and it might have been him flying with Smythe. It could just as easily have been another McNaughton who was no relation to the general.

4. The NRMA draft categories changed over the course of the war. According to Major-General E.L.M. Burns in *Manpower in the Canadian Army 1939–45*, the minimum call-up age was quickly dropped from 21 to 19. In August 1943, after Canadian troops became involved in the Italian campaign, the draft was expanded to include 18.5-year-olds. After D-Day, married men became draft-eligible for the first time, with single and married men 18 to 31 and single men 31 to 42 liable to be called up.

5. The problems the Canadian army had as an essentially British institution in attracting French-Canadian recruits and officers is explored more thoroughly in Granatstein's *The Generals*, and is addressed as well in Keegan's *Six Armies in Normandy*.

6. The memorandum on officers with Great War experience is preserved in the Ralston papers.

7. Harry Crerar's opinion of conscription is cited in Granatstein's *The Generals*.

In Uniform

1. Smythe's letter to Maple Leaf players encouraging them to join a militia, and the quote provided, is drawn from his memoirs. No copy of the letter survives in Smythe's papers.

2. No copy of the flyer prepared for Maple Leaf season ticket holders that is referred to by Smythe in his letter to Frank Ahearn on October 2, 1940, survives in Smythe's papers.

Recruits

1. Maurice Richard's rejection for military service was related to the author by former Maple Leaf Billy Harris, who played oldtimers' hockey with Richard (and whose father was shot down and killed over Holland while serving in the RCAF in 1944). Richard would neither confirm nor deny having made this statement to Harris, saying only that he had many injuries over his career.

To Serve and to Fight

1. This statement does not survive in the Smythe papers. The figures are drawn from daily reportage at the time of its release. A draft summary of Maple Leaf Gardens box office receipts for the 1942/43 season in the Smythe papers indicated a far smaller number of amateur events, 110, which nonetheless generated $74,287.76 in revenue. It may be that the figures quoted in the daily press referred to games in all amateur sports,

which would have included lacrosse. It's worth noting that the Gardens was also hosting lacrosse games by military teams.

2. The account of the hockey exploits of the 228th Battalion in the Great War is drawn from *The Trial of the Stanley Cup*.

3. The military orders bringing an end to armed forces hockey teams participating in league play that would lead to an Allan Cup appearance are preserved in the Ralston papers.

Incoming

1. Power makes brief note of his hockey days in his memoirs. The playing records of the Power brothers are drawn from *The Trail of the Stanley Cup*. (Power's brother Rockett appears as "Rocket" in *The Trail*.)

2. The account of Smythe having been visited in his room by a staff officer who informed him he faced court-martial is drawn from the one recorded by Smythe himself in his memoirs. He did not name the officer, and the account cannot be corroborated. No list of officers and their regiments could be located in his papers.

3. The full account of McNaughton's downfall appears in Granatstein's *The Generals*, from which this truncated version is drawn.

Firefight

1. The effect of the Italian campaign on Germany's ability to wage war on the eastern and western fronts is, as noted, still debated. Keegan in *Six Armies in Normandy* cites the need for Germany to allocate 50 of 300 divisions to Italy and the Balkans. Brian Holden Reid, in *The Oxford Companion to World War II*, calls the record of the Italian campaign in contributing to the Allied victory "mixed," asserting it had "no appreciable impact on the Eastern Front," and noting that the Germans were able to muster twenty-six divisions for the Ardennes offensive of December 1944 (the Battle of the Bulge) without drawing upon their Italian forces.

2. Ralston's movements and related activities are recorded in the diaries of Colonel Dyde and Brigadier Weeks, the relevant portions of which were provided to Ralston and preserved in his papers. Related reports and memos are also preserved in his papers.

3. Weeks's war diary recorded: "The RSM stated that in a recent draft of 72 men which joined the Bn, only 7 were found to be fully trained, as the result of being checked by unit NCO's." Dyde's diary gave a slightly different tally: "RSM Crossley spoke about the training of the rfts. He said that 62 out of 70 men arriving at the Bn had not thrown grenades."

4. Maple Leaf Gardens Ltd. purchased $50,000 in Victory Bonds on March 2, 1942. A Gardens statement of September 25, 1943, preserved in the Smythe papers, avows: "Today, we have $200,000 of Canada Victory Loan bonds, compared with $50,000 last year." Year-end financial statements through to the end of the war, however, only showed the initial $50,000 investment.

5. R.D. Grant was interviewed by the author to help determine the legitimacy of Smythe's allegation regarding training of armoured

reinforcements. He saw action in his Sherman for nearly a full month, from the D-Day landing until his wounding at Carpiquet, and was then out of action for several months. When he returned to active duty, he was placed in charge of an echelon squadron behind the lines as a result of his wounds. "There was never a problem with reinforcements to my recollection," he told the author. "I never heard any real complaints. We didn't hear about [the complaints] until we got back to England." Grant noted the fact that Shermans were replaced by Fireflys as they were lost. Tank production details in the accompanying footnote are drawn from *Encyclopedia of World War II*.

6. The use of "wastage rates" based in large part on the British army's experiences in North America, and the casualty rate as of July 14, 1944, are found in Major-General E.L.M. Burns's *Manpower in the Canadian Army 1939–45*. Defence department analysis of casualties in August and September 1944 is contained in the Ralston papers. Granatstein's *The Generals* notes the assumed rate of return of infantry from hospital.

7. The meeting between Ralston, Weeks and Leese was recorded by Weeks in the portion of his war diary preserved in the Ralston papers.

8. The Surgeon General's report on battle fatigue is noted in Gilbert's *Second World War*.

Into the Breach

1. The QOR regimental history outlines its losses (and those of the Chaudières) under the USAAF shortbombing on August 7. Granatstein and Morton in *A Nation Forged in Fire* set Canadian and Polish casualties at 300. Hastings in *Overlord* sets Canadian, Polish and British casualties in this instance of friendly fire at "over 300."

2. Casualties for the Queen's Own and the North Shore at Quesnay Woods are set at "almost 200" by Copp in *A Canadian's Guide to the Battlefields of Normandy*. Granatstein and Morton place the regiments' losses at 165 in *A Nation Forged in Fire*.

3. The details of Ralston's visits to No. 19 and 23 Canadian hospitals were recorded by Colonel Dyde.

Curragh, Hurrah

1. Major-General E.L.M. Burns's authoritative 1956 study, *Manpower in the Canadian Army 1939–45*, turned up striking differences between the fighting efficiencies of the Canadian and U.S. armies. Burns revealed that at the time of the conscription crisis there were 389,873 soldiers and officers in general service in the Canadian army. This figure boiled down to 158,000 men in the field formations, and of those, only 37,817 in the infantry, whose high casualty rate was the root of the conscription crisis. "These figures mean that with some 390,000 'general service' (GS) men on its strength, the Army could not find the bodies to reinforce the 38,000 infantry." He noted that 28.2 per cent of manpower in arms and services in the Canadian army overseas in November 1944 was consumed by headquarters and "overhead" non-fighting posts, compared to

only 11.6 percent in the U.S. army as of March 31, 1945. In the Canadian army, 34 per cent of men were in the fighting line, compared with 43.5 per cent in the U.S. army. He also noted that the U.S. army used smaller, more efficiently structured divisions in the field. A Canadian infantry division had 18,376 men, compared with 14,037 men in an American formation. There was a similar disparity in armoured divisions, with 14,819 in a Canadian one and 10,670 in an American one.

2. The circumstances of Hextall's one-season absence from the NHL is based on contemporary news reportage.

3. Pope's observations were made in his memoirs.

4. Crerar's western tour was outlined in a confidential memo, written December 26, 1944, labelled "Notes for the record on the recent crisis in the Government over reinforcements." The memo was provided to J.L. Ralston and survives in his papers. The author was anonymous, but the memo was written in the first person, and particular details make it plain that Crerar produced it.

Our Souls Torn Out

1. The confusion over the number of available reinforcements is underlined by the fact that, in the King diaries in these weeks, the total general service men in Canada varies between 120,000 and 130,000. Major-General E.L.M. Burns, in *Manpower in the Canadian Army 1939–45*, set the general service ranks in Canada in November 1944 at 135,631. He also set the number of NRMA men at 59,699.

2. The partisan campaign waged against the King government by the *Globe and Mail* was suspended for an editorial extending sympathy to Gardiner on the loss of his wife. Her cause of death, however, was not specified.

The Saint Comes Marching In

1. According to his military records, Broda was admitted to the Second Canadian General Hospital in Britain on May 24, 1944, two weeks before D-Day, when he appeared to be on the verge of going into the field. Broda had been taken on strength by the Canadian Artillery Holding Unit on May 8, and his next of kin were verified on May 22. He does not emerge from the hospital until August 25, one month after Hatten was wounded. Thus the most likely period for the hospital encounter between Hatten and Broda would be between Hatten's wounding on July 24 and Broda's release from hospital on August 25.

2. There is no doubt about the profitability of Maple Leaf Gardens Ltd. during the war years. Financial figures shown below indicate solid earnings as well as burgeoning fan loyalty, given the steady increase in deferred income from subscription sales to Maple Leaf season tickets. Net profits were also up over the war, despite soaring excess profit tax payments.

Oct. 31 year end:	1945	1944	1943	1942	1941	1940	1939
Net operating inc.	354,037	271,277	280,719	267,644	213,190	226,912	232,070
Net earnings	315,763	259,225	261,456	253,911	201,088	214,086	192,274
Excess profit tax	174,185	123,375	136,056	104,016	71,794	68,500	24,205
Net profit	90,783	88,252	74,683	86,176	48,136	60,466	81,190
Deferred income	151,569	121,102	83,678	90,427	78,128	63,867	45,335

(Maple Leaf ticket subscriptions)

3. Crerar's observations were made in the confidential memo on the conscription crisis written December 26, 1944 (See endnote, Curragh, Hurrah, number 4.)

4. The letter from Drew to McNaughton is cited by Granatstein in *The Generals*.

The Plot Thickens

1. Granatstein in *The Generals* observes that "the 355 officers and 6012 other ranks who were killed, wounded or captured [in the Scheldt offensive] would require almost all the men who remained in Stuart's reinforcement pool to replace." Elsewhere in *The Generals*, Granatstein sets total army casualties (which would include non-Canadians under the command of the First Canadian Army) in the fighting to clear the Scheldt at 13,000.

2. Smythe still had not forgiven Selke for dealing away Frank Eddolls for Ted Kennedy when he dictated his memoirs at the end of his life. In them, he offered the explanation that his anger stemmed from the fact that Selke had not sought the approval of the executive committee for the trade. This is contradicted by the survival in the Smythe papers of the trade agreement which is signed on the Leafs' behalf by Hap Day; Selke's signature appears nowhere. Selke might have engineered the deal, but Hap Day, at least, was fully aware of it. There seems to have been little excuse for the firing of someone who had made so many contributions to the success of the Leafs. It has been suggested that Smythe could not even have built the Gardens without Selke, who made the project possible by convincing unionized labourers to take a portion of their wages in Maple Leaf Gardens stock. As it turned out, Selke became the outstanding general manager of the great Montreal Canadiens teams from 1946/47 to 1963/64.

3. Montgomery's opinion of Pearkes is cited by Granatstein in *The Generals*.

The Cross He Bears

1. Crerar's experiences were recorded in his memo of December 26, 1944. (See endnote, Curragh, Hurrah, number 4.)

Deliverance

1. The travails of the American Hockey League during the Second World War are outlined well by Kiczek in *Forgotten Glory*.

2. Pope expressed his opinions in his memoirs.

3. Details of the loss of the *Shawinigan* and Able Seaman Garrett are drawn from a letter written August 28, 1945, to Garrett's father by the secretary of the Naval Board, which is preserved in Garrett's military records. According to the book *Corvette Canadians*, the captain of the *Burgeo* drew criticism for failing to report immediately that the *Shawinigan* had not appeared for the rendezvous. *Corvette Canadians* also states that the *Shawinigan* was sunk by a single acoustic torpedo. The loss of the *Shawinigan* helped draw Defence Minister McNaughton into a public disagreement with Navy Minister Macdonald over the wafety of shipping in the Gulf of St. Lawrence.

4. Smythe's visit to Maple Leaf Gardens is discussed in his memoirs.

5. The *Winnipeg Free Press*'s editorial likely had more than a little of Chubby Power's wisdom in it. Power was close to Grant Dexter, Ottawa editor of the *Free Press*, and saw fit to send him a confidential memo explaining his resignation.

Counterattack

1. The conservative press treated the Grey North by-election as an issue of national importance, and provided tenaciously detailed coverage. The author is particularly indebted to the work of J.H. Fisher of the *Toronto Telegram*.

2. Any losses NHL teams suffered in personnel were overwhelmingly among future stars such as Red Tilson, who were not yet established in the professional game. The Red Wings, for example, were rocked by the loss of goaltending standout Joe Turner. In 1937/38, he led the OHA Junior A in goals-against, and posted the league's best shutout record in 1938/39. He was starring with the Indianapolis Capitals of the American league when the U.S. entered the war. The Capitals won the 1941/42 league championship with Turner, who was named a first-team All Star. He was called up for one game by the Red Wings in 1941/42, allowing three goals. The Red Wings like what they saw but Turner, though a Canadian citizen, decided to join the U.S. Marines. He was listed as missing in action in Holland in January 1945. After the war, the International league named its championship trophy in his memory.

Over the Top

1. Raymond is quoted in Hastings's *Overlord*. Corporal Raymond was actually an American who crossed the border to enlist in January 1942. He chose the Canadian army because it had "a reputation for not asking many questions" according to Hastings, and at the time Raymond was only sixteen. He was dismissed after a month, but made a second enlistment attempt and was successful. He went ashore on Juno Beach on June 7, 1944, in a draft of reinforcements and was assigned as a machine gunner to the Stormont, Dundas and Glengarry Highlanders. He survived the war.

2. The important factor in criticism of the Gardens' war charity record is that there appears to have been no events in which actual Gardens

revenues were donated to any cause, although there were non-hockey events for which use of the Gardens was donated. No gate receipts from any regular-season Maple Leaf game, in whole or in part, seem to have been turned into a donation. It must be noted, however, that Smythe's experiences with his own wounds made him deeply sympathetic to the plight of handicapped children, and he became a generous supporter of related charities after the war. And in official circles, the efforts of Smythe (and the Gardens) to promote enlistment and Victory Bonds purchases was much appreciated. The province of Ontario (with George Drew its premier) held a dinner in honour of the Gardens war efforts in 1947.

3. King's diary entry is somewhat ambiguous here. The actual transcription reads: "I told him Ralston should have dealt with Connie Smythe at once. Could have got along in the crisis if there had not been determination on the part of some to force conscription." The author has left this passage open to interpretation. King might have been speaking of himself and Ralston or of himself and Graydon (or of the Liberals and the Conservatives in general) when he wrote "Could have got along...."

Citizen Soldiers

1. The author is indebted to John Keegan for his delineation of soldier types in *A History of Warfare*.

The Final Offensive

1. This statement is from the draft of a speech made to the Toronto Maple Leaf Hockey Club banquet in October 1945, preserved in the Smythe papers.

SOURCES

Military Records

Under the Privacy Act, military records of personnel who have been deceased for more than twenty years are unrestricted and can be obtained from the National Archives of Canada. The author filed for, and received, the military records of the following individuals:

Walter "Turk" Broda
James Dickinson "Dick" Irvin
Albert "Red" Tilson
Dudley "Red" Garrett
Charles Joseph "Joe" King

In addition, the author was provided with the military records of Bob Carse, which were secured from the National Archives by Mr. Carse himself.

The author was unable to access any records pertaining to military service deferrals. These were all destroyed on May 7, 1964, under Treasury Board authority.

The author thanks Louise Brazeau, May Boris and Greg McCooeye of the National Archives of Canada for their assistance in securing the above military records and in helping interpret their contents. Mr. McCooeye was particularly helpful in sorting out acronyms and explaining underlying nuances of curt record entries.

Personal Papers

The following public collections were used by the author in researching this work:

The Conn Smythe Papers, Archives of Ontario
The A.E.L. McNaughton Papers, National Archives of Canada
The J.L. Ralston Papers, National Archives of Canada
The Mackenzie King Diaries, National Archives of Canada
   and University of Toronto

In addition the author was granted access to the private papers of the family of Bob Carse.

Military and Political History

Accounts of military and political events in this work have been constructed from a wide variety of sources. For the theatre of war, these include official regimental histories of the Highland Light Infantry of Canada, the Regina Rifles, the Royal Winnipeg Rifles, the 6th Light Anti-Aircraft Regiment and the Queen's Own Rifles of Canada. The author is indebted to Buck Houle for providing a copy of the collected issues of *FLAK*, the 6th L.A.A. newsletter published weekly in the field during the war. Daily press coverage was also evaluated.

The author has relied upon the following published works:

Manpower in the Canadian Army 1939–45, by Major-General E.L.M. Burns

A Nation Forged in Fire: Canadians and the Second World War 1939–1945, by J.L. Granatstein and Desmond Morton

The Oxford Companion to World War II, I.C.B. Dear, General Editor

Overlord: D-Day and the Battle for Normandy 1944, by Max Hastings

Encyclopedia of World War II, John Keegan, General Editor

A Canadian's Guide to the Battlefields of Normandy, by Terry Copp

Second World War, by Martin Gilbert

Six Armies in Normandy: From D-Day to the Liberation of Paris, by John Keegan

The Generals: The Canadian Army's Senior Commanders in the Second World War, by J.L. Granatstein

Soldiers and Politicians: The Memoirs of Lt. Gen. Maurice A. Pope

Patton: A Genius for War, by Carlo D'Este

A History of Warfare, by John Keegan

The Battle for History: Re-Fighting World War Two, by John Keegan (The Barbara Frum Lectureship)

A Party Politician, by Charles Gavan Power

Post-Confederation Canada: The Structure of Canadian History Since 1867, by D.N. Sprague

A special note of thanks is due to J.L. Granatstein, for his personal advice on primary sources and his assistance in assessing the origin of certain documents examined by the author. Professor Granatstein also wrote a superb book in *The Generals*, which the author found invaluable as a field guide to the many characters wandering through the papers and diaries noted above. Anyone who wishes to know more about this era and its complex participants and events is encouraged to read it.

Military Facts and Figures

It is rarely possible to be firm about casualty figures, army strengths and the like when writing about the Second World War. The essential chaos of war defies unequivocal answers. The author has striven to choose figures from reliable sources; where he felt it pertinent, he has noted those sources in the endnotes.

Hockey History

The author thanks the staff of the Hockey Hall of Fame, in particular Craig Campbell, for their continued assistance in his researches. Player clipping files, historical documents and various historical publications were examined at the Hockey Hall of Fame Archives in the course of researching this book.

Noteworthy among published works:

The Trail of the Stanley Cup, by Charles Coleman
The Complete Encyclopedia of Hockey, Zander Hollander, Editor
If You Can't Beat 'Em in the Alley, by Conn Smythe, with Scott Young
The National Hockey League Official Guide and Record Book
American Hockey League Official Guide and Record Book
The Stanley Cup, by D'Arcy Jenish
Hockey Night in Canada, by Foster Hewitt
Maple Leaf Gardens: Fifty Years of History, by Stan Obodiac
Forgotten Glory: The Story of Cleveland Barons Hockey, by Gene Kiczek

The Daily Printed Record

The author relied for facts and opinions on the daily reportage of newspapers during the period. Owing to their particular political slant, the Toronto *Globe and Mail* and *Toronto Telegram* were especially helpful in tracking the unfolding Conn Smythe campaign in favour of full conscription. General McNaughton was a conscientious collector of press clippings, and his personal papers provided the author with a broad source of reportage and commentary by the daily press in Canada on the conscription crisis of 1944.

The *Toronto Telegram* was an invaluable resource for its political and sports coverage.

The author also found the *New York Times* invaluable for its coverage of the crisis in American professional sports over 4-F ratings that broke in December 1944.

Other Sources

Other published works the author found insightful were:

The Canadian Encyclopedia
The Rise and Fall of the British Empire, by Lawrence James
Ancient Wisdom Revived: A History of the Theosophical Movement, by Bruce F. Campbell
Who's Who in Canada

Interviews

The author is grateful to Ted Kennedy for his time and the reminiscences he provided on his own life during the period this work covers, including details about the life and military career of his half-brother, Joe King. Maurice Richard consented to a Q&A fact check on previously published items about his life in the period this book describes. For this courtesy, and for the elaborations he provided, the author thanks him. Bob Davidson, always courteous, invited the author into his Toronto home and provided helpful reminiscences about the era and its characters. The author also spoke with Don Metz regarding his military service.

The Carse family of Cleveland was enormously helpful in helping the author come to grips with Bob Carse's hockey and military careers. Three of four Carse daughters still living in Cleveland—

Sharon, Brenda and Nancy—granted interviews and assistance. The author thanks them for their time and efforts, for the privilege of meeting their father, and for permitting access to family papers. The author must also thank Ken Bergin, who was interned as a prisoner of war with Bob Carse and consented to be interviewed about his experiences.

Anke Wolfe freely provided translation services for German military documents contained in Bob Carse's military records (which came into the possession of Canadian authorities between 1949 and 1951), and for this the author is most thankful.

The men of Conn Smythe's 30th Battery were a terrific help. Don "Shanty" Mackenzie introduced the author to surviving battery members, and the author thanks the following members for the interviews they granted: Geoffrey Archer, Buck Houle, Bernie Dunn, Nick Hatten and Sherwood Wright. The author also thanks fellow author Brian Kendall for helping introduce him to the men of the 30th, and for supplying him with a copy of an article he wrote on the Battery which appeared in *The Beaver*. The author interviewed R.D. "Bob" Grant, a former major with the Fort Garry Light Horse, to gain his perspective on the allegations regarding poor training of tank crews in 1944.

Finally, the author thanks his editor, Meg Masters, for letting him say the things he felt he should, and not letting him say the things she knew he shouldn't.

INDEX